CAREER
OPPORTUNITIES
IN
TELEVISION,
CABLE, VIDEO,
AND
MULTIMEDIA

CAREER OPPORTUNITIES IN TELEVISION, CABLE, VIDEO, AND MULTIMEDIA

FOURTH EDITION

By Maxine K. and Robert M. Reed

General Editor
Lee Phenner

Checkmark Books™
An imprint of Facts On File, Inc.

CAREER OPPORTUNITIES IN TELEVISION, CABLE, VIDEO, AND MULTIMEDIA, FOURTH EDITION

Copyright © 1999 by Maxine K. Reed and Robert M. Reed

Checkmark Books
An imprint of Facts On File, Inc.
11 Penn Plaza
New York NY 10001

Library of Congress Cataloging-in-Publication Data

Reed, Maxine K.
    Career opportunities in television, cable, video, and multimedia /
by Maxine K. and Robert M. Reed and Lee Phenner.—4th ed.
        p.   cm.
    Rev. ed. of: Career opportunities in television, cable, and video.
3rd ed. c1990.
    Includes bibliographical references and index.
    ISBN 0-8160-3940-2 (hardcover).—ISBN 0-8160-3941-0 (pbk.)
    1. Television—Vocational guidance. 2. Cable television—
Vocational guidance. 3. Television film recording—Vocational
guidance. 4. Video tape recorder industry—Vocational guidance.
I. Reed, Robert M. II. Phenner, Lee. III. Reed, Maxine K. Career
opportunities in television, cable, and video. IV. Title.
HE8700.4.R43   1999
388.55′023′73—dc21   98–51425

Cover design by Nora Wertz

Printed in the United States of America

VB FOF 10 9 8 7 6 5 4 3 2 1
    (pbk) 10 9 8 7 6 5 4 3 2 1

This book is printed on acid-free paper.

To
Bob, Rick, and Deri,
whom we have counseled and
from whom we have learned—
and who make it all worthwhile,
and to
Forrest and Jessie
and
Carl and Hazel,
who started it all.

CONTENTS

PREFACE

Premise and Purpose

The more than 100 jobs described in the fourth edition of *Career Opportunities in Television, Cable, Video, and Multimedia* come out of some of the most exciting technological developments in our modern world. Some observers call today's environment the "information age," or the "electronic era," and whatever the name, there's little doubt that this emerging digital economy will characterize the new millennium.

The incredible number of electronic devices that affect and influence our lives represents a new entertainment and information society that is vital and dynamic. In just over 50 years, broadcast television has become a ubiquitous presence in American homes. In the past 20 years, we have seen the full development of cable and pay television and videocassettes. Satellites beam programming to an increasing number of outlets, and the family television set has become a display mechanism for video games, World Wide Web access, and home computing. Education, health, corporate, and government agencies draw on new technologies with increasing frequency, and high-definition television is now a reality, as broadcasters make the transition from analog to digital output.

Underlying all of these new entertainment and information services are people. Television, with all its show business allure, is often seen as a high-paying, glamorous field. The talented performers who appear in our living rooms every day become a part of our lives. But for every individual we see on the air, there are hundreds of workers behind the scene who make the appearance possible.

The rapidly growing television, video, and multimedia industries rely on trained engineers, talented programming and production professionals, skilled craftspeople, diligent clerical workers, and aggressive managers. News and advertising specialists are in demand, as are persuasive salespersons. Health, private industry, education, and government media centers need individuals who can harness new technologies to satisfy specific training and information objectives.

The fourth edition of this book describes the changing employment opportunities in these dynamic fields. No radio positions are listed, and jobs in public relations, film, journalism, and theater are included only as they relate to television, video, and multimedia. The job descriptions are at once more complete and more concise than those that are often found in similar career opportunity sources. An attempt has been made to present hard facts in the context of this expanding job market.

The purpose of the book is to serve as a guide to the most common occupations in these new fields. High school or college students who are interested in a career in these areas should be able to learn who does what in a television, video, or multimedia operation. Those who are currently employed in these professions should also find the information useful as they plan their career paths.

Methods

The communications field is rapidly growing and ever changing. This new edition has been carefully revised and expanded to include up-to-date information on salaries and job opportunities. A new comprehensive analysis of all media was conducted to evaluate current job opportunities and assess the immediate future of individual sections of the media. Particular attention was devoted to the creation of realistic job opportunity ratings. While it is often distressing to report that job opportunities in some communications fields are temporarily poor, we have opted for factualism rather than optimistic cheerleading.

The information for the fourth edition was gathered from printed job descriptions, employment documents, research studies, salary surveys, and tables of organization from more than 100 sources in the communications field. These data were carefully analyzed by the authors. Information from that material and from discussions with more than 50 professional colleagues were used in developing this revised edition. The career descriptions are not theoretical; they represent current practice and reflect the actual structure of jobs in the industries covered.

General Organization

The book is divided into an introduction and three main parts. The introduction provides an overview of the broadcast and cable television, video, and multimedia industries and the career opportunities within them through the coming decade; the remainder of the book consists of a part on broadcast television, a second on cable and video, and a third on multimedia. Each part is prefaced by an industry outlook.

Part I—Television Broadcasting contains 69 job descriptions organized in 8 sections, each representing a function within television or an advertising agency. The sections are Management and Administration; Programming; Production; News; Engineering; Advertising Sales; Advertising Agency; and Performance/Arts/Crafts.

Part II—Cable, Video, and Multimedia contains 38 job descriptions, organized in 7 sections, each of which represents the major cable, video, or multimedia areas under discussion: Cable Television and Multichannel Multipoint Distribution Service; Consumer Electronics and Home Video; Education; Private Industry; Government; Health, and Multimedia Development.

The careers discussed in this book have been included because they are most frequently found within a TV, cable, video, or multimedia-related industry or department. Titles, however, are not universally consistent and their definitions often overlap from setting to setting. These crossover job titles are most commonly used in today's professional environment.

The positions in Part I describe functions in broadcasting, but many are also found in other television-related operations; for example, a Producer or a Camera Operator may work with programs produced for cable television or health care communications as well as for commercial or public broadcasting. Each job description notes when there are opportunities for a position in other areas.

Whenever a title that is discussed in the book is mentioned, it appears with an initial capital letter. This will enable the reader to easily identify and refer to a related career. If a position is referred to but is not discussed in a separate description, it is printed in lowercase only.

Following Part II's job descriptions, there are three useful appendixes that provide additional sources of career information. Appendix I—Degree and Nondegree Programs lists Colleges and Universities; Workshops and Seminars; Internships, Scholarships, and Fellowships; and Training Programs and Schools. Appendix II—Unions and Associations includes all organizations mentioned in the book as well as others that might be important to particular careers. Appendix III—Bibliography lists essential books and periodicals in categories that parallel the industry and department sections used in the book. In addition, an index helps the reader to locate all positions discussed and cross-references alternate job titles.

Job Descriptions

These represent the heart of the book and warrant a detailed statement of the elements and criteria used. Each description has three major elements: Career Profile, Career Ladder, and a Narrative Text.

1. Career Profile

This is a quick reference to help the reader judge whether the position is of interest and warrants further reading. It presents a concise summary of the major facts contained in the full text and includes

Duties: a brief synopsis of the major responsibility/responsibilities of the job

Alternate Title(s): commonly used additional titles for the position

Salary Range: high and low extremes that are discussed in the Salaries section of the text

Employment Prospects and *Advancement Prospects:* rate the overall opportunities for moving into and out of the job. The ratings—Excellent, Good, Fair, or Poor—indicate the chances for employment or advancement in terms of competition for the job, supply and demand, relative turnover in the position, and the number of jobs available. They may be generally interpreted as follows:

Excellent: demand greater than supply and/or high turnover

Good: demand somewhat greater than supply; some competition and less turnover

Fair: demand and supply balance out; quite competitive; little turnover

Poor: supply exceeds demand; very specialized skills needed; highly competitive; little turnover

The ratings represent the subjective evaluation of the authors, based on the statistical evidence available, discussions with professionals in the occupation, and the viewpoints of industry observers.

Prerequisites: highlights three sets of criteria for obtaining the job, including

Education: minimum schooling required and preferred

Experience: the type of work and length of service usually needed

Special Skills: the major aptitudes and attributes that are useful in obtaining the job

2. Career Ladder

Each Career Ladder shows the job(s) to which the position often leads, and the job(s) or schooling that usually lead to the position. Career employment and advancement, however, depend entirely on the individual and his or her skills, initiative, ambition, and luck. The jobs listed in the Career Ladder indicate the most common or most direct routes to employment or advancement, but they are certainly not the only ones. The variables and the opportunities for career branching are many. Some of the positions in the Career Ladder are not fully discussed in the book because they are not specifically concerned with television, cable, video, or multimedia, or they occur too infrequently to merit full descriptions. The job(s) on the lower "rung" of the Ladder are usually referred to in the Employment Prospects or Experience/Skills portions of the text. The middle rung is always the position under discussion in the job description. The upper rung position(s) is usually mentioned in the paragraph on Advancement Prospects.

3. Narrative Text

Each job description contains the following eight categories.

Position Description: This is the core of each profile and describes the nature of the work. It presents an overview of what the job entails, including the environment, the reporting lines, whether it is supervisory in nature, and the main responsibilities of the position.

Salaries: Whenever available, ranges, average annual earnings in particular settings, and starting salaries are included. High and low extremes for the position are provided to show the broad range of salary possibilities and do not necessarily represent industry standards. It is noted if payment for work is on an hourly, per project, weekly, or per diem basis. When salaries are dependent on specific education and seniority, that is also mentioned. Fringe benefits, commissions, and prerequisites are included when the information is helpful. Most salary information is based on 1997 or 1998 surveys and is the most recent data available.

Employment Prospects: The rating in the Career Profile is elaborated upon here. The opportunities for employment are discussed in terms of the number of positions available nationally, the estimated amount of turnover, and the demand for special skills or talents. This section usually states whether individuals are promoted to the position from within or recruited from school, college, or other industry positions. As a rule, the routes to and probabilities of getting the job are discussed. Often immediate prior experience is mentioned here (or in the Experience/Skills section), and the competition is noted.

Advancement Prospects: The Career Profile rating is discussed in this section. The possibilities of advancement from the position are explained in terms of turnover at the next level, the special skills or experience required, and other career tracks that an individual might pursue. When career advancement is tied to an individual's geographic mobility, the text contains that information.

Education: The minimum educational requirements and any specific educational background or training preferred by employers are noted. Required courses, certifications, or training programs are listed, and recommended courses or degrees are indicated. To complement the Education section, Appendix I contains a list of institutions and organizations offering relevant degree and nondegree programs, training courses, seminars, workshops, internships, and apprenticeships.

Experience/Skills: This section indicates the nature and the amount of experience and vocational skills usually needed to obtain the job. There is also an assessment of the specific talents or intangible abilities that are generally expected by employers.

Minority/Women's Opportunities: The percentage of women and members of minority groups holding the position has been included when the information is available from national, government, or industry sources. Other information and estimates supplied by industry observers are also provided. In addition to current statistics, trends are supplied whenever possible.

Unions/Associations: The required craft, technical, or performing union membership is listed. Since union requirements vary considerably from job to job and among geographic locations, individuals interested in particular jobs are urged to contact local chapters or national headquarters for information. Many people advance their careers and enhance their professional growth through membership in associations, and the groups most commonly associated with the job are included. The full address and phone number, as well as the World Wide Web address if applicable, for each union and organization mentioned are listed in Appendix II.

Education/Training

Nearly all the jobs described in this book require a high school education, and for at least 80 percent, a college degree is preferred or required. Even if an entry-level position does not require one, the advancement opportunities are often brighter with a degree. The more training and education an individual acquires, the easier it is to obtain a position or advance in these challenging fields. A college education today is a job tomorrow.

Liberal arts degrees are valuable and job candidates are often required to be versatile, but specialization is becoming increasingly important. Targeted courses for specific jobs can also be useful. Courses in television and multimedia production are beneficial for anyone entering the programming or production fields. Those involved in advertising sales benefit from courses in advertising and marketing. Individuals seeking opportunities in a news department should take courses in political science and government. An ambitious person with an interest in engineering should have course work in the sciences and technology. Courses and levels of education are recommended in the appropriate job descriptions in this book.

A major in communications is even more valuable. More than 1,000 four-year colleges (see Appendix I) offered such study in 1998. The *1998–99 Occupational Outlook Handbook,* published by the U.S. Department of Labor's Bureau of Labor Statistics, said that most computer occupations, including multimedia, are expected to grow much faster than average through the year 2006; prospects for employment in television and cable are also very good.

Historically, the Federal Communications Commission (FCC) had issued broadcasting licenses for first-, second-, or third-class Radio Telephone Engineers. An examination was required for each level of competence. In late 1981, however, the FCC eliminated these distinctions, replacing them with a General Radio Telephone Operator and Broadcast Service designation. In the mid-1980s, the FCC again revised its rules and initiated a new license designation called the Restricted

Radio Telephone Operator permit. This license is required by all persons operating a television transmitter, and many employers also require it for other engineering employees. The license does not require an examination. Most employers prefer, however, that the applicant for an engineering job have a certificate from one of the industry certification programs operated by the Society of Broadcast Engineers (SBE), the International Society for Certified Electronics Technicians (ISCET), and other associations. Such certification requires study and successful completion of examinations.

Word processing skills are also important for a number of jobs profiled in this book because office computers as well as many types of telecommunications equipment operate with standard computer keyboards. Positions in Administration (Accountant, Bookkeeper), Programming (Program Manager, Publicity/Promotion Assistant), Production (Producer, Associate Producer), News (Reporter), Advertising Sales (Traffic/Continuity Specialist), and Education (Media Librarian) rely heavily on such equipment.

Given the prevalence of computers throughout the workplace and the increasing shift to digital production and broadcast standards, coursework or training in computers, with specific, job-related hardware and software, is virtually essential.

General Comments

We have sorted through mounds of data and talked with many people in the field to develop the latest and best material and to provide a realistic picture of job responsibilities, opportunities, and environments. It is assumed that the typical reader will not be interested in every position described but will scan the book selectively for specific information. For this reason, there is a deliberate repetition of terms, names of organizations and agencies, and acronyms in the job descriptions.

This book is the result of a lifetime of involvement in the communications field and of counseling and advising young people, formally and informally, about career opportunities. Specifically, it is the result of rising to the challenge of three children who dared us to put down on paper all those dinner table conversations. Our world is changing, and television, cable, video, and multimedia are vital parts of that change. A few decades ago, in the 1967 movie *The Graduate,* a family friend whispered "plastics" to the film character of Dustin Hoffman. Today he might more accurately shout "Multimedia!"

—Maxine K. and Robert M. Reed
East Northport, New York
Lee Phenner, General Editor
Cambridge, Massachusetts

ACKNOWLEDGMENTS

The authors gratefully acknowledge the following individuals who contributed research materials, job descriptions, tables of organization, and advice and counsel in the preparation of this book. Without their contributions in time, effort, and patience, the project could not have been completed.

Thanks to Paula Aguilera, multimedia producer; Robert Bailey, manager of industry research, Corporation for Public Broadcasting; P. William Bane, Mercer Management Consulting; Stephen P. Bradley, Harvard Business School; Thomas J. Bringola, vice president/business manager, WCVB-TV; Jeannie Buntin, Corporation for Public Broadcasting; Michael Butzgy, interactive writer; Cindy Buzby, president, New Media Artists Agency, Inc.; Ben Church, software engineer; David J. Collis, Harvard Business School; Jill Cooney, multimedia developer; Patricia Corrigan, assistant director of career services, Emerson College; Parthavi Das, manager of association outreach, Women in Cable & Telecommunications; Robert Hilliard, professor of visual and media arts, Emerson College; Gavin Koon, executive director, Scenic, Title, and Graphic Artists Local 816; Allan Kotmel, software engineer; Robin Shapiro Loeb, communications director, American Bar Association/Commission on Women in the Profession; Jean McCarthy, executive producer, Design Team, Microsoft Studios; Jack Stanley, vice president of communications, International Brotherhood of Electrical Workers; Vernon Stone, professor emeritus, University of Missouri/Columbia School of Journalism; Anne Forbes Van Nest, vice president, New Media Artists Agency, Inc.; Alisha Haydn Vera, partner, Black Bean Studios; and Chuck Warren, director of communications, Directors Guild of America.

In addition to the individuals cited above, the following associations and organizations graciously provided research materials, salary information, employment surveys, and study documents for the preparation of this book. Their contributions are gratefully acknowledged: Advertising Age; Affiliated Property Craftspersons Local 44; American Association of Advertising Agencies; American Artists; American Guild of Authors and Composers; Black Broadcasters Alliance; Broadcast Engineering; Broadcasting Training Program; Cable Telecommunications Association; Cablevision; Center for the Advancement of Hispanics in Science and Engineering Education; Communications News; Communications Today; Communicator; Computerworld; Corporation for Public Broadcasting; Directors Guild of America; Federal Communications Commission; HTML Writers Guild; Institute of Electrical and Electronics Engineers; Interactive Digital Software Association; Interactive Marketing & Research; Interactive Publishing/Catchup! Communications; International Alliance of Theatrical Stage Employees; Law School Admission Council; MCP Magazine; Minority Career Network; Multimedia Producer; National Action Council for Minorities in Engineering; National Association of Broadcast Employees and Technicians; National Association of Broadcasters; National Association of Minorities in Communications; National Broadcast Association for Community Affairs; National Cable Television Association; National Science Foundation; Oregon Multimedia Association; Planetary News; Radio & Television News Directors Association; Screen Actors Guild; Society of Broadcast Engineers; Television Bureau of Advertising; U.S. Consumer Electronics Industry Today; U.S. Department of Commerce/Secretariat on Electronic Commerce; U.S. Department of Labor/Bureau of Labor Statistics; U.S. News & World Report Online; University of Georgia/Henry W. Grady College of Journalism and Mass Communication; Videography Online; Video Systems; Web Techniques; Women in Cable & Telecommunications Foundation; Working Woman; Writers Guild of America, West; WUTR-TV; www.cfstaffing.com; www.collegeedge.com; www.inform.umd.edu/diversityweb; www.jobsearchtech.miningco.com; www.jobsmart.org; www.petersons.com; and www.w3.org.

PART I
TELEVISION
BROADCASTING

INDUSTRY OUTLOOK

HISTORY

Experiments in sending pictures through the air were conducted as early as 1884, but the first real television broadcast occurred in 1927. The first major telecast is generally considered to have been the transmission of President Franklin D. Roosevelt opening the 1939 World's Fair in New York City.

The number of over-the-air electronic transmissions that can be made without interfering with one another are effectively limited by the "physics of scarcity." The federal government, therefore, in accordance with the Communications Act of 1934, established the Federal Communications Commission (FCC)* to regulate radio and television stations. The FCC licenses stations to operate "in the public interest, convenience, and necessity," and assigns them to specific frequencies and power. The FCC also limits stations to particular communities, assigns their call letters, allocates channels, processes requests to transfer control of a station to another party, and monitors all stations to ensure that they are in compliance with its rules and technical regulations. At license renewal time, the FCC reviews a station's record to verify that it is operating in the public interest.

By the end of World War II, the available television channels were becoming crowded, and in 1948, the FCC imposed a ban on all new license applications. Finally, in 1952, it adopted a plan that allocated about 2,000 TV channels to 1,300 communities, and the age of television was born. By 1955, there were 448 stations on the air. Forty-four years later, 1,569 stations were licensed and operating throughout the United States (see Table I-1).

Television stations broadcast on assigned channels 2 through 13 in the VHF (very high frequency) band and on channels 14 through 83 in the UHF (ultra high frequency) band. The majority operate in the VHF band.

Public (educational) noncommercial TV (PTV) stations account for one-quarter of the licensees and are operated by universities, schools, state agencies, and community groups. These stations were originally designed and licensed to serve the educational needs of local communities. The first such station began broadcasting in 1953. With passage of the Public Broadcasting Act by Congress in 1967, the Corporation for Public Broadcasting (CPB)* was formed as an administrative funding agency, and the Public Broadcasting Service (PBS) was started as the programming agency. Today, most PTV stations transmit instructional television (ITV) programs during the day, and offer cultural programs, documentaries, art, and drama series during the evening as an alternative to commercial TV fare. All public stations are members of PBS, which serves as a national source of programming to the interconnected PTV stations.

Commercial television stations and networks make their money primarily by selling portions of their air time to advertisers. Public TV stations, on the other hand, sell no commercial time. Their incomes are derived from federal, state, and local governments, viewer donations, and grants from corporations and foundations.

Local television programming is created by station staffs, by independent producers, and by production companies who conceive and develop programs that are sold to commercial and some public TV stations. Many of the larger independent production firms produce shows and sell the broadcast rights to national syndication companies that, in turn, make the programs available to individual stations. Some national independent production companies produce programs for the networks, which then sell time on them to sponsors through advertising agencies.

In 1998, more than 96 million homes in the United States—more than 98 percent of the total—had a television set, more than 67 percent had more than two, and some 96 percent of the homes had a color TV set. The average household

---

* The Federal Communications Commission is an independent federal agency headed by seven commissioners who are appointed by the president with the advice and consent of the Senate. No more than four commissioners can belong to the same political party.

* The CPB is a nonprofit corporation responsible for administering federal funds for public broadcasting stations and for research and development, interconnection, and training programs.

Table I-1—Television Stations on the Air as of January 31, 1998

	Commercial TV	Public TV	Total
VHF	557	125	682
UHF	645	242	887
Total	1,202	367	1,569

Source: FCC

watched TV for 6 hours, 57 minutes a day, according to the National Association of Broadcasters.

TYPICAL ORGANIZATIONAL STRUCTURES

Commercial Networks

The four major commercial networks are ABC (the American Broadcasting Company), CBS (formerly called the Columbia Broadcasting System), NBC (the National Broadcasting Company), and FOX (the FOX Broadcasting Company). WB (Warner Bros.) and UPN (Paramount) are emerging networks. All maintain corporate headquarters in New York City and have studio facilities there and in Hollywood. The networks supply programming to their affiliated stations via satellite and coaxial cable or by microwave relay.

The networks are large corporate entities with staffs the equal of any major company. A typical Table of Organization (TO) is complicated and undergoes constant alterations to reflect changes in business emphases as well as the company's involvement in both media- related and nonmedia-related industries. For a recent simplified example, see Table I-2. Reporting to the executives shown in the chart are additional vice presidents in charge of advertising sales, programs and talent, and production, as well as many program managers and executives in charge of comedy, daytime programs, drama, children's programs, variety shows, and specials. Their efforts are supported by staffs that often number 50 or more.

Commercial Television Stations

Each of the networks also owns and operates a few local television stations. Many commercial stations, however, are nonaffiliated "independents." Most local stations, although affiliated with one of the commercial networks, are inde-

pendently owned. The station signs an affiliation agreement with a specific network and agrees to carry programs in certain time periods. The network can then obtain advertising sponsors for commercials within those programs by promising that they will be seen by a large national audience comprised of their local affiliates' viewers.

Regardless of its affiliation status, each station operates as a separate business and is usually organized into five major departments: Advertising Sales, Engineering, Business, News, and Programming. Every station, however, has its own specific structure and practices. The TOs in this outlook reflect some of the more common organizational patterns in the industry.

Table I-3 shows a typical TO for a commercial TV station. Reporting lines are clearly shown, although not all stations follow these lines of authority. We have attempted to show positions in terms of their relative importance by drawing lines of varying lengths. This is not precise and the reader should consult each job description to get a sense of the significance of each position, salary levels, and reporting lines.

Many small commercial stations employ 25 people or less who double and triple in various jobs. Major market stations may employ staffs of 150 or more.

The number of employees often depends on the amount of local production originated by the station or on its emphasis on news programming. In most stations, the engineering and news departments have the largest numbers of employees.

Public Television Stations

In general, public stations have fewer employees and a somewhat simpler organizational structure. Most PTV stations operate a separate department known as development (fund-raising). The emphasis on local production at public TV stations has led many of them to consider the production area

---

Table I-2—Typical Commercial Television Network Table of Organization

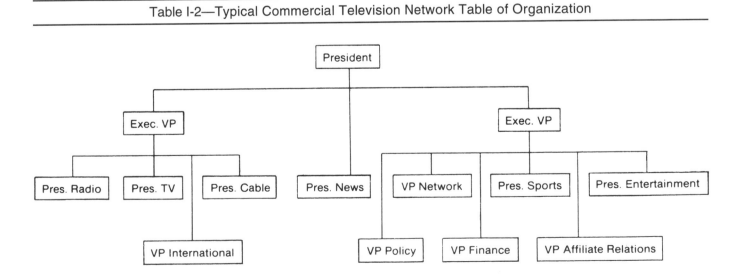

Table I-3—Typical Commercial Television Station Table of Organization

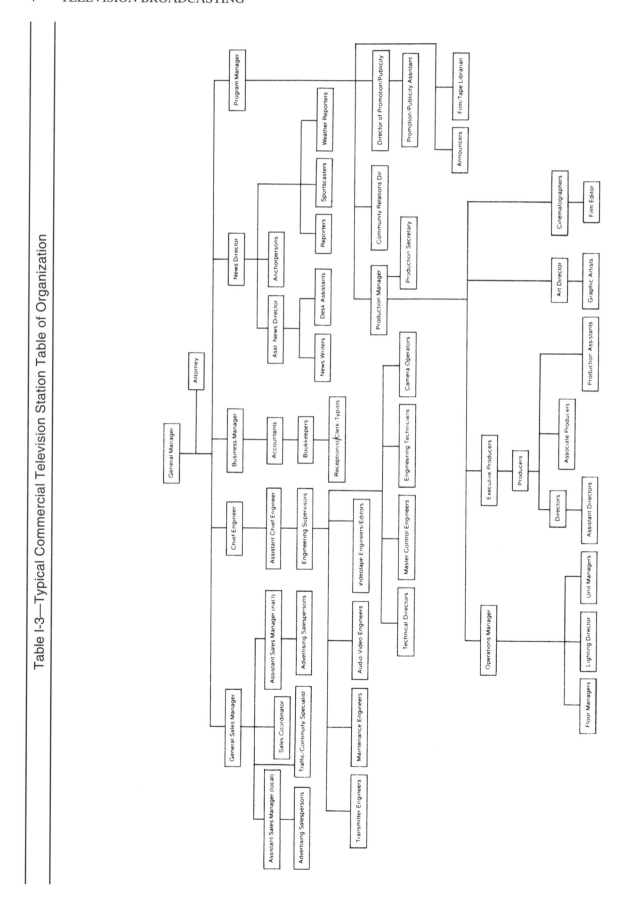

Table I-4—Typical Public Television Station Table of Organization

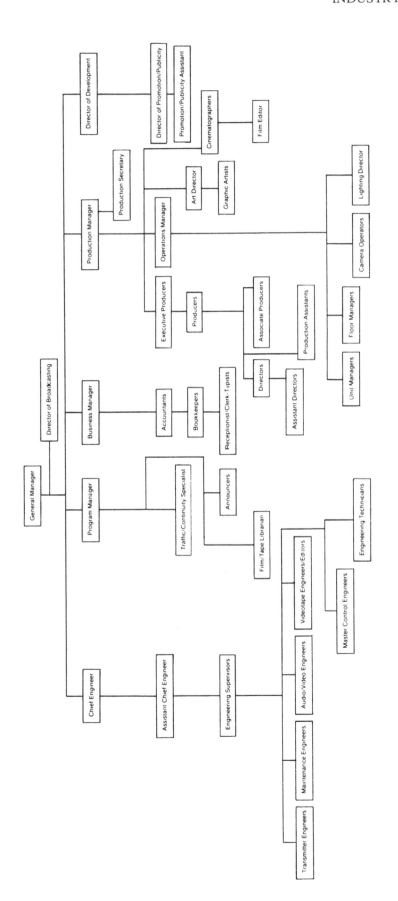

as a separate department, reporting directly to the General Manager.

Few public stations employ in-house Attorneys. Normally there is no news department. Most do not have Community Relations Directors either, inasmuch as the entire station staff is actively engaged in these duties because all of PTV programming is designed to serve community needs.

In commercial stations, the Traffic/Continuity Specialist normally reports to the General Sales Manager and schedules commercials as well as station breaks and programming. Since public TV stations do not deal with advertising sales, the Traffic/Continuity Specialist handles only programming and station breaks and reports directly to the Program Manager. At most commercial stations, engineering and technical employees are represented by a union and, as part of an engineering/technical contract, that union often represents Camera Operators. Engineering and technical staff members in public television are usually not represented by a union. In addition, the heavier emphasis on production at most PTV stations requires that Camera Operators report to, and be part of, the production department.

As a rule, the production and engineering departments at a public television station have the largest staffs. Total employment at public television stations in 1998 was 10,666, a 1.3 percent increase over the previous year, according to the Corporation for Public Broadcasting.

A public TV station is likely to have the following people reporting directly to the General Manager. Chief Engineer, Director of Broadcasting, Program Manager, Business Manager, Production Manager, and Director of Development. Table I-4 depicts a typical Table of Organization for a public TV station. As with the TO for a commercial station, reporting lines are clear but the reader should look at the job descriptions to get a more accurate picture of the relative importance of each position, salaries, and lines of authority.

PRODUCTION AND FACILITIES COMPANIES

Production

The vast majority of the programming seen on televsion broadcast stations or cable systems is not produced by the networks, individual stations, or cable companies but by independent production companies.

Large production companies produce original half-hour situation comedies, made-for-TV movies, or specials for sale to and transmission by the cable or commercial networks. Others produce game shows or first-run syndication programming. Some companies produce half-hour programs for syndication or cable television as well as taped segments for insertion into long-form network or cable programs.

Many companies specialize in the production of comercials for advertising agencies. Others specialize in making programs for corporate or private TV, government, or health organizations. Some specialize in producing music videos, fine arts programs, or documentaries. Some specialize in productions for public television. Some companies specialize in videotape production and others in films. Many produce programs in both formats.

The companies can be as small as one person with an idea to large multimillion-dollar corporations with sizable full-time staffs.

Most independent production companies maintain small full-time staffs, which include a Producer, Director, Lighting Director, and, sometimes, Camera Operators, augmented by freelancers workinig on a per-project basis. Full-time employment is rare, however, in an industry in which most people are generally "between assignments."

Periodic jobs are available in the Performance/Arts/Crafts area and, to a lesser extent, for the production jobs listed in Table II-2, Crossover/Communications Jobs. With a seemingly insatiable appetite for programming in all areas of television, cable, and video, opportunities should grow during the next five years. As in the other parts of the communications industries, Engineers will be in particular demand.

Production Facilities

Very few independent production companies own and operate their own facilities. Although some firms often have a few items of basic equipment, most rent production and postproduction facilities for most of their work. An independent production company uses the studios, remote truck, and editing equipment of a facilities company, which is often called a production house.

One of the largest users of facilities companies are AV centers in corporations (see the Industry Outlook in Part II). Bottom line–oriented corporations are less likely today to invest in large video studios and full-time staffs. Since prodution costs are easier to write off than capital expenditures, the staff farms out much of the work and utilizes production facilities companies.

Some firms offer full production as well as postproduction services, including editing and duplication of videotape (dubbing), and are called full-service companies. Some specialize in postproduction, others in renting remote trucks and equipment, and still others concentrate on film-to-tape transfers. Even within these sub-areas, some houses will rent very specific editing equipment or provide unique music or computer animation services. These smaller and quite specialized houses are often known as boutiques.

Overall, there are an estimated 1,300 full-service production facilities companies in the United States. This total almost matches the number of broadcast television stations in the United States, which also sometimes rent equipment and services from facilities companies. At least 600 key companies provided audio and video teleconferencing equipment, facilities, and services in 1998, according to industry sources.

ADVERTISING AGENCIES

Advertising is big business. Domestic expenditures of all advertising (print, billboards, television, radio), which totaled only $113 billion in 1988, reached $175 billion in 1998. Nearly 25 percent of the sum was spent on television advertising.

Television networks and stations, however, produce very few of the commercials seen on the air. Most are created by advertising agencies under contract from a specific sponsor. The agencies research the product and its potential customers, write the advertising copy, and produce the commercial on tape, digital media, or film using their own or independent production facilities. They usually rent production equipment and facilities.

The ad agency also recommends the frequency and periods when the commercial should be broadcast, contracts with a network or station for air time, and researches the effectiveness of the advertising campaign. For their services, ad agencies usually receive 15 percent of the amount spent by the sponsor in the advertising campaign.

EMPLOYMENT STATISTICS

In 1997, 149,975 people were working in television broadcasting in the United States, according to the FCC. This represented an increase from 146,616 in 1996. More than 20 percent of those employed served as officials and managers in 1996, and 33 percent, as professionals. More than 17 percent were employed as technicians, 15 percent as sales workers, and 12 percent as office/clerical workers. For a numerical analysis, see Table I-5.

WOMEN AND MINORITIES

The employment of women and members of minority groups in both commercial and public television has increased slightly in the past few years. The percentage of women occupying positions at broadcast television stations increased from 36.2 percent in 1988 to 40.8 percent in 1996, according to the FCC.

The growth in employment of minorities at both commercial and PTV stations did not increase as much during the same period. The FCC includes in the classification of minorities those people who are Black, Asian American, Pacific Islander, American Indian, and Hispanic. The percentage of minority groups occupying positions at commercial television stations increased very slightly, from 18.4 percent in 1988 to 19.9 percent in 1996. The percentage of minority employment in each occupational category in broadcast television is indicated in Table I-5.

EMPLOYMENT TRENDS

General

Total employment is expected to increase by 18.6 million jobs from 1996 to 2006, a 14 percent increase, according to the Bureau of Labor Statistics (BLS). The fastest-growing occupations are in service producing sectors, such as business, health care, and social services. Rapid growth in business services is led by computer and data processing services.

American workers will continue to be a diverse group. Minority group members in the year 2006 will make up an even larger share of the job market than in 1996. The Hispanic population will likely become the second-largest ethnic group, after whites, who are expected to comprise 73 percent of the U.S. labor force in 2006, compared with 75 percent in

	Total	Male	Female	Minority Percentage
Officials and Managers	29,572	19,109	10,463	14 %
Professionals	48,939	31,703	17,236	18.8
Technicians	25,417	21,636	3,781	23.8
Sales Workers	22,690	10,594	12,096	14
Office/Clerical	18,050	2,121	15,929	32.2
Craftspeople	696	588	108	32.2
Operatives	622	534	88	35.5
Laborers	178	158	20	54.5
Service	452	365	87	62.2
TOTAL	146,616	86,808	59,808	

Table I-5—Employment in Broadcast Television, 1996

Source: 1996 Broadcast and Cable Report

1996. The percentage of blacks, Asians, Native Americans, and others will also increase.

Women will continue to increase their share of the workforce. By the year 2006, they are expected to account for 47.4 percent of the workforce.

The influence of the "baby boomers" will continue to be felt through 2006, even as they grow older. For the first time in 25 years, though, the number of young workers (age 16 to 24) will be growing faster than the overall labor force. And they will be better educated. While the economy will generate jobs at all educational levels, employment in occupations requiring an associate's degree or higher will grow faster than those with lower educational requirements, according to the BLS.

The emphasis on education will continue. Because of the increasing role of technology, the fastest-growing job categories will require the highest levels of education and skill.

Communications

Employment in the broadcast communications industry through 2006 is expected to grow from 10 to 20 percent, according to the 1998–99 *Occupational Outlook Handbook.*

There have been a number of mergers and consolidations among television companies and networks, and the increased competition has created a need for more "bottom line" efficiencies, resulting, in some cases, in reductions in personnel.

This has been partially true at the middle management level at the networks and group broadcasters. Still, most entry-level jobs will remain open and available for young people.

A considerable number of jobs in television broadcasting will occur through normal attrition. Station structure and top management are in a period of transition. There have been several prominent retirees in the past few years, and their successors are younger. Job retirement is also positively affecting middle-management job opportunities, particularly in engineering and news. But commercial television broadcasting is a continuing and vital part of the American communications scene.

Commercial Television

At the beginning of the 1990s, the full-power commercial television broadcast industry was besieged by competitive technological innovations. Emerging new media, including low-power television stations, cable systems, and home video, were seen as the hot new challenges to broadcast television's traditional dominance of American homes.

The new technologies have made inroads. The networks' share of the prime time audience dropped from a high of 92 percent in 1978 to 60 percent in 1998, and more than 11 million consumers were serviced by a noncable multichannel video provider—in other words, direct broadcast satellite—representing 14 percent of the multichannel video market. Full-power television broadcasting, however, will still claim the mass audience that is vital to advertisers. And the jobs to support and

maintain affiliated stations and to create new programs will not diminish. These jobs are profiled in Part I of this book.

While jobs at the commercial networks may decrease, there will be opportunities in some of the ad hoc and semipermanent small "networks" of independent and affiliated stations, as well as in cable and satellite operations. These coalitions are expected to increase through 2006.

Public Television

The job outlook in public television is not bright. Few new PTV stations are expected to be constructed in the next five years. The jobs available will largely depend on the growth of the current stations and their ability to increase their fund-raising from federal and state governments, corporations, gifts, grants, and their dedicated and loyal viewers. Ironically, PTV viewing is at an all-time high and is expected to increase. Faced with declining federal support, however, PTV stations are engaging in entrepreneurial activities, including teleconferencing and the selling of production services, to increase their financial support and growth. While PTV jobs will not increase appreciably in the coming decade, some positions will be available to support the new endeavors, as well as through normal attrition.

Low-Power Television Stations

During the next five years, the FCC will continue to authorize the construction of low-power television (LPTV) stations. These stations are designed to provide the opportunity for small rural communities to establish their own stations. Called "community TV," the stations are often operated as a cross between a local newspaper and an FM radio station. Additional LPTV stations may be constructed in some major cities to serve specific audiences with specialized language, religious, minority, ethnic, or video music programming. Operating with limited power and covering a distance of less than 20 miles, the small LPTV stations are less expensive to construct, maintain, and operate. Some stations are operated as nonprofit organizations, while others are commercial ventures dependent upon advertising. Still others scramble their signals and charge viewers a monthly subscription fee, similar to cable television

The FCC began accepting LPTV construction permit applications in 1980 and, despite a partial freeze on new applications a few months later, it was flooded with more than 12,000 requests. Although most were returned on technical grounds, the FCC was forced to develop a complicated lottery system to award construction permits.

By September 1996, there were 6,872 LPTV stations on the air, according to the FCC. Most do local programming. Some 7,000 stations could be on the air by 2006. Each station employs 10 to 15 people. There will also be opportunities for part-time positions (paid or volunteer). While the stations require fewer staff members, many of the jobs profiled in Part I of this book will be available at these new LPTV operations.

In addition, some jobs at small network program headquarters, created to serve LPTV stations, may become available.

Production

The production facilities business is highly competitive, with each company vying with others to provide the latest state-of-the-art equipment. As a result, client services are emphasized and there is a major focus on recruiting and retaining a good personnel.

The facilities business is also a unique service business, inasmuch as the clients are actively involved in the work. The production company or corporate department brings along a few key people, including a Director, to produce the program at the facility. Most facilities companies operate with relatively small but expert staffs, ranging from 10 to 20 people. Freelancers are routinely employed to flesh out the crew or postproduction sequence on a project-by-project basis.

While the emphasis is on engineering and technically skilled personnel at most facilities houses, the in-house staff is often supplemented by many of the jobs profiled in the Performance/Arts/Crafts section in Part I.

Videotape Engineer/Editors are in particular demand, along with qualified Media and Maintenance Engineers, to operate and maintain the equipment. Although the field is extremely competitive, the need for on-line experts at computerized editing and special effects remains constant and is predicted to grow in the next five years. With the increased sophistication of equipment have come simpler operating procedures. Most top-line Videotape Engineer/Editors today do not have full-fledged engineering backgrounds.

Although no specific jobs are profiled in this book, the individual seeking a job at production and postproduction facilities companies should review the profiles for Production and Engineering positions in Part I and also the Crossover Job chart in Part II. The opportunities for positions in this area of communications are good.

Advertising Agencies

According to the American Association of Advertising Agencies (4As), there were 13,000 advertising agencies in the United States in 1998. One-third of them are small (essentially one-person operations), and one-third have an average of only five employees. But many are large organizations employing more than 1,000 employees each.

There were more than 500,000 people employed in advertising in 1997, according to the BLS; that figure could be increased as thousands more are employed at the national, regional, and local levels in media production and facilities companies and service and supply organizations.

The growth of advertising agencies has slowed in recent years, and there have been a number of mergers. While entry-level jobs are still available, the opportunity for mid-level jobs has declined, due to the consolidations. Advertising is a labor-intensive business. Salaries constitute the major expense at advertising agencies, and the loss of an account often means the loss of jobs.

Advertising is also a stressful occupation, full of uncertainties, particularly in the executive jobs where there are no clear, accepted standards for evaluating work. There is a high rate of turnover at agencies, as well as actual departures from the "ulcer gulch" industry of "Mad Avenue," according to industry observers.

Advertising, however, has grown in stature and respectability in the past 20 years. A major in advertising is offered at more than 190 universities, according to Peterson's website. Creative, exciting jobs do exist. The agency business is essentially a young person's field; the average age of employees is under 40.

Ad agencies are generally divided into four departments. The creative department develops and produces the actual advertising, and the media department analyzes and purchases advertising time and space in the various media. These two departments are supported by the research department, which conducts market studies. The account service department coordinates all activities and acts as the liaison with the clients.

In a study, the 4As discovered 96 separate job titles at the agency executive level and 93 at the nonexecutive level. Five representative positions are profiled in the Advertising Agency section of Part I of this book.

Performance/Arts/Crafts

At any one time in 1996, actors held an average of about 105,000 jobs in motion pictures, stage plays, industrial shows, and commercials, according to the BLS. Most actors, however, were "between jobs." And the Screen Actors Guild (SAG) reported that its members' average annual income earned from acting was less than $5,000.

In the same period, professional musicians held, at any given time, an average of about 274,000 jobs. Many more were "between engagements." Most Performers also work in unrelated occupations in order to maintain a reasonable standard of living.

The increasing demand for programming to fill all of the new channels of technology, however, should see an increase in the number of opportunities through 2006. Jobs for Performers in television and the related industries are expected to grow at a faster-than-average rate through 2006, according to the BLS.

Job opportunities at production/facilities companies, developing syndicated first-run programs for distribution to commercial stations, should increase, along with jobs in the production of commercials (see Part II). In addition, more jobs in the newer nonbroadcast media and multimedia (also described in Part II) will become available. Craft and technical jobs (Musical Director, Costume Designer, Makeup Artist, Property Master, Stagehand/Grip) will also increase slightly in the next five years to support the rising demand for new programming to serve the growing number of communications outlets.

As in the past, the majority of jobs will be in the major markets—in particular, in New York and Los Angeles. Other jobs will be available in Chicago, Orlando, and Nashville. There will also be an increase in engineering on-location positions at production companies during the next five years, according to industry observers.

The large numbers of people desiring Performance/Arts/Crafts jobs, and the lack of formal entry requirements, along with the relatively smaller number of job openings, will continue to create keen competition. Some jobs will occur by attrition as older personnel leave the professions. Only the most talented newcomers, however, will find regular employment.

SUMMARY OF OPPORTUNITIES

Opportunities in television broadcasting and all its related areas are expected to increase slightly in the next five years. The competition, however, is expected to be intense. More people are in the job market than ever before, and the communications industry has traditionally attracted a large number of applicants. This trend will continue. Some of the related nonbroadcast jobs (described in Part II of the book) may offer more opportunities. Severe competition for *all* communications positions will probably raise the requirements for jobs, so that those with more training and education will have a better chance of getting positions.

THE JOB DESCRIPTIONS

The 69 positions discussed in Part I of this book are divided among eight sections. Six of the sections reflect major divisions indicated in the Table of Organization charts for typical commercial and public television stations. These six are labeled: Management and Administration, Programming, Production, News, Engineering, and Advertising Sales. A seventh section contains discussions of jobs at an Advertising Agency. Section eight, Performance/Arts/Crafts, comprises descriptions of those specialty positions that are usually found only at networks, independent production companies, and some major market stations, and occasionally in cable, video, and nonbroadcast and nonprofit operations.

GENERAL MANAGER

CAREER PROFILE

Duties: Overall management of a television station

Alternate Title(s): Station Manager; Vice President/General Manager

Salary Range: $66,000 to $259,000

Employment Prospects: Poor

Advancement Prospects: Poor

Prerequisites:

Education—Undergraduate degree in communications, advertising, or business; master's degree preferable

Experience—Minimum of 10 years in television management

Special Skills—Leadership qualities; business judgment; extensive broadcasting knowledge

CAREER LADDER

```
┌─────────────────────────────────────┐
│ General Manager (Larger Station);    │
│ Network Executive;                   │
│ Program Syndication Executive        │
└─────────────────────────────────────┘

┌─────────────────────────────────────┐
│ General Manager                      │
└─────────────────────────────────────┘

┌─────────────────────────────────────┐
│ Program Manager; Business Manager;   │
│ General Sales Manager                │
└─────────────────────────────────────┘
```

Position Description

The General Manager (GM) is in charge of the overall management and operation of a television station. Responsibilities include all business and financial matters, including income, expenses, short- and long-range planning, budgeting, forecasting, and profitability. This person runs the station in accordance with all federal, state, and local laws, including Federal Communications Commission (FCC) regulations. The General Manager is also responsible for establishing and maintaining the station's image.

If the station is affiliated with a network, the General Manager has an obligation to uphold the policies of the affiliation agreement and to maintain contact with network officials. The person in this position also supports relationships with community leaders, advertisers, contributors, advertising agencies, program suppliers, and other outside station contacts.

The responsibilities of the General Manager are similar in commercial and in public broadcasting except in generating income. In commercial TV, the General Manager is in overall charge of producing advertising revenues, and must constantly evaluate the effectiveness of the sales department. At a public station, the General Manager prepares and defends budgets submitted to legislatures or other public entities and solicits funds from the viewing public, corporations, and foundations. Increasingly, however, PTV General Managers are supervising rental of facilities and other profit-making

ventures to bolster the stations' income. At commercial low-power television (LPTV) stations, the General Manager serves in a capacity similar to that of the GM at a full-power station, only on a much smaller scale.

The General Manager hires the major department heads and establishes their goals, monitors their performance, and approves their budgets. Although they have day-to-day responsibility, the General Manager oversees each department's activities. In programming, the GM approves what is produced locally, which syndicated programs are bought, and what should be broadcast in the future and evaluates the schedule in response to competition and audience ratings. For production, the General Manager monitors program budgets. In news, formats and editorial policies must be approved. In engineering, the General Manager approves of the investment in new equipment and facilities. For advertising sales, the GM determines advertising policies, tracks income, evaluates the rate structure of the station and its competition, and helps identify potential advertisers.

General Managers are selected and employed by boards of directors at public TV stations, and, in commercial broadcasting, by the chief executive officer of the company that owns the station.

Additionally, the General Manager

- delivers editorials on air;

- keeps up with changes in communications technology; and
- represents the station at industry conferences.

Salaries

In keeping with the demands of the position, General Managers are paid well.

The median base salary for General Managers at commercial stations in 1997 was $127,307, according to the National Association of Broadcasters (NAB). The median bonus paid to the individual was $32,660. Most individuals were paid by a salary-plus-bonus arrangement and had an expense-account, a company profit-sharing plan, a fully paid pension plan, and company-paid life insurance.

General Managers at public TV stations are generally less well paid than their commercial counterparts. According to a 1998 Corporation for Public Broadcasting (CPB) study, the median annual salary was $85,884. The range was from $26,671 at smaller school-owned stations to $240,918 at the larger community-owned companies. Most General Managers of noncommercial stations contribute to their medical, life insurance, and pension plans, and, of course, do not participate in profit sharing. Salaries for General Managers at the new LPTV stations ranged from $25,000 to $35,000 in 1998.

Employment Prospects

Opportunities in both commercial and public broadcasting are extremely limited. There are only 1,569 full-power stations that employ General Managers. Some opportunities will become available at the newer LPTV stations, which, in 1997, numbered 6,800 and are located mostly in rural areas.

Advancement Prospects

The majority of General Managers have reached the peak of their careers. Most are between 45 and 60 years of age. Some younger people take more responsible positions as General Managers at larger stations, as network executives involved in sales or relations with affiliated stations, or as managers in program syndication companies. Some establish their own advertising agencies or consulting firms. Still others purchase their own broadcasting stations. Because of the mergers and acquisitions spurred by the Telecommunications Act of 1996, opportunities for advancement are better than 10 years ago, with many GMs opting to move within the parent corporation.

Education

As a rule, the minimum requirement is an undergraduate degree, especially in communications, advertising, or jour-

nalism. Marketing or business degrees are also useful, and many General Managers have received a master of business administration (MBA), or have taken graduate level business courses. A few have law degrees.

Experience/Skills

At least 10 years of supervisory work in various television positions are necessary. In commercial TV, the General Manager frequently comes from the sales or business areas. In public broadcasting, he or she often has a middle-management background in programming or fund-raising and development. A General Manager's experience should include a successful track record in the specific position of Program Manager, Business Manager, or General Sales Manager.

Leadership, sound business judgment, a deep knowledge of broadcasting, a sense of responsibility, honesty, and an ability to motivate people are essential qualities for a General Manager.

Minority/Women's Opportunities

The majority of General Managers in television broadcasting are white males; however, minorities and women have made marginal gains in recent years. Of the total full-time broadcast employees in the upper-four job categories (which includes General Managers), the number of women increased from 34.1 percent to 34.4 percent, and the number of minorities increased from 17.5 percent to 17.8 percent from 1995 to 1996, according to the FCC. The CPB reported that from 1996 to 1997, the employment of minority officials and managers increased by 12.1 percent. Meanwhile, although BLS figures reveal that women overall still earn only 72¢ for every dollar that a man earns, the *Working Woman* 1995 Salary Survey states that professional/managerial women were earning between 80¢ and 90¢ for every dollar a man earns. Industry experts note that few women and minorities hold these top posts, and therefore, inroads should be possible.

Unions/Associations

There are no unions that serve as bargaining agents or representatives for General Managers. Some belong to the National Association of Television Program Executives (NATPE). Most are active in various network-affiliate committees and boards, and some are members of the International Radio and Television Society (IRTS) and the National Academy of Television Arts and Sciences (NATAS). In public television, General Managers are often members of regional networks and associations.

ATTORNEY

CAREER PROFILE

Duties: Advising and representing a communications company or government regulatory agency on legal matters

Alternate Title(s): Lawyer

Salary Range: $40,000 to $100,000+

Employment Prospects: Fair

Advancement Prospects: Poor

Prerequisites:

Education—Law degree

Experience—Two to three years in communications law

Special Skills—Interpersonal skills; logical reasoning; sense of responsibility; writing and verbal abilities

CAREER LADDER

```
┌─────────────────────────────────┐
│   Attorney (Larger Law Firm,     │
│   Larger Station, or Network)    │
└─────────────────────────────────┘

┌─────────────────────────────────┐
│           Attorney               │
└─────────────────────────────────┘

┌─────────────────────────────────┐
│ Junior Associate; Research Assistant; │
│           Law Clerk              │
└─────────────────────────────────┘
```

Position Description

Attorneys provide legal counsel to and represent an outside company, employer, or public agency active in the communications field. They minimize the legal risks clients face and generally protect their interests in all legal matters. Attorneys are technically officers of the courts and must balance the needs of their clients with the requirements of the law. An Attorney specializing in communications addresses issues relating to contracts, copyright, and libel, as well as regulations of the Federal Communications Commission (FCC) and other government agencies. The position may be within a communications company or a regulatory arm of the government.

Attorneys are usually on staff only at networks, major market stations, or multiple system operators (MSOs), companies that own a number of cable TV systems. Attorneys also work at home video companies. The majority of television stations do not have a staff Attorney but are represented by outside law firms. Most public and commercial stations also retain a law firm in Washington, D.C., that specializes in communications law and that represents the client in all federal regulatory matters, particularly with the FCC.

An Attorney representing a station must advise the client on how to protect and renew its FCC license. Another responsibility may be to handle copyright issues to protect the station from copyright infringement. An Attorney is usually in charge of, prepares, and negotiates contracts. These often include employment, equipment or program purchase, and advertising agreements. An Attorney is also frequently asked to review materials to be aired to make certain they are not libelous.

Many Attorneys work in federal, state, and local government regulatory agencies that oversee broadcasting or telecommunications. They assure that stations and cable TV systems are in compliance with all regulations. Attorneys working for these agencies help to write the rules, oversee compliance with federal, state, and local laws, and pass on various broadcast license or cable franchise applications.

Attorneys give clients or employers advice about their legal obligations, interpret the law, analyze problems and proposals, and suggest possible actions. When necessary, an Attorney develops strategies for and prepares and argues cases in court for a communications company or a regulatory agency.

Additionally, the Attorney

- handles real estate transactions, tax matters, and other noncommunications legal issues;
- researches and investigates cases, precedents, and rulings; and
- writes reports and briefs regarding the legal aspects of business activities.

Salaries

There has been an increase in salaries offered to new lawyers. In 1996, starting salaries for law school graduates were usually above $40,000. The average earnings for experienced communications Attorneys is approximately $60,000, and heads of legal departments at networks, MSOs, or large stations earned more than $100,000.

In the federal government, the starting salary for entry-level Attorneys employed by the federal government was $34,500 in 1996. The average salary for general attorneys employed by the federal government was $72,700 in 1997.

Employment Prospects

There were more than 622,000 jobs held by Attorneys in the United States in 1996, with 7 out of 10 practicing privately, according to government estimates. Two-thirds of all lawyers in the world are in the United States. Growth in the yearly number of law school graduates has continued, and lawyers will face keen competition through 2006. Still, government statistics indicate that employment for lawyers will grow. Most beginning communications Attorneys start work as junior associates, research assistants, or clerks in communications law firms. The prospects of employment are fair.

Advancement Prospects

There is relatively little turnover in communications law, and the chances for advancement are poor. It is often necessary to relocate to advance a legal communications career. Most of the large private firms specializing in communications law are in Washington, D.C., New York City, and Los Angeles.

Some Attorneys with communications law experience at private law firms in small or middle market communities obtain positions at specialized communications law firms in major market cities. Others join in-house legal staffs at networks or MSOs and some obtain communications law positions with the federal government. A few become partners in communications law firms after 6 to 10 years. Still fewer establish their own firms. A small number become General Managers at commercial TV stations, MSOs, or home video companies.

Education

To practice law in the courts of any state, an individual must be admitted to its bar. To qualify for the bar examination, an applicant must complete at least 3 years of college and graduate from 1 of the nearly 180 law schools approved by the American Bar Association (ABA) or the proper state authorities. Law school graduates receive a degree of either juris doctor (JD) or bachelor of law (LLB). An undergraduate degree in mass communications or electrical engineering is helpful, as are studies in business, economics government, and public speaking.

Experience/Skills

Most communications law firms or network legal departments require that candidates have two to three years of work in communications law, usually as a junior associate, research assistant, or clerk. Actual experience in dealing with the FCC and its regulations is also necessary.

Attorneys should possess good interpersonal skills to deal with clients, and excellent writing and verbal abilities. They must be able to reason logically, handle complex issues, and be responsible individuals with integrity and good judgment.

Minority/Women's Opportunities

In 1998, only 4 percent of practicing attorneys were members of minority groups, according to the Law School Admission Council. To promote diversity within the profession, LSAC-member law schools seek qualified minority students, and despite the glut of law school graduates crowding the field in the 1980s and 1990s, the *Wall Street Journal* reports that increased demand for minorities among senior management translates into plentiful opportunity in the coming decade.

The American Bar Association Commission on Women reports that in 1995, 23 percent of attorneys were women, far exceeding the 13 percent practicing in 1985. And the future looks promising, as 45 percent of law students in 1996–97 were women.

Unions/Associations

There are no unions that represent communications Attorneys. Some lawyers themselves serve as legal counsel to communications unions.

Many belong to the ABA or to their state and county bar associations to share industry concerns and make business contacts. Those in the Washington, D.C., area often belong to the Federal Communications Bar Association for the same purposes.

BUSINESS MANAGER

CAREER PROFILE

Duties: Managing all financial activities and planning for a television station, home video operation, or production/facility company.

Alternate Title(s):   Comptroller; Vice President of Business Affairs; Treasurer

Salary Range: $29,000 to $98,000

Employment Prospects: Fair

Advancement Prospects: Good

Prerequisites:

Education—Undergraduate degree in accounting, business administration, or management

Experience—Minimum of five years in business and accounting, preferably in TV or related field

Special Skills—Understanding of business and finance; knowledge of computer operations; management ability; detail orientation; analytical skills

CAREER LADDER

```
┌─────────────────────────────┐
│      General Manager         │
│   TV, Cable, Home Video      │
└─────────────────────────────┘

┌─────────────────────────────┐
│      Business Manager        │
└─────────────────────────────┘

┌─────────────────────────────┐
│         Accountant           │
└─────────────────────────────┘
```

Position Description

The Business Manager of a television station is responsible for the management of all financial transactions, including accounts receivable and payable, general ledgers, journals, and vouchers, and is immediately responsible for all financial planning. Other duties are supervising the preparation of all billings and developing and analyzing the financial statements and records of various station operations.

A Business Manager may also work at a home video operation, low-power television (LPTV) station, or production/facilities company. At a TV station, the Business Manager is the primary aide to the General Manager. The Business Manager develops short- and long-range plans and budgets and modifies and interprets financial data on a weekly, quarterly, and yearly basis. These plans enable the General Manager and the station's ownership to make financial projections.

The Business Manager develops and supervises all accounting policies and procedures, including the valuation of plant, equipment, programming, and other assets and prepares reports for the Internal Revenue Service and for corporate balance sheets. The responsibilities of the position include the development of profit and loss and cash flow statements and the monitoring of all departmental expenditures.

In performing these duties, the Business Manager supervises all members of the business department, including Accountants, Bookkeepers, billing clerks, and benefits personnel; hires support staff; and oversees the station's personnel policies.

Additionally, the Business Manager

- assists the Sales Manager and the General Manager in establishing realistic advertising rates for the station;
- provides accurate data and records for union negotiations concerning arbitration and contracts;
- oversees the management of the station's physical plant, including furniture and equipment; and
- establishes credit policies that achieve maximum sales results while reducing the number of late payments or defaults.

Salaries

Annual salaries for Business Managers/Comptrollers at commercial stations are reasonably high, in keeping with their responsibilities. The average salary was $53,485 in 1997,.

while the median salary was $50,000 in that year, according to the National Association of Broadcasters (NAB). Business Managers at major market stations, home video, and MSO cable companies often make $98,000 or more per year. Most Business Managers are paid a salary and a yearly bonus.

Salaries for business or financial officers are about the same in public television. The median in 1998 was $52,190, according to Corporation for Public Broadcasting (CPB) surveys. Figures ranged from $42,777 in small stations to $167,000 in major market community stations.

Employment Prospects

The opportunity to obtain a position as a Business Manager of a television station is limited.

In small market TV stations, both commercial and public, the Business Manager is usually someone who has been promoted from within the station's business department and who has an intimate knowledge of the station's particular financial operations.

In major market commercial and public stations, business executives are sometimes recruited from other stations or associated media companies, or are brought in by corporate headquarters to improve a station's financial condition. The opportunities for individuals from outside a station are generally fair, and the competition is heavy.

Advancement Prospects

Some Business Managers are promoted to the position of General Manager at their own stations, or join a smaller market station, sometimes owned by the parent corporation, in that capacity. The specific skills and experience acquired as Business Manager are readily transferable to other TV-related fields, including multichannel multipoint distribution service (MMDS) companies and cable TV systems, as well as to commercial production companies and LPTV stations.

Few Business Managers at television stations were initially trained in communications and many view the position as broad-based and applicable to many fields. As a result, they often seek nonmedia business opportunities to advance their careers.

Education

Almost all Business Managers in commercial or public television have an undergraduate degree in accounting, business administration, or management. In larger market stations, a master's degree in business administration (MBA) is often a prerequisite for being hired or promoted.

Many are Certified Public Accountants (CPAs) and some have law degrees in addition to their undergraduate business education. A substantial number have had extensive education in computer science, and a few have degrees in this field. In general, however, an education in accounting is the primary academic background required for Business Managers.

Experience/Skills

Most Business Managers are detail-oriented fact finders, who see things in black and white and are "bottom-line" oriented. They are concerned with maximum productivity. Today, the majority have some experience and skills in computer science. Interpersonal skills in personnel management and the ability to deal fairly and effectively with people are also considered to be major advantages. Some employers require candidates to have experience in labor negotiations and some knowledge of law.

At most stations, prospective Business Managers are required to have at least five years of prior experience in business and accounting, preferably in television broadcasting or a related media field. Personal integrity, reliability, accuracy, and a realistic view of television as a business are also considered important qualifications. The Business Manager is profit-oriented and aware of the time value of money.

Minority/Women's Opportunities

Industry observers estimate that in broadcast and cable television, women comprise upward of 40 percent of this once male-dominated position. Minorities have not made similar gains. The percentage of women serving as officials/managers (including Business Managers) was 34.4 percent in 1996, according to the Federal Communications Commission (FCC). This was an increase from 30.3 percent in 1988. Male and female minorities constituted 12.5 percent of the workforce in 1996, an increase from 11.6 percent in 1988.

In public television, the percentage of female officials/managers grew from 38 percent in 1989 to 41 percent in 1994, and the percentage of minorities increased significantly—from less than 1 percent in 1989 to 11 percent in 1994.

Unions/Associations

There are no unions that serve as representatives or bargaining agents. Business Managers in commercial television, however, often belong to the Broadcast Cable Financial Management Association (BCFMA), an organization devoted to developing new concepts of financial management. In public TV, the Public Telecommunications Financial Management Association (PTFMA) provides a similar forum.

ACCOUNTANT

CAREER PROFILE

Duties: Assisting the Business Manager in billings, payroll, and accounts receivable and payable at a TV station, media center, cable system, or LPTV station

Alternate Title(s):   Assistant Business Manager

Salary Range: $28,000 to $50,500

Employment Prospects: Good

Advancement Prospects: Good

Prerequisites:

Education—Minimum of an undergraduate degree in accounting or a related field

Experience—Minimum of two years of accounting work

Special Skills—Mathematical aptitude; accuracy; reliability; detail orientation; analytical mind; computer skills

CAREER LADDER

```
┌─────────────────────────────┐
│    Business Manager;         │
│    Public Accountant         │
└─────────────────────────────┘

┌─────────────────────────────┐
│         Accountant           │
└─────────────────────────────┘

┌─────────────────────────────┐
│    Bookkeeper; School        │
└─────────────────────────────┘
```

Position Description

An Accountant in a commercial or public television station is in charge of specific financial transactions. In performing these activities, the Accountant works closely with the General Sales Manager and with Advertising Salespersons. An Accountant usually reports directly to the Business Manager. Accountants are also employed at cable systems, multiple system operators (MSOs), low-power television (LPTV) stations, home video firms, and at production/facilities companies. They are also employed in some education and health media organizations (see Part II). At a station, an Accountant usually directly supervises the accounting and business staff, including Bookkeepers and billing, accounts receivable/payable, and payroll clerks. An Accountant often functions as a troubleshooter, working to solve specific day-to-day problems in the financial section of the station.

The role of an Accountant varies from station to station. Some large market stations have three or more Accountants, each with a specific responsibility and authority. At top market stations, an Accountant is sometimes assigned primary responsibilities for billing and accounts receivable.

At smaller stations, an Accountant's responsibilities are broader and encompass almost all activities in the business department, often including the direct supervision of clerical and support personnel and the management of office supplies, furniture, and equipment.

One of the major duties of an Accountant is to develop improved methods of cost accounting in specific financial areas so that the Business Manager can analyze specific problem areas more effectively. An Accountant systematically gathers and maintains financial data that provide a basis on which management can itemize income and expenses.

Many Accountants are skilled in computer science and word processing techniques, which improve financial data gathering and increase the speed with which such data can be analyzed. Still others have strengths in such accounting areas as inventory assessment, assets and liabilities, and profit and loss statements, and are assigned specific responsibilities in those areas.

Additionally, the Accountant

- double-checks vouchers, purchase orders, payroll timesheets, and invoices for accuracy prior to the approval of the Business Manager;
- reviews network accounts and agency and client payments and accounts;
- prepares data and summaries of financial reports for the Business Manager;
- maintains records for Federal Communications Commission (FCC) reports, income tax returns, and insurance claims; and
- continually monitors department budgets to balance expenses with allocated resources.

Salaries

The salary scale for Accountants in commercial TV is relatively low, ranging from $26,000 at small market stations to $47,000 in the major markets, according to industry estimates. Salaries increase proportionately with certification, a master's degree, or specialized expertise. For example, the National Association of Colleges and Employers' 1996 survey found that bachelor's degree candidates received starting offers averaging $29,400, whereas master's degree candidates averaged $33,000. Accountants with 1 to 3 years of experience earned between $27,000 and $46,000 in 1997, according to a survey conducted by Robert Half International.

Employment Prospects

In spite of competition, the opportunity to obtain or be promoted to the position of Accountant at a commercial or public television station is good. The majority of Accountants are normally not recruited from outside the station staff unless specific skills, such as computer science training or tax expertise, are required. For recent college graduates with accounting or related degrees, employment opportunities are also good at cable TV systems. Accounting positions in nonmedia-related companies are also available. Accounting jobs in all types of firms will grow by 10 to 20 percent by 2006, according to the Bureau of Labor Statistics (BLS).

Advancement Prospects

The top promotion for an Accountant at a television station is to the position of Business Manager. The opportunities for this move, however, are somewhat limited because of the general stability of such employees and the severity of the competition. Some Accountants assume the role of Business Manager at a smaller station or join a commercial production firm or media-related organization in a similar capacity. Still others use their experience to move into a top financial spot in an unrelated business.

Education

A minimum of an undergraduate degree in business administration or accounting is usually required. Business Managers seek individuals who have training in computer science.

Courses in bookkeeping, personnel management, or human resources are also valuable. Many Accountants have undergraduate degrees in business administration from one of the educational institutions accredited by the American Association of Collegiate Schools of Business. Others study and pass the exam and requirements for certification as a Certified Public Accountant (CPA) or a Certified Management Accountant (CMA).

Experience/Skills

Most Accountants are young—between the ages of 25 and 30—and the promotion to Accountant is their first career advancement. In many instances, they have worked as a Bookkeeper in the business department of the station for at least two years and have taken additional coursework and training in accounting. Today, all have had training and experience with computer business programs.

In large stations and media organizations, promising young college graduates are employed in the position.

An Accountant should be a bright, alert individual with a particular speciality in business, accounting, law, or computer science. Accuracy, reliability, and aggressiveness are prime requisites for the position. A successful Accountant is a fact finder and problem solver who can bring new ideas and techniques to a financial operation.

Minority/Women's Opportunities

The employment opportunities for women and minority group members are good. According to FCC statistics, 34.4 percent of all professionals (including Accountants) in commercial television were women in 1996. Minorities constituted 17.8 percent in this category in 1996; in fact, in 1997, accounting was listed by *Minority Career News* as the second "hottest" career in terms of salary, growth potential, and openness to inclusion. In public television in 1997, 50 percent of professional positions, which include Accountants, were held by women, and 50 percent by minorities, according to the CPB.

Unions/Associations

There are no unions that serve as bargaining agents for Accountants. Many individuals, however, belong to the Broadcast Cable Financial Management Association (BCFMA), which is devoted to developing new concepts of financial management. The Public Telecommunications Financial Management Association (PTFMA) provides a similar function for Accountants in public television.

BOOKKEEPER

CAREER PROFILE

Duties: Financial record-keeping at a television station, cable system, home video company, media center

Alternate Title(s): None

Salary Range: $22,000 to $38,000

Employment Prospects: Good

Advancement Prospects: Good

Prerequisites:

Education—Minimum of an associate's degree in business

Experience—Minimum of one year of bookkeeping experience preferable

Special Skills—Mathematical aptitude; accuracy; reliability; ability to work rapidly under pressure; computer literacy

CAREER LADDER

```
┌─────────────────────────────────┐
│         Accountant              │
└─────────────────────────────────┘

┌─────────────────────────────────┐
│         Bookkeeper              │
└─────────────────────────────────┘

┌─────────────────────────────────┐
│    Business School/College;     │
│  Bookkeeper (Another Station    │
│        or Business)             │
└─────────────────────────────────┘
```

Position Description

The basic duties of a Bookkeeper are to maintain journals, ledgers, and financial books for use by a television station's management in day-to-day operations and budget forecasting. TV stations and nonbroadcast organizations employ from 2 to 10 Bookkeepers, depending upon the size of the operation and the market. Bookkeepers report to the Business Manager or, at larger stations, to an Accountant.

At larger stations, the Business Manager or Accountant assigns Bookkeepers to specific areas of responsibility. An important specialty for a Bookkeeper can be maintaining the station's advertising billing accounts and files. Other individuals may be responsible for the preparation of all payroll elements, including time sheets, vacation and sick leave records, payroll and Social Security deductions, and overtime compensation. Some Bookkeepers may be assigned to accounts payable, where they post bills received at the station, including telephone bills, subscriptions, power and lighting bills, invoices for videotape, and other normal operational expenses. The Bookkeeper records all bills, matches them with purchase orders or vouchers, and checks their accuracy with the department head who purchased the items or services.

Some Bookkeepers are assigned to maintain the day-to-day accounts of a specific department, such as engineering or programming. In most stations, the programming department is the most expensive unit in terms of salaries, program purchases, licensing fees, shipping costs, line charges, production expenses, and other program-related costs. A Bookkeeper may be assigned specifically to monitor all income and expenses of that department.

At some small stations, the Bookkeeper works in all areas of accounting, including payroll, accounts payable and receivable, and advertising billings.

Today computers are a basic tool in station operations. Bookkeeping functions are routinely done on a computer, and a Bookkeeper must have knowledge of the processes and software.

Additionally, the Bookkeeper

- keeps accurate backup records of all invoices or bills and related documents for reference purposes;
- maintains an ongoing file of past-due accounts receivable or payable for use by the Business Manager or Accountant; and
- manages an inventory file of facilities, supplies, and equipment used or purchased by the station.

Salaries

Salaries for this position are somewhat low in commercial TV. The average yearly payment in 1996 was $20,700 according to the Bureau of Labor Statistics (BLS). Higher salaries are usually paid to beginners who have an undergraduate degree in accounting or to Bookkeepers who have been at the station for some time.

Bookkeeper salaries vary widely, depending on the region of the country, size of the city, and type and size of the media company. The level of industry or technical expertise required and the complexity and uniqueness of a clerk's responsibilities may also affect earnings.

Employment Prospects

This is frequently an entry-level position and job possibilities at a television station or in a related media or video operation are good. Most stations employ two or more Bookkeepers, and with 1,569 television stations on the air, there are opportunities available for bright young business school graduates.

Positions open up frequently as the station's Bookkeepers are promoted or move to other television or media positions. The necessary skills are readily transferable to related jobs at multichannel multipoint distribution service (MMDS) firms, cable TV companies, or low-power TV (LPTV) stations, and a large number of jobs also exist in nonmedia business organizations. Bookkeeping positions are expected to decline through 2006 because of the spread in office automation. Nevertheless, because of high turnover through career mobility, hundreds of thousands of positions will become available each year, according to the BLS.

Advancement Prospects

The possibilities for advancement are good, but the competition is heavy. Once a beginning Bookkeeper learns the job or becomes a specialist in various accounting areas within the business department, promotion is possible. The promotion may be to a specific bookkeeping responsibility with a higher salary or to the job of Bookkeeper in charge of a single departmental area within the station.

Some Bookkeepers, with further training and education, advance to the position of Accountant after apprenticing in all areas of the business department. Still others advance their careers by joining advertising agencies or other television-related organizations. Some use their business and accounting experience to assume more responsible positions outside the television and video industries.

Education

A minimum of an associate's degree in business, with the major emphasis of study in bookkeeping and accounting, is usually essential. An undergraduate degree in accounting, or in business administration with a major in accounting, is sometimes required at major or middle market stations. Courses in computer science/software training are extremely valuable as well as some education in personnel management. A solid educational background in accounting and bookkeeping, however, is the prime requisite for the position.

Experience/Skills

While some stations recruit experienced individuals from other stations or media companies, extensive experience is not the primary requirement for bookkeeping. Many Bookkeepers are between the ages of 22 and 30, but some are much older and have been in the position for a number of years.

At least one year of experience, either part-time during school or college or full-time as a bookkeeper in another business, is very helpful. Successful Bookkeepers must be bright, accurate, reliable, and able to work rapidly. Above all, however, they must be good at and enjoy working with figures and understand accounting software.

Minority/Women's Opportunities

The employment opportunities for minority group members and particularly women in this position are fair to good. The Minority Career Network in 1998 identified Accounting as a "hot" career for the next 10 years, and Bookkeeping is one pathway to that field. Federal Communications Commission (FCC) statistics indicate that over 88 percent of the office clerical employees (including Bookkeepers) in commercial television in 1996 were women. Minority group employment amounted to 32.2 percent of all persons in this job category in that year.

In public television, 80 percent of those employed in support positions, which include bookkeeping, were women in 1994, while 32 percent were members of minority groups.

Unions/Associations

There are no unions or professional organizations that represent Bookkeepers in commercial or public television.

RECEPTIONIST/OFFICE CLERK

CAREER PROFILE

Duties: Greeting customers and visitors and providing clerical support at a television station or media organization

Alternate Title(s): none

Salary Range: $15,300 to $26,200

Employment Prospects: Excellent

Advancement Prospects: Good

Prerequisites:

Education—High school diploma

Experience—Part-time office work

Special Skills—Word processing ability; familiarity with office equipment

CAREER LADDER

```
┌─────────────────────────────────┐
│           Secretary             │
└─────────────────────────────────┘

┌─────────────────────────────────┐
│    Receptionist/Office Clerk    │
└─────────────────────────────────┘

┌─────────────────────────────────┐
│   High School; Business School; │
│              College            │
└─────────────────────────────────┘
```

Position Description

A Receptionists/Office Clerk greets customers and visitors at a communications company and determines their needs. In most small office circumstances, the Receptionists/Office Clerk also operates the telephone switchboard and connects incoming calls to the proper staff individual. The responsibilities of the position also include word processing, filing, and general office work.

Receptionists/Office Clerks are employed at all public and commercial television stations. They are also employed at most of the other organizations described in this book.

As a part of their Receptionist duties, personnel in the position arrange appointments, screen telephone calls, take messages, and help unscheduled visitors. They may provide temporary identification cards and arrange for staff escorts to take visitors to the proper offices.

Individuals in the position often arrange for express mail pickups and handle such deliveries. In many media office situations, a part of the Receptionist's time is spent in opening and sorting the daily incoming mail.

When they are not busy with telephone callers, visitors, or the mail, Receptionists may type on the computer correspondence or reports, collate mailings, address envelopes, or type labels and lists. On occasion, they prepare travel vouchers or do simple bookkeeping.

The responsibilities of an Office Clerk vary. Some work in specific departments of a media operation, while others are a part of a pool of such personnel. The Clerk helps to maintain the rapid flow of written communications that is essential to the modern office. Beginning Clerks often process and print mailing labels, orders and invoices, and headings on form letters. In addition, they operate office copying machines, calculators, and other office equipment.

More experienced Clerks do work that requires a great deal of accuracy and independent judgment. They often work from rough handwritten drafts that are difficult to read or that contain considerable technical or budget detail. They may plan and word process complicated statistical tables, combine and manage materials from different sources, or prepare master copies to be reproduced on office copying machines.

In some large media organizations, word-processing centers handle the transcription and typing of several departments. Clerks in these circumstances use software such as Microsoft Word or WordPerfect to secure a finished copy.

Most media companies, however, are relatively small in size; few are large enough to maintain a word-processing center. More often the Receptionists/Office Clerks operate in a single location but do work for many individuals.

Additionally, a Receptionists/Office Clerk

- maintains files containing correspondence, rough drafts, orders, invoices, and business records; and
- listens to recorded dictation and transcribes it.

Salaries

Median annual earnings of full-time general Office Clerks, which include Receptionists, were about $19,300 in 1996; the middle 50 percent earned between $15,300 and $26,200 annually. The Bureau of Labor Statistics (BLS) reports that a survey of workplaces in 160 metropolitan areas found that beginning general Office Clerks had median annual earnings of about $14,200 in 1995, with the middle half earning about $12,500 to $16,400 a year. The most experienced general Office Clerks had median annual earnings of about $25,300, with the middle half earning about $21,800 to $29,000 a year.

Employment Prospects

The opportunities for employment are excellent. The positions are almost always considered entry-level jobs, and there are fine opportunities for beginners and those returning to the job market. Every commercial and public television station employs a Receptionist and most employ at least three Office Clerks. Some larger stations employ as many as 15 personnel in clerical support functions.

Opportunities also exist at production facilities firms, corporate television centers, and at government, health, and education media centers, as well as at cable TV systems. The position offers excellent opportunities to break into the field of communications on a part-time basis.

Receptionists/Office Clerks will find plentiful opportunity in the coming decade because of high turnover rates. Receptionist positions are expected to increase 21 to 35 percent nationally in all areas of the economy by 2006, according to the BLS, while Office Clerk jobs are expected to increase by 1 to 9 percent by that time.

Advancement Prospects

The prospects for advancement for bright, alert people are good. The responsibilities of the position require that the individual learn many aspects of the media operations, and many Receptionists/Office Clerks use the position to scout other opportunities.

Some are promoted to Production Secretary or Production Assistant and others to Bookkeeper or Desk Assistant. Those with a talent for sales work often advance to Sales Coordinator or Traffic Continuity Specialist. Many move to comparable positions in the nonbroadcast companies described in Part II of this book.

Education

The minimum requirement for the position of Receptionists/Office Clerk is a high school diploma. Some employers require some training in a business school. Many employers prefer to employ individuals who have had some education in communications or who have an undergraduate degree in media or TV, in order to train them for more responsible positions.

Experience/Skills

Most employers do not require extensive experience for this position. Word processing is essential, and good spelling, grammar, and punctuation are important skills in the job. Familiarity with standard office equipment and procedures is an asset. A neat appearance and good interpersonal skills are helpful.

Minority/Women's Opportunities

The majority of Receptionists/Office Clerks at public and commercial television stations are women. More than 80 percent of support positions at public television stations, which include Receptionists/Office Clerks, were filled by women in 1994, according to the Corporation for Public Broadcasting (CPB). More than 33 percent were minorities in that year. In commercial television, 88.2 percent of the office clerical workers were women in 1996, according to the Federal Communications Commission (FCC), with female minorities holding 28 percent of the office clerical positions, and male minorities, 4.3 percent in that year.

Unions/Associations

There are no unions or professional associations that represent Receptionists/Office Clerks.

PROGRAM MANAGER

Duties: Selecting and scheduling of all programming broadcast by a TV station

Alternate Title(s): Program Director; Vice President of Programming

Salary Range: $26,000 to $101,000

Employment Prospects: Fair

Advancement Prospects: Good

Prerequisites:

Education—Undergraduate degree in communications, radio-TV, theater, journalism, business, or marketing

Experience—Minimum of five years in television production and sales

Special Skills—Creativity; extensive knowledge of TV programming; organizational ability; sound judgment; good taste

```
┌─────────────────────────────────────┐
│  Program Syndication Salesperson;    │
│         General Manager              │
└─────────────────────────────────────┘

┌─────────────────────────────────────┐
│                                      │
│         Program Manager              │
│                                      │
└─────────────────────────────────────┘

┌─────────────────────────────────────┐
│        Executive Producer;           │
│        Production Manager            │
└─────────────────────────────────────┘
```

Position Description

The Program Manager, who reports to the General Manager, is responsible for all local, network, independent, and syndicated programming broadcast by a television station and must ensure that it is in compliance with all Federal Communications Commission (FCC) regulations. Primary responsibilities include selecting and scheduling all programs and trying to create a mix that will guarantee the largest possible viewing audience and highest ratings. At a commercial station, the Program Manager works closely with the sales department to determine the programming that is most marketable to advertisers during various times in the broadcast schedule.

The Program Manager keeps informed about the needs of the audience from sign-on to sign-off and monitors the quality, type, and profitability of programs broadcast by the station, staying constantly aware of the competition for the audience from other local stations. The Program Manager uses local and national research organizations, reports, and ratings services to define the demographics of the station's viewing audience at various times during the broadcast day and to measure the success or failure of a particular program. Increasingly, these analyses are done with the aid of computers.

The Program Manager decides which film packages, syndicated shows, reruns of previously aired network programs, and locally produced programs will be selected, produced, or purchased to provide the overall programming balance. The person in this position also supervises the scheduling of spot announcements, commercials, public service announcements, and station breaks, often with the aid of information technology systems.

The Program Manager must also create and schedule local public affairs programs to comply with the station's obligation to operate in the "public interest, convenience, and necessity" under FFC regulations, and must, therefore, understand the community's needs and problems and select programs accordingly.

Additionally, the Program Manager

* controls the programming budget and keeps within the station's affordable limits;
* negotiates with independent producers and program syndicators to purchase programming for the station; and
* evaluates local program ideas for possible production.

Salaries

Despite the demands and responsibility of this position, Program Managers are relatively low paid. Those at independent commercial stations are usually paid more than individuals at network-affiliated stations because of their increased responsibility in selecting programs.

The average base salary for Program Managers at commercial stations was $47,828, according to the National Association of Broadcasters (NAB). Most commercial-station Program Managers are paid a combination of salary and bonus.

Salaries for Program Managers in public TV are similar to those of their counterparts in commercial broadcasting, even though they generally have more responsibility. The 1998 median was $46,440, according to a Corporation for Public Broadcasting (CPB) survey. The range was between $19,153 and $119,333. Program Managers in public television in the top 50 markets whose stations were community owned earned more than their peers in college- or school-licensed stations in smaller markets.

Employment Prospects

With only 1,569 television stations on the air, the opportunities for employment are fair. Cable TV and multichannel multipoint distribution service (MMDS) operations offer some possibilities. Additional opportunities may become available at low-power television (LPTV) stations. Still, the number of new available positions is not expected to rise dramatically in the near future, and the competition is severe.

Advancement Prospects

Opportunities for advancement are good. Most Program Managers at both commercial and noncommercial stations move on to more responsible positions in broadcasting or become Program Managers at larger stations at higher salaries. The typical Program Manager in commercial TV starts at a smaller station and moves to progressively larger stations in the same capacity. Most believe they have not reached the top of their profession.

Some commercial-station Program Managers join network program staffs, and many become salespersons of syndicated programs. Still others join or form their own TV production companies. In recent years, some Program Managers have moved to similar positions in cable TV to advance their careers.

In public television, Program Managers are often next in line for the job of General Manager. Many Program Managers move to smaller stations to assume the top post at a higher salary, while others wait until normal attrition makes the position available at their own stations.

Education

Today, virtually all Program Managers have an undergraduate degree, and many have graduate degrees—usually in mass communications- media arts.

An undergraduate degree in communications, radio-TV, theater, journalism, business administration, or marketing is recommended. Study in speech, drama, and writing, coupled with courses in sales and marketing, can provide very useful background for a Program Manager.

Experience/Skills

Prospective Program Managers should have at least five years of experience in television production and, for commercial broadcasting, in sales. Many Program Managers now working in commercial stations have held the job of General Sales Manager and have had some on-air experience in radio or television. Most have worked at their jobs for 10 years.

In public broadcasting, the majority of Program Managers have been Executive Producers and Production Managers at some time in their careers. Some have worked as Writers or Directors.

A Program Manager is expected to have creativity, taste, organizational ability, a firm knowledge of television programming, show business savvy, and sound business skills.

Minority/Women's Opportunities

Program Managers at both commercial and public television stations are usually white males between the ages of 35 and 45. In 1996, some 35.4 percent of the officials and managers (including Program Managers) in commercial TV were women, while 14 percent were members of minorities, according to FCC statistics.

In public television, 11 percent of the Program Managers in 1994 were minority group members and 41 percent were women, according to the CPB.

Unions/Associations

There are no unions that serve as representatives for Program Managers. Most commercial and some public television Program Managers belong to the National Association of Television Program Executives (NATPE) to share mutual concerns and to learn about programs available for purchase.

FILM/TAPE LIBRARIAN

CAREER PROFILE

Duties: Acquiring, prescreening, and shipping commercials, film, tape, and digital programs at a television station or facility

Alternate Title(s): Media Librarian; Film/Tape Specialist; Film Director

Salary Range: $18,000 to $32,000

Employment Prospects: Fair

Advancement Prospects: Good

Prerequisites:

Education—High school diploma; technical school training helpful

Experience—Operation of audiovisual equipment and videotape machines helpful

Special Skills—Attention to detail; timing ability; record keeping accuracy

CAREER LADDER

```
Traffic/Continuity Supervisor;
Operations Manager;
Engineering Technician
```

```
Film/Tape Librarian
```

```
High School/Technical School
```

Position Description

The Film/Tape Librarian keeps track of all commercials, film, videotape, and digital format programs and prepares them for broadcast at a public or commercial television station. The librarian's duties include ordering, receiving, filing, and shipping films and tapes from and to a variety of sources and getting all on-air media to the proper location at the station in time for airing or to the client on time.

At a station, a major responsibility of the Film/Tape Librarian is to prescreen all incoming tape and film materials and evaluate their technical quality prior to their being broadcast. Television relies on split-second timing. A film or tape program that runs too long or too short can interfere with the entire station operation. A commercial on film that is aired scratched or dirty could cause the station to have to rerun it at no cost to the client. The Film/Tape Librarian ensures that all films and tapes are correctly timed and ready for broadcast.

In some stations, the Film/Tape Librarian also serves as a projectionist and checks, cleans, and loads the film chain (a TV projection system for film and slides) for programming and station breaks. In others, the person in this position receives and processes new, incoming blank videotapes (both in cassette and reel-to-reel formats) assigns control numbers, and readies them for technical evaluation by the engineering

department. When they have been returned, the Film/Tape Librarian inventories the tapes for use by the production department.

The use of film at broadcast stations and in other areas of commercial communications organizations has diminished considerably. Although the job title implies the use of film, many people occupying the position deal mostly with videotape and increasingly, with digital media. Although 1-inch tape is still the standard in broadcast, and 3/4 inch in cable, digital tape format (DTF) represents a new class of recording and storage technology whose use is increasing rapidly.

The Film/Tape Librarian works closely with the Traffic/Continuity Supervisor and reports to the Program Manager or to the Operations Manager. In either case, the Film/Tape Librarian reviews the daily advance log prepared by the programming department to determine that all scheduled tapes and films are in the house and ready for broadcast.

In the large postproduction facilities and tape dubbing operations, the Film/Tape Librarian may supervise others in handling and shipping videotapes to clients. In such circumstances, the group operates as a team to ensure that the videotapes are sent to the clients on time by the most economical means.

Additionally, the Film/Tape Librarian

- maintains an accurate and up-to-date inventory of all prerecorded tapes, films, and digital media, and notes their location and disposition;
- edits feature and syndicated films to conform with logged time and commercial breaks;
- edits and inserts commercials into film programs; and
- assembles and labels all taped or film commercials scheduled for station breaks and edits them onto a single reel in advance of broadcast.

Salaries

Income for Film/Tape Librarians in commercial and public television is low, approximately $18,000 to $32,000, although industry observers estimate that earnings are higher for those working in private industry, postproduction facilities, and government agencies.

Employment Prospects

Most TV stations employ only one or two Film/Tape Librarians. Since this is often considered an entry-level job, opening do occur as people are promoted. A few cable TV systems also employ Film/Tape Librarians, as do many large advertising agencies. A few low-power television (LPTV) stations may employ such personnel. The networks often employ more than 30 people in a videotape library handling nearly a thousand pieces of tape each day. Postproduction houses (described in Part II) also employ Film/Tape Librarians, as do videotape dubbing facilities. The overall opportunities for employment, however, are only fair, but the position is one of the easier entry-level jobs to obtain.

Advancement Prospects

Some Film/Tape Librarians advance to become Traffic/Continuity Supervisors. Individuals with some engineering skill and talent sometimes obtain licenses from the Federal Communications Commission (FCC) and eventually move to more responsible positions as Operations Managers or Engineering Technicians. Still others utilize this entry- level position to learn about the station or postproduction facilities and move into production and programming jobs. The opportunities for advancement are good but are dependent upon the individual's initiative, skills, interests, and attitudes.

Education

Most employers require a high school diploma. Some additional training in electronics or film at a technical school is helpful. At larger stations or the networks, a degree in communications is helpful.

Experience/Skills

Most employers provide on-the-job training for this entry-level position under the supervision of the Program or Operations Manager. Some experience operating audiovisual equipment, including 8mm and 16mm projectors, slide and videotape machines, digital Betacams, and associated gear is helpful. Some knowledge of common transportation carriers and shipping procedures is useful. Experience with home videocassette machines is most helpful.

A Film/Tape Librarian must be careful and detail-oriented. It is essential that he or she be able to keep accurate records and time programs precisely. A diligent attitude is necessary, and the individual must like working as a part of a team in the larger organizations.

Minority/Women's Opportunities

The majority of Film/Tape Librarians at commercial and public television stations in 1996 were male, but women have found increasing opportunities in this area. During the past 10 years, employment of minority group members has also increased, according to industry sources, particularly in major urban centers and at production/facilities companies. In public television in 1994, women held 23 percent of the technical and sales positions, which include Film/Tape Librarian, and minorities, 19 percent, according to the Corporation for Public Broadcasting (CPB).

Unions/Associations

There are no unions or professional organizations that represent Film/Tape Librarians.

ANNOUNCER

CAREER PROFILE

Duties: Providing the spoken portion of station identifications, public service announcements, and programs at a television station

Alternate Title(s): None

Salary Range: $20,000 to $120,000

Employment Prospects: Fair

Advancement Prospects: Poor

Prerequisites:

Education—Undergraduate degree in communications, drama, or speech preferable

Experience—Minimum of one year of varied radio or television announcing

Special Skills—Good control of voice and diction; acting ability; good personal appearance and style

CAREER LADDER

```
┌─────────────────────────────────────┐
│      Anchorperson; Reporter;         │
│    Sportscaster; Weather Reporter    │
└─────────────────────────────────────┘

┌─────────────────────────────────────┐
│             Announcer                │
└─────────────────────────────────────┘

┌─────────────────────────────────────┐
│         Radio Announcer;             │
│              Actor                   │
└─────────────────────────────────────┘
```

Position Description

An Announcer's voice is heard on station identifications and public service announcements at commercial or public television stations. Responsibilities of the position are to provide artistically satisfying, technically sound, and professionally acceptable spoken portions of broadcasts. A wide variety of assignments are handled. The Program Manager supervises Announcers.

In addition to their other duties, Announcers may also host or emcee programs and sometimes appear on camera as Performers. They might assume character roles for children's programs or introduce horror movies, special films, or other station-produced programs. At some smaller stations, Announcers do live or taped commercials for local station clients, often demonstrating products on camera. Sometimes they fill in for absent Sportscasters, Reporters, or Weather Reporters. Announcers also do freelance work on specific projects for advertising agencies, cable TV systems, and multichannel multipoint distribution service (MMDS) companies.

Announcing positions are also available at national cable satellite companies, usually on a part-time basis, for voice-over work. In addition, project-by-project work is available at production companies, corporate TV centers, and health, education, and government media operations. Much of this work calls for off-camera narration.

A good television Announcer learns to develop eye contact with the camera and reads copy easily from a TelePrompTer or cue cards with a good sense of timing and at an appropriate pace. The Announcer marks up scripts, edits, and delivers written copy, rephrasing as necessary to avoid awkward word usage and to provide a smooth and intelligent reading.

Most good Announcers try to read concepts, not just phrases, and groom their styles to provide a natural quality rather than a hard-sell delivery. They use a variety of speech techniques, including variation in the rate at which they speak, emphasis of key words and phrases, and grouping of words into meaningful sub-ideas. A good Announcer uses inflections appropriately, pronounces words clearly and accurately, and makes it all appear effortless.

Frequently, an Announcer is required to work without a prepared script and must, therefore, be quick thinking and have a good vocabulary, charm, and a style appropriate to the situation. Body movement, voice qualities, gestures, and personality all provide audience identification with the program.

Announcers are known by their voices. An individual's other qualities—wit, style, and knowledge—find expression through the delivery of spoken words.

Additionally, the Announcer

- narrates opening or closing credits for locally produced programs; and
- conducts, on occasion, interviews for a newscast or documentary.

Salaries

Salaries in commercial television averaged $54,300 in 1997, according to industry observers. Some personalities in the top 50 markets make considerably more. In public television, the median payment was $41,899 in 1998, according to the Corporation for Public Broadcasting (CPB). The range was from $23,985 to $110,466.

Employment Prospects

There are usually more Announcers available than there are opportunities, and the prospects for employment are only fair.

The position of staff Announcer at a TV station is not usually an entry-level job. Experience in radio announcing or acting is often required.

Most TV stations employ only one or two staff Announcers. At many small outlets, Announcers from local radio stations handle the daily voice-over duties on a freelance basis.

Advancement Prospects

Opportunities for advancement are poor and depend on the individual's talent and skill as well as on being in the right place at the right time.

Most staff Announcers seek higher-paid jobs as regular on-camera Anchorpersons, Reporters, Sportscasters, or Weather Reporters. The competition, however, is severe. Some Announcers advance their careers by moving to the same position at a larger market station, or by obtaining an on-camera position at a smaller station. Most freelance in commercials for advertising agencies and many also work at local radio stations owned by the TV company. A few move to larger stations that have special projects or programs. Announcers who have developed a distinct on-air or voice-over personality have better chances for advancement. A particular style is often sought by employers.

Education

While a formal education is less important than a facility with language, the majority of Announcers have an under-graduate degree in communications, drama, or speech. A broad liberal arts background is important, and courses in diction and phonetics are helpful, along with courses in a foreign language.

Experience/Skills

At least one year of working in radio or television, in various announcing formats and under a number of conditions, is usually required. Many television stations prefer to employ experienced professionals with three or more years of announcing assignments in smaller markets.

Announcers must have a quick memory and an ability to work under distracting conditions. They must also have clear voices without regional characteristics for most assignments, but they must be capable of doing dialects and special character voices. Most Announcers are good actors, understand microphone techniques, and have a knowledge of television or film production. They are capable of precise timing, have excellent speech and language skills, a good personal appearance and style, and are able to project a youthful quality, authority, and enthusiasm.

Minority/Women's Opportunities

Opportunities for women and members of minorities have increased greatly during the past 10 years. Although the majority of staff Announcers in commercial television are white males, more women and minority group members are occupying these positions each year, with the U.S. Department of Labor's Women's Bureau reporting that women constituted 14.7 percent of the 70,000 people employed in this occupation in 1997.

In public television, 50 percent of the individuals in the category of professionals, which includes Announcers, were women in 1994, while minorities constituted 18 percent, according to the CPB.

Unions/Associations

In markets where Announcers are represented by unions for bargaining purposes, some individuals belong to the American Federation of Television and Radio Artists (AFTRA). Others are members of the Screen Actors Guild (SAG), and some belong to the American Guild of Variety Artists (AGVA).

DIRECTOR OF PUBLICITY/PROMOTION

CAREER PROFILE

Duties: Responsibility for all public relations and promotion at a television station

Alternate Title(s): Director of Information; Director of Public Relations; Director of Advertising/Promotions; Director of Creative Services

Salary Range: $24,000 to $84,000

Employment Prospects: Fair

Advancement Prospects: Fair

Prerequisites:

Education—Undergraduate degree in public relations, advertising, or communications

Experience—Minimum of three years in public relations, advertising, promotion, or publicity

Special Skills—Writing or editing ability; sales talent; interpersonal skills; imagination; creativity

CAREER LADDER

```
Director of Publicity/Promotion or
Marketing
(Large Station, Network, Cable TV, or
Nonmedia Field);
Director of Development (PTV)
```

```
Director of Publicity/Promotion
```

```
Publicity/Promotion Assistant
```

Position Description

A Director of Publicity/Promotion plans and executes comprehensive public relations campaigns to promote a television station's image, its programs, and its activities. A variety of methods are used to help increase the audience for the station to attract new advertisers. Duties of the position normally evolve in response to current and projected broadcast schedules and to the promotion needs of the station.

On a continuing basis, a Director of Publicity/Promotion promotes the station, its programs, and its on-air personalities to current and potential audiences through imaginative campaigns, using many types of advertising and on-air and print promotional techniques. Duties include the conception, planning, and editing of printed materials such as press kits, news releases, posters, fliers, fact sheets, and feature articles. Consumer advertising, using billboards, newspapers, radio, and consumer and trade magazines, must also be generated.

The Director of Publicity/Promotion ensures that program listings and schedule changes are promptly distributed to the media and that they are printed accurately. To further promote upcoming shows and events, the Director oversees the production and scheduling of promotional spot announcements to be aired on the station during the broadcast day. The Director of Publicity/Promotion also previews and selects tape and film excerpts from other sources and selects talent and Announcers to promote the station.

At a commercial station, the Director of Publicity/Promotion works closely with the General Sales Manager to increase advertisers' awareness and with the art department to produce print and promotional materials to attract new advertisers. With the Community Relations Director, the person in this position coordinates public functions and provides printed materials and other public relations support. If the station is affiliated with a network, the Director of Publicity/Promotion collaborates with the network's promotion and publicity department to advertise the station's programs.

In the past few years, effective promotion has become more of an exact science, rather than intuitive exploitation. As a result, the Director of Publicity/Promotion often plans and oversees research on audiences, media research, and rating demographics, and also works closely with the traffic/continuity department in scheduling spot announcements promoting the station.

At a public TV station, the Director of Publicity/Promotion works closely with the volunteer coordinator, the Director of Development, and other members of the staff to promote the station and its image, and also interacts with the publicity and promotion staff at the Public Broadcasting Service (PBS).

The Director of Publicity/Promotion usually reports to the Marketing Director, Program Manager, or directly to the General Manager. Because of the importance and complexity of the job, from two to five (or more) assistants are usually employed who specialize in different media or techniques of promotion and publicity.

Additionally, the Director of Publicity/Promotion

- prepares and administers the departmental budget;
- supervises special promotion events, including parades and appearances of on-air talent at public functions;
- arranges interviews in other media for the station's personalities;
- provides advance screenings of unique and special programs; and
- speaks at public or community functions on behalf of the station.

Salaries

Salaries at commercial stations in 1997 averaged $43,806, according to the National Association of Broadcasters (NAB). Directors of Promotion/Publicity were considered department heads at most stations, and many made considerably more at major market stations.

In public television, the 1997 income ranged from $16,467 to $91,416 for those who were considered officials, according to the Corporation for Public Broadcasting (CPB). The median was $34,433.

Employment Prospects

Opportunities for moving into this position are only fair. Although all of the 1,569 TV stations in 1997 had promotion and publicity employees, there is not much movement out of the top positions, and openings do not occur that frequently. Talented and ambitious Publicity/Promotion Assistants can, however, move into the job at their own stations or within the parent company's organization. Some opportunities also exist for qualified people in other public relations fields to transfer into television as Directors of Publicity/Promotion. Positions are also available at cable systems and networks and at home video companies (see Part II) and at some low-power television (LPTV) stations.

Advancement Prospects

Opportunities are fair in both public and commercial television. At a commercial station, this is often the top job in publicity and promotion, and there are few opportunities to advance within the station organization. Some individuals obtain higher-paid jobs in the same position at larger stations or at the network level. An increasing number find opportunities in cable TV. Some move into other public relations fields or to more responsible public relations positions in other media-related organizations. In public television, some Directors of Publicity/Promotion move to fund-raising positions, such as Director of Development, at their own stations or at other stations in smaller markets.

Education

An undergraduate degree in public relations, advertising, or communications is usually mandatory. Courses in writing, photography, printing, and speech are valuable. Art and design courses are most helpful, and some courses in media research are desirable.

Experience/Skills

A minimum of three years of experience in all phases of public relations, advertising, promotion, or publicity is mandatory. Knowledge of the World Wide Web and print design is useful, and some experience with outside vendors is helpful.

A candidate for the job must have a vivid imagination, possess solid writing and editing skills, and, in addition, be a good salesperson who is poised, articulate, and capable of dealing with a variety of people in relatively sophisticated environments. The successful candidate must also be creative, personable, persuasive, enthusiastic, and ingenious. A flair for developing concepts and themes is essential.

Minority/Women's Opportunities

The prospects for women to obtain this position in commercial TV have improved dramatically over the past 10 years, according to industry sources, and are now excellent. More than 40 percent of the positions in commercial television in 1996 were held by women, according to the FCC. Opportunities for minority group members are increasing at a slower pace. Blacks and other minorities held approximately 19.9 percent of the positions in 1996, according to the FCC. In public television, 41 percent of the officials and managers, including Directors of Publicity/Promotion, in 1994 were women and 11 percent were minorities, according to the CPB.

Unions/Associates

There are no unions that specifically represent Directors of Publicity/Promotion in commercial or public television. Many belong, however, to ProMax International, Inc., to share mutual concerns and advance their careers.

PUBLICITY/PROMOTION ASSISTANT

CAREER PROFILE

Duties: Handling the details associated with public relations, promotion, and publicity at a television station/media company

Alternate Title(s):   Promotion Specialist; Assistant Promotion Director; Public Information Assistant

Salary Range: $15,000 to $54,000+

Employment Prospects: Fair

Advancement Prospects: Good

Prerequisites:

  Education—Undergraduate degree in public relations, journalism, English, advertising, or communications

  Experience—Some promotion and public relations work helpful

  Special Skills—Writing talent; language and television production skills; familiarity with media including the World Wide Web

CAREER LADDER

```
┌─────────────────────────────────────┐
│    Director of Publicity/Promotion   │
└─────────────────────────────────────┘

┌─────────────────────────────────────┐
│    Publicity/Promotion Assistant     │
└─────────────────────────────────────┘

┌─────────────────────────────────────┐
│      Media or Nonmedia Promotion/    │
│       Public Relations Position;     │
│         College; Secretary           │
└─────────────────────────────────────┘
```

Position Description

A Publicity/Promotion Assistant handles all the detail work involved in providing public relations, promotion, and publicity services for a television station in support of its programs and other activities. The Assistant reports to and assists the Director of Publicity/Promotion in assigned tasks. A similar position exists at many larger cable TV systems and multichannel multipoint distribution service (MMDS) operations.

Small commercial stations often employ only one Promotion/Publicity Assistant who performs many and varied tasks. In middle market commercial and public TV stations, three or more Assistants are employed, and each usually has a specified major responsibility, such as on-air promotion, public relations/publicity, or advertising. Most publicity/promotion departments are relatively small, however, and the Assistant performs many duties to attract new viewers and advertisers to the station.

At commercial stations, the Publicity/Promotion Assistant works closely with the Community Relations Director, the traffic department, and the art department to implement promotion and public relations projects. At a public station, day-to-day working relationships are with the coordinator of volunteers and the Director of Development to help raise money effectively.

Some of the Publicity/Promotion Assistant's tasks include writing press releases and feature articles and compiling and distributing press kits. Other responsibilities are making arrangements for special events and appearances and conducting tours of the studio or station. It is up to this person to maintain up-to-date mailing lists of the station's advertisers, viewers, volunteers, and supporters.

A Publicity/Promotion Assistant establishes and is in daily touch with a wide variety of media contacts in order to publicize and promote station activities and usually spends at least one-quarter of the working day outside the station. When inside, a considerable amount of time is spent on the telephone.

Often, a Publicity/Promotion Assistant creates, develops, and edits on-air promotion spots and slides that publicize the station's upcoming programming. Due to the increasingly competitive environment among the many media, on-air promotion has increased dramatically in the past five years. The Publicity/Promotion Assistant now routinely works with the Videotape Engineer/Editor to create sophisticated spots. Some Publicity/Promotion Assistants specialize in the creation of computer-generated promotional announcements. The Assistant also writes boldface listings, program schedules, and schedule changes and distributes them regularly to newspapers in the station's coverage area. The Publicity/Promotion Assistant is usually responsible for writing program announcements (overcrawls) to be superimposed on the video image during newscasts and other programs. Other responsibilities include writing and designing fliers, brochures, direct mail pieces, and other promotional literature. The Publicity/Promotion Assistant also works with the sales staff to develop meaningful research information for advertising agencies and clients.

Additionally, the Publicity/Promotion Assistant

- responds to viewer comments, complaints, suggestions, and questions about programming;
- maintains all promotion and publicity files, photographs, stories, national press releases, and taped promos;
- makes speeches and represents the station at community and business affairs; and
- arranges advertising barter or trade agreements.

Salaries

Earnings in 1996 ranged from $15,000 for entry-level employees at small market stations to more than $54,000 for experienced individuals with seniority at major market operations, according to the Bureau of Labor Statistics (BLS). Median annual earnings were about $34,000 in 1996, with the middle 50 percent earning between $25,000 and $54,000 annually.

Employment Prospects

Chances of getting a job as a Publicity/Promotion Assistant are generally fair. Keen competition for these jobs will likely continue among recent college graduates with a degree in communications—marketing, public relations, advertising, or a related field—as the number of applicants is expected to exceed the number of job openings.

Employment in this field is expected to increase 21 to 35 percent through the year 2006. Recognition of the need for good promotion in an increasingly competitive business environment should spur demand for specialists even at the entry level.

Advancement Prospects

The opportunities for advancement for bright, capable Publicity/Promotion Assistants are good, particularly for those with imagination, flair, and specialized skills. Some become Directors of Publicity/Promotion at their own sta-

tions after some years of successful experience, while others move to better-paid positions at major market stations at higher salaries. Some individuals move to cable TV or to multichannel multipoint distribution service (MMDS) operations as Directors of Publicity/Promotion. Still others find rewarding and more responsible positions in nonbroadcast companies, including home video and production firms. Some may find positions at the low-power television (LPTV) stations. Many use their television experience to obtain more rewarding positions in public relations or promotion at companies, organizations, or associations outside the media field.

Education

An undergraduate degree in public relations, journalism, English, advertising, or communications is often required. Courses in all the liberal arts are helpful, but writing courses are mandatory. Courses in art and design (including layout and web design) are extremely helpful.

Experience/Skills

Some experience in promotion and public relations at a media- or nonmedia-related organization is expected, and experience in promoting a nonprofit organization, even on a part-time basis, is helpful. In many circumstances, however, an undergraduate degree and some background in writing can replace full-time experience.

Candidates should be enthusiastic and creative individuals who are versatile, dependable, and adaptable to many situations and assignments. Ability to write short articles and press releases and good language skills are required. Interpersonal skills and social talents are helpful. All Publicity/Promotion Assistants must be competent with word processing software.

Minority/Women's Opportunities

Opportunities for women are excellent. The majority of Publicity/Promotion Assistants at commercial stations in 1996 were women, according to industry estimates. The Corporation for Public Broadcasting (CPB) reports that in 1994, 17 percent of professionals working at public television stations, a category that included Publicity/Promotion Assistants, were minorities, and 42 percent were women.

Unions/Associations

There are no unions that act as bargaining agents for Publicity/Promotion Assistant. Many, however, belong to ProMax International, Inc., to improve their skills and advance their careers.

COMMUNITY RELATIONS DIRECTOR

CAREER PROFILE

Duties: Determining local public needs and creating programs and announcements to meet them at a TV station

Alternate Title(s):   Public Service Director; Director of Community Affairs

Salary Range: $19,000 to $69,000

Employment Prospects: Poor

Advancement Prospects: Fair

Prerequisites:

　Education—Undergraduate degree in government, urban affairs, sociology, or communications

　Experience—Minimum of two years in community, civic, cultural, or service organizations

　Special Skills—Sensitivity; excellent writing and speaking abilities; service orientation; interpersonal skills

CAREER LADDER

```
┌─────────────────────────────────────┐
│           Producer;                  │
│       Program Manager                │
└─────────────────────────────────────┘

┌─────────────────────────────────────┐
│    Community Relations Director      │
└─────────────────────────────────────┘

┌─────────────────────────────────────┐
│ Director of Service or Civic Organization │
└─────────────────────────────────────┘
```

Position Description

A Community Relations Director is directly responsible for developing a continuing program of station services in response to the needs and interests of the local community. The Director is usually the station's primary liaison with public and private agencies, businesses, and professional organizations in the station's viewing area. The position of Community Relations Director is a unique one in communications, usually found only at commercial television stations. The responsibility of this individual is to keep a finger on the pulse of the community. This person also represents the station's point of view to the community.

All commercial and public television stations are licensed by the Federal Communications Commission (FCC) to operate "in the public interest, convenience, and necessity." Stations meet this responsibility by broadcasting local programs, public service announcements (PSAs), and special events coverage that address local needs and interests. Much of the Community Relations Director's time is spent in representing the station at public meetings in order to determine these needs and interests.

As the direct communications link with business associations, civic organizations, social service agencies, and youth organizations, the Community Relations Director is responsible for the effective use of specialized station programming to meet the interests of these groups.

Most Community Relations Directors are responsible for planning and producing the public affairs panel programs, interviews, or talk shows that deal with community-oriented issues. In many instances they serve as hosts for these programs. They also develop the necessary informal and contractual relationships to involve individual organizations in station programming.

The Community Relations Director oversees the production of all local public service announcements, and screens those that are produced elsewhere to determine their quality and appropriateness for broadcasting by the station.

Community Service Directors deal with a variety of groups daily. They must sympathetically evaluate requests for promotion and help from many worthy organizations. They are service-oriented people concerned with using television to deal effectively with community needs.

Because they deal with many special interest groups, Community Relations Directors must have a good understanding of FCC regulations, including the Fairness Doctrine and equal-time provisions. Often the most difficult aspect of the job is the ability to say "no" to requests for station time while avoiding negative repercussions for the station. Because of their close contact with the community, Community Relations Directors often research and develop station editorial positions on community issues. The position is partly that of a public relations professional and partly that of an ombudsman, reflecting both the needs of the station and those of the community.

A Community Relations Director is usually employed only at middle or major market commercial stations, generally reporting to the Program Manager. At smaller market stations, the Program Manager and the General Manager often share the duties. In public television, a station's entire programming operation is designed to be responsive to community needs. The duties of a Community Relations Director are, therefore, usually performed by a number of people, including the General Manager, the Program Manager, the Director of Publicity/Promotion, and the Director of Development.

Additionally, the Community Relations Director

- administers all ascertainment files (comments by community members about the station's programming), as required by the FCC;
- arranges and conducts station tours for organizations and groups;
- establishes and trains a speaker's bureau from the station's employees and schedules their appearances at public or organization meetings; and
- plans and organizes public service events to discuss the station's programming with community members.

Salaries

Salaries at commercial stations averaged $39,856 in 1997, according to the National Association of Broadcasters (NAB). Smaller salaries are usually paid to individuals who have fewer responsibilities.

Employment Prospects

Opportunities are poor. There were relatively few openings in commercial television specifically for a Community Relations Director at the 1,202 commercial TV stations on the air in 1998.

At many stations the position is filled by a director of a service or civic group with an understanding of local problems and of the organizations that deal with them, or by another individual experienced in community relations. Some positions may become available at the low-power television (LPTV) stations in the future, but most of those stations will be too small to support a Community Relations Director.

Advancement Prospects

Opportunities for advancement to other broadcast-related positions are fair. Some Community Relations Directors become full-time Producers of public affairs or news programs. A few use their television skills and knowledge of programming to become Program Managers. Still others use their knowledge to obtain better-paid public relations positions at nonprofit organizations or government agencies.

Education

An undergraduate degree in government, urban affairs, or sociology is usually necessary, although a degree in communications or public relations is sometimes required. A broad liberal arts background with courses in the social sciences, government, and public affairs is helpful.

Experience/Skills

Most Community Relations Directors have at least two years of previous experience as a director or a public information officer for a community, civic, cultural, or service organization. They should have experience in dealing with a wide variety of social problems and a familiarity with the structure of local business, community, and governmental groups.

Candidates must be sensitive individuals with a strong desire to assist in alleviating problems. They should be good listeners and adept in acting as mediators. They should also possess excellent speaking and writing skills and be able to appear on camera with poise. Good social skills are also required. Above all, a Community Relations Director should be service-oriented and capable of dealing with a large number of organizations and people in an understanding manner.

Minority/Women's Opportunities

Opportunities for women and members of minority groups are excellent. Most Community Relations Directors are women, and many inroads have been made by minorities, according to several industry observers. The FCC reports that in 1996, 35 percent of all officials and managers, which include Community Relations Directors, were women, and 14 percent were minorities. In public television, 37 percent of officials and managers were women in 1994, and 16 percent were minorities.

Unions/Associations

There are no unions that serve as bargaining agents for Community Relations Directors. Many individuals join the National Broadcast Association for Community Affairs, a professional organization, as well as a variety of civic and service organizations in the course of performing their duties.

PRODUCTION MANAGER

CAREER PROFILE

Duties: Responsibility for all local studio and remote productions at a television station or media organization

Alternate Title(s):   Production Director; Production Supervisor; Production Coordinator

Salary Range: $27,000 to $68,000

Employment Prospects: Fair

Advancement Prospects: Good

Prerequisites:

　Education—Undergraduate degree in radio-TV, communications, or theater; graduate degree preferable at some stations

　Experience—Minimum of five years in TV production

　Special Skills—Creativity; organizational ability; leadership qualities; taste

CAREER LADDER

```
┌─────────────────────────────┐
│      Program Manager;        │
│     Operations Manager       │
└─────────────────────────────┘

┌─────────────────────────────┐
│     Production Manager       │
└─────────────────────────────┘

┌─────────────────────────────┐
│     Executive Producer;      │
│          Producer            │
└─────────────────────────────┘
```

Position Description

The Production Manager's primary responsibility is to conceive, design, and develop ideas for local television productions that result in entertaining and informative programs. This individual is in charge of developing and complying with detailed budgets for all local productions, including costs for materials, capital equipment, supplies, and talent.

As overall manager of the station's production schedule, the Production Manager coordinates the creation of locally produced commercial spots, public affairs programs, entertainment shows, specials, and remote coverage of sporting events. Duties also include overseeing the design of sets, art, and prop elements to ensure quality design and workability in a studio or at a remote location. This involves directing and coordinating the creative efforts of many people during the planning and execution stages of television productions.

The Production Manager often supervises Executive Producers, Directors, Lighting Directors, Production Secretaries, the Art Director, Graphic Artists, and other production support personnel, including Camera Operators, Production Assistants, and Floor Managers, and at many stations, the Operations Manager. The Production Manager also negotiates with many individuals from outside the station, including Performers, Writers, and Musicians.

At a smaller commercial station that has few local productions, the Production Manager typically reports to the Pro-

gram Manager. In many public television stations, where local productions are more frequent, the production unit is a separate department.

Additionally, the Production Manager

- monitors standards of quality on all local productions;
- coordinates equipment and facilities requirements for local productions; and
- develops and manages the departmental budget.

Salaries

Salaries for Production Managers at both commercial and public television stations are relatively low.

At some small market commercial stations, the Production Manager is viewed as a glorified Operations Manager with scheduling duties, and the salary is correspondingly low. The average salary was $39,437 in 1997, according to the National Association of Broadcasters (NAB).

At most public television stations, this is a more important position because of the greater involvement with local productions. The Production Manager, however, is not well compensated.

According to a Corporation for Public Broadcasting (CPB) survey, Production Managers' median salary ranged from $31,435 to $65,650 at noncommercial stations in 1998. The overall median was $44,100. In general, the higher-paid positions are in the top markets, which place an emphasis on locally originated programs.

Employment Prospects

The job of Production Manager is not an entry-level position. Opportunities for employment are generally fair and competition is heavy. There are 1,569 Production Managers in television, and most have been promoted from within the ranks of the production department of their stations.

As a result of some turnover, there are a few positions open for the more talented Operations Managers or Executive Producers. A typical route to the Production Manager's position at a local station is from Production Assistant to Camera Operator to Floor Manager to Assistant Director to Director to Executive Producer to Production Manager.

The skills of a Production Manager are transferable to cable TV systems and independent production companies, and some Production Managers are employed at health, media, and occasionally at education and government media centers (see Part II).

Advancement Prospects

The opportunities for advancement are good. Most Production Managers at commercial or public TV stations move on to more responsible positions, either within the station or in a smaller market. Some assume similar positions at larger stations. Still others form their own production companies or join established commercial or independent production companies.

At public television stations, a Production Manager may be promoted to Program Manager or move to that position at another public station. Occasionally a Production Manager moves to a higher-paying position as Director of Instructional Television at an educational telecommunications center, as Director of Media Services in private industry, or as a Media Resource Manager or Media Specialist in a health organization.

Education

While it is not essential for the job, most Production Managers have a college degree in radio-TV communications, theater, or a related liberal arts field. Many have graduate degrees. This is particularly true in public television, where increased emphasis is placed on the role and responsibilities of a Production Manager. A degree is less important at commercial television stations, but some education other than on-the-job experience is usually required.

Experience/Skills

In general, Production Managers are between the ages of 25 and 35. Most have had extensive prior experience in television production. Having spent time at all levels in a production crew, a Production Manager is better able to coordinate all the elements and individuals that are involved in a station's locally originated program schedule.

Experience in cinematography or theater staging is helpful. In most cases, however, the Production Manager is hired from within the industry and has had at least five years of experience in television production.

Creativity, organizational ability, leadership, and taste are important talents in a Production Manager. The ideal candidate for this position will combine a sense of esthetics with pragmatism and logic, be excellent at working with a variety of people in highly complex tasks, and be able to transform elusive ideas and concepts into visually exciting programs.

Minority/Women's Opportunities

The opportunities for employment as a Production Manager at a local television station for women and minority group members are better than ever. It's no longer uncommon for women and minority college students to concentrate on production while earning their bachelor's degree; consequently, in recent years, industry observers say many have become television producers upon graduation and have then moved into production management.

The NAB reports that 14 percent of officials and managers, which include Production Managers, working in 1996 were minorities, while 35 percent were women. In public television, 11 percent were minorities in 1994, and 41 percent were women.

Unions/Associations

Some Production Managers at commercial stations have belonged to the National Association of Broadcast Employees and Technicians AFL-CIO (NABET) and a few have been members of the American Federation of Radio and Television Artists (AFTRA), but most become inactive when they reach this level. Some belong to the National Association of Television Program Executives (NATPE). There is no union or professional organization that specifically represents Production Managers.

EXECUTIVE PRODUCER

CAREER PROFILE

Duties: Conceiving, developing, and producing a television series, complex program, or special production

Alternate Title(s):   None

Salary Range: $23,000 to $150,000+

Employment Prospects: Fair

Advancement Prospects: Fair

Prerequisites:

Education—Minimum of undergraduate degree in mass communications, radio-TV, or specialized subject area

Experience—Three years as a television Producer

Special Skills—Creativity; leadership qualities; interpersonal skills; organizational ability; business acumen; financial orientation

CAREER LADDER

```
┌─────────────────────────────────────────┐
│  Production Manager; Program Manager;     │
│  Executive Producer (Production           │
│  Company)                                 │
└─────────────────────────────────────────┘

┌─────────────────────────────────────────┐
│         Executive Producer                │
└─────────────────────────────────────────┘

┌─────────────────────────────────────────┐
│              Producer                     │
└─────────────────────────────────────────┘
```

Position Description

An Executive Producer is responsible for conceiving and developing ideas for television series, individual complex programs, or special productions that meet defined audience objectives. The individual in this position formulates the rationale for the project, determines the format, frames the budget, arranges the financing, and oversees the promotion.

Many Executive Producers work with independent production companies that create programs for network or cable broadcast syndication or at home video companies (see Part II). Some Executive Producers for commercial television and syndicated programs are owners of production companies. A few are staff members at major market stations in charge of news, documentary, or public affairs programs. Some are employed at the networks in charge of developing shows for specific audiences (children) or in specific subjects (religion or sports).

At PTV stations, Executive Producers are often in charge of programs or series that have more-than-local appeal and are created for distribution or for PBS.

The responsibilities of the Executive Producer last through the life of the project. This person seeks and identifies ideas that can be creatively developed into entertaining or informative shows, researches them, determines whether they can be produced within the available technical resources and facilities, and writes, edits, or approves the program scripts.

The overall budget is established by the Executive Producer, who carefully monitors all expenses concerned with the project and often finds and convinces sponsors to fund the broadcast. The Executive Producer exploits all of the resources of television, arranges for facilities, equipment and personnel, and supervises every aspect of the project to ensure smooth, interesting, and entertaining broadcasts.

The Executive Producer is a "deal maker" who conceives, develops, cajoles, and fights for each project with programmers and advertisers. Often, more time is spent in the development of a project than in its actual production. The Executive Producer is a master of "who can do what" and of negotiating rights for television programs.

One or more Producers are selected by the Executive Producer to interpret and execute the concepts of individual shows or segments. The Executive Producer however, acts as final arbiter in the selection of Writers, Directors, Performers, and special technical/craft and production staff, including Music Directors, Costume Designers, and Scenic Designers. An Executive Producer has the ultimate responsibility for the success or failure of the project as it is seen on the air, in syndication, or on home video.

Additionally, the Executive Producer

- approves the completed program(s) prior to broadcast;
- monitors all promotion and publicity for the program(s); and

• Evaluates audience response to the show(s).

Salaries

In keeping with the talent and versatility needed for the position, Executive Producers are well paid. The lowest pay is at major market local commercial television stations, where the few full-time Executive Producers' salaries ranged from $30,000 to $60,000 in 1998, according to industry sources. Some Executive Producers of network or syndicated programs earn well over $150,000 yearly at a production company. Additional compensation comes from the licensing of rights to other media, including cable and home video. In public television, 1998 salaries ranged from a low of $23,227 at the smaller university- or school-owned stations to $117,115 for Executive Producers of programs designed for broadcast on the Public Broadcasting Service (PBS) system, according to the Corporation of Public Broadcasting (CPB). The median salary was $44,100 in that year.

Employment Prospects

The opportunities for employment as an Executive Producer are generally fair. Only the brightest and most capable achieve the position, and competition for the job is heavy. While some major market public and commercial TV stations employ two or more Executive Producers, there is little opportunity in small market stations or in government, education, or health media units, where Producers and Producer/Directors often perform the roles of Executive Producers. Nevertheless, with 1,569 television stations, as well as the recent establishment of networks such as Warner Brothers and cable networks including the Discovery Channel and the History Channel, content—which is developed and managed by Executive Producers—is in demand.

An Executive Producer is usually promoted from within the station's ranks. Having produced a variety of successful programs, a bright and talented individual may be given overall responsibility for high-budgeted productions. Some entrepreneurial individuals with great initiative and exciting ideas (and, often, a sponsor) are hired from outside the station to be Executive Producers for series or specials.

Advancement Prospects

The possibilities of advancement from Executive Producer to Production Manager or Program Manager are fair. Some individuals, however, obtain those positions in smaller market stations, although the assumption of these largely administrative posts reduces their creative activities as Executive Producers. Still others are able to get better-paying positions at independent production companies. Some experienced people form their own companies and develop programs for syndicated sale to stations, to networks, or to home video. A very few are skilled and talented enough to obtain staff Executive Producer positions at the commercial networks.

Education

Most employers require that candidates have a minimum of an undergraduate degree in mass communications or radio-TV. Many Executive Producers have training and education in the subjects for which they develop programs. A degree in a particular area is often necessary for an Executive Producer of specific kinds of broadcasts, such as political science for news programs or theater arts for dramatic productions.

Experience/Skills

Most Production Managers or Program Managers expect a candidate to have at least three years of experience as a television Producer. The individual must have a thorough practical knowledge of all stages involved in producing a TV program and an understanding of television or film technology.

The Executive Producer is an idea person and must be creative and able to develop concepts, ideas, and formats for television programming. The Executive Producer must have leadership capabilities and great interpersonal skills to manage creative and technical people effectively and must have an organized mind and a sound business sense. An Executive Producer should be able to estimate costs and develop budgets for television productions.

Minority/Women's Opportunities

Increasing numbers of Executive Producer positions in commercial television were occupied by women or members of minority groups in 1998. Cable networks including Lifetime and Black Entertainment Television emphasize programming for women and minorities, which has resulted in greater opportunities for members of these groups to take on production and management roles.

Unions/Associations

There are no unions or professional organizations that represent Executive Producers. Many belong to the National Association of Television Program Executives (NATPE) and to the National Academy of Television Arts and Sciences to exchange ideas and sell programming.

PRODUCER

CAREER PROFILE

Duties: Creating and developing individual television productions

Alternate Title(s):   Producer/Director

Salary Ranges: $22,000 to $100,000+

Employment Prospects: Fair

Advancement Prospects: Fair

Prerequisites:

Education—Undergraduate degree in radio-TV, communications, theater, or journalism

Experience—Minimum of three years as a Director or Associate Producer

Special Skills—Leadership qualities; creativity; interpersonal skills; organizational abilities; orientation to detail; financial expertise; business acumen; television judgment

CAREER LADDER

```
┌─────────────────────────────────────────┐
│ Production Manager; Executive Producer    │
└─────────────────────────────────────────┘

┌─────────────────────────────────────────┐
│              Producer                     │
└─────────────────────────────────────────┘

┌─────────────────────────────────────────┐
│      Director; Associate Producer         │
└─────────────────────────────────────────┘
```

Position Description

A Producer is the overall manager and arranger of an individual television production or of one that is part of a series. The person in this position conceives and develops ideas for a program consistent with the theme established by an Executive Producer or Production Manager, and, in addition, ensures that the program meets all of the station's objectives and is compatible with audience interests. Producers also work for cable and home video companies and in business, health, education, and government media organizations (see Part II).

A Producer is a skilled professional who may be selected by an Executive Producer to generate a single program or segment of a larger project. Producers are usually staff members of a TV station, a network, or an independent production company that creates shows for networks, syndication, or home video. Most commercial and public stations employ several full-time Producers. At network and independent production companies, two or three producers may be responsible for individual programs within a series and may have alternating responsibilities on a daily or weekly basis, depending on the complexity of the productions.

Virtually all types of programs require Producers, including variety shows, soap operas, talk shows, dramas, situation comedies, news, public affairs, sports, and all other categories of TV programming. Within the parameters of a series's or program's goals, the Producer has considerable latitude in developing ideas, selecting Performers, creating scripts, choosing Directors, and determining the specific approach and format of each production.

It is the job of Producers to keep programs within budget and on schedule. They take care of all business arrangements and they are responsible for contracts with Performers, handle clearances, order technical facilities and equipment, and schedule rehearsals and performances. Producers supervise negotiations with personalities and other Performers, as well as with professional and technical people needed for a production. They select Performers who will appear on camera, including guest hosts, and musicians. They also coordinate production assignments and supervise Directors. On occasion, a Producer may act as on-air talent—that is, as a host, interviewer, or Reporter.

For newscasts and documentaries, Producers are frequently involved in selecting the stories and special event to be covered. They often decide on the issues to be discussed, supervise background research, and help to choose individuals to be interviewed.

Additionally, the Producer

- supervises the development of promotional material for the program; and
- ensures that the program meets production quality standards.

Salaries

In commercial broadcasting, Producers/Directors earned an average of $30,794 in 1997, according to the National Association of Broadcasters (NAB). The average starting salary was $23,976. Some Producers of sports, special events, or entertainment programs at major market stations make more than $40,000 per year. Producers at networks and at independent production companies earn $100,000 or more.

In public television, the median 1998 salary for a Producer was $33,000, according to the Corporation for Public Broadcasting (CPB).

Producers of training, public information, instructional, and health programs in private industry, government, health, and educational organizations usually receive slightly lower salaries.

Employment Prospects

The Producer's position is highly coveted at most stations, and competition for the job is heavy. Most television stations employ from two to eight Producers who work on specific assignments or on special programs during a given period. In addition, some Producers move to similar positions at independent production companies, advertising agencies, video production operations, or larger market stations, so jobs become available at some stations. Because of the expertise and training required and the extensive competition, employment prospects for a Producer in TV broadcasting are generally fair.

Government, health, private industry, and educational video production operations employ Producers who are often specialists in particular subject areas. The opportunities for employment in these nonbroadcast settings, although usually better than at TV stations, are only fair.

Advancement Prospects

Many Producers view the position as the final step in their careers. Some, however, become Executive Producers or Production Managers at smaller market stations. Still others seek administrative, production, or program responsibilities at independent production companies or at private educational, health, and governmental media organizations.

A number of Producers specialize in news and public affairs, commercials, sports, or entertainment programs and advance their careers by working on higher-budgeted or more prestigious shows where they have expertise in the subject covered. A very few Producers with great talent and ability obtain positions at the network level or with independent production companies that produce programs for network, cable TV, or home video.

Education

Most employers require that a Producer have a degree in radio-TV, communications, theater, or journalism. He or she should have a broad exposure to the liberal arts and some specific education in the subject area of the assigned program.

Experience/Skills

A candidate for a Producer's job should have a minimum of three years of experience as a Director or Associate Producer. The aspiring Producer needs a thorough practical knowledge of TV production, should be familiar with budget estimation, and should have experience in all stages of program development, from conception to videotape editing.

Producers must demonstrate leadership qualities and be creative and original in developing new formats and techniques for TV production. They must be able to coordinate a number of individuals, including Performers and technical and production people. Producers must be well organized, detail-oriented, and financially astute, and must have good business and television judgment.

Minority/Women's Opportunities

According to industry sources, the majority of Producers at commercial stations in 1997 were white males, although women and minority group members are increasingly employed in the position, particularly at smaller market stations. In public television, 50 percent of professionals, including Producers, were female and 18 percent were members of minorities in 1994, according to the CPB. As programming for minorities and women increase, industry observers predict growth in opportunities for them as Producers.

Unions/Associations

Some Producers who also work as on-air talent are members of the American Federation of Television and Radio Artists (AFTRA). A few are members of the Directors Guild of America (DGA). In the majority of instances, however, Producers are not represented by a union or professional organization.

ASSOCIATE PRODUCER

CAREER PROFILE

Duties: Providing administrative and professional support to a television Producer

Alternate Title(s): Assistant Producer

Salary Range: $18,000 to $50,000

Employment Prospects: Fair

Advancement Prospects: Fair

Prerequisites:

Education—Undergraduate degree in mass communications or radio-TV

Experience—Minimum of two years in a variety of production positions

Special Skills—Creativity; organizational aptitude; leadership qualities; writing ability; cooperativeness

CAREER LADDER

```
┌─────────────────────────────────────┐
│              Producer                │
└─────────────────────────────────────┘

┌─────────────────────────────────────┐
│         Associate Producer           │
└─────────────────────────────────────┘

┌─────────────────────────────────────┐
│ Production Assistant; Floor Manager  │
│   Unit Manager; Assistant Director   │
└─────────────────────────────────────┘
```

Position Description

An Associate Producer provides general administrative and professional support to the Producer of a TV program. This person acts as the Producer's chief aide in conceiving, developing, and producing a TV show recorded on tape or broadcast live from a studio or remote location. In the Producer's absence, the Associate Producer assumes full responsibility. An Associate Producer may also be employed at a larger cable production company or at a production or home video company (see Part II). The smaller media organizations in business, health, education, and government seldom employ Associate Producers, although some staff members temporarily assume the job for particular projects.

Some complex TV productions employ several Associate Producers, each of whom has a specific function during various production stages. In addition to helping others work out their concepts, Associate Producers also develop their own original story lines and ideas and, often, are given full responsibility to create taped elements or segments to be inserted into the finished show.

Associate Producers help to prepare the budget, organize the production schedule, and occasionally supervise Camera Operators, Cinematographers, Videotape Engineers/Editors, and other members of the production team. They also evaluate scripts and program proposals, help design set and lighting plots, and, sometimes, select music for bridges and inserts. They often negotiate rights for film, slide, or tape inserts, Musician or Performer "step-up" fees (residual payments for wider distribution of a program), and, on occasion, the rights for cable TV or home video distribution.

The television and film industries resist standardization in production job categories. The process of developing and shooting a program is complex and ever changing. Each project provides different challenges and requires varied techniques and methods. As a result, Associate Producers find themselves in different roles, depending on the production.

As a rule, an Associate Producer is given wide latitude in helping to develop the production. The Associate Producer usually reports to a Production Manager and is assigned to one Producer for specific projects or programs. Program responsibilities can include news, sports, documentaries talk shows, and entertainment specials. In almost every instance, the emphasis for a particular project is different.

The Associate Producer can be an important member of a station's news department and may be called upon to assist a Producer or Reporter in developing a story or documentary by providing some of the research and doing part of the writing. The Associate Producer may also conduct background interviews and supervise the filming or videotaping of segments to be used in the finished program. At private production companies and in home video production, the

Associate Producer is often assigned more responsibility for the budgetary control of the project expenses.

Additionally, the Associate Producer at a station

- works with the Operations Manager in scheduling facilities and equipment;
- assists in film or videotape editing of a final production; and
- participates in research of audience acceptance of the program.

Salaries

Salaries for Associate Producers range from $18,000 for beginners in smaller market commercial stations or production companies to more than $50,000 for experienced individuals who work on major TV programs or films for network broadcast.

In public television, Associate Producers' earnings ranged from $16,000 for entry-level employees at smaller school or university stations to $38,000 at major market community-owned stations for those working on major program projects for PBS system distribution in 1998, according to industry observers.

Employment Prospects

Although some smaller market stations view the Associate Producer as a person involved in detail work, most TV production operations require more experienced individuals. To become an Associate Producer, therefore, one needs a thorough knowledge of TV production, which can usually be gained by working as a Production Assistant, Floor Manager, Unit Manager, or Assistant Director.

Although many stations and independent production companies employ more than one Associate Producer, competition for the position is usually quite strong. There is, however, considerable mobility among Associate Producers, and through attrition a number of positions become available. Advertising agencies also employ Associate Producers. The overall opportunities for employment are fair.

Advancement Prospects

Most Associate Producers are ambitious, have considerable experience in TV production, and actively seek more responsible positions, usually as Producers. The more creative and talented move to Producer positions at smaller market stations or become Producers of news, public affairs, or sports programs at their own stations. The competition for these jobs is great, however, and only the best and the brightest advance. Some Associate Producers move to advertising agencies or corporations or to education, health, or government TV operations as Producers of specific or specialized programs. The opportunities for advancement are generally fair for the ambitious, dedicated individual.

Education

Television stations most often hire Associate Producers who have undergraduate degrees in mass communications or radio-TV. A broad liberal arts background is useful. Some theater training is desirable, and courses in writing are also helpful. An Associate Producer who wishes to work in a specialized area such as news, sports, or music has a better chance with some educational background in that discipline.

Experience/Skills

Most employers require a minimum of two years of varied experience in television production. An Associate Producer usually has experience as a Production Assistant, Floor Manager, or Unit Manager and has operated film and tape editing equipment. The majority have had some experience as Assistant Directors.

Employers seek bright and aggressive people with original ideas for programs. An Associate Producer must be creative and well organized and should demonstrate leadership abilities, versatility, persistence, writing skills, and an ability to work well with a variety of people.

Minority/Women's Opportunities

The opportunities for women and members of minority groups to gain employment as Associate Producers in commercial television are excellent. This is particularly true at middle and major market stations and at production and home video companies.

Unions/Associations

There are no unions or professional groups that represent Associate Producers.

DIRECTOR

CAREER PROFILE

Duties: Orchestrating all technical and creative elements of a television production

Alternate Title(s): Producer/Director

Salary Range: $16,600 to $100,000+

Employment Prospects: Fair

Advancement Prospects: Good

Prerequisites:

Education—Undergraduate degree in radio-TV or communications

Experience—Minimum of two years in television production

Special Skills—Creativity; technical knowledge; organizational and leadership qualities; motivational skills

CAREER LADDER

```
┌─────────────────────────────────────────┐
│                Producer                   │
└─────────────────────────────────────────┘

┌─────────────────────────────────────────┐
│                Director                   │
└─────────────────────────────────────────┘

┌─────────────────────────────────────────┐
│   Assistant Director; Unit Manager;      │
│            Floor Manager                  │
└─────────────────────────────────────────┘
```

Position Description

A Director plays a critical role in any television production. It is the Director's responsibility to turn a concept or script into a cohesive and interesting program creatively, effectively, and within budget. Working in a complex, pressure-filled environment, this person is the unifying force during the planning, shooting, and completion of a TV program. The show's final success is largely due to the Director's talent and ingenuity.

The Director coordinates all elements, facilities, and people during rehearsal and actual production and gives significant and detailed instruction to the studio or location crew and talent. A Director is usually assigned to a Producer for a particular show or program but sometimes also assumes the Producer's role.

The work begins in preproduction planning stages, when the Director meets frequently with the Producer and sometimes the Writer to develop a workable program. The Director collaborates with important members of the team to determine production elements, including equipment and engineering requirements, lighting needs, the number of cameras necessary, music, costumes, and sets. The Director also hires or approves of the cast. Working with a floor plan, the Director plots camera shots, placement of equipment, and blocking of Performers.

During rehearsals and productions, Directors oversee all production and engineering personnel from the control room and communicate with the studio via headphones. They select all camera shots and movements that will eventually be seen by the audience and combine all preplanned creative and technical elements into smooth and polished shows. In the postproduction phases, Directors supervise videotape editing of programs.

A Director's role is somewhat different in news and documentaries. The Producer chooses what stories or events will be covered and selects the film or videotape segments to be shown. The Director then organizes the preedited pieces and studio elements into a unified broadcast.

Directors are employed on staff by all networks and virtually every station. At some smaller outlets, one or two staff Directors may be responsible for all locally produced programs. At others, one Director may be in charge of a continuing program or series or may specialize in a particular format such as news or sports. Independent production companies usually employ Directors on staff and often hire freelance Directors for specific projects.

Additionally, the Director

- assists in the design of the set and lighting plot;
- reviews the script with Performers and conducts rehearsals; and
- selects slides, artwork, graphics, and tape and film inserts for the program.

Salaries

Salaries in 1997 in commercial television for the related position of Producer/Director (the one often used in surveys) averaged $30,794, according to the NAB. Some experienced people at major market stations earned over $60,000. The few Directors of major TV programs for network release make considerably more. Most such individuals work on one or two productions annually but can earn more than $100,000 if they work six months or more a year.

In public TV, 1998 salaries for Directors ranged from a low of $17,811 in small university- or school-owned stations to $74,840 for experienced individuals with seniority at major market community-owned stations, according to the Corporation for Public Broadcasting (CPB). The median was $31,982 in that year.

Employment Prospects

Most commercial and public stations employ from two to six Directors, and increasing numbers of production companies are expanding opportunities. The job requires considerable experience and skill, and competition for the position is strong. Most Directors are promoted to their positions after working as Assistant Directors, Floor Managers, or Unit Managers.

Some additional opportunities exist at cable systems and independent production companies, as well as at education, government, health, and corporate TV operations. The overall chances of becoming a Director are fair.

Advancement Prospects

For some, the position of Director is considered the peak of a successful career. A considerable number, however, become Producers, and others assume more responsibility as producer/directors. Usually a Director obtains one of these positions at a smaller market station at more salary, although some move into comparable positions at independent production houses at higher salaries. Some Directors specialize in a particular kind of program, such as news, sports, variety, or cultural shows, and they command higher salaries for more complex productions. In general, opportunities for advancement are good.

Education

An undergraduate degree in radio-TV or communications is usually required to be hired as a Director. Many individuals have some education in theater and others come from a journalism background. While a degree is not an absolute requirement, a broad education, usually in the liberal arts, is extremely useful for Directors, who must work with programs that involve various subjects, styles, and formats. Few directors are employed straight out of college or broadcast training school.

Experience/Skills

Many television Directors are between the ages of 25 and 30 and have had at least two years of production experience. They often apprentice in all positions on a production crew, including Camera Operator, Floor Manager, Unit Manager, and Assistant Director.

Directors must have fast reflexes to give instructions to a number of people working in a variety of tasks under severe time constraints. They should have a thorough knowledge of the medium and be well organized, methodical planners with excellent leadership qualities and an ability to motivate others. They must act decisively under pressure, be creative and flexible, and have a good eye for the composition of images.

Minority/Women's Opportunities

In 1997, Directors Guild of America president Jack Shea stated that "[e]mployment levels for DGA women and minorities are simply unacceptable," and took a step to address the situation through a "Summit on Diversity." The conference examined how to recruit and hire more minorities and women into the ranks of film and television directors, as well as assistant directors, unit managers, and floor managers—the positions in which most aspiring directors gain fundamental experience. In 1996, only 21 African-American women were DGA members; women directors working in television represented 24 percent of DGA membership (but only 9 percent of film directors were women), and only 6 percent of television directors in 1996 were members of minority groups—down from 9 percent in 1986.

Heightened awareness and recruiting programs are expanding these numbers. At CBS in 1997, 16 of the 26 new shows had "women, minorities or both on their staff as directors," according to Leslie Moonves, president of CBS Entertainment. And with 150 more television stations on the air than a decade ago and the emergence of several cable networks, programming for a larger, more diverse and specialized audience is now being developed more than ever before, which is beginning to open more doors for women and minority directors, according to industry observers.

Unions/Associations

Directors working for networks, independent production companies, and some major market stations are usually represented by the DGA. The majority of Directors, however, are not represented by a union or professional organization.

ASSISTANT DIRECTOR

CAREER PROFILE

Duties: Assisting the Director in television productions

Alternate Title(s):   Associate Director

Salary Range: $18,000 to $50,000+

Employment Prospects: Fair

Advancement Prospects: Fair

Prerequisites:

Education—Undergraduate degree in mass communications, radio-TV, or theater

Experience—Minimum of two years as a station Unit Manager, Floor Manager, or Production Assistant

Special Skills—Firm knowledge of TV production; organizational ability; facility with details

CAREER LADDER

```
┌─────────────────────────────────────┐
│    Director; Associate Producer      │
└─────────────────────────────────────┘

┌─────────────────────────────────────┐
│        Assistant Director            │
└─────────────────────────────────────┘

┌─────────────────────────────────────┐
│   Unit Manager; Floor Manager;       │
│      Production Assistant            │
└─────────────────────────────────────┘
```

Position Description

The Assistant Director helps the Director to coordinate the production elements of a TV program and makes certain that Performers, equipment, sets, and staff are ready for rehearsals and shooting, serving as the Director's right hand prior to, during, and immediately following the production. Usually, the Assistant Director reports to a Production Manager at a station and is assigned to a Director on a project or program basis.

For major productions for network TV, a first Assistant Director and a second Assistant Director are usually hired by the independent production company. In all situations, the primary role of the Assistant Director is to specifically organize the preproduction preparation of the program. Television production is often a series of compromises, and the Assistant Director is called upon to effect those compromises, often between the Director and the crew. The Assistant Director is usually employed for managerial expertise within a creative environment.

A major responsibility of the Assistant Director is to make sure that all film segments, slides, tapes, inserts, and electronic titles have been assembled and timed in the preproduction stage. This individual assists in the development and preparation of scripts, times rehearsals, and prompts Performers. The Assistant Director helps the Director block camera shots and Performer movement on the floor plan. In short, he or she ensures that the details are taken care of so that the creative work can proceed.

For a remote production or a complex dramatic film, the Assistant Director scouts locations and works with the Unit Manager in organizing arrangements for transportation, lodging, facilities, and personnel. For studio rehearsals, the Assistant Director takes notes and transmits the Director's production requirements to Production Assistants, Technical Directors, Floor Managers, Makeup Artists, Lighting Directors, and other production team members.

During rehearsals and actual production, the Assistant Director is often in the control room and is in charge of timing the various elements of the program and relaying time cues to the Floor Manager and other production personnel. On location, the Assistant Director often directs background action and supervises crowd control. The Assistant Director is also responsible for securing minor cast contracts and releases from extras. In the absence of a Technical Director, the Assistant Director is responsible for presetting and readying camera shots and cueing film, tape, and slide inserts, and helping the Director in postproduction editing of a videotaped or filmed TV show.

Additionally, the Assistant Director

- coordinates all deadlines related to the production;
- handles immediate emergencies pertaining to sets of Performers;
- ensures that all elements of the production blend into a cohesive, smooth process; and
- prepares a daily shooting schedule and determines cast and crew call times.

Salaries

Some small market stations, both commercial and public, with relatively simple news or interview programs offered low annual salaries of $18,000 to $22,000 for the few staff positions available in 1997, according to industry estimates. The accomplished Assistant Directors working on major TV films or complex entertainment specials for independent production companies command much higher salaries. Minimum payments for first Assistant Directors were $2,849 a week in 1998, according to the Directors Guild of America (DGA). For on-location work, the weekly minimum was $3,987. These individuals work on assignment for one or two projects a year as contract personnel, usually for 26 weeks. They are not part of a regular station staff.

Employment Prospects

The Assistant Director job is a coveted one in most commercial or public TV stations and independent production companies because it often leads to higher production positions. The competition among Floor Managers, Unit Managers, and other production workers is, therefore, very heavy.

Most major TV or film productions require more than one Assistant Director on a project-by-project basis. Only major market stations, networks, and some independent production companies hire them as full-time staff members. Very few advertising agencies, cable TV, health, government, and educational TV operations use them. Since many good Assistant Directors move on to more responsible positions at smaller market stations, positions are usually available for qualified people. Because of the competition, however, employment prospects are considered to be only fair.

Advancement Prospects

An Assistant Director is likely to view the job as a stepping-stone to becoming a Director, and some obtain that position at smaller market stations. Still others become Associate Producers at their stations or take similar positions at independent production companies.

There are not as many openings for either Director or Associate Producer positions as there are qualified candidates, and only the best Assistant Directors are likely to be promoted. Because of the general competition, overall prospects for advancement for Assistant Directors are only fair.

Education

Production Managers usually require an undergraduate degree in radio-TV, mass communications, or theater in promoting or hiring a person as an Assistant Director at a station. Although a degree is not required at smaller market stations, mostly employers select applicants who have had some post–high school training in television production or in the theater. On large-scale network productions, the DGA operates a formal, on-site, paid training program for Assistant Directors under the supervision of the Second Assistant Director.

Experience/Skills

Most employers in major market stations or independent companies require a minimum of two years of experience as a Unit Manager or Floor Manager for promotion to Assistant Director. In some stations, however, an experienced Production Assistant may be promoted to the job.

In addition to having a sound background in all aspects of TV production, Assistant Directors must be well organized and detail oriented in order to follow through on the complex elements involved in working on a program. Above all, they must be inventive and be capable of dealing with a variety of other creative as well as technical people in pressure situations.

Minority/Women's Opportunities

While educators note that more women and minorities than ever before are today pursuing the Director's track, which usually includes learning the responsibilities of Assistant Director, Unit Manager, and Floor Manager, industry observers state that by and large, most of these positions are still held by white males. The DGA has established steering committees to examine and recommend solutions to the dearth of women and minorities in the director's chair and the critical positions, such as Assistant Director, that prepare one for it, and most observers are optimistic about expanding opportunities.

Unions/Associations

In the majority of instances, there are no unions or professional organizations that represent Assistant Directors. For many major made-for-TV dramatic films or taped specials, however, the DGA serves as the bargaining agent.

UNIT MANAGER

Duties: Overseeing logistics and budget control of a television production or series, usually on location

Alternate Title(s):   Studio Supervisor; Remote Supervisor; Unit Production Manager; Unit Supervisor

Salary Range: $17,000 to $75,000+

Employment Prospects: Fair

Advancement Prospects: Fair

Prerequisites:

Education—High school diploma; TV or film production training; some college preferable

Experience—Minimum of two years TV/film production

Special Skills—Technical aptitude; organizational and administrative skill; financial management ability

```
┌─────────────────────────────────────┐
│         Associate Producer          │
└─────────────────────────────────────┘

┌─────────────────────────────────────┐
│            Unit Manager             │
└─────────────────────────────────────┘

┌─────────────────────────────────────┐
│  Floor Manager; Production Assistant │
└─────────────────────────────────────┘
```

Position Description

A Unit Manager is the primary logistics organizer of all elements of a television production and also serves as the person immediately in charge of budget expenditures, ensuring that all production costs are within budgetary limitations.

Unit Managers are employed at some commercial television stations, at some major public television stations, and at the networks. They are also employed at production companies that produce made-for-TV programming (see Part II).

Usually, a Unit Manager at a station is immediately responsible for all preproduction scheduling and for the setup, maintenance, and operation of all facilities and equipment. The Unit Manager organizes staging and lighting personnel, Camera Operators, Production Assistants, and other production employees in the preparation of rehearsals and in preproduction activities. A Unit Manager usually reports to an Assistant Director or Associate Producer.

A Unit Manager must be able to manage the diverse technical and practical elements of a television production efficiently and effectively.

Although Unit Managers are most often responsible for on-location film or remote television productions, the title is sometimes used in major market stations for the people in charge of a daily in-studio television production. They over-

see the budget and physical organization of a continuing series of television productions.

Unit Managers who are employed by major independent production companies on a project-by-project basis break down and prepare preliminary shooting schedules and budgets. For on-location shooting, they oversee preliminary searches and surveys and coordinate arrangements for the transportation and housing of cast, crew, and staff. During production, they supervise the completion of production reports for each day's work, as well as reports on the overall status of the production. A Unit Manager in these circumstances reports to the Producer and supervises all aspects of the production from a cost control standpoint. In these situations, the Unit Manager works closely with and sometimes supervises the Assistant Director.

Additionally, the Unit Manager

- arranges the rental of remote locations;
- organizes the delivery and setup of all equipment, including cameras, lights, audio equipment, monitors, sets and scenery, easels, props, and other items necessary for a production;
- checks and monitors all facilities and crew during production to ensure a smooth operation; and
- organizes the strike (dismantling) of a remote production and the return of all equipment and personnel.

Salaries

Unit Managers in commercial television were paid from $18,000 in smaller markets to more than $50,000 for experienced personnel in the major markets and production companies in 1998, according to industry sources.

The salaries at public TV stations for employees functioning as Unit Managers were approximately the same. Payments for these people, often titled Unit Supervisors or Studio Supervisors, ranged from $17,190 to $68,383 in major market public TV stations in 1998, according to the Corporation for Public Broadcasting (CPB). The median salary was $29,800 in 1998. Salaries for Unit Production Managers employed on a project basis at production companies are considerably higher. The weekly salary was $3,118 for studio work and $4,366 for on-location work in 1998, according to the Directors Guild of America (DGA).

Employment Prospects

The position of Unit Manager is not normally an entry-level job, and opportunities are only fair for diligent and ambitious production employees at a station. Unit Managers are often assigned from the production staff to specific remotes, or to a continuing series of in-studio programs. Because of this, there are sometimes opportunities for a production employee to be assigned periodically as a Unit Manager to various projects during a year. In addition, some major market stations maintain standing production units for continuing series, and efficient Floor Managers or Production Assistants are sometimes promoted to Unit Managers on a permanent basis. Each commercial network usually employs more than 100 Unit Managers on a full-time basis, but employment there and at independent production companies is difficult to obtain.

Advancement Prospects

Most Unit Managers are aggressive and have a penchant for organization. In large stations, the opportunities for advancement to Associate Producer or to other responsible production posts are fair. A series of successful assignments often impresses a superior enough to promote the Unit Manager to a more responsible position. Some Unit Managers seek advancement in smaller stations as Production Managers. Still others freelance at larger independent film or television commercial production organizations to further their careers.

Education

A high school diploma and some evidence of technical training in television or film production is helpful for employment in or promotion to the position. Major market stations and the networks prefer an undergraduate degree in radio-TV, mass communications, or theater. Courses in theater staging and lighting can also be useful. Experience in television production, however, is often more important than formal education.

Experience/Skills

New Unit Managers are usually expected to have at least two years of experience in television or film production and a thorough knowledge of TV equipment and facilities.

The position also requires an ability to work well with people on both an individual and a collective basis, and to organize personnel for complex and interrelated tasks in pressure situations. The Unit Manager must understand budgets, be highly organized, and have a good mind for detail.

Minority/Women's Opportunities

The majority of Unit Managers in commercial television in 1997 were white males, according to industry estimates. The number of women holding the job has increased slightly and should continue to do so.

At public television stations in 1994, 50 percent of the professionals, which include Unit Managers, were white females and 18 percent were minority group members, according to the CPB.

Unions/Associations

Unit Managers working on television films for network release are classified as Unit Production Managers, and as such are represented by the DGA. Most Unit Managers in local commercial or public television stations, however, do not belong to a union.

FLOOR MANAGER

CAREER PROFILE

Duties: Coordination of Director's instructions with studio and remote production activities

Alternate Title(s):   Stage Manager; Crew Chief; Floor Director

Salary Range: $16,000 to $50,000+

Employment Prospects: Fair

Advancement Prospects: Fair

Prerequisites:

Education—High school diploma; some college preferable

Experience—Minimum of one year in television production

Special Skills—Versatility; cooperativeness; organizational ability; cool-headedness

CAREER LADDER

```
┌─────────────────────────────┐
│     Assistant Director;      │
│        Unit Manager          │
└─────────────────────────────┘

┌─────────────────────────────┐
│                              │
│       Floor Manager          │
│                              │
└─────────────────────────────┘

┌─────────────────────────────┐
│      Camera Operator;        │
│    Production Assistant       │
└─────────────────────────────┘
```

Position Description

The Floor Manager is responsible for coordinating the Director's instructions with all crew and talent activities on the studio floor or on remote location during rehearsals and actual production. A major function of the Floor Manager is to follow along with the script and cue Performers, both in rehearsal and, silently, during production. It is one of the most important positions on the production team, especially during actual production. Floor Managers are usually assigned to a particular show by the Production Manager. During the rehearsals and production, the Floor Manager reports to the Director.

Prior to the production, the Floor Manager supervises all staging activities for each program, including the setup of scenery and all production-related equipment and devices. The Floor Manager works closely with the Art Director or Scenic Designer for on-the-spot construction, painting, and modifications of the set and verifies that all props and costumes are accounted for and are on hand. In small studio talk shows, the Floor Manager applies simple makeup to guests and places lavaliere microphones on the host and interviewees.

During actual production, the Floor Manager positions easels and graphics, operates the TelePrompTer, places props, and gives timing signals and other cues to Performers.

Wearing headphones and acting as the on-site extension of the Director, the Floor Manager relays instructions by hand signals and cue boards to the crew and Performers.

The Floor Manager is ultimately responsible for all studio activity before and during production, making some independent, immediate decisions regarding the solution of production problems that occur in the studio during rehearsal or actual production. As the Director's on-site representative, this individual must behave calmly and efficiently so that any tensions related to the production are not transmitted to the Performers or crew.

Additionally, the Floor Manager

- assists the Lighting Director in the transport, setup and placement of lights and accessories;
- positions video monitors during rehearsal and production; and
- directly supervises the dismantling and storage of set pieces and production equipment.

Salaries

In keeping with the necessary experience and skills required for the position of Floor Manager, it is a reasonably well-paid job in commercial and public TV. At commercial stations, the average salary for the position was $25,458 in

1997, according to the National Association of Broadcasters (NAB). The average starting compensation was $20,213.

In public television in 1998, Floor Managers' salaries ranged from $16,000 for beginners to $50,000 for experienced senior people, according to industry estimates that year. Because they often act as de facto Unit Managers at public television stations, they are sometimes paid more than at commercial stations.

Employment Prospects

The chances of employment are only fair. The position of Floor Manager is not an entry-level job in either commercial or public television.

Most employers require that candidates have a minimum of one year of experience in a production crew, usually as a Camera Operator or Production Assistant. Many stations promote only their most experienced crew members to the job. While some major market stations employ more than one Floor Manager for various programs or shifts, most small stations have only one individual for whom this job is his or her primary responsibility. They work on the stations' news programs and in the production of commercials. Public television stations do more local production, but the shows are scheduled so that fewer Floor Managers are needed.

Some Floor Manager positions are available in larger production facility companies, at cable television systems, in corporate television, and in education, health, and government television units where a significant amount of production is scheduled.

Advancement Prospects

Opportunities for advancement are fair for competent, talented individuals. The position of Floor Manager is often a stepping-stone for ambitious, professional younger people employed in television production. The majority of individuals in such positions were between the ages of 24 and 30 in 1997, according to industry estimates. A bright Floor Manager often moves up to Assistant Director after a year or two in the job. Some Floor Managers switch to major market stations or to independent production companies for more responsible positions, such as Unit Manager. The competition for such jobs, however, is heavy. Most Floor Managers ultimately seek to become Directors.

Education

A high school diploma and some college training in theater or radio-TV are often required. An undergraduate degree in mass communications or radio-TV is particularly useful in obtaining the job at major market commercial or public television stations. Courses in theater arts (staging and lighting, in particular) are helpful, as are courses in cinematography.

Experience/Skills

A minimum of a year of experience as a member of a production crew is usually required. A Floor Manager needs a good knowledge of all aspects of television production, including lighting, staging, makeup, and camerawork. An ability to organize many elements into a smoothly running operation is a necessity. In addition, the Floor Manager must be resourceful, have initiative, and be capable of independent action in managing the complex aspects of a studio production. Above all, the Floor Manager must appear calm and confident during a hectic television production.

Minority/Women's Opportunities

While the majority of Floor Managers in commercial television are white males, women are occupying the position in growing numbers, according to industry estimates. Members of minorities are also increasingly being hired for the position in commercial television.

In public television, 23 percent of the technicians, including Floor Managers in 1994, were women, and 19 percent were minority group members, according to the Corporation for Public Broadcasting (CPB).

Unions/Associations

The majority of Floor Managers in commercial and public TV are considered members of the production department and thus are not represented by a union. At some major market stations, they are members of and are represented by the National Association of Broadcast Employees and Technicians AFL-CIO (NABET) or the International Brotherhood of Electrical Workers (IBEW).

PRODUCTION ASSISTANT

CAREER PROFILE

Duties: Assisting in the production of studio and remote television programs

Alternate Title(s): Staging Assistant; Floor Assistant; Floor Person

Salary Range: $15,000 to $30,000+

Employment Prospects: Good

Advancement Prospects: Good

Prerequisites:

Education—High school diploma; undergraduate degree preferable

Experience—Some theater, photography, or film experience

Special Skills—Resourcefulness; organizational ability; cooperativeness; initiative; word processing skills

CAREER LADDER

```
┌─────────────────────────────────────┐
│   Camera Operator; Floor Manager;    │
│  Associate Producer; Assistant Director │
└─────────────────────────────────────┘

┌─────────────────────────────────────┐
│        Production Assistant          │
└─────────────────────────────────────┘

┌─────────────────────────────────────┐
│   High School/College; Production    │
│              Secretary               │
└─────────────────────────────────────┘
```

Position Description

The Production Assistant aids in the creation of a local, network, or independent television production in a variety of ways to help achieve a smooth, polished, and professional program. The individual holding this position helps the Floor Manager, Unit Manager, Producer, or Director to schedule, coordinate, and set up a TV production. As an apprentice, the Production Assistant has the opportunity to gain experience in a wide assortment of TV programming, including news, documentaries, talk shows, and entertainment specials. The Production Assistant is usually assigned to a particular program project by the Production Manager and works with that project until its completion.

The major responsibility of this position is to assist the production staff in nonengineering matters by providing effective and timely support in all phases of a production. Production Assistants often act as the principal message and communications liaison between various staff members, and, as such, they work with the Camera Operators, Assistant Director, Associate Producer, Director or Producer, and Floor Manager. During the preparation of a program, they often report to the Producer or Director. During actual production, however, they report to the Assistant Director, Floor Manager, or Unit Manager.

Although Production Assistants usually work on assignment in the studio or on remote on a specific program, some also assist in the planning, scheduling, coordination, and daily operation of the production department or unit.

The role of Production Assistant is one of continuing importance to the orderly flow of a production. It is a jack-of-all-trades job in which the individual may do research or copywriting, assist in casting or scheduling guests, and work on sets, costumes, and makeup. Duties also include helping in the control room or studio by placing monitors on easels, and prompting devices, holding cue cards and slate cards, and performing other production duties. The Production Assistant is a vital part of the production team.

Additionally, the Production Assistant

- prepares and distributes daily shooting schedules and notifies the crew of all script changes and production arrangements;
- records all production shot sheets, detailing the timing of various program segments;
- assists in the setting up, lighting, and eventual strike (dismantling) of the set;
- assists in the research, development, coordination and finalization of program scripts;
- Collects files and records upon completion of a production, including visual materials, photos, personnel worksheets, on-air talent releases, and other related material; and

- Occasionally operates the character generator keyboard during a production.

Salaries

Wages for Production Assistants are rather low. The average payment for Floor Persons on commercial TV in 1997 was $19,795, according to the National Association of Broadcasters (NAB).

In public TV, 1998 earnings ranged from $15,000 to $32,000 for a full-time Production Assistant, according to industry estimates.

Employment Prospects

Chances of getting this job are good. It is generally considered an entry-level position in most commercial and public TV stations. Production Secretaries, however, are often promoted from within the station to Production Assistant. Opportunities for employment often depend on being in the right place at the right time.

Most stations employ from 3 to 12 Production Assistants, depending on the size of the market and on the amount of production work. In addition to the opportunities at TV stations, all independent TV production companies employ Production Assistants. Some cable TV systems, as well as some government, health, corporate and educational media centers that produce programs, offer possibilities for employment.

Advancement Prospects

The opportunity for advancement from the position of Production Assistant to other production and programming positions is good. A bright and enthusiastic person may be promoted to Camera Operator (in nonunion shops) or to Floor Manager, Associate Producer, or Assistant Director. The experience gained in all aspects of television production, coupled with resourcefulness, often leads to promotion.

Competition for more responsible production positions is heavy, and while there is considerable turnover among Production Assistants, only the more experienced and reliable

are promoted. Some move to smaller stations or production units in order to gain more responsible production positions.

Education

A high school diploma is usually a minimum requirement. Many large market public and commercial stations prefer to hire the recent college graduate who has majored in mass communications, radio-TV, or theater.

Experience/Skills

Since Production Assistant is an entry-level position, most employers do not require extensive experience in television production. Some background in theater staging and lighting, photography, or film work is helpful.

A Production Assistant must be bright, resourceful organized, and able to plan and think intuitively and effectively. The individual must also be able to work under pressure with a variety of people and get a job done cooperatively and creatively. Some typing ability is also usually required, and knowledge of word processing equipment is helpful. Above all, a Production Assistant must be eager and willing to operate in a teamwork atmosphere.

Minority/Women's Opportunities

Opportunities for women and members of minorities as Production Assistants are excellent. In commercial television, more than 50 percent of the Production Assistants in 1998 were women, according to industry estimates. While those in union commercial and public stations are often white males, minority group members are occupying the position in increasing numbers.

Unions/Associations

The majority of Production Assistants are considered part of the production department at many stations and are not represented by unions. In a few major market commercial and public TV stations, however, they are represented by the National Association of Broadcast Employees and Technicians AFL-CIO (NABET).

PRODUCTION SECRETARY

CAREER PROFILE

Duties: Providing clerical support for a television production department or unit

Alternate Title(s): None

Salary Range: $16,000 to $41,000

Employment Prospects: Good

Advancement Prospects: Good

Prerequisites:

Education—High school diploma; minimum of one year of business school preferable

Experience—Minimum of one year as a secretary in TV or an ad agency

Special Skills—Word processing ability; shorthand or speed writing; familiarity with office equipment; organizational ability; computer literacy

CAREER LADDER

```
┌─────────────────────────────────┐
│      Production Assistant        │
└─────────────────────────────────┘

┌─────────────────────────────────┐
│      Production Secretary        │
└─────────────────────────────────┘

┌─────────────────────────────────┐
│   Receptionist/Office Clerk;     │
│   High School/Business School    │
└─────────────────────────────────┘
```

Position Description

A Production Secretary is an integral part of the production team and is responsible for the office support of the production department at a television station or independent production company. This person coordinates much of the work within the department and provides general secretarial assistance, including word processing, filing, transcribing, taking dictation, and general office work. Production Secretaries schedule appointments, give information to callers, fill out forms, route mail, and answer telephones. In addition, they compile and maintain reports and prepare correspondence. Production Secretaries also gather and refine production schedules and data, using word processing equipment.

As a rule, the Production Secretary reports directly to the Production Manager and, in small and middle market stations, may also provide general clerical support for Producers, Directors, and other production people. The vast majority of Production Secretaries work for more than one individual. While the position requires standard secretarial skills, the Production Secretary must also be knowledgeable about current practices, terms, and nomenclature used in TV and must be resourceful and organized in dealing with staff, talent, guests, and others involved in a production.

The Production Secretary often works independently in researching and developing the basic material and information needed for the timely development of a program script, which includes preparing and organizing the script from draft through final form, then duplicating, collating and distributing it to the production staff.

Sometimes the Production Secretary is assigned on a temporary basis to perform the duties of a Production Assistant.

Additionally, the Production Secretary

- assists in obtaining clearances for remote locations;
- schedules talent and guests;
- monitors the production schedule;
- maintains the production files containing scripts, program information data, contracts, business records, talent sheets, and other records; and
- occasionally operates the character generator during production.

Salaries

Production Secretaries are considered support personnel and, as such, are relatively low paid in comparison with other television positions. In commercial TV, salaries for all secretaries averaged about $22,000 in 1997, according to observers.

Employment Prospects

The opportunities for employment are generally good. There will be a need for all types of secretaries in the next 10 years, according to the Bureau of Labor Statistics (BLS). Secretarial jobs in all types of firms will be plentiful through 2006, according to the BLS; projected growth will vary by specialty and industry. Although the position is not usually considered an entry-level job, smaller market stations sometimes employ beginners and provide on-the-job training. At some large market commercial or public stations, various program units within the production department employ Production Secretaries. In addition, all independent production companies and most government, health, and education television operations that are engaged in production have them on staff (see Part II). Opportunities are also available in corporate media centers, at advertising agencies, and at low-power TV (LPTV) stations.

Advancement Prospects

The prospects for advancement for bright, alert people are good. The responsibilities of the position require that the individual learn all aspects of television production, and many Production Secretaries become Production Assistants or move to other, more responsible positions within the production department. Some Production Secretaries are promoted to Assistant Director or Associate Producer, usually within the station or unit, while others use their experience to obtain more responsible positions at other production organizations and at advertising agencies.

Some Secretaries become "professional" and advance their careers within a television or media company by becoming Executive Secretaries to administrative executives. A few advance their secretarial careers by passing a series of exams from Professional Secretaries International and becoming Certified Professional Secretaries (CPS).

Education

The minimum educational requirement for the position of Production Secretary is a high school diploma. Most employers prefer at least one year of training in a business school or an associate's degree. Major market commercial and public TV stations usually employ individuals who have had some education in mass communications or who have an under-graduate degree in theater or radio-TV. Some training in word processing is helpful.

Experience/Skills

Employers in some middle and major market commercial stations require at least one year of experience as a Receptionist/Office Clerk in a television station, advertising agency, or media center. In many such stations, an undergraduate degree in radio-TV is acceptable in lieu of experience.

In smaller market commercial and public television stations or independent production companies, the position is sometimes considered an entry-level job, and little experience is required. The individual must possess good secretarial skills, however.

A knowledge of standard office equipment, including photocopy, transcribing, postal meter, and teletype machines is necessary. A Production Secretary must also be able to type at least 50 words per minute and have some experience in shorthand or speed writing. In today's office environment, a knowledge of word processing software is necessary. Some employers provide on-the-job training with such resources. Production Secretaries must also be proficient in spelling, punctuation, and grammar. A good command of the English language is necessary, as well as an aptitude for numbers. The ability to organize work and develop priorities among often conflicting assignments in the hectic television production environment is helpful.

Minority/Women's Opportunities

The vast majority of Production Secretaries in commercial TV in 1997 were female, according to industry estimates. Minority women represent a significant percentage. In public TV, 80 percent of all secretaries were females in 1994, and 33 percent were members of minorities, according to the Corporation for Public Broadcasting (CPB).

Unions/Associations

There are no unions or professional organizations that represent Production Secretaries.

LIGHTING DIRECTOR

Duties: Lighting studio and remote television productions

Alternate Title(s): Staging/Lighting Supervisor; Lighting Direction Engineer

Salary Range: $20,000 to $40,000+

Employment Prospects: Fair

Advancement Prospects: Fair

Prerequisites:

Education—High school diploma; Second-Class FCC license helpful

Experience—Two years as a Camera Operator or Engineering Technician

Special Skills—Technical aptitude; creativity; physical strength; cooperativeness

```
┌─────────────────────────────────────────┐
│  Floor Manager; Technical Director;      │
│  Lighting Director (Large Station,       │
│  Independent Production Company, or      │
│  Full-Service Production Facility)       │
└─────────────────────────────────────────┘

┌─────────────────────────────────────────┐
│           Lighting Director              │
└─────────────────────────────────────────┘

┌─────────────────────────────────────────┐
│      Camera Operator; Engineering        │
│              Technician                   │
└─────────────────────────────────────────┘
```

Position Description

The Lighting Director designs and executes the lighting for television productions, either in the studio or on remote locations. Since the transmission of a TV picture is dependent on the illumination of a subject, the job is a vital one. The person fulfilling these duties must balance the technical limitations of TV with creativity to achieve sparkle and brilliance in lighting effects and complement the overall purpose and design of a production. Lighting Directors are employed at public and commercial TV stations. They also work in full-service production facilities, where they are often among the key people.

Incorporating theatrical lighting techniques to sharpen, balance, and add dimension, the Lighting Director uses spotlights, floodlights, filters, a light meter, and other equipment and accessories to provide the lighting. The Lighting Director must ensure that the tonal qualities and color needs of faces, furniture, backdrops, props, and other set elements work together to achieve the desired lighting effects.

To obtain the correct results, the Lighting Director works with a floor plan, created by the Scenic Designer and Director, and a copy of the script, which must be annotated to indicate lighting needs. The Lighting Director then designs and lays out a lighting plot for the program. This is a complex and detailed version of the floor plan showing how and where each lighting instrument will be placed. In some stations and full-service production facility companies, the lighting design is accomplished with the aid of computer technology.

Usually supervising a part-time or on-assignment crews of two to five people to install and position lighting instruments, the Lighting Director makes certain that the lighting is properly focused and balanced and sets up a cue sheet of instructions. Adjustments are made in rehearsal and, as needed, during the actual production.

Virtually all TV stations employ individuals whose primary responsibility is lighting, but at some smaller stations they often have additional responsibilities in staging, engineering, camera work, or other production activities. In some cases, the duties of the Lighting Director are handled by members of the production crew.

Some stations consider the Lighting Director to be part of the engineering staff, while others consider the position a production job. Depending on the station, a Lighting Director reports either to an Engineering Supervisor or to a Production Manager, but during the actual production the Lighting Director reports to the Director of the program.

Additionally, the Lighting Director

- cues the lighting control board operator during production to alter lighting as necessary;
- oversees the striking (dismantling) of lighting equipment at the completion of a program;

- maintains the inventory of lights and accessories and purchases replacement parts and supplies; and
- performs routine maintenance on lights, electrical equipment, and accessories.

Salaries

At network-affiliated TV stations in 1997, the salaries for Lighting Directors ranged from $18,000 to $35,000, depending on whether additional responsibilities were required and if the position was considered part of the engineering or the production staff. In union stations, the pay scale was much higher. Lighting Directors' salaries for network shows are usually higher.

In public TV, the duties of the Lighting Director are often combined with others into a position called Staging/Lighting Supervisor. Salaries for such employees are generally lower than those of their commercial counterparts.

Employment Prospects

This position is seldom an entry-level job at a station or other production-related organization. Openings at small public and commercial TV stations, where the Lighting Director might have additional production duties, occur infrequently. Even at small independent production firms or cable TV systems where programs are produced, the opportunities are limited since these duties are often handled by members of the production crew.

The possibilities for getting a job as a Lighting Director are only fair and are largely confined to middle and major market stations or large production organizations where a full-time person is employed in this position. Many larger stations employ more than one Lighting Director for various units or production teams. Top Lighting Directors are also employed at the full-service production facility companies.

Advancement Prospects

In spite of the somewhat ambiguous nature of the position at smaller stations, the opportunities for advancement are generally fair to good. An alert Lighting Director has the opportunity for promotion to Floor Manager in the production department or to Technical Director or other middle-management positions in the engineering department. Good Lighting Directors often move to larger market stations or to larger independent film or TV production organizations in order to advance their careers in this specific job. The best find employment at the networks or at full-service production facilities (see Part II).

Education

A high school diploma is a minimum prerequisite. The individual should have a basic knowledge of the electronic and technical aspects of television transmission and operation.

Experience/Skills

Two years of previous experience as a Camera Operator or Engineering Technician are usually required. The experience gained in actual TV production of in-studio and remote programs is invaluable in obtaining the position. A background in theater staging and lighting is very helpful, and many supervisors seek such experience when hiring a Lighting Director.

The Lighting Director must be able to combine a thorough knowledge of the technical requirements of television with a creative and esthetic sense and be detail-oriented and well organized. Other requirements are the physical strength to handle lighting equipment and the ability to work cooperatively with production and engineering personnel in pressure situations.

Minority/Women's Opportunities

The vast majority of Lighting Directors in commercial and public broadcasting are men. The physical demands of the job have been a factor in keeping the representation of women low; however, their numbers are increasing. The percentage of minority males in the position is increasing, according to industry estimates.

Unions/Associations

In some major market commercial stations, Lighting Directors are part of the engineering department and are represented by the National Association of Broadcast Employees and Technicians AFL-CIO (NABET) or by the International Brotherhood of Electrical Workers (IBEW). Some Lighting Technicians working on network productions are represented by the International Alliance of Theatrical Stage Employees (IATSE). In many smaller commercial and public television stations where the individual reports to the production department, such employees are not represented by a union.

ART DIRECTOR

CAREER PROFILE

Duties: Conceiving and shaping the visual elements of a TV production and the visual style of a TV station or media center

Alternate Title(s): Broadcast Designer; Graphic Arts Supervisor; Senior Artist; Graphic Arts Manager

Salary Range: $26,000 to $60,000+

Employment Prospects: Fair

Advancement Prospects: Fair

Prerequisites:

Education—Minimum of an undergraduate degree in commercial art, fine art, or design.

Experience—Minimum of five years as a Graphic Artist in TV production

Special Skills—Creativity; sense of esthetics; administrative abilities; technical aptitude

CAREER LADDER

```
┌─────────────────────────────────┐
│   Art Director (Ad Agency);      │
│   Owner (Art/Design Company)     │
└─────────────────────────────────┘

┌─────────────────────────────────┐
│          Art Director            │
└─────────────────────────────────┘

┌─────────────────────────────────┐
│         Graphic Artist           │
└─────────────────────────────────┘
```

Position Description

The Art Director is responsible for the design of all television programs produced and broadcast by a station. While much of the work is directly related to TV production, the Art Director is also usually in charge of the visual representation of a station in promotional material. This includes advertising rate cards and displays, promotion/publicity brochures, booklets, pamphlets, stationery that project the station's corporate image, and websites.

The Art Director conceives ways of visually portraying television production ideas and supervises the execution of all design, layout, and art materials for the station. As an administrator, the Art Director supervises a staff of two to eight full- and part-time employees who produce all art and visual materials in various formats. In association with other Graphic Artists and the station's production, promotion, and technical staffs, the Art Director combines talent and technical knowledge to complete creative projects on time and within budget.

The Art Director is the final authority on the appropriateness of all materials produced by the art department, and must create, develop, and maintain the station's overall visual representation in all types of internal and external presentations.

Additionally, the Art Director

- conceives and supervises the execution of all visual elements of photography, scenic design, and animation;
- develops story boards, layouts, and rough sketches for television, print, and film productions;
- consults with Producers, Directors, and other production and technical personnel on graphic design for local productions;
- supervises the design and construction of new sets and the modification of existing scenery;
- develops and administers the art department budget and allocates funds for specific projects;
- orders, installs, operates, and maintains all art equipment and supplies; and
- assists in determining purchases of electronic video art equipment.

Salaries

Art Directors are not very well compensated in the field of television. Salaries in commercial TV averaged $40,830 in 1997, according to the National Association of Broadcasters (NAB).

In public television, Art Directors tended to be paid somewhat lower on average, according to the Corporation for Public Broadcasting (CPB).

The annual salary for the comparable position of Art Director in an advertising agency averaged $50,100 in 1997, according to *Advertising Age.*

Employment Prospects

Overall, the chances for employment are fair. The position of Art Director at a television station requires considerable knowledge and experience in all phases of commercial art, particularly in TV production. With 1,550 operating television stations, the opportunities are somewhat limited. Some very small market stations use only freelance Graphic Artists as the occasion demands. Cable television systems and multichannel multipoint distribution service (MMDS) and low-power TV (LPTV) stations occasionally employ Art Directors for specific projects, but few are large enough to require a full-time person. There are also part-time, project-by-project jobs available at some of the full-service production and postproduction facilities.

Advancement Prospects

The possibilities for advancement are fair in television. An Art Director is generally confined to the creation and execution of various formats of the visual arts. While the position requires a knowledge of production, the opportunity for promotion within a station to Production Manager or other supervisory job (Producer or Director) is seldom available. Some Art Directors in smaller television stations move to similar positions in larger markets and thus gain greater responsibility and a larger salary. Some use their experience to form their own commercial art/design firms or join independent television production agencies that create artwork for specific clients.

Education

Most Art Directors have undergraduate degrees in commercial art, fine art, or design. While a degree is less important than taste, ability, and visual style, the Art Director's background usually includes some college level courses in the liberal arts.

In lieu of such education, a year or two of training at a commercial art school is usually a requisite for obtaining the position of Graphic Artist and for eventual promotion to Art Director. Courses and education in all the visual art media and in computer graphics are helpful.

Experience/Skills

When hiring an Art Director, most employees require at least five years of experience in television production artwork. In addition, wide experience in various art forms (layout, sculpture, scenic design, cartooning, drawing, etc.) is usually required.

Art Directors should demonstrate a clean style that is visually appealing and that conforms to the image desired by the station. Sophisticated taste in the visual arts, strong technical skills, and an ability to organize and manage a diverse group of creative subordinates are required. In addition, an Art Director must be able to work in cooperation with other production and technical people, on- air talent, and promotion and public relations personnel.

In the 1990s employers began to seek Art Directors with experience in computer and digital video effects (DVE) devices. Experience with computer graphics is often a requirement in obtaining the position.

Minority/Women's Opportunities

In commercial television in 1996, 35 percent of officials and managers, a category that includes Art Directors, were women, and 14 percent were minorities. In public television, 41 percent of officials and managers were women in 1994, while 11 percent were minorities. Industry observers note that minorities holding this position are few but that opportunities for recruitment are better than ever.

Unions/Associations

Some Art Directors are members of the National Association of Broadcast Employees and Technicians AFL-CIO (NABET). A few at major market stations are represented by United Scenic Artists for bargaining purposes. In Hollywood, some are represented by the International Alliance of Theatrical Stage Employees (IATSE). In both commercial and public TV, however, most are not represented by a union. Many commercial television Art Directors are members of the Broadcast Designers Association International in order to share mutual professional concerns.

GRAPHIC ARTIST

CAREER PROFILE

Duties: Design and creation of television art and related visual materials

Alternate Title(s): Television Artist; Staff Artist's Illustrator

Salary Range: $18,000 to $30,000+

Employment Prospects: Good

Advancement Prospects: Fair

Prerequisites:

Education—Minimum of an associate's degree in commercial art; undergraduate art degree preferable

Experience—Minimum of one year as a commercial artist

Special Skills—Creativity; versatility; talent for illustration

CAREER LADDER

```
+-------------------------------+
|         Art Director          |
+-------------------------------+

+-------------------------------+
|        Graphic Artist         |
+-------------------------------+

+-------------------------------+
|   School; Commercial Artist   |
+-------------------------------+
```

Position Description

The Graphic Artist in a commercial or public television station creates, designs, and executes a variety of visual art forms to enhance, and often serve as the focal point of, a television production. This includes the creation of charts, graphs, title cards, maps, and three-dimensional objects, as well as set design and construction.

Graphic Artists also work at postproduction facilities and in health, education, government, and private industry positions. The Graphic Artist may be responsible for the design, layout, and execution of art for newspaper advertising, publicity brochures, program guides, billboards, web sites, and other advertising and promotional displays. In these areas, the Graphic Artists may be involved with graphic design software, photography, photo laboratory developing, color separations, typography, and other print-oriented art requirements.

Graphic Artists are primarily illustrators of ideas and concepts. They must translate the basic thoughts and perceptions of a variety of people into finished art that improves the visual image of a program or print campaign and clearly communicates ideas to the viewer or reader. Graphic Artists work in a variety of styles, including cartooning, realistic renderings, decorative background painting, and sculpting. They are versatile executors of a variety of art techniques within the framework of the television medium.

Increasingly, the Graphic Artist is called upon to work with computer graphics equipment, in association with the Videotape Engineer/Editor. This computer-controlled gear creates pictures and effects such as shading or airbrushing. Animation, graphs, and charts are often developed electronically with today's sophisticated software. Nearly all artists use computer graphics to produce commercial art today.

At TV stations, Graphic Artists work with in-house slide stands and in-house printing and film animation equipment.

Additionally, the Graphic Artist

- performs the layout of printed materials;
- operates various types of art equipment, including airbrushes, and dry mount machines;
- designs and creates backdrops, set pieces, and props for television production; and
- operates electronic paint and animation editing systems and digital video effects (DVE) devices.

Salaries

Salaries for Graphic Artists in Commercial television stations averaged $28,358 in 1997, according to the National Association of Broadcasters (NAB).

In public television, 1998 salaries ranged from $18,000 at small market school or university stations to more than $30,000 at the larger metropolitan stations. In general salaries for Graphic Artists are lower in public TV, regardless of location.

The median salary for Graphic Artists in 1996 in general was $27,100, according to the Bureau of Labor Statistics.

Employment Prospects

The position of Graphic Artist is often an entry-level job in the art department of a television station. The chances for employment are quite good. Most small market stations employ at least two Graphic Artists and major market stations may have more than five on staff. According to a survey by the NAB, the average commercial station employed two in 1997. Part-time positions are also available. Graphic Artist positions are also available at cable TV systems and at the commercial networks, particularly in electronic graphics work. Some opportunities exist in instructional and closed circuit television (ITV and CCTV). In addition, TV operations in business, health, and government settings usually have at least one Graphic Artist. Postproduction facilities employ people with a graphics background as videotape editors.

Advancement Prospects

The opportunities for advancement for creative and diligent Graphic Artists at a commercial or public TV station are only fair. The relative scarcity of Art Director positions and the competition tend to limit advancement. In addition, the skills and talents required by an artist are not usually transferable to other production or technical positions within the station.

Promotion to positions in other TV-related industries, however, is often available for an experienced Graphic Artist. Many utilize the experience gained in television art, as well as in print media, to excellent advantage in obtaining positions in advertising agencies, public relations firms, or postproduction houses. Still other Graphic Artists advance their careers by moving to larger stations at higher salaries or by becoming Art Directors at smaller market operations. Advancement into project management is also a possibility.

Education

Most stations require a minimum of a high school diploma and at least an associate's degree in commercial art when employing a Graphic Artist. Some employers require an undergraduate degree in commercial or fine art, as well as some evidence of private study in specific art techniques and styles.

Experience/Skills

An extensive background in television art is not essential, although some middle or major market stations do require at least a year of experience.

Facility in a variety of commercial art techniques and styles, as well as considerable versatility in print art, is often a prerequisite to obtaining the position. The Graphic Artist should display a portfolio containing a variety of different projects. A clean, clear style is important. Experience with basic art equipment and an ability to work rapidly and meet deadlines are advantages. Experience with computer-generated graphic systems is a must. Good eye-to-hand coordination is a must. Some film animation skills are helpful in working with video animation.

Minority/Women's Opportunities

This is one of the areas in television in which opportunities for women are excellent. In 1997, more than 50 percent of the Graphic Artists in commercial and public TV were female, according to industry estimates. Minorities have made some gains but are still quite underrepresented, industry observers note.

Unions/Associations

Some Graphic Artists belong to and are represented by the National Association of Broadcast Employees and Technicians AFL-CIO (NABET). In most instances, however, Graphic Artists in commercial and public television are not members of a union. Many people in public and commercial TV belong to the Broadcast Designers Association International to share mutual concern and to improve their skills.

CINEMATOGRAPHER/VIDEOGRAPHER

CAREER PROFILE

Duties: Shooting and editing of film, tape, and digital formats at a TV station or communications center

Alternate Title(s): Videographer/Film Cameraman; News Photographer; Film Camera Operator; Cinevideographer

Salary Range: $16,000 to $50,000+

Employment Prospects: Fair

Advancement Prospects: Fair

Prerequisites:

Education—Undergraduate degree in television or media arts

Experience—Minimum of one year of shooting and editing

Special Skills—Creativity; technical skill; originality; resourcefulness

CAREER LADDER

```
┌──────────────────────────────────────┐
│  Producer (Film/Tape Production);     │
│  Film/Tape Director                   │
└──────────────────────────────────────┘

┌──────────────────────────────────────┐
│  Cinematographer/Videographer         │
└──────────────────────────────────────┘

┌──────────────────────────────────────┐
│  Assistant Cameraperson (Film         │
│  Production); Production Assistant;    │
│  Film Editor                          │
└──────────────────────────────────────┘
```

Position Description

A Cinematographer/Videographer is responsible for shooting and editing film/tape inserts to be used as elements of the news or special events programs broadcast on television. This person may also shoot commercials for a station or ad agency's clients. A Cinematographer/Videographer works on major productions, including documentaries, sports, movies, or other special programming created for TV on a project-by-project basis for an independent production company (see Part II).

During the past 10 years, most stations have begun to add digital cameras and editing equipment to their portable electronic news gathering (ENG) equipment for most of their short, on-location productions. This equipment is used for the majority of news coverage and interviews shot outside a studio. In most stations Cinematographers/Videographers have switched from shooting film and routinely use ENG systems. (Camera Operators also operate ENG equipment on news assignments.) Cinematographers/Videographers are often still responsible for a station's black and white and color still photography.

Most commercial and public television stations employ Cinematographers/Videographers for news coverage, commercial production, and special programs. At some commercial stations, they are part of special units that provide production services for advertising clients. Often they are members of the production or programming departments. Still other Cinematographers/Videographers are assigned permanently to a station's news department.

The Cinematographer/Videographer's overall responsibility is to produce quality images for use in various types of television productions and to interpret the needs of the Director, Producer, or Reporter in developing cinematic approaches to a script or news story. The Cinematographer/Videographer chooses the cameras, lenses, accessories, and film or tape stock or digital resources (diskettes) appropriate for each shooting assignment.

Additionally, the Cinematographer/Videographer

- selects angles and shot composition to achieve desired effects;
- directs the selection and placement of lights;
- performs minor repairs on film and tape equipment; and
- maintains an inventory of raw film stock, videotape and other visual news gathering supplies.

Salaries

Income for Cinematographers/Videographers is relatively low. At commercial stations the average payment for news photographers was $25,958 a year in 1997, according to the National Association of Broadcasters (NAB).

In public television, 1997 salaries ranged from $16,000 for beginners at small stations to more than $40,000 for experienced individuals at major market community stations, according to the Corporation for Public Broadcasting (CPB).

Salaries for Videographers at corporate television centers in 1997 ranged from $20,000 to $50,000, according to industry estimates. Cinematographers/Videographers (First Cameramen) working on commercials and network TV programs on an annual basis are paid more, since they are often members of a union.

Employment Prospects

Overall opportunities for employment are only fair. An assistant cameraperson in commercial film production or a talented and knowledgeable Production Assistant can sometimes become a Cinematographer/Videographer. The use of film, however, is a thing of the past at commercial stations. Fortunately, the techniques and skills required of a Cinematographer/Videographer are easily transferable to ENG technology. Some stations even use the term "cinevideographer" for an individual who uses the techniques of film production in operating portable video camera equipment.

Opportunities are good at major market stations that have a heavy news schedule. Often, five to eight news crews work for a station, and each crew has at least one Cinevideographer/Videographer. The average commercial station employed nine news photographers in 1997, according to NAB.

Opportunities for Cinematographer/Videographers are also available at public television stations, where many documentaries are still shot on film. In addition, many independent production firms and advertising agencies prefer film and continue to use it to shoot commercials. There are some additional opportunities for Cinematographer/Videographers in government, education, and health video settings and corporate media centers.

Advancement Prospects

The opportunities for Cinematographer/Videographers to advance in production are fair. Some seek to create longer-form feature, artistic, or documentary films for theatrical presentation and use their TV experience as Producers at independent production firms. In television stations that have large departments, they can be promoted to director in charge of other Cinematographer/Videographers or to the position of Producer specializing in on-location productions.

Education

An undergraduate degree in film or communications with some training in television production techniques is often required. Courses in film production, editing, film history, and film as an art form are helpful. Courses in television production using ENG equipment are extremely useful.

Experience/Skills

Most employers require at least one year of experience in shooting and editing motion picture film and tape. Familiarity with many types of cameras and related audio tape recorders is helpful. A background in still camera equipment and techniques, processing, and film chemistry is also useful.

Cinematographer/Videographers are often given considerable independence and latitude in shooting film/tape/diskette for television. Individuals who are imaginative and have a feel for composition and the esthetics of shooting and editing film and tape are good employment prospects. A Cinematographer/Videographer must be original and resourceful in dealing with a variety of different circumstances during film/tape production.

Minority/Women's Opportunities

According to a survey by the Radio-TV News Directors Association (RTNDA) in 1994, some 36 percent of news personnel were women and 48 percent were minorities. While minority representation has grown, the majority of Cinematographer/Videographers in commercial television were white males in 1994. The minority share was twice as great at Fox and independent stations, and media educators note that more women and minorities are entering the ranks of news production teams.

Unions/Associations

Some Cinematographer/Videographers in commercial television are represented by the National Association of Broadcast Employees and Technicians AFL-CIO (NABET) or the International Alliance of Theatrical Stage Employees (IATSE), which act as bargaining agents. Many Cinematographer/Videographers belong to the American Film Institute (AFI), the Association of Independent Video and Filmmakers (AIVF), and other local, state, and national film councils to share ideas and advance their careers.

FILM/TAPE EDITOR

CAREER PROFILE

Duties: Editing/cutting film, tape and digital content at a television station, production/facilities company, or non-profit media center

Alternate Title(s):   Video Film Editor

Salary Range: $20,000 to $65,000+

Employment Prospects: Fair

Advancement Prospects: Good

Prerequisites:

Education—High school diploma; some film training; college degree preferred

Experience—At least one year of experience in film editing

Special Skills—Dexterity; creativity; ability to work with a variety of people; flexibility; organizational skills

CAREER LADDER

```
┌─────────────────────────────────────┐
│      Director; Cinematographer;      │
│      Film/Tape Editor (Theatrical)   │
└─────────────────────────────────────┘

┌─────────────────────────────────────┐
│           Film/Tape Editor           │
└─────────────────────────────────────┘

┌─────────────────────────────────────┐
│       Assistant Film/Tape Editor     │
└─────────────────────────────────────┘
```

Position Description

The Film/Tape Editor is responsible for the editing, splicing, and cutting of 16mm or 35mm film, videotape, and digital segments to create a visually coherent, effective program. The major responsibility of the position is to assemble, sort, and align a vast amount of footage shot by a Cinematographer into a complete and finished product.

A Film/Tape Editor works at a commercial or public television station and at production/facilities companies. Film/Tape Editors are also employed at corporate television centers and at some of the nonprofit media centers at the health, education, and government organizations described in Part II. Some Film/Tape Editors freelance and work on a project-by-project basis, and a few operate their own editing companies.

Film/Tape Editors are seldom found at multipoint multichannel distribution service (MMDS) stations, or at low-power television (LPTV) stations. A few are employed at the larger cable and satellite systems, and some are employed at advertising agencies.

A Film/Tape Editor works on many types of programs, including entertainment programs, documentaries, and minidramas as well as on promotional spots and news shows. A few work on made-for-TV movies or full-length theatrical motion pictures. Most editing work in television involves much shorter films. Film Editors work on short inserts, commercials, and occasionally on 30- or 60-minutes programs.

Film/Tape Editors usually deal with a project from the pre-production stage through the "work print," "rough cut," "second cutting," and "answer print" stages. They work with and for Cinematographers, Directors, and Producers.

Film/Tape Editors work with edge-numbered film at an editing bench and with adjacent "trim bins" that are used to hold the various sections of film footage. They use film synchronizers (to synchronize the sound and picture tracks), a Moviola machine or "flat bed" editing table, film splicers, splicing tape and cement, leader and academy leader, a film footage/time calculator, and grease pencils. Armed with the script and written logs of the completed scenes, they view the pieces of film that have been shot from various angles (long shot, close-up, etc.) for a particular scene. They examine the options, select and trim the various shots they wish to use, and splice them together in the proper sequence to form a continuous smooth exposition of the scene. The process is then repeated for each individual scene, and the scenes are finally assembled in a continuous running series of scenes and sequences that make up a finished film.

Although the principles, organization, and logistics are similar to editing on videotape, the process of film editing is more mechanical than electronic. Many Film Editors, however, are embracing videotape editing and, in doing so, fulfilling many of the responsibilities of the Videotape Engineer/Editor.

Increasingly, broadcast and production outfits are investing in digital nonlinear editing systems produced by such companies as Avid Technology, Inc., and Media 100, which enable the editor to sit at a computer and perform frame accurate trimming, interactive timeline editing, the linking of scripts into the digital capture and editing process, quick searches and instant integrated compositing, among other tasks. Today's sophisticated editing hardware, software, and networking capabilities allow for segments of film and tape to be digitized, then cut, pasted, and manipulated to create a seamless content flow.

Additionally, a Film/Tape Editor

- assembles "dailies" (film footage from a day's shooting); and
- supervises all contacts with the motion picture laboratory that processes the undeveloped footage.

Salaries

The salaries for Film/Tape Editors at television stations are relatively low. The annual salary for a Film/Tape Editor at a commercial station averaged $24,872 in 1997, according to the National Association of Broadcasters (NAB). Those who were members of a union, however, were paid much more. In public television, the salaries ranged from $20,206 to more than $60,000, according to the Corporation for Public Broadcasting (CPB). The average was $32,878 in that year. Music and effects editors were paid slightly less in that year, and those working on commercials were paid less than those who worked on features and long-form television programs.

Employment Prospects

The employment prospects are only fair. The typical commercial television station employed three Film/Tape Editors in 1997, according to the NAB, and the use of film in both public and commercial television stations has declined in the past 10 years as videotape and digital platforms have replaced the older medium. Some nonprofit media centers, however, continue to do original productions on film, and some opportunities exist at the larger cable systems and corporate television centers. In general, however, there are usually more applicants than there are jobs available for this particular position.

Advancement Prospects

Many Film/Tape Editors seek to become Cinematographers and Producers or Directors of film programs. They are, by nature, filmmakers. Many of the personnel who hold those positions have spent some time "at the bench." Some Film Editors seek to advance their careers by moving into the editing of full-length theatrical features. Some stay in television, however, and advance their careers by moving to larger stations at higher salaries. A few start their own film editing companies. The skills and aesthetics learned in the job are applicable to many other higher-level production jobs in television and film, and the opportunities for those with skill, dedication, and ambition are good.

Education

A high school diploma is required. Most employers prefer some college training in film production and film editing; in fact, most require an undergraduate degree. Courses in film appreciation, film shooting, production techniques, and film processing, as well as film editing, are required.

Experience/Skills

Most employers require at least a year of experience in film editing and many require more than two years of prior work.

The process of editing is both an art and a craft. It requires a logical and organized mind as well as a sense of story-telling and drama. Creativity and a sense of film aesthetics are required in addition to manual dexterity. An ability to concentrate for long hours on a complex task in a closed room is necessary, as are interpersonal skills.

Minority/Women's Opportunities

Women have traditionally held many of the jobs as Film Editors in both commercial and public television. Women held more than 40 percent of the freelance jobs in editing full-length motion pictures in 1997, according to industry observers. They also note that minorities continue to be underrepresented in this field.

Unions/Associations

Some Film Editors belong to the International Alliance of Theatrical Stage Employees (IATSE), while others at commercial stations are members of the National Association of Broadcast Employees and Technicians AFL-CIO (NABET). In public television, some individuals are members of a union, but most are not represented by any group. Some Film Editors belong to the American Film Institute (AFI) and the Association of Independent Video and Filmmakers (AIVF) to share ideas and advance their careers.

OPERATIONS MANAGER

Duties: Scheduling and coordinating all technical and production facilities at a television station

Alternate Title(s):   Operations Supervisor; Director of Operations

Salary Range: $27,000 to $94,000+

Employment Prospects: Fair

Advancement Prospects: Fair

Prerequisites:

Education—Minimum of technical school or college training; college degree preferable

Experience—Minimum of two years in various TV station positions

Special Skills—Organizational ability; logical mind; detail orientation; scheduling talent; cooperativeness; leadership qualities

```
┌─────────────────────────────────┐
│      Production Manager;         │
│    Director of Broadcasting      │
└─────────────────────────────────┘

┌─────────────────────────────────┐
│       Operations Manager         │
└─────────────────────────────────┘

┌─────────────────────────────────┐
│   Floor Manager; Film Manager;   │
│ Unit Manager; Engineering Supervisor │
└─────────────────────────────────┘
```

Position Description

The Operations Manager allocates the facilities and resources at a television station to achieve and maintain a smooth and professional operation and maximize production opportunities. The person in this position schedules all production, engineering, and technical facilities from sign-on to sign-off and coordinates the station's on-air activities. The Operations Manager also arranges for the leasing of telephone lines for the distribution of programs to and from networks and other locations.

The Operations Manager's responsibility is to schedule production studios, control rooms, videotape machines, film projectors, and other equipment and, in some cases, operating staff as well. Periodically coordinating the activities of the traffic/continuity, program, film, production, and engineering departments are additional functions of the position. At some stations, the Operations Manager oversees the activities of the Film/Tape Librarian and periodically supervises some members of the engineering and production staffs on a temporary basis.

In addition, the Operations Manager acquires, processes, and distributes all program information, including the station logs, slides, films, or tapes for station breaks. Other duties are establishing the procedures for the prompt procurement, scheduling, and delivery of commercials for broadcast and the recording of programs or program elements from network and other sources.

The duties of an Operations Manager vary from station to station. In some PTV stations, the job has been incorporated into the position of Director of Broadcasting. In some small settings, the Manager is considered a glorified traffic coordinator whose main functions are the delivery of tapes and films and the setup of slides, films, and commercials for station breaks. In most middle and major market stations with heavy production schedules, however, there is considerable responsibility. At some stations, the Operations Manager reports to the Program Manager or Production Manager. In others, the immediate supervisor is the Assistant Chief Engineer.

Additionally, the Operations Manager

- supervises the station's library of videotapes, films, and records and oversees cataloging procedures; and
- schedules staff announcers.

Salaries

Operations Managers in commercial television earned an average of $53,161 in 1997, according to the National Association of Broadcasters (NAB).

In public television, 1997 salaries ranged from $33,940 at small market stations to more than $126,000 for a few experienced personnel at major market stations with heavy national and local production schedules, according to the Corporation for Public Broadcasting (CPB). The median salary was $55,328 in 1997.

Employment Prospects

The chances of getting a position as an Operations Manager are fair. This is not an entry-level job. In most stations, the position is held by an experienced individual who has a broad knowledge of station operations and a thorough understanding of each department's functions. A talented Floor Manager, Film/Tape Librarian, or Unit Manager already on the station's staff is likely to be promoted to the position should an opening occur.

Most cable television, multichannel multipoint distribution service (MMDS), and other production organizations do not maintain operations that are as complex as those at broadcasting stations. As a result, opportunities for employment as an Operations Manager in those settings are extremely limited.

Operations Managers are usually not employed at the smaller education, health, or government media centers, at corporate TV centers, or at low-power television (LPTV) stations. They are occasionally employed at production facility companies (see Part II), where the position is more involved with scheduling than with operational work.

Advancement Prospects

Possibilities for advancement are fair. Diligent Operations Managers who are efficient and experienced sometimes move to the position of Production Manager. Some obtain similar positions at larger stations with more responsibility and better salaries. Still others advance their careers by moving to smaller stations in more responsible positions, such as Director of Broadcasting. Since each station operates in a slightly different manner, the skills acquired at one station are not automatically transferable. In the majority of instances, Operations Managers are not highly mobile and they seek promotion within their own stations.

Education

All employers require a high school diploma. Some call for technical school training or college courses in radio-TV or mass communications. Most now prefer an undergraduate degree.

Experience/Skills

Most employers require a minimum of two years of experience in the engineering, production, or programming departments within the particular station when promoting an individual to Operations Manager. Many Operations Managers gain experience as Floor Managers, Film/Tape Librarians, or Unit Managers, while others earn valuable experience in the traffic/continuity department. Some serve as Engineering Supervisors and acquire experience in scheduling and supervising operating and technical people.

Employers seek alert and responsible individuals with a thorough understanding of the operation of every department in the station as well as a knowledge of production and engineering equipment. The candidate should be well organized, logical, and able to create and manage a detailed schedule of people and equipment. Most important, the individual must be cooperative and have leadership qualities to deal with a variety of people in day-to-day pressure situations.

Minority/Women's Opportunities

While the majority of Operations Managers are white males, the number of women in this position in commercial TV has increased over the past few years. Minority group member representation has also increased, according to industry sources.

From 1996 to 1997, minority employment among public TV officials and managers, a category that includes Operations Managers, increased by 12.1 percent. Overall, 19 percent of all staff were members of minority groups, according to the CPB.

Unions/Associations

A few Operations Managers are considered part of the engineering department at major market stations and are members of the National Association of Broadcast Employees and Technicians AFL-CIO (NABET) or of the International Brotherhood of Electrical Workers (IBEW). In the majority of stations, however, they are considered members of the programming or production department and are not represented by a union or professional organization.

NEWS DIRECTOR

CAREER PROFILE

Duties: Directing of all activities of a television station's news department

Alternate Title(s):   News and Current Affairs Director

Salary Range: $35,000 to $183,000+

Employment Prospects: Poor

Advancement Prospects: Fair

Prerequisites:

Education—Undergraduate or graduate degree in political science, journalism, or mass communications

Experience—Several years in other television news positions or in print or radio news

Special Skills—Sound news judgment; inquisitive mind; imagination; administrative abilities; objectivity; integrity

CAREER LADDER

```
┌─────────────────────────────────────┐
│  News VP (Large Station or Network); │
│         General Manager              │
└─────────────────────────────────────┘

┌─────────────────────────────────────┐
│          News Director               │
└─────────────────────────────────────┘

┌─────────────────────────────────────┐
│      Assistant News Director         │
└─────────────────────────────────────┘
```

Position Description

The News Director is the senior executive in charge of a television station's news department and serves as the final authority for the choice of all news, interviews, documentaries, and special events programs broadcast by a station. The decisions of the News Director determine what events will be covered, which stories will be broadcast, and how and when they will be presented.

Supervision, coordination, and evaluation of the performances of the news staff are the prime responsibilities of a News Director. The typical TV station had a staff of 30 full-time staff members in 1997, according to the Radio-TV News Directors Association (RTNDA). In some major market stations, however, the news staff includes 75 or more Reporters, Anchorpersons, Sportscasters, Weather Reporters, News Writers, film and video Camera Operators. Cinematographers/Videographers, and a sizable number of other professionals and support personnel. The News Director must, therefore, be able to supervise and communicate with a news team that is very often composed of individuals with strong personalities. The position is often more that of management than of journalism.

When selecting particular stories and news events to be covered, the News Director must rely on strong journalistic instincts, assessing the importance of a story and deciding how best to utilize the available talent and technical resources of the station. The individual must also be capable of making quick decisions about fast-breaking events. At smaller market television stations, the News Director is often involved in actual on-the-air reporting.

Additionally, the News Director

- develops and administers the news department budget;
- monitors the progress of in-depth investigative research and reporting and of special events coverage;
- reviews and approves news film, videotape stories, and edited news copy from all sources;
- resolves production and technical problems with the production and engineering departments; and
- coordinates news department activities with the traffic/continuity and programming departments.

Salaries

News Directors' salaries vary considerably, depending on the size of the station, its geographical location, and the extent of local news coverage. The average base salary was $73,298 in 1997, according to the National Association of Broadcasters (NAB).

The larger the market or the larger the news staff, the higher the salaries. News Directors in the smallest markets ranked number 151 out of 211 and had an average base salary of $45,743 in 1997, according to the NAB. Those in the top 10 markets averaged $137,667 annually.

In public television, the median salary for the related position of News and Current Affairs Director was $42,717 in 1998, according to the Corporation for Public Broadcasting (CPB).

While these salaries are respectable, News Directors are generally paid less than the superstar of local and network news—the Anchorperson. News Directors, however, are often Anchorpersons, particularly at midsize and small stations, and are paid accordingly.

Employment Prospects

Television News Director positions are available at the 1,202 commercial stations, hundreds of cable networks, and the few public stations that broadcast news. The news profession is filled with individuals who are capable and aggressive, and the competition is fierce. Only exceptionally talented people become News Directors, usually with the help of some breaks. Most often, a successful Assistant News Director is promoted to the top position. There is, however, a high turnover rate among News Directors. The average newsperson held the same position only three to four years in the early 1990s, according to the RTNDA.

The demand for higher ratings in a highly charged competitive marketplace and the economic value of news to a station's income create a continuing search for new formats, different air personalities, and new News Directors. Not surprisingly, most News Directors are in their 30s.

Advancement Prospects

Although there is a fairly high turnover rate among News Directors, there are few positions to which they may advance. Some move to print journalism to advance their careers. A few become news vice presidents at the very large TV stations or the networks, and, in some recent cases, News Directors have been promoted to the top general management position at stations and networks.

To many individuals, the position of News Director is the climax of a successful career. Because of the relatively few opportunities currently available, advancement from this position is presently considered only fair. However, with the growing popularity of and increase in television news, and with the expansion of cable news, opportunities for News Directors are actually better than 10 years ago.

Education

An undergraduate degree is essential in attaining the position of News Director, and a graduate degree is extremely helpful. Most News Directors have an undergraduate degree,

according to the RTNDA. The major areas of study should be in political science, journalism, or mass communications. A solid liberal arts background and courses in law, economics, and sociology are helpful.

Experience/Skills

Several years of hard work, imagination, and initiative in lower-level news department positions are essential for promotion to News Director. Previous employment and experience in radio news or in print journalism or as a Reporter for a wire service is also good training.

Experience, energy, an inquisitive mind, and sound journalistic judgment are expected of a News Director, as are good communication skills, objectivity, and a willingness to assume responsibilities. Also necessary are a thorough knowledge of Federal Communications Commission (FCC) regulations involving fairness and equal time; an understanding of libel, slander, and copyright law; and familiarity with the intricacies of the Freedom of Information Act.

Minority/Women's Opportunities

Female News Directors, almost unheard of 25 years ago, constituted nearly 25 percent of all News Directors in 1996, according to researcher Vernon Stone. This showed an increase from 17 percent, as reported in a comprehensive 1992 survey Stone conducted for the RTNDF. So the glass ceiling is being cracked; however, the "white ceiling" remains: only 8 percent of News Directors in 1997 were minorities—with negligible representation from Asian Americans and Native Americans, according to the annual RTNDF/Ball State University Survey. Minority television News Directors were more than eight times as likely to work at an independent station as at a network affiliate, which generally pays more.

In public television in 1994, 11 percent of officials and managers, which include News Directors, were minorities, while 41 percent were women. Organizations such as the Black Broadcasters Alliance are charged with advocating increased representation of minorities throughout the mass media, particularly in decision-making positions.

Unions/Associations

As members of management, News Directors are not represented by a union for bargaining purposes.

RTNDA is the professional membership association for News Directors and other professionals in the field. The association sets standards for its members, encourages college students who are preparing for broadcast news careers, operates a placement service, and acts to secure and protect the right to report the news.

ASSISTANT NEWS DIRECTOR

CAREER PROFILE

Duties: Making news coverage assignments; supervising newsroom operations

Alternate Title(s): Assignment Editor; Desk Editor; TV Managing Editor

Salary Range: $18,000 to $93,000

Employment Prospects: Fair

Advancement Prospects: Good

Prerequisites:

Education—Undergraduate degree in journalism, political science, or mass communications

Experience—Several years as a Reporter and in other news functions

Special Skills—Leadership qualities; sound news judgment; communication skills; objectivity; organizational ability

CAREER LADDER

```
┌─────────────────────────────┐
│       News Director         │
└─────────────────────────────┘

┌─────────────────────────────┐
│   Assistant News Director   │
└─────────────────────────────┘

┌─────────────────────────────┐
│         Reporter            │
└─────────────────────────────┘
```

Position Description

Most commercial and some public television stations employ an Assistant News Director. Large cable systems and news gathering organizations also employ Assistant News Directors, as do national cable and broadcast networks. The majority, however, have jobs at local TV stations. The responsibilities vary from station to station, but nearly every Assistant News Director selects and assigns Reporters, News Writers, and commentators to cover specific news and special events.

The Assistant News Director oversees the daily operation of the newsroom, coordinating wire service reports, network feeds, taped or filmed inserts, and stories from individual News Writers and Reporters. This person monitors all of the assignments and activities leading to each newscast and schedules work shifts that keep the newsroom functioning at all times. At some stations, the Assistant News Director also has the responsibility for designating the technical crews for each assignment as well as for selecting a Producer for each newscast segment. Assistant News Directors also work closely with specialty Reporters such as medical or consumer specialists in coordinating their stories and reporting them on the station's newscasts.

The Assistant News Director often has direct supervisory control over the video and film news units and develops procedures to improve and strengthen the technical aspects of news gathering.

Most of the duties that are outside the normal daily routine of the Assistant News Director are carried out in consultation with the News Director. The Assistant usually assumes complete supervision of the news staff when the News Director is away from the station and when fast breaking stories are developing.

The newsroom's computer systems instantly transmit assignments to and from field Reporters and display on a terminal the nearest crew to a "breaking" story. The system also constantly monitors all news gathering logistics, as well as automatically searching and mailing to Reporters on assignment incoming wire stories. As computer systems have replaced typewriters, the Assistant News Director's job has changed so as to improve the speed, flexibility, and efficiency of the TV news operation.

Additionally, the Assistant News Director

- analyzes news reports, determines their significance and the extent of coverage necessary for an individual story;

- evaluates finished stories, film inserts, and taped reports and selects significant stories for use on a newscast; and
- searches for any reportorial mistakes or misinterpretations in order to provide creditable and balanced news reporting for the station.

Salaries

Salaries for Assistant News Directors ranged from $18,000 in the smallest markets to $93,000 at network affiliates in the largest markets in 1997, according to the Radio-Television News Directors Association (RTNDA). The average salary was $49,700. Salaries for the related job of Assignment Editor averaged $27,100 in 1997. Earnings vary depending on geographic location, the ranking of markets, and the relative size of individual stations. Salaries at smaller market stations and in public television are generally lower.

Employment Prospects

Most major market stations employ more than one Assistant News Director, with each responsible for a specific news area. There are, however, many ambitious and able Reporters competing for the job at stations of all sizes, and the opportunities for employment are generally fair. Some experienced Reporters do find such positions at cable television news operations.

Advancement Prospects

With television news enjoying a greater popularity and higher ratings than ever before, with both local stations, commercial networks, and cable networks seeking to expand their news broadcasts, and with technological advances that include all-news cable television channels (as well as on-line services), the opportunities for advancement are good.

The relatively high turnover rate of News Directors increases the possibility of direct promotion. The wire services, government, and information and public relations fields also represent advancement possibilities for people who have had some management experience in broadcast news. Some Assistant News Directors move to magazine or newspaper positions to advance their careers.

Education

An undergraduate degree in journalism, political science, or mass communications is essential in obtaining the job. Equally important is a strong background in liberal arts.

While history courses contribute a sense of perspective and studies in English improve language skills, many employers also look for some educational background in business administration or economics.

Experience/Skills

The Assistant News Director job is not an entry-level one. It is most frequently filled by promotion from within the news department at a television station. Several years of experience as a Reporter and in various other newsroom positions is usually required.

Some Assistant News Directors are recruited from a TV station in a smaller market or from print journalism. In the latter case, some prior experience in broadcast news is usually necessary.

The position of Assistant News Director is demanding and challenging and requires an inquiring mind and qualities of leadership and communications, as well as the awareness and initiative of a good Reporter.

Employers seek well-organized and experienced people who can bring a balanced perspective to television journalism and who are capable of good judgment under pressure. An ability to coordinate many activities on a tight schedule and experience with computers are also required.

Minority/Women's Opportunities

Employment for women and minority group members in reportorial, writing, and on-air news positions has increased during the last decade. In 1997, women represented 37 percent of all those working in local television news, while minorities represented 21 percent, according to the RTNDA. Minorities in television news most often hold the positions of reporter, photographer, or anchor, but like women are beginning to make inroads into news management roles.

Unions/Associations

If their duties involve any news writing or news reporting on the air, Assistant News Directors may be members of the Writers Guild of America (WGA) or the American Federation of Television and Radio Artists (AFTRA). This is particularly true at some large market stations or at the network level. Assignment Editors at CBS are members of the International Alliance of Theatrical and Stage Employees (IATSE).

Membership in the RTNDA is open to Assistant News Directors. Some also belong to the Society of Professional Journalists.

NEWS WRITER

Duties: Writing and editing of news stories and continuity for newscasts

Alternate Title(s):   None

Salary Range: $25,000 to $70,000

Employment Prospects: Good

Advancement Prospects: Good

Prerequisites:

Education—Undergraduate degree in journalism or mass communications with strong liberal arts background

Experience—Occasionally entry level; minimum of one year as a Desk Assistant or related position preferable

Special Skills—Good, concise writing style; talent for research; ability to meet deadlines; computer skills

```
+-----------------------------+
|          Reporter           |
+-----------------------------+

+-----------------------------+
|         News Writer         |
+-----------------------------+

+-----------------------------+
|   College; Desk Assistant   |
+-----------------------------+
```

Position Description

A News Writer writes and edits the news stories, commentaries, continuity (transitional phrases and sentences), introductions, and descriptions that constitute the oral portions of a regularly scheduled newscast.

At most television stations, News Writers do not write advertising or commercial copy, the continuity for station breaks, or other locally produced television programming; they write primarily for newscasts and, occasionally, for public affairs and documentary programs produced by the news department. They do not write all of the news stories; very often, the Reporter who gathers the information and delivers the report on the air writes or assists in writing the story. Often Reporters in the field ad-lib their reports from notes and add voice-over narrative (which they have written) in the editing process at the studio. The Writer, therefore, often concentrates on reportorial copy for on-camera Anchorpersons and in-studio Reporters. A Writer also provides voice-over narrative copy for tape or film inserts and transitional copy between stories and between Reporters' appearances. Sometimes a News Writer may be asked to follow through on a particular story and will act as Producer or Reporter.

The News Writer must be able to use language effectively, conveying a thought in concise phrases and sentences, and must know where to acquire information and how to translate that information into clear, understandable prose. News writing differs from other forms of expression. The Writer must compose brief, descriptive sentences with correct adjectives and adverbs.

Television is a visual medium, and the writing of a story is most often accomplished after the visual material has been selected and edited. The News Writer is then confronted with the job of matching words to video images for the silent portions of the story. At the same time, transitionary "lead-ins" and "lead-outs" must be provided for on-camera sound interviews that are incorporated into the story. Timing is thus extremely important. The News Writer must be adept at intuitively measuring and matching the beat and meter of a phrase with the speech patterns and pace of the Reporter or Anchorperson, who will usually deliver the lines. News writing must be clean, crisp, and descriptive. The language used must be informally formal, to allow the viewer to clearly understand the story and to believe that it properly reflects the facts of the matter.

Since journalism at its best often concerns itself with controversial concepts and ideas, the News Writer must be accurate and thorough and be able to write under pressure and deadlines with skill and a feeling of controlled panic.

Additionally, a News Writer

• utilizes such resources as printed material, electronic storage and retrieval systems, including on-line wire services, and personal and telephone interviews in gathering information;

- verifies the accuracy of questionable facts for news broadcasts; and
- obtains additional relevant details of news events by research and questioning.

Salaries

News Writers are generally paid less than the more visible on-air members of the news team, and women are still at a significant disadvantage in terms of pay equity. According to researcher Vernon S. Stone, experience as indicated by years in news—a measure he has found to have the greatest effect on salaries—is about the same for white and minority newspeople in television, typically eight years. A few years ago, TV newswomen, including News Writers, typically earned 16 percent less than their male counterparts in 1991, although this discrepancy can be attributed to the fact that men, whose median age was 32 versus the women's median age of 26, were older and had more experience. According to a 1998 survey conducted by the Radio-Television News Director's Association, the median salary for News Writers was $24,000.

Employment Prospects

Large television stations employ several News Writers. The best of these people often advance to more prestigious positions, opening up entry-level jobs for the fledgling writer. The networks also employ News Writers, and the trend toward increasing the length and frequency of newscasts and the emergence of all-news cable television networks indicate opportunities in news. Prospects for employment are good for potential News Writers.

Advancement Prospects

In spite of the recent downsizing of news staffs at the major networks, industry predictions about the growth potential of the entire news profession are guardedly optimistic. News Writers can look forward to opportunities in the future, either at the station level, in cable TV news, or with one of the wire services. Today, some ambitious News Writers with a desire to move in front of the cameras are becoming Reporters or Producers at their own stations or in larger markets.

Education

An undergraduate degree in journalism or mass communications is almost a necessity, particularly if the News Writer wishes to grow and advance in the profession. A strong background in English, economics, political science, and the humanities is also recommended.

Experience/Skills

Talented people are occasionally hired as News Writers right out of college. A candidate with at least one year as a Desk Assistant or similar news function, however, stands a better chance for employment. This experience could be acquired outside of television broadcasting, but a knowledge of TV news is helpful.

A crisp journalistic writing style and the ability to translate complex ideas into meaningful copy are the primary skills needed by a News Writer. Research skills and the ability to work under the pressure of regular deadlines are also most important. Experience with a word processor or computer is mandatory.

Minority/Women's Opportunities

Opportunities are good for minorities and women. The percentage of minority news staffers, including News Writers, stood at 18 percent in 1994 and has remained steady through the 1990s, according to Vernon Stone's 1998 University of Missouri School of Journalism study "Minorities and Women in Television News." Women have made significant gains, securing 1,000 of the 2,200 new positions that opened between 1990 and 1994.

Unions/Associations

The National Association of Broadcast Employees and Technicians AFL-CIO (NABET) and the Writers Guild of America (WGA) represent News Writers for bargaining purposes at a few major market stations and at the network level. The Radio-Television News Directors Association (RTNDA) is also open to News Writers and promotes professional growth and offers support.

DESK ASSISTANT

Duties: Providing general assistance to the news department of a television station

Alternate Title(s): News Assistant

Salary Range: $14,000 to $22,000

Employment Prospects: Good

Advancement Prospects: Good

Prerequisites:

Education—High school diploma; some college or business school preferable

Experience—Any news-related activities helpful

Special Skills—Typing ability; writing aptitude; organizational skills; computer skills

```
┌─────────────────────────────────────┐
│  News Writer; Production Assistant   │
└─────────────────────────────────────┘

┌─────────────────────────────────────┐
│           Desk Assistant             │
└─────────────────────────────────────┘

┌─────────────────────────────────────┐
│  High School/Business School/College │
└─────────────────────────────────────┘
```

Position Description

The Desk Assistant is an all-around helper in a television news department. The position is often an entry-level apprenticeship for one who has a specific interest in a broadcast news career.

Desk Assistants perform general office duties in the newsroom. These include answering telephones and taking messages for staff members, opening and distributing mail, delivering newspapers and magazines, ordering office supplies, and filing scripts and correspondence. They are also responsible for collecting wire service copy and distributing it to News Writers and Reporters.

Desk Assistants are usually considered to be general messengers. They may have to pick up food for newsroom employees and deliver packages both inside and outside the station. They can also be called on to deliver film or videotape to and from editors, the library, the videotape room, laboratories, and studios. Often Desk Assistants are involved in logging incoming and outgoing news film and tape and seeing that it is delivered to the proper location for shipping or for use at the station. On occasion, they may go to an airport, train depot, or bus terminal to ship or pick up news film and tape.

Helping with script preparation can also be part of the job. The Desk Assistant may word process updated sections of the script for a newscast, special report, or documentary and deliver them to appropriate staff members. They may also be called on to transcribe the audio portion of a film or videotape

interview into typewritten form so that a Reporter or Producer can select the segments to be included in the final production.

The Desk Assistant sometimes collects routine data such as sports scores and weather information for inclusion in a newscast, does occasional background research for a particular project, and locates library film or videotape footage for use in a report or documentary.

In larger stations and at the networks, the Desk Assistant can be assigned on a regular basis to a specific news show or special unit. In most outlets, however, the job is involved in the entire newsroom operation.

The Desk Assistant position can offer an excellent introduction to the news profession. The capable, aggressive individual will find it a challenge and an invaluable opportunity to become familiar with many aspects of television news.

Additionally, the Desk Assistant

- assists studio and control room personnel during production; and
- accompanies a Reporter to an on-location assignment to rush film or videotape back to the station or to a laboratory.

Salaries

Salaries are comparable to those of many other entry-level positions. In 1997, they ranged from $14,000 to $22,000, according to industry estimates. Seniority, the size of the station and market, and geographical differences all affect the salary scale. As in other news positions, the larger the market or the larger the staff, the higher the salaries.

Employment Prospects

Opportunities are currently good. Although competition is stiff—the average commercial television News Director reported receiving about 60 applications for every entry-level hire in the early 1990s—positions are often available in the small, middle, and large market commercial television stations because there is relatively rapid turnover in the job as individuals are promoted or decide to pursue careers in other fields. In addition, as never before, job seekers can explore opportunities in low-power television stations (LPTV), which numbered 6,850 in 1997, according to the Federal Communications Commission, and at cable and on-line news operations, whose numbers are burgeoning.

Advancement Prospects

Industry sources are cautiously optimistic about the future of news personnel. There will be a need for some qualified professionals at all levels over the coming years in the increasing numbers of cable, LPTV, and on-line services, and a bright, ambitious Desk Assistant should find the opportunities good for promotion to a higher-ranking position. Some with the necessary skills become News Writers. Others move into news production as Production Assistants. Still others find advancement opportunities in cable TV news or at newspapers, wire services, or news magazines.

Education

A high school diploma is required, and a year or two of college or business school education is helpful for obtaining a Desk Assistant position. In order to prepare for a better-paying, higher-level television news position, however, candidates should consider the educational requirements for News Writers, Reporters, Anchorpersons, and News Directors. An undergraduate degree in journalism or political science with a heavy liberal arts emphasis is recommended.

Experience/Skills

Part-time or college extracurricular experience in a news-related field is extremely useful in obtaining a Desk Assistant position. Word processing, writing, and organizational skills are important. Initiative, an inquisitive mind, and an enthusiastic manner are also helpful.

Minority/Women's Opportunities

Neither women nor members of minority groups are finding discrimination in the hiring practices of television news departments today. This is particularly true for entry-level positions, such as Desk Assistant. Both groups were well represented in the mid-1990 surveys within the television news industry.

Women made up 37 percent of the television station news force in 1997, while minorities totaled 21 percent, according to the Radio-Television News Directors Association (RTNDA). In addition, 96 percent of television news staffs employed women, and 87 percent employed minorities—although most minorities work in large urban markets, which skews salary averages and indicates a lack of representation in small and midsize markets.

Unions/Associations

At network owned-and-operated stations and certain other major market stations, Desk Assistants are represented, for bargaining purposes, by the National Association of Broadcast Employees and Technicians AFL-CIO (NABET). At most outlets, however, they are not represented by a union or professional organization.

ANCHORPERSON

Duties: Reporting the news and introducing reports on the air; serving as focal point for a newscast

Alternate Title(s): TV Newscaster

Salary Range: Under $20,000 to $314,000+

Employment Prospects: Poor

Advancement Prospects: Poor

Prerequisites:

Education—Undergraduate degree in mass communications, journalism, or political science, with a strong liberal arts background

Experience—Many years in various TV newsroom positions

Special Skills—Attractive appearance; good speaking voice; ability to communicate authoritatively; integrity; pleasant personality

```
┌─────────────────────────────┐
│      Anchorperson           │
│  (Large Station or Network) │
└─────────────────────────────┘

┌─────────────────────────────┐
│      Anchorperson           │
└─────────────────────────────┘

┌─────────────────────────────┐
│        Reporter             │
└─────────────────────────────┘
```

Position Description

The main functions of an Anchorperson are to host regularly scheduled newscasts, report some of the major news stories, provide lead-ins for other stories, and serve as the personality around whom the entire newscast revolves. The Anchorperson has extremely high visibility in a community and can even achieve star status.

As one of the most coveted jobs in television newscasting, the Anchorperson's position appears to be high-paying, glamorous, and easy. In fact, it is sometimes high-paying, occasionally glamorous, and almost never easy. In smaller and middle-market stations, the Anchorperson often does the legwork necessary to research news stories or constructs reports from wire service copy or network feeds. Even at stations with large news staffs and at the network level, the talent usually writes or rewrites some material.

The person holding this position must have a particular appeal to viewers and be able to speak to them in a satisfying and authoritative manner. The Anchorperson must have a thorough understanding of all news developments locally, nationally, and internationally and must be able to identify trends and significant events, analyze and interpret them, and convey such information clearly to the viewing audience.

With news escalating in importance and stations involved in ratings wars, the Anchorperson has become the most important element of a newscast. An attractive and popular individual brings more viewers to the newscast, and thus a larger consumer audience to the station or network.

Additionally, the Anchorperson

- takes part in determining the order of stories and the content of a newscast;
- provides voice-over commentary for filmed or taped clips of a particular story or event;
- conducts in-studio or on-location interviews; and
- hosts documentary productions and special news reports.

Salaries

The salary range is very broad, with small market stations paying near the bottom of the scale and the major networks near the top. Some network personalities earn more than $2 million per year. Apart from the superstars at the network level, the average Anchorperson's salary was $71,937 in 1997, according to the National Association of Broadcasters (NAB). Salaries are a reflection of the market size and the size of the news staff. Salaries ranged from $20,000 in the smallest markets to an average of $313,712 in the 10 largest markets in 1997, according to the NAB. The average annual pay at the network affiliates in the markets ranked 51 to 75 for Star Anchors was $68,559 in 1997.

Employment Prospects

The anchor position at any television station or network is a very attractive post and is considered the height of a television Reporter's career. It is well paid, highly visible, and frequently accompanied by substantial benefits. Competition is extremely fierce, and only a small percentage of aspiring Reporters become Anchorpersons.

There were approximately two Anchorpersons at the typical middle-market TV station in 1992, according to the Radio-Television News Directors Association (RTNDA). Because of the constant emphasis on ratings, there is considerable turnover.

Advancement Prospects

Until recently, the networks were considered the ultimate goal for Anchorpersons, but with current trends toward higher salaries and better quality in local news, the rush to join a network has diminished. In cable TV and on-line news, opportunities for Anchorpersons will increase in the future. Current advancement possibilities, however, are quite poor.

Education

An undergraduate degree is necessary, and a graduate degree is preferable, for the position of Anchorperson. The major field of study should be mass communications, journalism, or political science, but with a strong liberal arts education. Many News Directors recommend that up to three-quarters of an aspiring Anchorperson's college coursework should be in such areas as English, speech, government, sociology, and the humanities.

Experience/Skills

A considerable number of years of newsroom experience at smaller market stations is usually required before promotion to Anchorperson, and many more years of news work are necessary as an individual moves up the ladder to larger market stations. This experience includes news writing and reporting in all content areas and in various market sizes. Anchorpersons often have some experience in radio news or, less often, in print journalism.

A large part of an Anchorperson's success is based on appearance and delivery. An Anchorperson must look attractive on camera, speak in a clear and authoritative manner and project integrity and a pleasant personality.

Minority/Women's Opportunities

As with most on-camera news positions, opportunities for women and minorities have improved in recent years, with both groups enjoying a strong presence on the air. Women anchors surveyed by Vernon Stone in 1991 had an average of 7.4 years' experience and a median salary of $31,250, while men's experience averaged 14.2 years and a median salary of $50,000. With the exception of small television news staffs of 1 to 10 employees, an RTNDA 1997 survey found that 80–100 percent of news staffs employ women and minorities.

Despite recent gains, blacks, Hispanics, Asian Americans, and Native Americans remain underrepresented in broadcast news.

Unions/Associations

When represented by a union, Anchorpersons may be members of the Writers Guild of America (WGA) or the American Federation of Television and Radio Artists (AFTRA).

The RTNDA is very active in promoting the professionalism of broadcast news, and many Anchorpersons belong to that organization. Some are also members of the Society of Professional Journalists.

REPORTER

Duties: Gathering of news from various sources; analyzing and preparing news and features for television broadcast; on-air reporting

Alternate Title(s):   Correspondent

Salary Range: $20,000 to $85,000

Employment Prospects: Fair

Advancement Prospects: Fair

Prerequisites:

Education—Undergraduate degree in political science or journalism with strong liberal arts background

Experience—Minimum of two years as a News Writer in television or radio or in print journalism

Special Skills—Good writing and speaking ability; inquiring mind; dependability; persistence

```
┌─────────────────────────────────┐
│    Assistant News Director;      │
│         Anchorperson             │
└─────────────────────────────────┘

┌─────────────────────────────────┐
│           Reporter               │
└─────────────────────────────────┘

┌─────────────────────────────────┐
│         News Writer              │
└─────────────────────────────────┘
```

Position Description

A television Reporter is a working journalist who gathers news from many different sources, organizes each report, sometimes writes it, and reports it on the air at a local station or network. At the major market station and network level, a Reporter assigned to an outlying area or overseas is usually called a correspondent or, occasionally, a foreign correspondent. In many stations, Reporters serve as their own Producers for specific television news coverage.

The day-to-day responsibilities of a Reporter vary considerably from station to station and from market to market. In a small station that does not employ News Writers, the Reporter will write the stories and deliver them on the air. In a larger station with several Reporters and News Writers on staff, each Reporter may specialize in a particular area such as politics, economics, health, or consumer information. In those instances, News Writers help develop the Reporters' stories for delivery on the air.

Reporters' assignments may vary in importance from covering a civic luncheon or a local fire to in-depth investigative reporting on corruption in local government or the significance of national economic policies to a local community. Reporters acquire information through library research, telephone inquiries, interviews with key people, observation, and questioning. Covering news conferences and press briefings, researching feature stories, and reporting on special events are part of the Reporter's responsibilities.

A Reporter is skilled in investigating and gathering the news; in developing the information into an understandable report; and in broadcasting it in a clear, concise, and credible manner.

Reporters must be accurate and must constantly search for the facts. They often report to an Assistant News Director from the "Chicago school of journalism," who is inclined to insist, "You say your mother loves you? Check it out!"

Additionally, the Reporter

- determines the slant or emphasis of a particular news story;
- examines significant news items to determine ideas for features and news reports and evaluates leads and tips in developing story ideas;
- conducts live, taped, or filmed interviews in the studio and presents stand-up live, taped, or voice-over reports from the site of a news event; and
- follows through on the developments of a previously reported story for news updates and additional reports.

Salaries

All news position salaries have increased in recent years, and industry sources believe they will continue to do so.

Reporters, however, are paid substantially less than the top Anchorpersons. There is also a wide variance in Reporters' salaries between small local stations and the top market stations and networks, where salaries may reach $50,000 to more than $100,000. The average salary for a News Reporter was $33,223 in 1997, according to the National Association of Broadcasters (NAB).

According to the 1996 Annual Survey of Journalism and Mass Communication Graduates (Gerald M. Kosicki and Lee B. Becker), the median income of the 1996 bachelor's degree recipient 6 to 8 months after graduation was $21,500. As in other news jobs, the larger the market and news staff, the higher the salary. Reporters tend to make more than news Producers in the 100 largest markets, while Producers have higher salaries in the smaller 100 markets.

Employment Prospects

Although the position is sometimes considered an entry-level job at small market stations, most Reporters have had experience as television News Writers. Midsize and large market stations employ several Reporters, as do the networks. The typical station employed seven Reporters in 1997, according to the National Association of Broadcasters (NAB). Some opportunities are opening up in cable television news operations. There is also a high turnover rate in this position at TV stations, and opportunities are fair for employment as a replacement Reporter, particularly for those who specialize in particular topics such as health or consumer reports.

Advancement Prospects

The career goal of nearly every television Reporter is to become an Anchorperson. Prospects for that particular promotion, however, are poor because of the limited number of anchor positions available, the reluctance of Anchorpersons to vacate those positions, and the extremely heavy competition for the few openings that do occur.

Yet it is possible to advance by moving to a larger market station, and thus to a higher salary and more prestige. Earning more money in television news reporting almost always requires moving to the major market stations, according to the Radio-Television News Directors Association (RTNDA). Salaries are much higher at stations in the top 50 markets. Promotion to Assistant News Director and ultimately to News Director at a smaller station is also a possible career track.

For many Reporters, the position represents the peak of their careers. Some large stations in the major markets have Reporters on staff who have retained their jobs for years.

Education

A television Reporter must have broad knowledge in many areas. An undergraduate degree in political science or journalism with considerable coursework in all of the liberal arts is a necessity. Graduate study is useful for those who specialize in reporting on political or economic affairs. Writing courses are essential.

Experience/Skills

Two or three years of experience in a television station's news department as a Desk Assistant or News Writer is usually preferred by employers, although some entry-level reporting positions do exist at smaller market stations. Actual news experience in college at a student newspaper or radio station is helpful. Some Reporters move to television reporting from a successful career in a newspaper reporting.

Employers look for a bright, alert individual with an inquiring mind, a considerable degree of curiosity, and a great deal of persistence. A Reporter must be dependable, have an excellent knowledge of the English language, a reasonably good speaking voice, and good diction. Above all, the applicant must be able to write good, succinct copy.

Minority/Women's Opportunities

Reporter is one of the top-three positions filled by minorities in television news, with the other two being Anchor and photographer. Of the 20,500 people comprising the news workforce in 1994, minorities represented only 18 percent, 9.9 percent of which were minority men and, 8.1 percent, minority women. Researcher Vernon Stone's detailed analysis found minority representation to be as follows: 10.2 percent black, 5 percent Hispanic, 2.1 percent Asian, and .7 percent Indian.

In public television, 48 percent of professional positions (which include Reporters) were held by women in 1994, and 18 percent were held by minorities; the increase in minority representation was 5.6 percent from the previous year, according to the Corporation for Public Broadcasting.

Unions/Associations

News personnel who write or perform are sometimes members of the Writers Guild of America (WGA) or the American Federation of Television and Radio Artists (AFTRA).

Television Reporters are also eligible for membership in RTNDA and other professional associations. Many Reporters have belonged to Phi Delta Epsilon, an honory college journalism fraternity; Kappa Tau Alpha, a journalism scholastic society; or Pi Gamma Kappa or Alpha Epsilon Rho, student broadcasting fraternities.

WEATHER REPORTER

CAREER PROFILE

Duties: Reporting of weather conditions and forecasts as a part of a regularly scheduled TV newscast

Alternate Title(s):   Weathercaster; Meteorologist

Salary Range: $20,000 to $150,000

Employment Prospects: Poor

Advancement Prospects: Poor

Prerequisites:
   Education—Undergraduate degree in meteorology required at major market stations and networks
   Experience—Some public speaking
   Special Skills—Pleasant appearance and manner; good verbal ability; distinctive style

CAREER LADDER

```
┌─────────────────────────────┐
│      Weather Reporter        │
│  (Large Station or Network)  │
└─────────────────────────────┘

┌─────────────────────────────┐
│      Weather Reporter        │
└─────────────────────────────┘

┌─────────────────────────────┐
│         Announcer            │
└─────────────────────────────┘
```

Position Description

Weather Reporters range from the personable, attractive college graduate at some local stations to the highly qualified, knowledgeable meteorologist employed by half of the country's TV stations, networks, and cable systems. They are also employed at the national cable service, The Weather Channel. Some television stations fill this position with an experienced staff Announcer who is permanently assigned to the post and who is regularly responsible for the subject.

The Weather Reporter usually reports to the Assistant News Director. Responsibilities of the position include gathering information about weather conditions on a daily basis. A Weather Reporter is also responsible for the much-maligned forecasts of future weather probabilities. The forecasts are made for the following five days or a week and predict trends or changes in weather patterns. In some parts of the country, the weather is an important factor in the economy, and in those locations it is reported on regular newscasts as well as in short summaries several times during the day. Extensive weather coverage of the entire country is usually reported three times a day during major newscasts. Industry studies have indicated, however, that most viewers are interested in weather conditions in other locations only if something unusual has occurred.

The Weather Reporter gathers information from national satellite weather services, from local or regional government agencies, from wire services, and through reports from Reporters in the field. In larger stations, the weather department maintains its own equipment to measure and gauge local weather conditions. Some weather departments at television stations are actually separate, independent companies that are located at the stations. They provide weather information/reports for the stations and usually for the radio stations in the area.

A Weather Reporter uses a variety of visual devices to illustrate weather conditions, including radarscopes to show storm conditions; dials and charts that indicate temperature, humidity, wind velocity, barometric pressure, and pollen count; computer graphics; transparent plastic overlays; and satellite photographs of the continental United States. A Weather Reporter works with the station's production team and Art Director to develop new techniques of making weather information more interesting and informative for the viewer.

Additionally, the Weather Reporter

- works with the production crew and Director in setting up and changing or modifying weather visuals for a newscast; and
- checks with contacts in different parts of the station's coverage area for information on weather conditions in various locations.

Salaries

Weather Reporters' salaries vary with the size of a station, its geographic location, the importance with which weather is viewed by management as an audience-builder and the qualifications of the person holding the position. Salaries averaged $55,018 in 1997, according to the National Association of Broadcasters (NAB). The average starting salary was $31,531 in that year. Some Weather Reporters who are well known and have a distinctive style that attracts viewers are paid considerably more. Network Weather Reporters earn $500,000 or more each year.

Employment Prospects

The potential for employment is very limited. Some stations employ only one full-time Weather Reporter, with an Announcer filling in on early morning and some weekend newscasts. Others employ a weekend Weather Reporter on a permanent basis. Some major market stations that also operate AM and FM radio stations employ two or more Weather Reporters. The field is limited, however, to those existing stations and the few that will be constructed in the future. There are some opportunities in larger cable systems that originate local newscasts and at the few low-power television (LPTV) stations that provide local news origination.

Advancement Prospects

For the professional Weather Reporter, the most likely career path for advancement is to a larger market station or possibly to a network. Some Weather Reporters move to cable TV systems in larger markets to advance their careers. For the staff Announcer who is assigned the job, a good performance can help pave the way to promotion within the News Department. In general, however, most successful Weather Reporters remain in that position and the chances for advancement to another market or to a different television career are quite limited.

Education

Educational requirements vary little from station to station and from market to market. At most broadcast stations, an undergraduate or graduate degree, ideally in meteorology, is required. Membership in and certification by the American Meteorological Society (AMS) is sometimes required at mid-size stations. Courses in public speaking and mass communications are helpful.

Experience/Skills

The weather segment of a newscast is usually delivered without a script and with almost constant eye contact with the camera. Some public speaking experience and an ability to ad-lib with style, wit, and enthusiasm is generally required of Weather Reporters. Most News Directors seek articulate, attractive people who have pleasant voices and proper diction. An ability to relate to and attract a viewing audience is the primary requirement for the position. This requires developing a unique on-air personality.

Minority/Women's Opportunities

As with many on-camera positions in television news, both women and minority group members are finding more opportunities open to them as Weather Reporters. Some observers estimate that nearly half of on-air Weather Reporters are women. Minority representation, however, was not as high. In 1997, Weather Reporters were among those who made the most significant salary gains from the year before, according to the annual Radio and Television News Directors Foundation (RTNDF) Ball State University Salary Survey.

Unions/Associations

Some Weather Reporters are members of the American Federation of Television and Radio Artists (AFTRA). Most, however, are not represented by a union. For meteorologists, membership in the AMS is a prestigious affiliation that can enhance their career opportunities. Some Weather Reporters belong to the Radio-TV News Directors Association (RTNDA).

SPORTSCASTER

CAREER PROFILE

Duties: Reporting of athletic and sports events as part of a regularly scheduled TV newscast

Alternate Title(s): Sports Director; Sports Reporter

Salary Range: $25,000 to $100,000+

Employment Prospects: Poor

Advancement Prospects: Poor

Prerequisites:

Education—Undergraduate degree in journalism or mass communications with heavy exposure to the sports scene

Experience—Some newsroom and sports desk experience in television, radio, or newspapers

Special Skills—Extensive knowledge of all sports; writing and verbal ability; pleasant personality

CAREER LADDER

```
┌─────────────────────────────────┐
│      Sports Director            │
│  (Large Station or Network)     │
└─────────────────────────────────┘

┌─────────────────────────────────┐
│        Sportscaster             │
└─────────────────────────────────┘

┌─────────────────────────────────┐
│   Desk Assistant; News Writer   │
└─────────────────────────────────┘
```

Position Description

A Sportscaster's duties and responsibilities are similar to those of a Reporter, but in a highly specialized area—the sports world.

At small stations, the Sportscaster may be a department of one, reporting to the Assistant News Director. In this situation, considerable autonomy is permitted in selecting, writing, and preparing, as well as delivering, the sports news for each newscast. At major market stations and at the network level there may be several Sportscasters on staff, all of whom report to a sports director. Each person may specialize in a particular sport or event.

The duties of a Sportscaster go beyond merely reporting the outcomes of local games and contests to include coverage of such diverse subjects as a baseball strike, the major professional sports' annual drafts, local personalities who appear headed for national prominence, legislation that affects the athletic scene, professional players' contracts and salary arrangements, record-breaking events, and more. Generally, the Sportscaster covers any event that involves or affects the sports scene.

A Sportscaster gathers and edits information and is often required to separate the natural hype of the industry from the actual facts. A Sportscaster spends a considerable amount of time outside the station tracking down leads and stories.

Additionally, the Sportscaster

- reviews network feeds, syndicated sports clips, and wire stories on national and international sports news;
- selects video material for use on a newscast;
- provides play-by-play (description of action in an event as it occurs) or color (informative commentary) coverage for games broadcast by the station;
- interviews local and visiting sports personalities;
- maintains continuing contact and encourages good station relationships with local and regional sports figures—coaches, managers, athletic directors, and players; and
- originates and develops special sports commentaries, features, and documentaries.

Salaries

Salaries for all news personnel have risen over recent years, particularly at smaller market stations. Sportscasters, however, are still paid substantially less than Anchorpersons. Salaries for Sportscasters averaged $52,644 in 1997, according to the National Association of Broadcasters (NAB). The average starting salary was $31,117 in that year.

Exceptions to the above figures occur at major market stations and networks, where popular Sportscasters can be paid well over $200,000 per year. As in other news positions, the larger the market, the higher the salary.

Employment Prospects

Competition for sportscasting jobs in commercial television is fierce, and employment opportunities are poor. The position requires extensive background in athletics and solid reporting and writing skills. It is not considered an entry-level position, and most stations employ only two Sportscasters. There is, however, a high degree of interest in sports in this country. Technological advances in satellite transmission have created more opportunities in sports reporting, both at the station level and in the cable television industry.

Advancement Prospects

Sportscasting is generally not a stepping-stone to bigger and better positions within the news department. A Sportscaster may look forward to promotion to sports director at his or her station, if such a position exists, or at the network level, where salaries and prestige can be higher. Expertise and specialization in a particular sport are usually necessary.

Cable television news operations also offer advancement possibilities for the best and the brightest Sportscasters. The overall outlook for advancement, however, is considered poor.

Education

Sportscasters can no longer get by on a "dumb-but-charming-jock" image. They must be articulate and knowledgeable. Their writing skills must be highly developed, since Sportscasters often write their own copy. Most employers require an undergraduate degree in journalism or mass communications with coursework in speech, English, sociology, and psychology. Extensive exposure to, or training in, virtually all aspects of sports is essential.

Experience/Skills

Many Sportscasters gain general news experience as a Desk Assistant or News Writer before moving to sports reporting. Writing and speaking experience in television or radio is required. Newspaper sports reporting experience also provides background for the job. Part-time work in television or radio or at a newspaper while in college is useful training for those wishing to enter the field.

A Sportscaster should have an enthusiastic interest in sports and broad experience in a wide variety of athletic events, as well as an appealing voice, good intonation and diction, a personal style, and a distinctive on-air personality.

Minority/Women's Opportunities

Although the profession was long dominated by men, broadcast professionals such as Leslie Visser and Robin Roberts have made great strides for women and minority sportscasters. Some of this influence is noted at the local station level, although sports reporting in 1997 was largely dominated by male reporters. Male members of minority groups achieved acceptance as Sportscasters earlier than women did, and there is little evidence of racial discrimination in hiring practices at all levels of sportscasting.

Unions/Associations

Some Sportscasters may belong to the Writers Guild of America (WGA) or to the American Federation of Television and Radio Artists (AFTRA) at certain networks and at some network-owned stations in major markets. At small market stations, however, Sportscasters are not usually represented by a union.

Sportscasters may hold membership in the Radio Television News Directors Association (RTNDA), and other journalism organizations.

CHIEF ENGINEER

Duties: Overseeing of all engineering and technical operations at a television station or media facility

Alternate Title(s): Director of Engineering; Vice President of Engineering

Salary Range: $30,000 to $99,000+

Employment Prospects: Fair

Advancement Prospects: Fair

Prerequisites:

Education—Undergraduate degree in electrical engineering required; advanced degree preferable; training in broadcast equipment; certification; FCC license

Experience—Minimum of five years as an Assistant Chief Engineer

Special Skills—Technical aptitude; administrative and organizational ability; leadership qualities

```
┌─────────────────────────────────┐
│  General Manager; Engineering    │
│         Management               │
│        (TV Network)              │
└─────────────────────────────────┘

┌─────────────────────────────────┐
│        Chief Engineer            │
└─────────────────────────────────┘

┌─────────────────────────────────┐
│    Assistant Chief Engineer      │
└─────────────────────────────────┘
```

Position Description

The Chief Engineer is ultimately responsible for all of a television station's technical facilities, equipment, and services necessary to conduct its broadcast and programming activities. This person reports to the General Manager and is responsible for the administration and supervision of all engineering and operations personnel, and for keeping the station on the air during all broadcast periods.

The Chief Engineer is in charge of all long-range facilities planning, of systems design, of the budgeting and purchasing of technical equipment, and of making sure that station operations are in compliance with Federal Communications Commission (FCC) regulations and applicable local, state, and federal laws.

The Chief Engineer is instrumental in the design, construction, and installation of all engineering equipment; develops preventive maintenance programs for station facilities; and ensures the efficient and effective use of a station's equipment.

The Chief Engineer's job is one of managing personnel in the complex world of television engineering. The largest number of employees at most commercial and public television stations is usually in the engineering department. The number of Engineers ranges from as few as 10 to more than 75 at major market stations. The supervision, organization, and efficient management of personnel occupies a considerable amount of the Chief Engineer's work day.

A Chief Engineer is a forward-thinking individual with expertise in planning for the electronic future. Budgeting and planning for new equipment occupies a considerable portion of the Chief Engineer's time.

Additionally, the Chief Engineer

- coordinates and negotiates the use of outside telecommunications facilities with appropriate utility companies and private agencies; and
- prepares all technical applications, including FCC construction authorization permits, licenses, and the renewal or modification of licenses.

Salaries

In spite of their many responsibilities, Chief Engineers are not as well paid as other management personnel in broadcast television. The average base salary in commercial TV was $56,980 in 1997, according to the National Association of Broadcasters (NAB).

In public television, salaries for Chief Engineers ranged from $24,500 in small markets to $89,896 at some major market community stations in 1997, according to the Corporation for Public Broadcasting (CPB). The median salary was $49,538 in 1997. Salaries for those classified as chief of operations and engineering at community PTV stations ranged from $32,798 to $126,567 in 1997, according to the CPB. The median was $55,328 in that year.

Employment Prospects

The opportunity to become a Chief Engineer at any of the 1,569 commercial and public television stations is somewhat limited. Although qualified engineers are increasingly difficult to find, a minimum of five years of experience in all aspects of broadcast engineering is essential. Because of the high degree of technical expertise required, the position is often viewed as a climax to a successful career in engineering. There is relatively little turnover in this area.

Positions for Chief Technicians at cable or satellite television systems or at multichannel multipoint distribution service (MMDS) companies, however, are available in increasing numbers, sometimes at lower salaries. Other opportunities exist in government, health, or educational production organizations and in the low-power television (LPTV) stations that are going on the air. Other opportunities will occur in any new full-power commercial TV stations that will be constructed in the next five years. Because of the lack of qualified broadcast engineers, ambitious and diligent individuals who have the necessary experience and education should find additional opportunities in these newer areas.

Advancement Prospects

Many Chief Engineers view the position as a successful completion of a career. Some, however, move onward to the same position at a higher salary at a larger station. Still others transfer to networks or large production companies to advance their careers. A few obtain the position of General Manager at smaller market stations. Recently, a number of individuals have advanced by obtaining more financially rewarding positions of a similar nature in large cable TV operations.

Education

Most Chief Engineers have degrees in electrical engineering, physics, or a related science. A few have some graduate work or a graduate degree. All have had some technical training in broadcast engineering at a school or technical center and have a Restricted Radio Telephone Operator permit from the FCC and a certificate from one of the industry certification programs. The certificate requires study and successful completion of examinations.

Experience/Skills

Television engineering is not an exact science. The possibilities of breakdowns in transmission or technical equipment are high. Considerable experience with all types and models of electronic gear, a thorough understanding of the principles of electronics, and an ability to rapidly scan and decipher schematic drawings are necessities in this position. Most TV stations require a Chief Engineer to have at least five years of experience as an Assistant Chief Engineer.

The Chief Engineer must thoroughly understand all FCC regulations and be current on all state-of-the-art television equipment. In addition, the individual must be capable of designing various technical systems using interrelated components to improve engineering facilities and must demonstrate leadership qualities, be budget conscious, and be a capable administrator.

Minority/Women's Opportunities

The Society of Broadcast Engineers (SBE) estimated that its minority and women membership stood at less than 5 percent in 1998, but opportunities are better than they've ever been, according to industry experts. The 1996 National Science Foundation report *Women, Minorities, and Persons with Disabilities in Science and Engineering* states that only 8 percent of engineers (in all disciplines) were women and 3 percent were blacks; 1998 statistics show that Hispanics represent only 3 percent of the engineering and scientific community in the United States, and the number of American Indians, the other underrepresented minority, is negligible in the engineering professions.

Still, organizations such as the National Action Council for Minorities in Engineering, the Society of Women Engineers, and the National Science Foundation sponsor academic and professional advancement programs to cultivate greater numbers of women and minorities in the field. Experts observe that advancing to the position of Chief Engineer will become more likely as members of these underrepresented groups obtain advanced degrees and log more years of experience in the industry.

Unions/Associations

Chief Engineers are considered part of the management of a station and are not represented by a union or bargaining agent. Some have been members of the International Brotherhood of Electrical Workers (IBEW) or the National Association of Broadcast Employees and Technicians AFL-CIO (NABET). Most become inactive, however, upon becoming Chief Engineers.

Many belong to the SBE or the Society of Motion Picture and Television Engineers (SMPTE), sharing mutual concerns and increasing their technical knowledge.

ASSISTANT CHIEF ENGINEER

CAREER PROFILE

Duties: Day-to-day scheduling, maintenance, and operation of a television station's equipment and facilities

Alternate Title(s):   Assistant Director of Engineering

Salary Range: $25,000 to $80,000

Employment Prospects: Fair

Advancement Prospects: Good

Prerequisites:

Education—Undergraduate degree in electrical engineering or related field required; advanced degree preferable; training in broadcast equipment; FCC license; certification

Experience—Five years as an Engineering Supervisor

Special Skills—Technical aptitude; administrative and organizational ability; leadership qualities

CAREER LADDER

```
┌─────────────────────────────┐
│      Chief Engineer         │
└─────────────────────────────┘

┌─────────────────────────────┐
│  Assistant Chief Engineer   │
└─────────────────────────────┘

┌─────────────────────────────┐
│   Engineering Supervisor    │
└─────────────────────────────┘
```

Position Description

The Assistant Chief Engineer is usually the second in command in the engineering department at a commercial or public television station. As the senior technical staff member, this individual is directly responsible to the Chief Engineer for the day-to-day operation of the station and all scheduling of engineering employees and facilities. The person in this job also implements the department's budget and policies.

The Assistant Chief Engineer advises program and production personnel on the technical aspects of a TV program during the planning stages and implements the support systems necessary to mount a production. Other important functions include assisting the Chief Engineer in developing technical designs and specifications and creating (or supervising the creation of) the documentation necessary for installing or modifying equipment.

The Assistant Chief Engineer also helps to determine the satellite or land connecting services required for program distribution, directly orders them from the telephone or satellite company and other carriers, and keeps abreast of state-of-the-art broadcast equipment specifications and of the vendors, prices, and availability of such equipment. An Assistant Chief Engineer is a logistician who juggles personnel and schedules to meet the ever-changing demands of a television operation.

Because of the requisite supervisory skills and experience, the person in this position often acts as a troubleshooter and consults with the Engineering Supervisors in various engineering sections. An Assistant Chief Engineer is often the station's expert in computerized engineering equipment and directly supervises its installation and integration into the station's engineering system. Training employees in the operation and maintenance of new equipment, in conjunction with an Engineering Supervisor, is also one of the duties of the position.

As the second in command of the engineering department, the Assistant Chief Engineer directly supervises master control, editing, and transmitter operations and conducts tests to ensure that the station is operating in accordance with Federal Communications Commission (FCC) regulations.

Additionally, the Assistant Chief Engineer

- anticipates all possible contingencies in the studio or at the transmitter and develops procedures to minimize technical downtime;
- supervises equipment replacement and modification;
- assists in the installation of equipment;

- purchases engineering supplies and equipment;
- conducts transmission tests;
- oversees inventory of parts and components; and
- serves as backup for other engineering supervisory employees and for the Chief Engineer.

Salaries

Salaries for Assistant Chief Engineers are relatively good in broadcasting. At commercial television stations, they averaged nearly $45,000 in 1997, according to industry observers.

In public TV, 1997 salaries ranged from $25,000 at small market stations to $80,000 in the larger markets, according to industry estimates.

Employment Prospects

The opportunities for employment as or advancement to Assistant Chief Engineer in commercial or public television are fair. There is relatively little turnover in the position, and in many small market stations the Engineering Supervisor in charge of transmission also performs the duties of an Assistant Chief Engineer.

Positions in cable TV, satellite, or multichannel multipoint distribution service (MMDS) operations, however, are available and many government, health, and educational production units require management-level technical workers who have some broadcast experience. Because of the increasing need for engineering personnel in all areas of broadcast and nonbroadcast operations, the opportunities for employment in this or in a comparable position are improving for ambitious and qualified people.

Advancement Prospects

Most Assistant Chief Engineers seek advancement to the position of Chief Engineer. Some advance their careers by moving to a smaller market in a more responsible role and at a higher salary. Still others join independent production organizations or become Chief Technicians in cable TV or MMDS companies, which actively recruit broadcast-quality engineering managers. Advancement to the Chief Engineer position at the low-power television (LPTV) stations is also possible. Because of the relative lack of experienced personnel, Assistant Chief Engineers have a good chance of advancing their careers in a variety of technical settings.

Education

Most Assistant Chief Engineers possess an undergraduate degree in electrical engineering, physics, or a related science.

Some training by equipment manufacturers or at technical schools is required, and an individual should have a Restricted Radio Telephone Operators permit from the FCC, must have completed a study program, and have received a certificate from one of the industry certification programs, operated by the International Society of Certified Electronic Engineers (ISCET), the Society of Broadcast Engineers (SBE), or other groups.

Experience/Skills

A minimum of five years of experience involving all aspects of broadcast technology (usually as an Engineering Supervisor) is frequently required for employment as or promotion to Assistant Chief Engineer. In order to reach that position, a person must have a complete knowledge of currently used television equipment, systems, and components and a thorough understanding of FCC technical regulations.

In addition, the applicant must possess supervisory and leadership capabilities, must be organized and budget-conscious, and must be capable of dealing with a wide variety of individuals from various departments within a station. An Assistant Chief Engineer should also be experienced in dealing with manufacturers' representatives and electronic supply companies.

Minority/Women's Opportunities

At most, a handful of minorities and women hold this senior engineering position because, industry surveys point out, these groups have made inroads into the profession only recently; therefore, they don't have the same level of experience as their white male counterparts. Industry observers express hope that those statistics will change, and organizations such as the National Action Council for Minorities in Engineering are working to diversify the field. NACME scholarships, for example, have made it possible for 6,500 minority students to obtain engineering degrees since 1980.

Unions/Associations

Assistant Chief Engineers are usually considered part of management, and as such are not represented by a union, although at one time in their careers they may have been members of the International Brotherhood of Electrical Workers (IBEW) or the National Association of Broadcast Employees and Technicians (NABET). Most people in the position, however, belong to one or more professional organizations, including the SBE and the Society of Motion Picture and Television Engineers (SMPTE).

ENGINEERING SUPERVISOR

CAREER PROFILE

Duties: Supervision of Audio/Video, Maintenance, Master Control, Transmitter, or Videotape Engineers/Editors at a television station or facilities company

Alternate Title(s): Supervising Engineer; Engineering Coordinator; Broadcast Supervisor/Engineer

Salary Range: $25,000 to $60,000

Employment Prospects: Fair

Advancement Prospects: Fair

Prerequisites:

Education—High school diploma; one to two years of technical school training; undergraduate degree in engineering preferable; FCC license; certification

Experience—Minimum of two years as an Audio/Video, Maintenance, Master Control, Transmitter, or Videotape Engineer

Special Skills—Technical aptitude; supervisory skills; leadership qualities

CAREER LADDER

```
┌─────────────────────────────────────┐
│      Assistant Chief Engineer        │
└─────────────────────────────────────┘

┌─────────────────────────────────────┐
│      Engineering Supervisor          │
└─────────────────────────────────────┘

┌─────────────────────────────────────┐
│      Audio/Video, Maintenance,       │
│         Master Control,              │
│  Transmitter, or Videotape Engineer  │
└─────────────────────────────────────┘
```

Position Description

An Engineering Supervisor directs the day-to-day operation of electronic and technical equipment and of operating engineers at a television station or production/facilities company. In smaller market stations, one or two engineers supervise the entire engineering staff. In middle-market and major market stations, there are often four or more Engineering Supervisors, each of whom directs the activities of Audio/Video, Maintenance, Master Control, Transmitter, or Videotape Engineers/Editors. In some small and middle-market stations, the Engineering Supervisor of transmitter operations often serves as the Assistant Chief Engineer.

One of the major responsibilities of the position is to ensure the proper maintenance and operation of electronic equipment. An Engineering Supervisor is held responsible for the safe, efficient, and effective operation of all electronic and technical equipment under his or her jurisdiction.

The Engineering Supervisor often oversees the performance of five or more engineers, serves as the day-to-day manager of various shifts, schedules personnel, and determines assignments within each shift. Depending on the size of the station and of the department, the Supervisor may also be responsible for the actual running of equipment. In most cases, however, the person in this position serves as a backup and troubleshooter for a variety of operations.

Additionally, the Engineering Supervisor

- makes tests and calibrations to ensure the station's conformance to Federal Communications Commission (FCC) rules and regulations;
- supervises preventive and emergency maintenance and repair of all equipment under his or her supervision;
- maintains and reviews all discrepancy and technical reports to spot and correct technical problems; and
- installs new component parts and equipment, particularly computerized electronic gear.

Salaries

In keeping with their responsibility, Engineering Supervisors are relatively well paid. Salaries in commercial TV ranged from $25,000 at smaller market stations to $60,000 in major markets for people with experience and seniority in 1997, according to industry observers. Engineering salaries were up across the board in 1997, according to *Broadcast Engineering*'s annual salary survey.

Employment Prospects

The opportunities for employment as an Engineering Supervisor are fair. The position is not an entry-level job, and it requires considerable experience and knowledge of sophisticated broadcast equipment. Although most stations and the larger television production facilities organizations often employ more than four Engineering Supervisors, competition for the job is heavy. The position is usually acquired by the more diligent, competent, and experienced engineers from within the station. More opportunities for a similar position, however, exist at larger cable TV and satellite systems and multichannel multipoint distribution service (MMDS) companies. Some jobs are also available at education, government, and health television production organizations and in corporate television. Positions are often available in such organizations, where the equipment is less sophisticated and the Engineering Supervisor often acts as a de facto Chief Engineer. In addition, many Engineering Supervisor positions are open at production and postproduction facilities companies.

Advancement Prospects

The possibilities for advancement to the position of Assistant Chief Engineer or in some cases directly to Chief Engineer are generally fair. The ability to stay abreast of new technologies will distinguish those who want to advance.

The bright, alert, and diligent Engineering Supervisor who has earned a reputation in a specific area (such as videotape recording, digital editing, maintenance, or transmission) and who has shown interest in other engineering disciplines often finds promotional opportunities at his or her own station. Some use their skills and experience to obtain better-paying positions at larger market stations, while others advance by assuming more responsible engineering posts at smaller stations. Many experienced Engineering Supervisors obtain better positions at higher salaries in cable TV or at production and postproduction facilities companies which actively recruit broadcast-quality engineers.

Education

A minimum of a high school education and a year or two of training at a technical school is required for the position of Engineering Supervisor. A bachelor's degree in electrical engineering, physics, or a related field is preferable. Engineering supervisors have usually obtained a Restricted Radio Telephone Operators permit from the FCC and completed a certificate study program from one of the industry certification groups.

Experience/Skills

Most candidates for the position are expected to have a minimum of two years of experience as an Audio/Video, Maintenance, Master Control, Transmitter, or Videotape Engineer/Editor. A complete knowledge of the particular engineering specialty that the individual will supervise is required, as well as some understanding of other engineering functions. Most Supervisors have earned a reputation among their peers for skilled troubleshooting. Today, all have had experience with computerized electronic equipment.

Engineering Supervisors must have the ability to supervise other engineers in the installation, operation, and maintenance of complicated electronic equipment and must be organized and efficient. They should also be capable of dealing with a wide variety of technical problems and of determining effective solutions. At facilities companies, Engineering Supervisors must have the ability to interact positively with clients.

Minority/Women's Opportunities

There were but a handful of women Engineering Supervisors at commercial stations in 1997. The vast majority of the positions were held by white males. The number of minority group members, however, has increased in the past few years, particularly in the major urban areas, according to industry observers. College enrollment of minorities and women has increased during the last 10 years. The 20 institutions with the most female engineering students in 1994 included the University of Michigan, MIT, and the University of Puerto Rico.

Unions/Associations

Engineering Supervisors are sometimes considered to be management personnel and, as such, are not represented by a union. Others are represented by the International Brotherhood of Electrical Workers (IBEW). Some advance their knowledge and their careers by joining the associations listed in the Assistant Chief Engineering profile.

MAINTENANCE ENGINEER

CAREER PROFILE

Duties: Maintenance and repair of equipment at a TV station or facilities company

Alternate Title(s): Maintenance Technician

Salary Range: $20,000 to $55,000

Employment Prospects: Excellent

Advancement Prospects: Good

Prerequisites:

Education—High school diploma; certification

Experience—Minimum of one year as an Engineering Technician

Special Skills—Technical aptitude; troubleshooting and problem-solving ability; intuition; curiosity

CAREER LADDER

```
┌─────────────────────────────┐
│    Engineering Supervisor    │
└─────────────────────────────┘

┌─────────────────────────────┐
│    Maintenance Engineer      │
└─────────────────────────────┘

┌─────────────────────────────┐
│    Engineering Technician    │
└─────────────────────────────┘
```

Position Description

A Maintenance Engineer is responsible for the repair and maintenance of all broadcast-related equipment at a television station or at a production facilities operation. Under the direction of an Engineering Supervisor, the person in this position performs preventive maintenance on cameras, switchers, audio consoles, video monitors, microphones, videotape recorders, film chains, etc. This individual also designs, modifies, and repairs component parts, systems, and elements used in all production and transmission equipment.

A Maintenance Engineer is a problem solver and troubleshooter and must handle major repair problems, often reconstructing existing equipment to upgrade it to conform to state-of-the-art technology.

Responsibilities of the job are to see that equipment meets all design specifications and that there is as little downtime as possible. This person usually works in the engineering shop, which is often adjacent to the master control room at a TV station. A Maintenance Engineer also works at the transmitter location or (at a production facilities company) in a shop area.

The Maintenance Engineer is usually employed for a regular shift but is often on call to do major and complex repairs that require immediate attention.

Additionally, the Maintenance Engineer

- uses various testing monitors and meters to gauge the performance of equipment;

- maintains an inventory of parts and supplies needed to repair electronic equipment;
- keeps complete records of all equipment maintenance; and
- recommends the replacement of equipment that is outdated or that cannot be repaired.

Salaries

The salaries for Maintenance Engineers are usually higher than those for their peers who are involved in audio, video, or transmitter engineering. In 1997, the average hourly rate was $20.37, according to the International Brotherhood of Electrical Workers (IBEW). The minimum hourly was $10.98, and the maximum was $37.50.

Employment Prospects

Opportunities in all areas of television, video, and telecommunications are excellent. Qualified Maintenance Engineers are extremely difficult to find. Most commercial and public television stations employ four or more such people who are experienced electronic troubleshooters. Maintenance Engineers are also in demand at the production and postproduction facilities companies described in Part II. These houses often have more state-of-the-art equipment and a need for qualified personnel to maintain the gear. Today's TV equipment consists of hundreds of complex, interrelated components with computer elements. The ability to determine which element in the system has malfunctioned and how best to repair it is a rare talent. As a result, Maintenance Engineers are sought by commercial television stations as well as by educational, government, health, and corporate production organizations. Multichannel multipoint distribution service (MMDS) companies, cable TV systems, and low-power television (LPTV) stations also offer employment opportunities. Some Engineering Technicians with the necessary skills, and with further study and training, can become Maintenance Engineers.

Advancement Prospects

Creative and innovative Maintenance Engineers have numerous opportunities to advance their careers. Many assume more responsible positions at smaller market stations or move up at their own stations by becoming Engineering Supervisors in charge of equipment maintenance. In addition, there are opportunities for advancement to Engineering Supervisor jobs in cable and MMDS firms or in education, health, and other nonprofit settings such as government agencies. Positions are also open for Engineering Supervisors at the many private corporations that operate media centers. In addition, many advancement opportunities as Maintenance Engineers, often at higher salaries, are open for those familiar with state-of-the-art equipment at the production and postproduction facilities described in Part II.

Education

A high school diploma and some training in electronics at a vocational or technical school are required. Nearly all Maintenance Engineers have completed a certification study program and passed examinations by industry organizations such as the Society of Broadcast Engineers (SBE) or the International Society of Certified Electronics Technicians (ISCET).

Experience/Skills

A minimum of one year of television maintenance experience is expected in individuals promoted to the position of Maintenance Engineer. A solid knowledge of engineering test equipment and its functions is required. An ability to read and interpret schematic diagrams is useful. A knowledge of computerized electronic gear and "cards" or modules is required.

An inquisitive mind is most useful, as is the ability to analyze electronic problems. Most good Maintenance Engineers are excellent problem solvers who combine experience and intuition when troubleshooting malfunctions in complex electronic gear.

Minority/Women's Opportunities

The majority of Maintenance Engineers in commercial television are white males. In 1996 in commercial television, 14.9 percent of technicians, including Maintenance Engineers, were women, while 23.8 percent were members of minority groups. In public television, 23 percent were women, and 19 percent were minorities in 1994, according to the Corporation for Public Broadcasting.

Unions/Associations

Many of the Maintenance Engineers in commercial television are members of the National Association of Broadcast Employees and Technicians AFL-CIO (NABET) or the IBEW. In public TV most are not represented by a union, except in the major market community stations.

TRANSMITTER ENGINEER

CAREER PROFILE

Duties: Operating and maintaining a television transmitter

Alternate Title(s):   Field Service Technician; Broadcast Engineer

Salary Range: $20,000 to $55,000

Employment Prospects: Good

Advancement Prospects: Good

Prerequisites:

　Education—High school diploma; some technical training; FCC license; certification; bachelor's degree preferable

　Experience—Two years as an Engineering Technician

　Special Skills—Technical aptitude; mechanical skills; diligence

CAREER LADDER

```
┌─────────────────────────────────┐
│      Engineering Supervisor      │
└─────────────────────────────────┘

┌─────────────────────────────────┐
│      Transmitter Engineer        │
└─────────────────────────────────┘

┌─────────────────────────────────┐
│      Engineering Technician      │
└─────────────────────────────────┘
```

Position Description

A Transmitter Engineer is involved in all phases of the direct transmission of a television signal to the viewing audience. The person in this position is responsible for operating a TV transmitter and antenna system in accordance with Federal Communications Commission (FCC) regulations. In co-owned radio-TV stations, this person often operates the AM or FM transmitter as well.

Transmitter Engineers are the unsung heroes of broadcasting. All of the elaborate and expensive production efforts of hundreds of people are useless if the public cannot receive the broadcast signal. The Transmitter Engineer is seldom recognized until the station abruptly goes off the air. Then all hell breaks loose, and professional and rapid repairs and adjustments are made by the Transmitter Engineer to restore the signal. One of the Transmitter Engineer's continuing primary responsibilities is to ensure that such instances are few in number.

In some instances, the transmitter is located with the station's production, administrative, and other engineering facilities in a metropolitan area or suburb. In other circumstances, the transmitter tower and antenna are located in a remote spot (usually on high terrain) away from the main studio. A Transmitter Engineer works at either location, under the direction of the Engineering Supervisor in charge of the transmitter.

Transmitter Engineers are responsible for the actual broadcasting of a TV signal. They also handle the day-to-day maintenance of the transmitters, antennas, and associated equipment. One of the primary responsibilities of the position is to oversee the continuing monitoring of the studio-transmitter link (STL) microwave signal to assure continuous signals for retransmission. In addition, the Transmitter Engineer is often responsible for incoming satellite programs at the transmitter site.

A Transmitter Engineer is assigned to various shifts during the broadcast day. During a typical eight-hour period, responsibilities include making the immediate technical adjustments necessary to keep the station on the air and to ensure uninterrupted operation.

Additionally, the Transmitter Engineer

- makes proof of performance tests, measures transmitter and antenna output, and performs other tests in accordance with FCC regulations;
- conducts daily inspections of building, tower, and antenna lights to ensure continued operation;
- adjusts and repositions the equipment associated with microwave receiving and transmitting parabolas located on towers;
- adjusts and repositions a satellite transmission-receiving unit and associated equipment;

- designs, constructs, and installs prototype or experimental components and equipment and makes test measurements and reports;
- maintains hour-by-hour and program-by-program transmission records according to FCC rules;
- continually monitors all incoming and outgoing transmissions, including satellite, studio, network, or regional broadcasts; and
- keeps an inventory of supplies and parts for all electronic components and systems associated with television transmission.

Salaries

Salaries for Transmitter Engineers in commercial television varied from $20,000 for beginning personnel in small market stations to more than $55,000 in 1997, according to *Broadcast Engineering's* 1997 salary survey.

In public TV, salaries for Broadcast Engineers ranged from $17,900 at small, school-owned stations to $65,659 at major market community stations in 1997, according to the Corporation for Public Broadcasting (CPB). The median salary was $33,543 that year.

Employment Prospects

The possibilities for employment are good. There is generally a scarcity of qualified applicants, and with most broadcast, cable, and independent production facilities planning to install digital and high-definition television (HDTV) transmission capability, those who stay in step with new technologies will be in demand. Most stations employ three or more full-time Transmitter Engineers for various shifts and specific duties, and opportunities exist for an alert Engineering Technician or other individual with some broadcast experience. The remote locations of some transmitters also makes it difficult to attract personnel. In addition, there are new opportunities for Transmitter Engineers at multichannel multipoint distribution service (MMDS) companies and at low-power television (LPTV) stations.

Advancement Prospects

The opportunities for qualified and ambitious Transmitter Engineers to move to more responsible positions within an engineering department are good, but the competition is heavy. All Engineering Supervisors in charge of transmitters, Assistant Chief Engineers, and Chief Engineers have worked as Transmitter Engineers at some time in their careers. Because of their experience in broadcast technology, many

Transmitter Engineers are in demand at MMDS and LPTV operations. In addition, the new full-power television stations that will be constructed in the next few years will require some transmitter personnel.

Education

Most Transmitter Engineers have a high school diploma and some training in broadcast engineering from a trade or vocational school. Some coursework in electrical engineering and physics is also helpful. All have a Restricted Radio Telephone Operator permit from the FCC. While it can be obtained without an examination, most employers also require a certificate from one of the study programs of the industry certificate programs operated by the Society of Broadcast Engineers (SBE) or other groups.

Experience/Skills

Transmitter Engineers usually have at least two years of experience as Engineering Technicians with some of it at transmitters. They must be familiar with the specialized equipment used to keep a TV station on the air. Considerable experience with standard engineering test equipment is also required, as well as some ability at reading schematic diagrams. A Transmitter Engineer should also have some background and skills in the maintenance of electronic equipment.

Most employers seek conscientious, technically oriented individuals who are good with details and at solving problems.

Minority/Women's Opportunities

The vast majority of Transmitter Engineers were white males in 1997, according to industry sources. However, employment of women and minority group members in the position has increased somewhat in the past 10 years. In public television, more than 23 percent of the technicians and salespersons were women, and 18.6 percent, minorities in 1994, according to the CPB.

Unions/Associations

Most Transmitter Engineers at commercial television stations are members of and are represented by the National Association of Broadcast Employees and Technicians AFL-CIO (NABET) or by the International Brotherhood of Electrical Workers (IBEW). While the majority of such workers in public TV are members of neither union, some engineering employees at major market community-owned public televisions stations do belong to one of them.

AUDIO/VIDEO ENGINEER

CAREER PROFILE

Duties: Operating electronic audio and video equipment at a television station, production center, or facilities company

Alternate Title(s): Audio Technician; Video Technician

Salary Range: $20,000 to $70,000

Employment Prospects: Good

Advancement Prospects: Good

Prerequisites:

Education—High school diploma; technical school training; certification; bachelor's degree preferable

Experience—Minimum of one year as an Engineering Technician

Special Skills—Technical aptitude; quick reflexes; versatility

CAREER LADDER

```
┌─────────────────────────────────┐
│      Engineering Supervisor;      │
│       Technical Director;         │
│         Cable Technician          │
└─────────────────────────────────┘

┌─────────────────────────────────┐
│       Audio/Video Engineer        │
└─────────────────────────────────┘

┌─────────────────────────────────┐
│       Engineering Technician      │
└─────────────────────────────────┘
```

Position Description

An Audio/Video Engineer is responsible for operating all electronic controls of audio and video equipment used in a TV station's studio or on-location productions. Audio/Video Engineers are also employed at corporate television media centers, at education, government, and health agencies, and at production/facilities houses. Most engineering departments cross-train personnel, but Audio/Video Engineers usually concentrate on and are more experienced in one of the two functions.

The audio specialist is responsible for the sound portion of a production, which includes voices, music, and special effects. This specialist sets and places microphones, prerecords all necessary material, and, during production, monitors all sound levels and cues records and tapes. During videotape editing of a major show, prerecorded elements such as music may be added to the tape, and some portions may be modified ("sweeten the track") to improve overall sound quality.

The video specialist is in charge of the quality of the pictures that are created. Responsibilities are to set up and align cameras and, during production, control their brightness and color levels. Because of the sensitivity of video equipment, it must be monitored continuously to ensure that the best possible image is being broadcast.

Working in either speciality, the Audio/Video Engineer is a vital part of the production team. The job involves contributing to the overall technical quality of the production by providing professional expertise at particular electronic equipment.

The Audio/Video Engineer usually reports to an Engineering Supervisor who makes shift and project assignments. During rehearsals and actual production, he or she is responsible to the Technical Director.

During a studio production, the Audio/Video Engineer works in the control room. For on-location programs he or she is in a remote truck that contains all of the necessary equipment. In postproduction, the Audio/Video Engineer is usually found in the editing room or in the control room of the editing suite.

Additionally, the Audio/Video Engineer

- maintains and makes minor repairs on audio or video equipment; and
- assists the Director in achieving special sound or visual effects.

Salaries

Salaries for Audio/Video Engineers in commercial TV in 1997 ranged from $25,000 at small market stations for employees with one or two years of experience to $70,000 for experienced people with seniority at major market stations, according to industry sources.

In public television, the 1997 salaries for Audio/Video Engineers ranged from $16,000 for newer employees to $55,000 for experienced personnel with seniority, according to industry sources. The Society of Broadcast Engineers (SBE) reports that one of four engineers was SBC certified in 1997, which increases salaries across the board.

Employment Prospects

Most stations employ six or more Audio/Video Engineers. At least two are assigned to studio productions, one specializing in audio and the other in video. Complex studio or on-location productions require more individuals, particularly in the video area. In addition, the government, health, education, and corporate production operations that produce programs require Audio/Video Engineers. Cable TV systems that produce programs also employ such personnel. Audio/Video Engineers are also in demand at the production and postproduction facilities described in Part II. As a result of all of these possibilities, employment opportunities are quite good.

Advancement Prospects

Qualified Audio/Video Engineers are in demand, and those with experience, especially with digital technologies, have good opportunities to obtain more responsible engineering positions. Many alert individuals are promoted to Engineering Supervisors at their own stations, while some move to larger stations as Technical Directors. The opportunities for employment in middle management engineering positions at corporate production centers and health, government, or educational production studios are also good for those who exhibit leadership abilities. Competent Audio/Video Engineers are also sought as Technicians by cable TV and multichannel multipoint distribution service (MMDS) operations because of their general broadcasting experience, and at low-power television (LPTV) stations. Some move to higher-paying positions at production and postproduction facilities companies in New York or Los Angeles.

Education

A high school diploma and some training at a technical or vocational school are usually necessary to obtain the position of Engineering Technician and to be promoted to Audio/Video Engineer at a TV station. Some applicants study and receive a certificate from one of the programs offered by the SBE. With the increased sophistication and simplicity of the newer production equipment, however, many Audio/Video Engineers today do not have formal training in engineering but may have a bachelor's degree in mass communications. This is particularly true at corporate TV centers, in education, health, and government agencies, and at production and postproduction facilities.

Experience/Skills

A minimum of one year's experience as an Engineering Technician is usually required for promotion to the position. The individual must be thoroughly familiar with the operation of all audio and video equipment used in a television production and must be capable of routine maintenance.

In promoting personnel to the position, most Technical Directors and Engineering Supervisors look for young people who are versatile but display a particular skill in the operation of computerized audio or video equipment. Audio personnel should possess a discriminating "ear," and for both positions quick reflexes and an understanding and feel for television production are required.

Minority/Women's Opportunities

While employment of women and minority group members has increased in the position, the majority of Audio/Video Engineers in commercial television were white males in 1997. In public TV, 23 percent of the Audio/Video Engineer (and related) positions were held by women in 1997, and 18.6 percent by members of minorities, according to the Corporation for Public Broadcasting.

Unions/Associations

Many Audio/Video Engineers in commercial television are members of the National Association of Broadcast Employees and Technicians AFL-CIO (NABET), or of the International Brotherhood of Electrical Workers (IBEW). In public TV, some employees of major market stations also belong to one of these unions.

VIDEOTAPE ENGINEER/EDITOR

CAREER PROFILE

Duties: Operating videotape machines at a television station or production/facilities center

Alternate Title(s): Videotape Operator; Videotape Editor; Film/Tape Editor; Operating Technician

Salary Range: $16,000 to $55,000

Employment Prospects: Good

Advancement Prospects: Good

Prerequisites:

Education—High school diploma; some technical training

Experience—Minimum of one year as an Engineering Technician

Special Skills—Technical aptitude; creativity; ability to work with a variety of people

CAREER LADDER

```
┌─────────────────────────────────┐
│      Engineering Supervisor      │
└─────────────────────────────────┘

┌─────────────────────────────────┐
│    Videotape Engineer/Editor     │
└─────────────────────────────────┘

┌─────────────────────────────────┐
│      Engineering Technician      │
└─────────────────────────────────┘
```

Position Description

A Videotape Engineer/Editor is responsible for the setup and operation of all types of videotape machines and for recording, playback, and editing at a television station. Videotape Engineer/Editors are also employed at postproduction facilities companies. In such environments, the emphasis is on editing rather than operating. Responsibilities also include the evaluation of videotapes, the duplication (dubbing) of taped material, and the assembling of videotapes for production use and broadcast.

Videotape Engineer/Editors record programs being produced in studios at their stations or those from networks and other outside sources. They also assemble and edit commercials, promotional spots, and station breaks for each day's broadcasting. They work with Producers, Associate Producers, Directors, Assistant Directors, and Reporters in editing various pretaped segments into a finished program. They also provide dubbing services for the programming and sales departments and for the promotion and publicity departments.

At most television stations, the Videotape Engineer/Editor works in a clean and secure environment adjacent to the master control room. Two or more Videotape Engineer/Editors are assigned by an Engineering Supervisor to each shift. Depending on the number of machines and the production and dubbing schedule, the Videotape Engineer/Editors work on various assignments during each shift.

Videotape Engineer/Editors are among the busiest individuals in the engineering department during a broadcast day. It is their responsibility to juggle various videotape requirements among machines and to determine priorities necessary for a smooth and professional videotape operation.

Additionally, the Videotape Engineer/Editor

- sets up, aligns, adjusts, cleans, and monitors traditional and digital video machines prior to operation;
- files technical and malfunction reports; and
- works on remote productions (outside the studio).

Salaries

Salaries for operating technicians, which include Videotape Engineer/Editors, averaged $24,469 in 1997, according to the National Association of Broadcasters (NAB). In public television, 1997 salaries for the position ranged from $16,000 at small stations to $48,000 for those with seniority at larger stations, according to industry sources.

At postproduction/facilities houses, extremely skilled video editors earned a reported $60 per hour on a freelance basis in 1997. Since the work is almost constant, one can earn from $45,000 to more than $80,000 per year as a top editor in New York or Los Angeles.

Salaries for Editors in corporate television ranged from $22,000 to $65,000 in 1997, according to industry observers.

Employment Prospects

The majority of productions in today's television environment are prerecorded. As a result, the need for Videotape Engineer/Editors has increased dramatically in recent years. Videotape and digital format editing has become an art form in itself.

A station usually employs three or more Videotape Engineer/Editors. Large stations employ as many as 15, to cover all shifts and contingencies. Some Videotape Engineer/Editors are recruited from other stations. Opportunities for employment in this position are also available at government, education, or corporate organizations that are involved in production. Some cable TV and multichannel multipoint distribution service (MMDS) operations and low-power TV (LPTV) stations that originate programming on videotape also require Videotape Engineer/Editors. Additional opportunities are available in the production and postproduction facilities houses described in Part II. The positions usually involve sophisticated editing techniques with computerized electronic editing equipment, including digital nonlinear editing systems and digital tape format (DTF). The opportunities for Editors specializing in electronic graphics or art in the major markets' postproduction facilities are excellent. On-line editing jobs at smaller operations are also available.

Advancement Prospects

The chances for advancement from the position are generally good. Talented Videotape Engineer/Editors may seek advancement to the position of Engineering Supervisor. Others move to smaller market stations in more senior positions to advance their careers. Some use their skills and experience to move to more responsible positions at large advertising agencies that operate their own production or engineering units. There are also some chances for moving to a network or to more responsible engineering positions at MMDS and cable TV operations. Many Editors specialize in special effects, animation, or graphics and move to larger production and postproduction facilities companies to advance their careers. Some open their own video editing "boutiques" or teach advanced editing and postproduction skills at local colleges.

Education

Most employers require a minimum of a high school education and some post–high school technical or vocational training in employing or promoting personnel to the position. Many prefer that applicants have studied and passed a certification program from one of the industry organizations such as the Society of Broadcast Engineers (SBE) and undergone training for the emerging technologies. The dramatic increase in sophisticated videotape and editing devices has made them easier to operate once the systems have been learned. Many Videotape Engineer/Editors enter the field from production, art, and film backgrounds.

Experience/Skills

The position is usually not an entry-level one. Most Videotape Engineer/Editors are promoted to the spot after a year or two as Engineering Technicians or in some other engineering position at the station or facility. Sound knowledge of and experience with all types of videotape machines and computerized editing equipment is required, as well as basic engineering knowledge of other types of technical equipment.

Videotape Engineer/Editors must have technical aptitude and feel comfortable in working with broadcast equipment. They must also be capable of working well with a variety of nonengineering personnel in editing productions and must possess some creative instincts in assembling prerecorded segments into a polished program. A knowledge of the aesthetics of film editing is helpful.

Minority/Women's Opportunities

An increasing number of minority group members and women have assumed the position of Videotape Engineer/Editor in commercial television during the past 10 years, although one industry observer estimated that minorities and women still represented less than 5 percent of all broadcast engineers, which include Videotape Engineer/Editors, in 1997.

Unions/Associations

Many Videotape Engineer/Editors in commercial television are members of the International Brotherhood of Electrical Workers (IBEW) or of the National Association of Broadcast Employees and Technicians AFL-CIO (NABET). In public broadcasting, some individuals at large community-owned stations are members of one of these unions, but most are not represented by any group.

MASTER CONTROL ENGINEER

CAREER PROFILE

Duties: Coordinating all audio and video inputs for broadcasting at a station or network center

Alternate Title(s): Master Control Operator; Air Operator

Salary Range: $25,000 to $40,000+

Employment Prospects: Fair

Advancement Prospects: Fair

Prerequisites:

　Education—High school diploma; some technical training; FCC license

　Experience—Minimum of one year as an Engineering Technician

　Special Skills—Knowledge of broadcast equipment; decision-making ability; quick reflexes; sound judgment

CAREER LADDER

```
┌─────────────────────────────────────┐
│   Operations Manager; Engineering    │
│             Supervisor;              │
│         Technical Director;          │
│        Audio/Video Engineer          │
└─────────────────────────────────────┘

┌─────────────────────────────────────┐
│      Master Control Engineer         │
└─────────────────────────────────────┘

┌─────────────────────────────────────┐
│       Engineering Technician         │
└─────────────────────────────────────┘
```

Position Description

The Master Control Engineer is charged with the successful coordination of all audio and video input from various sources at a television station and with delivering their signals to the transmitter for broadcasting. As the chief operator in the nerve center of a TV station, the person in this position is directly responsible for ensuring that all transmissions are made in accordance with Federal Communications Commission (FCC) regulations.

The Master Control Engineer combines videotape, studio and on-location feeds, network programs, and prerecorded audio announcements. This individual also cues and rolls film and videotape programs and switches video and audio inputs from different sources. Another important function is to ensure the smooth transition from one program to another and to control the switching to and from station breaks. This includes coordinating the broadcasting of commercials, public service messages, slides, and promotional tapes, as well as cueing Announcers.

The Master Control Engineer is also responsible for handling all emergency situations, such as the loss of picture, program overruns and underruns, and equipment malfunctions. Immediate corrections have to be made so that broadcast interruptions are kept to a minimum.

In assuring the smooth transmission of all of the station's programming, the Master Control Engineer works with the Operations Manager, Videotape Engineer/Editors, the Film/Tape Librarian, Announcers, and the Traffic/Continuity Supervisor.

The Master Control Engineer position is more of an operational rather than a technical position. It involves the coordination of the activities and work output of many people, as well as the mixing and merging of a number of pieces of electronic equipment. The Master Control Engineer position is a cross between a logistician and a conductor, with responsibilities for the on-air look of the station and its public image as a smooth-running professional operation.

Additionally, the Master Control Engineer

- ensures that all scheduled program elements are ready prior to broadcast;
- operates the master control switcher and audio console during station breaks; and
- maintains the official station log and discrepancy records.

Salaries

Master Control Engineers are not as well rewarded financially as many of their peers. Salaries ranged from $25,000 to

$40,000 in commercial television in 1997, according to industry sources. In public TV, salaries ranged from $15,000 at small market stations to $60,000 for people with experience and seniority at major market community stations in 1997, according to industry observers.

Employment Prospects

Most stations employ three or more Master Control Engineers who work eight-hour day and night shifts. In complex major market station operations, two or more Engineers are usually assigned to each shift. The opportunities are fair for bright, alert Engineering Technicians who demonstrate good judgment in the operation of television equipment to become Master Control Engineers. Part-time weekend and holiday work is also available for Master Control Engineers.

Master Control Engineers are also employed at the few education, government, and health operations that regularly transmit programming. They are also employed at videoconferencing origination companies and at large national cable satellite program services, such as HBO or Showtime, and at the headquarters of satellite news networks.

Advancement Prospects

Opportunities for advancement are fair. Many Master Control Engineers move to smaller market stations as Operations Managers or become Engineering Supervisors at their own stations. Others advance to positions as Technical Directors or Audio/Video Engineers, usually at higher salaries. A few who have the requisite skills become Maintenance Engineers.

Education

Most Engineering Supervisors require a minimum of a high school education and some technical training in promoting employees to the position of Master Control Engineer. A Restricted Radio Telephone Operator Permit from the FCC is often required.

With the increased sophistication of equipment and its ease of operation, as well as the increasing trend toward automation, some stations require less background in engineering. Some Master Control Operators are recent college graduates from radio-TV or communications curricula with little engineering training.

Experience/Skills

A minimum of one year as an Engineering Technician is usually required for promotion to the position. Some major market stations require more engineering experience.

Master Control Engineers must have working knowledge of the limitations and operating characteristics of a wide variety of audio and video equipment. They must be alert and capable of making decisions quickly, must have good reflexes, and must display sound judgment.

Minority/Women's Opportunities

The opportunities for women and minority group members in obtaining the position in commercial TV have increased in the past 10 years, according to industry sources. The position, however, is still largely occupied by white males.

Unions/Associations

Some Master Control Engineers in commercial television were members of the National Association of Broadcast Employees and Technicians AFL-CIO (NABET) in 1997. Most personnel at PTV stations do not belong to a union.

ENGINEERING TECHNICIAN

CAREER PROFILE

Duties: Carrying out various engineering duties at a television station or production facilities center

Alternate Title(s): Engineer; Technician; Operating Engineer; Operator Technician

Salary Range: $21,000 to $72,000

Employment Prospects: Good

Advancement Prospects: Good

Prerequisites:

Education—High school diploma; some technical school

Experience—Familiarity with electronic and technical equipment

Special Skills—Mechanical aptitude

CAREER LADDER

```
┌─────────────────────────────────────┐
│      Audio/Video, Maintenance,       │
│           Master Control,            │
│  Transmitter, or Videotape Engineer  │
└─────────────────────────────────────┘

┌─────────────────────────────────────┐
│       Engineering Technician         │
└─────────────────────────────────────┘

┌─────────────────────────────────────┐
│     High School/Technical School     │
└─────────────────────────────────────┘
```

Position Description

Engineering Technician is usually the entry-level position in the engineering department at a commercial or public television station. Engineering Technicians are also employed in the education, health, and government organizations involved in television, at the larger independent production and postproduction facilities companies, and at low-power television (LPTV) stations. The person in this job is responsible for performing various technical tasks in one or more units of the operation. Engineering Technicians are responsible for the operation, maintenance, setup and construction of equipment. They install components and systems and collate and summarize test data. They also work on various pieces of equipment, including cameras, video and audio tape recorders, microphones, audio switchers and mixers, video switchers and special effects boards, transmission equipment, audio and video testing devices, lighting equipment, and slide and film projectors.

The average TV station employs several Engineering Technicians in various capacities. It is usually the goal of the engineering department to cross-train them so that each person can gain experience in as many areas as possible.

Engineering Technicians usually report to a Technical Director or to an Engineering Supervisor. After showing talent in a particular area, they are often trained to become Audio/Video, Maintenance, Master Control, Transmitter, or Videotape Engineer/Editors. In some stations where Camera

Operators are considered part of the engineering department, an Engineering Technician can also be trained for that position.

The responsibilities of the engineering department are diverse. The Engineering Technician can, therefore, work in almost any area of the station or production/facilities center and may be assigned to a studio, the videotape room, the transmitter, the master control room, the maintenance shop, or an on-location spot outside the station.

Additionally, the Engineering Technician

- collects engineering records, including Federal Communications Commission (FCC) program and transmitter logs, facilities utilization forms, and testing and monitoring reports; and
- maintains an inventory of engineering supplies and replacement parts.

Salaries

Salaries for Engineering Technicians are fairly good. The average hourly rate was $22.82 in 1998, according to the International Brotherhood of Electrical Workers (IBEW). In union shops the hourly rate ranged from $10.45 to $35.00 for those with experience and seniority.

Salaries in public television in 1998 tended to be lower, according to industry observers.

Salaries for Technicians at corporate television centers and at education, government, and health media operations ranged from $16,000 to $45,000 in 1998, according to industry observers.

Employment Prospects

There are usually more beginning engineering positions open than there are qualified candidates to fill them. The average commercial or public television station employs more than 12 Engineering Technicians, and many major market stations have more than 60 on the payroll. Opportunities are also available at production and postproduction/facilities houses, at education, government, and health operations involved in television (described in Part II), and at low- power television (LPTV) stations. The opportunities for bright, capable, and mechanically and electronically oriented young people are excellent.

Advancement Prospects

The opportunities for advancement to other Engineering positions are good. With application and diligence, an Engineering Technician can expect to be promoted to Audio/Video, Maintenance, Master Control, Transmitter, or Videotape Engineer/Editor after a year or two of experience.

In time, many Engineering Technicians move further up the career ladder to become Engineering Supervisors or Assistant Chief Engineers. Some are promoted to more responsible positions within their stations or move to better-paying positions at major market stations. The competition, however, is heavy. Some people seek promotion opportunities in cable TV, multichannel multipoint distribution service (MMDS) operations, or at large production/facilities companies.

Education

A high school diploma and some electronics training in a technical or vocational school are required by most employ-ers. Some stations operate intern programs to help train prospective employees. Individuals who have studied for and passed a certificate program from an industry organization particularly with digital technologies, are especially sought by employers.

Experience/Skills

Most stations do not require extensive experience for the position of Engineering Technician. Some interest in and understanding of electronics and the repair of mechanical and audiovisual equipment is helpful. A basic grasp of physics and the ability to read schematic diagrams are also useful. An aptitude for mathematics is helpful. Employers seek diligent, alert, and ambitious people who have a love of electronics and who enjoy working with equipment.

Minority/Women's Opportunities

The opportunities for members of minorities and women are excellent. An increasing number of minority group members has entered the field in the last 10 years and, according to the FCC, they held 23.8 percent of the Technician positions in 1996. While the increase in the employment of women has not been as rapid, more are being hired. Women occupied 14.9 percent of the technical positions (including Engineering Technician) in 1996 in commercial television, according to the FCC.

In public TV, 23.1 percent of the positions were held by women, and 18.6 percent, by minority group members in 1994, according to the CPB.

Unions/Associations

Many Engineering Technicians in commercial television are represented by the National Association of Broadcast Employees and Technicians AFL-CIO (NABET) or the IBEW. Some public television employees are represented by these unions, but most work in nonunion stations.

TECHNICAL DIRECTOR

CAREER PROFILE

Duties: Overseeing technical quality of a television production; operating production switcher

Alternate Title(s): Switcher

Salary Range: $21,000 to $52,000+

Employment Prospects: Fair

Advancement Prospects: Good

Prerequisites:

Education—High school diploma; some technical training

Experience—Minimum of one year as an Audio/Video Engineer, Lighting Director, or Camera Operator

Special Skills—Knowledge of TV production and engineering; quick reflexes; leadership qualities; cooperativeness

CAREER LADDER

```
┌─────────────────────────────┐
│   Engineering Supervisor;    │
│       Unit Manager;          │
│     Assistant Director       │
└─────────────────────────────┘

┌─────────────────────────────┐
│                             │
│     Technical Director       │
│                             │
└─────────────────────────────┘

┌─────────────────────────────┐
│    Audio/Video Engineer;     │
│      Lighting Director       │
│      Camera Operator         │
└─────────────────────────────┘
```

Position Description

The Technical Director is an important element in the production of a television show. The major responsibility of the position is to oversee the technical quality of the program and operate the production switcher, the unit that controls which camera images and special effects are broadcast or transmitted to videotape.

Technical Directors are employed at public and commercial television stations and at the large production/facilities companies described in Part II. They operate in a studio location or in a remote truck. A few education, government, and health organizations involved in larger productions also employ Technical Directors.

The Technical Director is the principal link between the Director and the technical crew assigned to the production. The individual usually supervises from three to nine engineers and assistants. At stations that do not have a Lighting Director, the Technical Director is often responsible for fulfilling that role.

During the preproduction stage, the Technical Director analyzes specific production requirements and makes technical recommendations to the Director. During rehearsals and actual production, the Technical Director usually sits on the right of the Director in the control room, transmits instructions (via headphones) to Camera Operators about the position of cameras, and directs all other studio and control room technical personnel. Other duties include operating the production switcher and following the Director's instructions about changing from one camera shot to another and about selecting other picture sources, such as film and videotape. The Technical Director also presets and controls the switcher for special electronic effects and transitions called for by the Director.

The person in this position normally reports to an Engineering Supervisor and is assigned to specific productions. During actual production, the Technical Director reports to the program's Director. In smaller stations where there is no staff Technical Director, the responsibilities are often shared by an Engineering Supervisor and an Assistant Director. Some midsize stations utilize a switcher rather than a Technical Director. The job is seldom supervisory in nature and does not demand the engineering expertise of a Technical Director. In those situations, the switcher often reports to the Production Manager for assignments but to the Director of the program during production. In very small stations, Directors frequently do their own switching.

Additionally, the Technical Director

- provides technical leadership during production emergencies;

- assigns and trains studio and control room crew members and monitors their performance; and
- prepares reports on the facilities used in a production for the Engineering Supervisor or Assistant Chief Engineer.

Salaries

Salaries for the position in commercial TV averaged $26,840 in 1997. The average starting salary was $21,184, according to the National Association of Broadcasters (NAB). In stations where Technical Directors are represented by a union, the average hourly rate was $28.74 in 1998.

Employment Prospects

The position of Technical Director is not an entry-level job. Some experience in TV engineering, and specifically in studio engineering, is usually required. Although some major market commercial and public television stations with heavy production schedules employ four or more Technical Directors, most large stations require only two on staff. In many smaller stations, there are none. Technical Directors are also employed by networks and major independent production/facilities companies, but they tend to hire experienced people. The opportunities for employment are generally only fair.

Advancement Prospects

Technical Directors usually seek advancement to the position of Engineering Supervisor or, in some major production organizations, they are promoted to Unit Manager. Since a good part of the job involves the positioning of cameras and the preparation of shots, many individuals use their experience to move into Director positions, usually by first becoming Assistant Directors. Some Technical Directors move to smaller market stations at higher salaries and in more responsible technical or production positions. Those occupying the position usually view it as a transitional job that will help them to move to more responsible positions in engineering or production. The opportunities are good for ambitious individuals with initiative.

Education

The minimum requirements for the position are a high school diploma and some education at a vocational or technical school. Courses in TV production techniques can be helpful.

Experience/Skills

Most Engineering Supervisors require a minimum of one or two years of experience as an Audio/Video Engineer, Lighting Director, or Camera Operator when promoting individuals to the position of Technical Director. Experience in professional studio and remote TV production is a must.

To be effective, the Technical Director must have a thorough understanding of all production and engineering aspects of putting together a television program. In addition, the applicant must be able to react to directions quickly and to make decisions rapidly in pressured situations. An ability to lead and to cooperate with other crew members is also important.

Minority/Women's Opportunities

There were only a handful of women employed as Technical Directors in commercial television in 1998. Male minority group members, however, are increasingly represented in the position, according to industry sources. Efforts such as the National Action Council for Minorities in Engineering's scholarship program and similar undertakings by the National Science Foundation aim to promote diversity within the technical professions.

Unions/Associations

Technical Directors in commercial TV are considered part of the engineering staff and are usually represented by the International Brotherhood of Electrical Workers (IBEW) or the National Association of Broadcast Employees and Technicians AFL-CIO (NABET). In public television, they are usually not represented by a union. Switchers are seldom represented by a union.

CAMERA OPERATOR

CAREER PROFILE

Duties: Setting up and operating television cameras on location or in a studio

Alternate Title(s): Cameraman; Cinevideographer

Salary Range: $18,000 to $60,000+

Employment Prospects: Fair

Advancement Prospects: Good

Prerequisites:

Education—High school diploma; training in photography or audiovisual equipment helpful

Experience—Some TV production, usually as a Production Assistant

Special Skills—Creativity; versatility; fast reflexes

CAREER LADDER

```
┌─────────────────────────────────┐
│  Floor Manager; Lighting Director; │
│      Audio/Video Engineer         │
└─────────────────────────────────┘

┌─────────────────────────────────┐
│        Camera Operator            │
└─────────────────────────────────┘

┌─────────────────────────────────┐
│      Production Assistant;         │
│     Engineering Technician         │
└─────────────────────────────────┘
```

Position Description

A Camera Operator is responsible for operating a television camera during the rehearsals for, and the actual production of, a TV program. This may be a full-size camera mounted on a tripod, dolly or crane, or a smaller minicam or Electronic News Gathering (ENG) camera used for on-location shooting.

Most operations have a minimum of two Camera Operators on staff. At some stations, more than eight are employed for various shifts and assignments. For some simple productions, only one or two cameras are used. For more complex programs, five or more cover various elements of the program.

Camera Operators are sometimes considered part of the engineering department and report to an Engineering Supervisor. At other stations, they are members of the production department and report to the Production Manager. Many commercial stations assign some Camera Operators to the news department, where they are given specific assignments by the Assistant News Director. In such circumstances, they operate more independently as Cinematographers/Videographers.

In most situations, however, the Camera Operator receives directions (via an intercom system and headset) from the Director or Technical Director during rehearsal and actual production of a program in the studio or on a remote. In news gathering operations, the Camera Operator usually follows the instructions of a Reporter when covering an on-location story. As an integral part of a television studio or remote production team, the Camera Operator is important to the continuing flow and appearance of any show or newscast. In addition to responding immediately to the Director, a good Camera Operator finds new, interesting, and imaginative angles and shots for use during a production.

Additionally, the Camera Operator

- assists the Audio/Video Engineer in the setup, technical check, and simple maintenance of television cameras;
- assists the Lighting Director in the setup of scenery, lighting equipment, and other accessories prior to a production; and
- assists the Floor Manager or Unit Manager in the strike (dismantling) of a production.

Salaries

The International Brotherhood of Electrical Workers (IBEW) reported that in 1998, camera operators' minimum hourly rate was $8.55, and the maximum, $29.18. The average hourly rate was $15.89. In public television, salaries ranged from $18,000 to $40,000, according to industry estimates.

Employment Prospects

Camera Operator is considered an entry-level job at some stations but, more often, an experienced Production assistant is promoted to the position. Sometimes an Engineering Technician is assigned to the job after some experience at a station. The number of openings depends on the amount of production done. Job openings for Camera Operators are particularly good at stations with a heavy news schedule, where the news department alone may employ five to eight news crews. Networks often employ more than 200 Camera Operators on a full-time basis. Camera Operator positions are also available at education, government, and health television studios and at many independent production firms. Cable systems that originate productions also employ full-time camera people. Because of competition, however, employment prospects are considered to be fair.

Advancement Prospects

Chances for moving up in television are good. Most Camera Operators seek a career in production. The usual advancement path for production-oriented individuals is to Floor Manager or Lighting Director. In stations where a Camera Operator starts as an Engineering Technician and is considered part of the engineering department, the track is often to Audio/Video Engineer. A Camera Operator often advances to a Cinematographer/Videographer position in the news or documentary unit of a television station, where there is more judgment and creativity required as well as increased independence.

Some advancement opportunities are also available in production or engineering roles at government, health, or education organizations.

Education

A high school diploma is required by most employers. Additionally, some training in photography (still or motion) or audiovisual equipment is helpful. Some employers seek evidence of study toward a certificate from one of the industry engineering organizations. Others seek bright young people who have had some informal training with home video and film cameras.

Experience/Skills

Most Camera Operators have some experience in television production, usually as Production Assistants, prior to assuming the position. They need to have a creative sense of composition and an ability to initiate imaginative angles when operating a TV camera. Camera Operators should have the ability to react rapidly to Directors during a production. A Camera Operator should also have considerable physical and mental stamina and be alert and versatile.

Minority/Women's Opportunities

Although there has been some increase in the number of women holding the job in commercial television during the past 10 years, the majority of Camera Operators in 1997 were male, according to industry sources. Minority male employment in the position has increased greatly in the past few years. In public television, many of the positions were occupied by women and minority group members in 1997, according to industry sources.

Unions/Associations

At some commercial television stations the position of Camera Operator is represented by the IBEW or by the National Association of Broadcast Employees and Technicians AFL-CIO (NABET). In public TV, the majority of Camera Operators are not represented by a union.

GENERAL SALES MANAGER

CAREER PROFILE

Duties: Responsibility for producing all advertising revenue for a television station

Alternate Title(s): Sales Director; Advertising Sales Manager

Salary Range: $35,000 to $150,000+

Employment Prospects: Fair

Advancement Prospects: Good

Prerequisites:

Education—Undergraduate degree in marketing, advertising, or business administration preferable

Experience—Minimum of five years of experience in broadcast advertising sales

Special Skills—Leadership qualities; aggressiveness; poise; perseverance; organizational ability; interpersonal skills

CAREER LADDER

```
┌─────────────────────────────────┐
│        General Manager           │
└─────────────────────────────────┘

┌─────────────────────────────────┐
│      General Sales Manager       │
└─────────────────────────────────┘

┌─────────────────────────────────┐
│     Assistant Sales Manager      │
└─────────────────────────────────┘
```

Position Description

The General Sales Manager of a commercial television station is responsible for generating the advertising revenue that enables a station to pay for programming, salaries, technical equipment, and operations by dealing with a limited inventory of commercial air time for advertising sales. The General Sales Manager works closely with the Program Manager and the General Manager in selecting programs during and around which such advertising can be sold.

A General Sales Manager is in day-to-day charge of all advertising sales activities and of the station's sales staff, usually from 2 to 15 or more employees. The General Sales Manager's duties entail administering and coordinating all local, regional, and national programming and spot commercial sales accounts with clients, advertising agencies, and the station's national representative (rep). This includes developing the station's overall advertising sales plan and targets, previewing programs, and directly supervising the effectiveness of all sales efforts.

The General Sales Manager reports to the General Manager of the station and, with that person, establishes the station's advertising policies. A General Sales Manager must know the local market and the competition in order to establish advertising rates that are competitive. In addition, the

General Sales Manager develops audiovisual and statistical sales tools to assist Salespersons in their work.

A General Sales Manager must be aware of economic factors, retailing, merchandising, barter and trade arrangements, programming trends, and audience demographics and psychographics at both the local and national levels and must work closely with advertising agencies, reps, and local clients to ensure a continuing and profitable relationship.

Additionally, the General Sales Manager

- monitors Arbitron and Nielsen ratings and research studies of the station's audience;
- supervises all commercial scheduling and copy writing;
- services top agency accounts in order to keep close to the selling scene; and
- ensures that the commercial time sold by the station conforms with National Association of Broadcasters (NAB) guidelines, Federal Trade Commission (FTC) regulations, and station policies.

Salaries

The General Sales Manager in a local commercial television station is usually the second highest paid employee. The compensation has increased steadily since 1980 and is expected to increase even more in the future.

According to the NAB in 1997, most General Sales Managers were paid a salary plus other compensation usually comprised of commission and bonus. The average salary that year was $87,481, augmented by $38,841 in other compensation.

Employment Prospects

The opportunity to acquire a position as a General Sales Manager in a commercial TV station is more limited than for other management personnel, and the competition is heavy. There is little turnover in the position.

Most General Sales Managers are promoted from within a television station organization, having first served as Assistant Sales Managers. Some are recruited from the sales staffs of larger market stations or even from competitors in the local community. Others are recruited from advertising sales forces in print or other media.

Advancement Prospects

The opportunities for promotion for General Sales Managers are good. The typical move is to the position of General Manager, although some individuals transfer to larger markets, rep firms, group-owned stations, or even into advertising sales management at a network.

The skills of a General Sales Manager are easily transferable to cable TV systems. Although opportunities are good, the compensation levels are not as high as in commercial television.

Education

A degree is less important in obtaining the job of General Sales Manager than is the ability to sell effectively and consistently. An applicant with a degree, however, is usually chosen over someone without a degree.

An undergraduate degree in marketing, advertising, or business administration provides an excellent background for entering into sales positions and for eventual advancement to a higher position. In larger market stations, some General Sales Managers have a master's degree in business administration.

Experience/Skills

Most General Sales Managers are expected to be profit-oriented administrators with proven track records. Successful experience in TV advertising sales is a prime requisite, as is the ability to organize and motivate a sales staff and to develop the station's sales efforts. The General Sales Manager usually has at least five years of successful TV sales experience as an Assistant Sales Manager, a good feel for organization and logistics, and an outgoing and positive personality.

Most successful General Sales Managers are able to analyze research data easily and are experienced in marketing, merchandising, and retailing. They are capable of and enthusiastically interested in actual sales. As a group, they are aggressive, proficient at controlling expenses, poised, and persistent.

Minority/Women's Opportunities

There has been considerable improvement in the opportunities for women and minority group members in the television sales field in the past four years. The majority of General Sales Managers in 1997, however, were white males. According to Federal Communications Commission (FCC) statistics, the percentage of women in all sales positions in commercial TV increased from 50.6 percent in 1992 to 53.3 percent in 1996. The percentage of minority group members in all commercial TV sales positions rose also, from 12 percent in 1992 to 14 percent in 1996. The General Sales Manager is a senior position. In 1996, 35.4 percent of all officials and managers, which include General Sales Managers, in broadcast television were women, and 14 percent were minorities, according to the FCC.

Unions/Associations

There are no unions or professional organizations that represent General Sales Managers.

ASSISTANT SALES MANAGER

CAREER PROFILE

Duties: Assisting the General Sales Manager in local and national advertising sales

Alternate Title(s): Local Sales Manager; National Sales Manager

Salary Range: $28,000 to $90,000+

Employment Prospects: Good

Advancement Prospects: Good

Prerequisites:

Education—High school diploma and some college; undergraduate degree in marketing or advertising preferable

Experience—Minimum of three years in television advertising sales

Special Skills—Analytical mind; motivational talent; leadership and supervisory abilities

CAREER LADDER

```
┌─────────────────────────────────┐
│      General Sales Manager       │
└─────────────────────────────────┘

┌─────────────────────────────────┐
│      Assistant Sales Manager     │
└─────────────────────────────────┘

┌─────────────────────────────────┐
│      Advertising Salesperson     │
└─────────────────────────────────┘
```

Position Description

An Assistant Sales Manager at a commercial television station assists the General Sales Manager in all aspects of the station's advertising sales activities. This person relieves the General Sales Manager of some burdensome details and personnel management so that the senior person can concentrate on long range sales planning. The Assistant helps the General Sales Manager establish and monitor quotas for each Advertising Salesperson and assigns each to particular accounts. An Assistant Sales Manager is usually an experienced professional who understands both the advertising business and the local market.

As a rule, an Assistant Sales Manager can be responsible for one particular account area, such as local, national, or spot sales, in addition to more general duties. In many large market stations, there are two or more Assistant Sales Managers, often with titles reflecting their area of responsibility, such as Local Sales Manager or National Sales Manager. When Assistant Sales Managers are responsible for local sales activities, they oversee local Advertising Salespersons and accounts. In developing, selling, and servicing such accounts they supervise from three to eight Salespersons and keep them informed about changing station policies and sales procedures. On a daily basis, they meet with the station's sales staff.

Assistant Sales Managers may specialize in air time for specific types of programs, such as news, special events, or sports. In some stations, they serve as troubleshooters in dealing with difficult accounts or in soliciting new business. They are often assigned direct consumer response sales or concentrate on persuading advertisers who are traditionally print-oriented to buy ads on television. In some of the larger stations, an Assistant Sales Manager is in charge of supervising the servicing of all accounts after they are sold.

Although the position is generally a supervisory one, Assistant Sales Managers also actively sell air time on a day-to-day basis and are responsible for continued sales to their own accounts. They are usually in charge of all sales efforts in the absence of the General Sales Manager. Additionally, the Assistant Sales Manager

- oversees all advertising proposals and contracts;
- maintains advertiser, agency, and prospect files;
- analyzes Arbitron and Nielsen ratings statistics;
- prepares competitive products studies, internal sales analyzes, and reports for specific clients; and
- monitors all available advertising air time.

Salaries

Most Assistant Sales Managers are paid on a salary-plus-commission, salary-plus-bonus, or salary-bonus-commission basis. Most of the local and national sales managers were compensated under such plans in 1997, according to the

National Association of Broadcasters (NAB). Commissions range from 10 to 25 percent with the majority at the rate of 15 percent of the advertising income received by the station. In almost all cases, Advertising Salespersons are allowed to retain their sales accounts upon promotion to Assistant Sales Manager and receive commissions accordingly. Upon the assumption of administrative duties, the initial employment contract is renegotiated to provide for a larger base salary and smaller commissions. Sometimes the commission rate is raised appreciably and the Assistant Sales Manager is given a modest salary increase.

Combined earnings for Assistant Sales Managers averaged $102,418 for local Sales Managers and $97,353 for national Sales Managers in 1997, according to the NAB. Most individuals have expense accounts, and many have company-paid life insurance and group health plans. The majority participate in company pension plans.

Employment Prospects

The possibilities are good for securing this position. Nearly 10 percent of the staffs of local TV stations are in the sales department. In general, however, only the brightest and most successful and experienced people within sales are promoted to Assistant Sales Manager. The relative scarcity of good salespeople and the high turnover rate in this area create good openings, but competition is strong.

Assistant Sales Managers are usually chosen from Advertising Salespersons within the station who have good sales records and experience with the department. Some are recruited from other stations where they have been successful in specific sales areas.

Advancement Prospects

Advancement opportunities are good. Most Assistant Sales Managers actively seek the position of General Sales Manager and, ultimately, of General Manager. The chances at commercial stations, however, are limited by the number of TV stations on the air and those that will be constructed in the next few years. Only the very able make the transition. Some Assistant Sales Managers move to smaller market stations as General Sales Managers or to network or syndicated program sales positions.

The skills and experience acquired in television time sales are readily transferable to other media-related industries. Cable television systems are increasingly moving into advertising sales, and they often recruit people who are experienced in TV advertising.

Education

A minimum of a high school diploma is usually required, along with some college work. Many employers prefer to hire and promote people who have an undergraduate degree in marketing or advertising. Some courses in business administration and communications are also helpful. In general, however, a degree is less important than the ability to generate sales effectively and consistently.

Experience/Skills

For promotion to Assistant Sales Manager, the candidate should have at least three years of experience with a consistent and successful track record in TV advertising sales and a special talent in a particular sales area.

An ability to analyze data quickly and to motivate other sales employees are prime requisites, as are competitive drive and demonstrated initiative. Supervisory and leadership skills are also important, since most Assistant Sales Managers oversee less experienced salespeople.

Minority/Women's Opportunities

Opportunities for women and minority group members in TV sales are increasing yearly. Women held 53.3 percent of all broadcast sales positions in 1996, according to the Federal Communications Commission (FCC). They are increasingly being employed in television sales, although promotions to Assistant Sales Manager jobs appear to be slower for women than for their male colleagues.

Members of minorities have made less progress. Minorities held 14 percent of all sales positions in 1996, according to the FCC. In general, the position of Assistant Sales Manager is occupied by white males between the ages of 25 and 35.

Unions/Associations

There are no unions or professional organizations that represent Assistant Sales Managers.

ACCOUNT EXECUTIVE/SALES

CAREER PROFILE

Duties: Selling advertising time locally, regionally, or nationally for a television station

Alternate Title(s):   Advertising Salesperson

Salary Range: $25,000 to $70,000+

Employment Prospects: Excellent

Advancement Prospects: Good

Prerequisites:

   Education—High school diploma; some college or undergraduate degree in marketing or advertising preferable

   Experience—Minimum of one year in retail or print advertising sales helpful

   Special Skills—Competitive drive; initiative; persuasiveness; persistence; gregariousness

CAREER LADDER

```
┌──────────────────────────────────┐
│      Assistant Sales Manager      │
└──────────────────────────────────┘

┌──────────────────────────────────┐
│      Account Executive/Sales      │
└──────────────────────────────────┘

┌──────────────────────────────────┐
│           Salesperson;            │
│ Advertising Salesperson (Print Medium) │
└──────────────────────────────────┘
```

Position Description

An Account Executive at a commercial television station is responsible for selling advertising air time to businesses or to advertising agencies acting on behalf of businesses, thus generating income for the station.

At most stations, Account Executive are assigned specific territories or responsibilities. Some concentrate on local sales, some on national sales, and others on obtaining sponsors for particular programs.

TV advertising time usually consists of 10-, 15-, or 30-second commercials, or the partial or full sponsorship of a television program. The Account Executive matches the station's available advertising air time with a client's need, selling a time slot or program that will improve the client's sales. The individual in the position analyzes a client's products or services, obtains detailed information about its business, and explains the size and type of audience that can be reached with particular advertising formats. To be effective, the Account Executive must understand many kinds of products and merchandising techniques.

Account Executives must also be familiar with the station's programming (syndicated, network, and local) and specific audience shares and ratings. They analyze all research data and devise sales presentations, including charts, graphs, ratings records, and other audience research data, and they often screen programs for clients.

At larger stations, the Account Executive works with and sells to the advertising agency representing the client. The agency actually prepares and produces the television commercial and delivers it to the station. In other instances, the Account Executive works directly with the advertiser in creating and producing commercial spots and announcements, using the station's production facilities.

Additionally, the Account Executive

- serves as the continuing liaison between the client and the TV station in all advertising and program matters;
- assists in or supervises the copywriting and production of spot commercials for the client;
- works with the Sales Coordinator and Traffic/Continuity Specialist to ensure proper scheduling for advertising; and
- attends regular sales staff meetings to exchange ideas, submit reports, and receive assignments.

Salaries

The remuneration for an Account Executive varies considerably according to market size and the individual's experience. The top 100 markets generally offer a chance for a better income, although some stations in smaller markets pay more because of special competitive or geographic circumstances.

Account Executives are less likely than Assistant Sales Managers to receive a salary. Most account executives are paid a straight commission or a "draw" against commissions. Many commissions are paid after the client is billed, but some are not paid until after the income is actually received by the station.

Commercial television stations employed an average of seven account executives in 1997, according to the NAB, and the average compensation for an account executive was $56,948. Because of commissions, the income for an individual may vary from year to year, and often from month to month. Most stations offer Account Executives the opportunity to contribute to life and medical insurance plans, and almost all provide them with expense accounts.

Employment Prospects

The chances of employment and eventual promotion in the field are excellent. Most small stations employ at least two Account Executives, and a sales staff of 12 or more is not unusual in a major market station.

There is a constant need in commercial television for effective Account Executives. It is often more difficult for station management to find qualified salespeople than it is to find other TV and media specialists.

In addition, there is a rapid turnover of sales personnel, and stations usually have openings, particularly in the fall. As a result, the general outlook for employment as an Account Executive in TV is much better than that of most other occupations in the medium.

Advancement Prospects

The majority of Account Executives actively seek advancement to Assistant Sales Manager or to General Sales Manager. The more aggressive and successful individuals move to higher administrative sales positions within their own stations or assume such positions at larger market stations. Some become General Sales Managers at smaller market stations. The skills necessary for a good Account Executive in broadcast television are readily transferable to other media firms, such as cable TV systems, where advertising time is increasingly being sold. In most instances, the personality of a successful Salesperson demands further advancement, and many easily obtain higher positions and salaries during their careers.

Education

Although a minimum of a high school education is usually required, the ability to sell is often more important than formal schooling in obtaining a position as an Account Executive. Having some college education, however, indicates that an individual is serious and motivated in pursuing a career. Employers at some major market stations look for candidates who have undergraduate degrees in advertising, marketing, or business administration. This is particularly true if the position to be filled is in national sales, where more complicated and sophisticated sales environments are the rule.

Experience/Skills

At least one year of sales experience in the retail field or in newspaper or other print advertising is extremely helpful for aspiring TV Account Executives. Some background in television production and programming can be very useful.

Most Account Executives have an extroverted personality, an ability to relate to others, and initiative and perseverance. They should have a good appearance, correct manners, and competitive drive. It is also important that they demonstrate confidence and imagination when making sales presentations and be able to express ideas well when speaking and writing. Above all, an Account Executive must like to sell and be interested in making money.

Minority/Women's Opportunities

The opportunities for women and minority group members in the television sales area are increasing yearly. In commercial TV 53.3 percent of all sales employees were women in 1996 and 14 percent were members of minorities, according to Federal Communications Commission (FCC) studies. The percentage of women employees in this field has risen 7.1 percent in the past 8 years; minority representation has increased 4.1 percent. While employment has not risen as fast for members of minorities, opportunities for them in the sales area are increasing as more stations seek wider audiences and advertising clients and a sales staff to reach them.

Unions/Associations

There are no unions or professional organizations that represent Account Executives.

SALES COORDINATOR

Duties: Coordinating all advertising activities for a television station

Alternate Title(s):   Traffic/Sales Assistant; Order Processor

Salary Range: $18,000 to $30,000

Employment Prospects: Good

Advancement Prospects: Good

Prerequisites:

Education—Minimum of a high school diploma; some business or secretarial training preferable

Experience—Some general office and retail sales work

Special Skills—Typing ability; good math skills; sales talent; organizational ability; detail orientation

```
┌─────────────────────────────────┐
│      Advertising Salesperson     │
└─────────────────────────────────┘

┌─────────────────────────────────┐
│        Sales Coordinator         │
└─────────────────────────────────┘

┌─────────────────────────────────┐
│            Secretary             │
└─────────────────────────────────┘
```

Position Description

At most middle and major market commercial television stations, the Sales Coordinator is in charge of all traffic within the advertising sales department and helps organize the activities of the Advertising Salespersons. Responsibilities include writing advertising orders, maintaining a schedule of available air time, and keeping track of all commercial advertising matters. In addition, this individual serves as a general assistant to the people in the sales department.

The Sales Coordinator must keep abreast of the changing status of all actual and potential sales, scheduled commercials, make-goods (advertising time provided free by a station to an advertiser whose commercials were preempted or were broadcast incorrectly), exceptions, and cancellations. The Coordinator maintains a master scheduling board or computer terminal giving the up-to-date lineup of all sales traffic for use by the sales department staff members. It is the responsibility of the Sales Coordinator to keep the traffic continuity department informed of all sales activities and to coordinate with the production department all dubbing of commercials for clients, commercial production schedules, and other client production services.

In addition, the Sales Coordinator maintains the master sales files and schedules, order control sheets, and contracts for the Advertising Salespersons. In many stations, the person in this position also serves as a telephone solicitor of advertising sales and as a backup for the Advertising Salespersons when they are absent from the office.

As a rule, the Sales Coordinator reports to the Assistant Sales Manager or directly to the General Sales Manager.

Additionally, the Sales Coordinator

- checks all sales contracts for accuracy against work orders, control sheets, and clients' time orders;
- researches competitive product and media reports for use by the sales department; and
- rearranges all prelog schedules to assist in clearing and changing commercial air time availabilities.

Salaries

According to industry sources, the salaries for Sales Coordinators are relatively low. Earnings in 1997 ranged from $16,000 at smaller market stations for beginning employees with no experience to $30,000 at major market stations for individuals with some experience and seniority. Sales Coordinators are often promoted to their jobs from within the station and carry with them their previous seniority and a modest increase in salary.

Employment Prospects

The position of Sales Coordinator is often the first promotion for a secretary in the Sales Department at a commercial station. In some settings it is considered an entry-level position.

TV sales people are generally quite mobile, with some 30 percent moving to other positions each year, according to industry observers. In addition, many major market stations often employ two or more Sales Coordinators in specific sales areas (such as national and local) who perform approximately the same duties. The opportunity for employment or promotion to the position at commercial stations is good. There are additional opportunities available at cable television systems, which are beginning to increase local advertising sales, and at some of the larger low-power television (LPTV) stations.

Advancement Prospects

Experience gained as a Sales Coordinator often leads to advancement in a television sales career.

The opportunities for a bright and alert Sales Coordinator to move into a more responsible position in the sales department are good, even though the competition is heavy. Individuals who work well with clients and assist in the servicing of accounts are often promoted to direct selling as Advertising Salespersons. The promotion to actual day-to-day sales, however, often depends entirely on an individual's aggressiveness and persistence, qualities needed by an Advertising Salesperson.

Other Sales Coordinators who are not specifically sales-oriented become specialists in "co-op" (cooperative) advertising, in which they help organize the complex deals made between local advertisers and national manufacturers to share advertising costs. The co-op coordinator at a commercial station earns considerably more and averaged $47,056 in 1997, according to the NAB.

Education

A minimum of a high school diploma is required for the position. Many employers look for some further education at a business or secretarial school. Some require previous training in computer terminal operations or in word processing equipment. A few seek a person with an undergraduate degree in business administration, marketing, or mass communications.

Experience/Skills

Some experience in general office work is helpful in getting the job, as is some background in sales at the retail level. Many employers promote the brightest and most able secretaries to the position.

Many employers look for proficiency with word processing and spreadsheet software applications, while others are impressed by the candidate's interest in and talent for actual sales work. All stations require that the Sales Coordinator be precise and well organized and have a penchant for detail.

Minority/Women's Opportunities

The vast majority of Sales Coordinators at smaller local television stations are women, many of whom began as administrative assistants; this common pathway likely accounts for the fact that 53.3 percent of all sales personnel in commercial television in 1996 were woman, according to industry observers.

The opportunities for minority group members as Sales Coordinators are plentiful. As of 1996, 14 percent of sales personnel were minorities.

Unions/Associations

There are no unions or professional organizations that represent Sales Coordinators.

TRAFFIC/CONTINUITY SPECIALIST

CAREER PROFILE

Duties: Scheduling programs and commercials, developing logs; and writing station identifications and announcements

Alternate Title(s): Continuity/Copywriter; Traffic Assistant

Salary Range: $15,000 to $30,000+

Employment Prospects: Good

Advancement Prospects: Good

Prerequisites:

Education—High school diploma; some college preferable

Experience—Writing; computer operation

Special Skills—Organizational ability; detail orientation; precision; computer literacy

CAREER LADDER

```
┌─────────────────────────────────┐
│      Operations Manager;         │
│    Advertising Salesperson;      │
│       Sales Coordinator          │
└─────────────────────────────────┘

┌─────────────────────────────────┐
│   Traffic/Continuity Specialist  │
└─────────────────────────────────┘

┌─────────────────────────────────┐
│        School; Secretary         │
└─────────────────────────────────┘
```

Position Description

The Traffic/Continuity Specialist is one of the most indispensable employees at a television station. Although the duties vary from large to small markets and between public and commercial stations, the position is vital to day-to-day operations.

The Traffic/Continuity Specialist is in charge of the detailed scheduling of all programming for the station, including programs, station breaks, commercials, and public service announcements. This individual prepares the daily operational Federal Communications Commission (FCC) log, which details the minute-by-minute broadcasting operation from sign-on to sign-off. In many circumstances, the Traffic/Continuity Specialist writes on-air promotional copy for the station announcers to use during station breaks and as transitions between programs.

At commercial stations the position usually reports to the General Sales Manager but may report to the Program Manager instead. The Traffic/Continuity Specialist keeps a continuous record of all available commercial air time and informs the sales department when slots are open and when they are sold and scheduled. The Specialist also ensures that there is a time separation between advertised products of a similar nature and that commercials adhere to FCC and Federal Trade Commission (FTC) regulations and to the station's broadcast standards.

Today, commercial stations rely on computer networks to help manage the complex traffic information involved in advertising sales and scheduling. Many midsize and major market stations separate the duties of continuity and traffic. The Continuity/Copywriter concentrates on preparing written copy, while the Traffic Assistant is heavily involved in scheduling and has no writing responsibilities. Both responsibilities are generally supervised by a Supervisor or Director of Continuity/Traffic.

At a public TV station, the Traffic/Continuity Specialist usually reports to the Program Manager and does not deal with the availability of commercial air time. The individual compiles all program information, creates and distributes the FCC log to engineering and operations personnel, writes the station identifications (IDs), and often writes and schedules all public service announcements and station promotional spots.

Additionally, the Traffic/Continuity Specialist

- assembles and processes all audio and video information needed to develop the station's operating log;
- creates, in cooperation with the programming or production department, slide, film, or videotape spots to accompany the audio for local station IDs; and
- schedules announcers for recording station breaks and promotional or live announcements.

Salaries

Traffic/Continuity Specialists are often classified as support personnel and thus, in spite of the responsibility, their salaries are rather low. In commercial television, salaries for Continuity/Copywriters averaged $20,833 in 1997, according to the National Association of Broadcasters (NAB). The average starting compensation was $17,346 in that year. The average salary for a Traffic Manager Supervisor was $33,374.

In public television, Traffic/Continuity Specialists' salaries are generally lower than in commercial television, according to industry observers. The median salary for the supervisory position of Director of Continuity/Traffic at PTV station was $26,676 in 1997, according to the CPB.

Employment Prospects

Traffic/Continuity Specialist is often an entry-level job at both commercial and public television stations. Attrition and promotion rates are high, and many opportunities are available for beginners. Some cable TV systems and multichannel multipoint distribution service (MMDS) operations have similar positions. Positions are also available at low-power television (LPTV) stations.

Many large market stations employ three or more people in their traffic/continuity departments, with each assigned specific duties and responsibilities. The typical commercial TV station employed three Continuity/Copywriters in 1997, according to the NAB. In many instances, secretaries and stenographers in the programming department are promoted to the position. The opportunities for employment in this job are good.

Advancement Prospects

Opportunities for advancement to other positions at a station are also good. In this spot, an individual has the chance to learn some of the most fundamental aspects of broadcasting.

Possibilities often exist for promotion to the more responsible job of Operations Manager. In addition, the alert and bright Traffic/Continuity Specialist can move into the sales department as an Advertising Salesperson or Sales Coordinator.

Education

The minimum educational requirement for a position as Traffic/Continuity Specialist is a high school diploma. Some employers in major market stations prefer an undergraduate degree in mass communications or advertising. Courses in broadcasting or marketing and in copywriting are also valuable.

Experience/Skills

Since the position is very often an entry-level one, employers do not require extensive television experience.

Most stations look for alert, bright young people who are extremely detail oriented and precise. Experience in computer operations or word processing can be very helpful, since most stations are using such equipment for traffic and continuity. A candidate should have some background in writing to be able to create good copy for promotional announcements and station breaks. In addition, a facility with numbers is important, since a Traffic/Continuity Specialist works with specific segments of a broadcast day.

Minority/Women's Opportunities

In 1996, 88.2 percent of office/clerical/support personnel, which includes the Traffic/Continuity Specialist, were women, and 32.2 percent were minorities. In public television, 80 percent of support personnel were women, and 32 percent were minorities.

Unions/Associations

There are no unions that serve as collective bargaining agents or representatives for Traffic/Continuity Specialists.

DIRECTOR OF DEVELOPMENT

CAREER PROFILE

Duties: Fund-raising and the selling of services for a public television station

Alternate Title(s):   Director of Marketing; V.P. or Chief of Development

Salary Range: $29,000 to $129,000+

Employment Prospects: Poor

Advancement Prospects: Fair

Prerequisites:

Education—Undergraduate degree in public relations, marketing, advertising, or communications

Experience—Minimum of three years in promotion, publicity, or fund-raising

Special Skills—Writing ability; sales talent; interpersonal and organizational skills; charm

CAREER LADDER

```
+----------------------------------+
|         General Manager          |
+----------------------------------+

+----------------------------------+
|      Director of Development      |
+----------------------------------+

+----------------------------------+
|   Director of Publicity/Promotion |
+----------------------------------+
```

Position Description

A Director of Development is in charge of all fund-raising for a public television station. The responsibilities of the position include designing and implementing campaigns to solicit operating and capital funds from the station viewers, corporations, and private donors. In addition, the Director of Development is often ultimately in charge of all promotion and advertising for the station.

The position of Director of Development is unique to public (nonprofit) television stations. No such position exists at cable TV or multichannel multipoint distribution stations (MMDS). Neither is the position found at health, education, or government media centers. Fund-raising activities at those nonprofit agencies are usually handled by an employee of the parent organization.

A Director of Development position is a combination of public relations, promotion, and sales. The "product" represented is the public television station's programming and services to the community or to firms in the area. A Director of Development enlists corporations to underwrite specific programs or periods of the broadcast day by giving funds to the station. In return, the corporation receives a credit before or after the program or time period and is acknowledged in the station program guide and other promotional pieces. Since all public television stations are nonprofit organizations, such gifts provide tax advantages to corporations.

The Director of Development also solicits funds from individual viewers. These fund-raising activities range from on-the-air auctions of merchandise donated by local companies to pledge weeks in which special programs are broadcast and the viewer encouraged to become an individual member of the station. Membership costs vary and premiums (goods such as umbrellas, tote bags, or books) are often given along with the membership to encourage viewers to donate funds. Potential members are also solicited by extensive direct-mail campaigns.

A Director of Development also solicits larger sums from individuals, who are encouraged to leave a portion of their estates to the PTV station. One of the responsibilities of the position is the writing of grant proposals for the funding of specific programs or prospects by local, state, or federal agencies. The Director of Development often works out the complicated arrangements for finding and obtaining funds from a variety of sources for the production of special programs or series for national broadcast by the Public Broadcasting Service (PBS). In addition, the Director of Development designs and leads capital fund-raising campaigns to replace the technical equipment and facilities at the station.

The Director of Development is responsible for estimating the amount of money that can be raised in any given year from a variety of sources to support the station's operating and capital budgets. The responsibilities also include the management of the budget for the development department and supervision of its staff.

Because the responsibilities of the position are so closely linked to promotion and publicity, the Director of Development is often in charge of those functions at a PTV station. This includes supervising the activities of a Director of Publicity/Promotion and Publicity/Promotion Assistants. Press releases, posters, fliers, fact sheets, and print advertising are some of the tools used to promote the station and its programming and the need for money. The Director of Development usually reports to the General Manager of the station.

Additionally, the Director of Development

- speaks at public or community functions on behalf of the station;
- organizes and supervises the volunteers assisting in fund-raising activities;
- maintains membership in and liaison with community groups; and
- makes on-the-air appearances to solicit funds.

Salaries

In keeping with the responsibilities and importance of the job, Directors of Development are quite well paid in noncommercial public television. Yearly salaries ranged from $29,133 to $129,300 in 1997, according to the Corporation for Public Broadcasting (CPB). The median was $51,858 in that year, which was 6.4 percent above the previous year. Salaries are highest at the larger market community-licensed stations.

Employment Prospects

The opportunities for obtaining the position are poor. Although almost every PTV employs an individual in this position, there are only 178 PTV station licenses. While there is some turnover in the position, most of the Directors of Development tend to stay within the field and move from station to station. There are occasional opportunities for those assistants in charge of specific fund-raising responsibilities, such as underwriting or volunteers, to move into the job. Some opportunities exist for qualified personnel from other nonprofit organizations to fill the position.

Advancement Prospects

The opportunities for advancement are fair. Because of the importance and responsibility of the position and the exposure to management problems, many Director of Development seek and obtain the position of General Manager at smaller PTV stations. Others move to larger PTV stations in the same position at higher salaries. Some advance their careers by obtaining fund-raising positions at larger nonprofit organizations at the state or national level.

Education

A minimum of an undergraduate degree in public relations, advertising, marketing, or communications is required for nearly all employees. Graduate work or a degree is preferred. Courses in writing, photography, printing, and speech are helpful.

Experience/Skills

A minimum of three years of experience in nonprofit fund-raising and all phases of public relations, advertising, and promotion and publicity is mandatory. A candidate for the position must be organized and resourceful. Since the job involves constant interaction with the public, the individual should be poised, articulate, and capable of dealing with a variety of people in relatively sophisticated environments. A Director of Development must be personable, persuasive, enthusiastic, and a good salesperson. Above all, the position requires a certain amount of charm.

Minority/Women's Opportunities

The opportunities for women in this position are excellent. Of the officials and managers (which includes Development Director) at PTV stations in 1994, 41 percent were females, according to the CPB. Minority employment was much lower and constituted only 11 percent in those positions in that year.

Unions/Associations

There are no unions which represent Directors of Development. Many belong to ProMax International, Inc., to share mutual concerns and advance their careers.

MEDIA DIRECTOR

CAREER PROFILE

Duties: Selection of different types of media; identification of target audiences for advertising campaigns

Alternate Title(s):   Director of Media Services; Media Supervisor; Media Department Head

Salary Range: $42,000 to $95,000+

Employment Prospects: Poor

Advancement Prospects: Poor

Prerequisites:

Education—Undergraduate degree in business, marketing, advertising, journalism, or mass communications; graduate degree preferable

Experience—Minimum of five years of advertising agency work

Special Skills—Leadership qualities; knowledge of all media; analytical mind

CAREER LADDER

```
┌──────────────────────────────────────────┐
│   Media VP or President (Ad Agency)        │
└──────────────────────────────────────────┘

┌──────────────────────────────────────────┐
│              Media Director                │
└──────────────────────────────────────────┘

┌──────────────────────────────────────────┐
│            Media Group Head                │
└──────────────────────────────────────────┘
```

Position Description

A Media Director in an advertising agency determines the specific market a client is trying to reach, the media that will most effectively reach that market, and how a commercial message should be positioned in various media in order to achieve maximum results.

Media are the channels through which products or services may be advertised. The Media Director determines the placement of advertising in broadcast media (television or radio) as well as in print media (magazines, trade publications, newspapers, displays and posters, direct mail) and new media (World Wide Web sites). This position requires a creative executive who relies on extensive research as well as on highly developed marketing instincts and extensive experience.

The selection of the media is made after an in-depth study of television ratings (Arbitron, Nielsen), surveys, demographic studies, and other analytical reports. Market surveys are carefully analyzed to define the type of consumers and the target audience. In considering television as a vehicle for the advertising message, the Media Director deals with the advertising sales departments at television stations, networks, and various cable systems. Responsibilities include supervising the media staff in computing the costs of placing the television commercial in various positions during the broadcast day. After these costs are analyzed the Media Director is involved in developing an overall media campaign that best fits the marketing goals and the budget of the client.

The Media Director in a large advertising agency supervises a staff that handles most of the detail work. In order to perform effectively, the Media Director must communicate regularly with other departments of the agency, culling information from the research staff and working closely with the account services department.

Additionally, the Media Director:

- oversees the selection of the specific type of advertising (spot announcement, partial program sponsorship, etc.);
- supervises the actual buying of all television time;
- possesses a thorough understanding of the client's product and its marketing environment;
- makes formal presentations to the client regarding specific media buys;
- works with the account services department in developing market target profiles;
- hires staff and conducts in-depth training programs for junior personnel;
- reviews and evaluates staff reports, flow charts, and recommendations; and
- gives direction in analyzing market research.

Salaries

According to a 1997 *Advertising Age* survey of the industry, Media Directors' salaries ranged from $42,100 at smaller agencies to $92,400 at agencies billing between $15.1 and $45 million per year. Most Media Directors had a generous expense account. Average earnings in 1997, including salary and bonus, were $63,300. At the lower end, however, starting salaries for Media Directors may be as low as $30,000, particularly in the small market areas. The position often includes additional benefits, such as bonuses, stock options, and profit-sharing plans. Other prerequisites may include a new company car every two years, club dues and assessments, and fully paid medical and dental benefits, as well as some company-paid financial services.

Employment Prospects

The Media Director's position is among the higher-ranking and better-paid jobs in an advertising agency. Competition is very heavy, and only the brightest and most capable people achieve this position. When openings do occur, they are usually filled by the promotion of an assistant media director or media planner, or by seeking a talented replacement from a smaller agency. The mergers of a number of advertising agencies in the mid-1980s resulted in a number of layoffs of mid- and senior-management positions, and there are fewer positions available today than in the past.

Advancement Prospects

Opportunities for promotion from the position of Media Director to other advertising jobs are poor except for an extremely talented person, whose services may be in demand at a larger, more prestigious agency. Occasionally, a Media Director will become a vice president of media and sometimes president of an advertising agency after serving in the vice presidential ranks for a time.

Education

An undergraduate degree in business, marketing, advertising, journalism, or mass communications is essential, and a graduate degree is preferable. Studies should include all of these disciplines as well as statistical courses and data processing.

Experience/Skills

Media Directors should be knowledgeable about all aspects of advertising. They usually have at least 5 to 10 years of agency experience. A background in time selling at a television station can be helpful. Previous experience in data analysis is essential, as is research, as well as an understanding of marketing philosophies and merchandising techniques.

Media Directors should be strong leaders and administrators. They must have a thorough understanding of all advertising media and how best to use them for successful product promotion.

Minority/Women's Opportunities

Employment in the advertising industry is based largely on personal talent and ability, and historically there is perhaps less gender discrimination within it than in some other businesses. According to *Advertising Age,* women held 106 of the 145 media director positions in 1996.

The promising influence of women in the advertising industry is reflected in the fact that 13 percent of the chief executives in 1996 were women, according to *Ad Age.* The average base salary for women Media Directors in 1997 was $56,900, shy of the $60,000 average for their male counterparts.

Minorities are not represented as well, industry observers say; however, efforts such as the Multicultural Advertising Intern Program run by the American Association of Advertising Agencies seek to improve diversity throughout the industry.

Unions/Associations

As part of management, Media Directors are not represented by a union. They may, however, look to such professional associations as the American Association of Advertising Agencies (4As) and the American Advertising Federation (AAF) for professional guidance and support.

MEDIA BUYER

CAREER PROFILE

Duties: Purchasing broadcast air time on television stations for an advertising agency

Alternate Title(s): Time Buyer

Salary Range: $21,000 to $45,000+

Employment Prospects: Good

Advancement Prospects: Good

Prerequisites:

Education—Undergraduate degree in marketing, communications, business or advertising; graduate degree desirable

Experience—Agency experience useful

Special Skills—Objectivity; good judgment; ability to interpret statistics; intuition; computer literacy

CAREER LADDER

```
┌─────────────────────────────────┐
│         Media Planner;          │
│  Assistant Account Executive    │
└─────────────────────────────────┘

┌─────────────────────────────────┐
│         Media Buyer             │
└─────────────────────────────────┘

┌─────────────────────────────────┐
│      College; Secretary         │
└─────────────────────────────────┘
```

Position Description

A Media Buyer in an advertising agency selects the proper media for the placement of advertising. In middle and large market areas, the Media Buyer sometimes specializes in the purchase of time for television advertising, and is responsible for negotiating and purchasing air time on TV and cable stations and networks for spot announcements and program sponsorship for the agency's clients.

The overall goal of the Media Buyer is to identify the best potential consumers and then to propose the most effective vehicles that will reach them at the best prices.

The most important asset of a Media Buyer is a comprehensive knowledge of television stations and networks—their audience ratings, rate cards, character, influence, image, types of programming, coverage, audience demographics, and general track records.

The Media Buyer must also have a thorough understanding of each client's product and marketing goals. Some considerations are the particular emphasis of the product to be advertised when selecting the appropriate TV air time, as well as the ages and income groups of the target audience. Television market research and statistics are valuable tools in this regard, and the Media Buyer must be able to study and interpret them, relating that information to the client's product and to the overall advertising campaign that has been devised for that product.

With the product and market factors clearly in mind, the Media Buyer decides which of the television possibilities will allow the commercials to reach the maximum number of potential customers at the best cost. The Media Buyer's knowledge of specific television rates and of the demographics and psychographics of each station's viewers are important factors in arriving at the decision.

After the station(s) or network(s) that will carry the client's message have been determined, the Media Buyer considers what position within the broadcast day will be most effective for spot announcements or, if the advertising will consist of program participation, what particular program will best serve the client's needs.

Additionally, the Media Buyer

- compares prevailing advertising rates and program sponsorship costs in order to stay within the allocated budget;
- studies and interprets market reports from various auditing and research organizations;
- consults with media representatives regarding specialized information about the station or network;
- evaluates and makes recommendations regarding specific proposals from media representatives; and
- conceives and develops flowcharts or time schedules of all media utilized by the client.

Salaries

Industry observers indicated that Media Buyers can earn as much as $45,000. Entry-level salaries were about $21,000 in 1997. An individual's income depends on years of experience and the size, billings, and importance of the agency, as well as the size of the market. The competitive climate between agencies in a particular market also has an influence on salaries.

Employment Prospects

The larger agencies have more than one Media Buyer. Some specialize in a particular medium (television, print, radio, etc.). There are also assistant positions in media buying and planning. Smaller agencies have fewer Media Buyers who purchase advertising on other media as well as on television. In very small agencies, the duties are often handled by another staff member, and often the duties of a media planner are combined with those of the Media Buyer. Many smaller agencies subcontract all media analysis and buying to an independent buying service. Positions, therefore, are sometimes available in these service companies.

Openings for Media Buyers occur in the larger agencies. One New York agency is reported to fill as many as 60 entry-level jobs a year in media. Employment opportunities can be considered good for advertising personnel at this level. Promotion to the position from within the agency is not uncommon, and the applicant who has a good understanding of marketing, merchandising, and television time sales should have little trouble attaining this position.

Advancement Prospects

The job of Media Buyer is rarely a terminal career position, and the brighter and more diligent individual may, after a number of years, be promoted to media planner or media group head. In some cases, a lateral move to the account service department occurs. Bright, diligent Media Buyers may also find themselves in demand at the more prestigious agencies at higher salaries and with more responsibilities. The opportunities for advancement are good.

Education

At most agencies, an undergraduate degree in marketing, communications, business, or advertising is preferred, as well as some training in statistical research and computer operation.

Experience/Skills

A knowledge of the advertising industry and of the various media is essential, either through college studies or through prior agency experience, most likely at the secretarial level.

Specific skills needed for the position include an analytical mind, the ability to grasp many details and synthesize them into a sound recommendation, and good communication talents. Data processing knowledge, as well as computer literacy, is also useful.

A Media Buyer should be objective and able to make sound decisions for a client. Also needed are good judgment, skill at interpreting statistics, and a good intuitive sense.

Minority/Women's Opportunities

Opportunities in advertising are predicated more on ability, talent, and performance than on sex or race. Women and minority group members should not find discrimination to be a problem when seeking Media Buyer positions.

Unions/Associations

No union serves as a bargaining agent for Media Buyers, but organizations such as the American Association of Advertising Agencies (4As) and the American Advertising Federation (AAF) provide professional support.

ACCOUNT EXECUTIVE/AGENCY

CAREER PROFILE

Duties: Overall supervision of the advertising campaign for an account; client liaison

Alternate Title(s): None

Salary Range: $36,000 to $75,000+

Employment Prospects: Good

Advancement Prospects: Fair

Prerequisites:

Education—Minimum of undergraduate degree, preferably in advertising or business administration

Experience—Minimum of four years of advertising agency experience

Special Skills—Organizational and leadership qualities; diplomacy; detail orientation

CAREER LADDER

```
┌─────────────────────────────────────┐
│        Account Supervisor            │
└─────────────────────────────────────┘

┌─────────────────────────────────────┐
│      Account Executive/Agency        │
└─────────────────────────────────────┘

┌─────────────────────────────────────┐
│    Assistant Account Executive;      │
│    Media Planner; Researcher         │
└─────────────────────────────────────┘
```

Position Description

An Account Executive (AE) represents an advertising agency in dealings with the client and combines marketing, salesmanship, and business skills in defining the client's needs to the agency. The AE looks after the client's interests, coordinates all of the creative and production work, meets deadlines, and controls costs. A thorough knowledge of the client's advertising and marketing problems is essential, as well as an understanding of how the agency can respond to and solve them. The creative staff relies on the Account Executive for product information, market analysis, and the timetable for the various stages and completion of the advertising campaign. The AE determines the basic facts about a product, analyzes them, and leads the creative team in developing the overall advertising strategy.

It is essential that Account Executives have a good understanding of all advertising media, including television, radio, newspapers, magazines, new media, and direct mail. When television advertising is called for, they work with the media department to determine the markets, time slots, stations, networks, audiences, shows, and frequency suitable to the clients' products and budgets. They are also involved in overseeing the creation of the commercial, from concept to storyboard (a rough representation of the frame-by-frame action) through production, and make certain that the television advertising complements the full campaign. As the client's representative, the AE must be satisfied with all elements before a presentation is made to the client.

While much of the detail work for an advertising campaign is delegated within the agency, an Account Executive must have a firm grasp of the entire operation and must be able to develop concepts that fulfill the client's advertising needs.

Additionally, the Account Executive

- develops the overall advertising strategy and sales message;
- analyzes the marketing, advertising, and quality of competing products;
- manages the allocated budget to the best advantage for the client;
- monitors the effectiveness of the campaign strategy and recommends alternatives as necessary; and
- promotes agency relationships with clients and the media.

Salaries

Salary surveys by *Advertising Age* in 1997 showed that Account Executives earned an average of $40,900 in that year, depending on experience and the size of the agency. Expense accounts can be healthy, and other benefits may include bonuses, stock options, profit-sharing, a company car, club dues, and other fringe benefits depending on the individual agency. While higher incomes are often associated with larger, more prestigious agencies, many small firms also maintain a respectable salary schedule. Some Account Executives earn more than $75,000 per year.

Employment Prospects

For the qualified, experienced individual, prospects for becoming an Account Executive are good. Openings are usually filled by people in similar or lesser positions at other agencies, although sometimes promotion within an agency is possible. In addition, some companies have their own in-house ad agencies that assign Account Executives to specific products or divisions.

Practical knowledge can be gained by working as an assistant account executive, media planner, or Market Researcher, but an Account Executive must also be well grounded in all aspects of advertising. Even with years of experience, only the most capable and versatile people who have strong instincts for business, marketing, and merchandising are qualified for this position.

Advancement Prospects

Although turnover among Account Executives is high, people tend to move from one agency to another at approximately the same level. Advancement opportunities, in general, are only fair. Some Account Executives advance to higher-paying and more responsible positions within the agency, either to account supervisor, management supervisor, or senior Account Executive.

Because of the nature of their work, Account Executives are extremely knowledgeable about all phases of agency operations, and many, therefore, aspire to manage their own agencies. Leaving the large corporate environment after promotion and years of experience, they open their own companies, usually starting with a small staff and a few reliable and stable clients.

Education

Within the industry, it is generally recognized that a top-notch Account Executive must have an undergraduate degree in advertising or business administration. Courses in journalism, broadcasting, and marketing are also useful. An MBA is especially helpful and will enable one to command a higher beginning salary.

Experience/Skills

There is no one training area that provides all of the knowledge an Account Executive must have; rather, the position demands several years of advertising agency experience and knowledge of media functions, copywriting, design, and production.

A successful Account Executive must be able to organize many elements, from creative to financial, into an effective advertising approach to satisfy a client's needs. Leadership qualities are essential in order to coordinate the efforts of the agency's departments, and the AE must feel comfortable with different types of clients in a variety of situations. The Account Executive has business acumen, marketing expertise, and a creative, facile mind that is capable of following through on many details.

Minority/Women's Opportunities

There is little statistical information on the status of minority group members and women as Account Executives. Although promotion to the higher levels can be slow, *Advertising Age* reports that women Account Executives outnumbered men AE's by nearly two-to-one in 1997. The top job—that of chief executive officer—was dominated by white males: only 13 percent of these posts where held by women in 1997, according to *Ad Age*.

Minorities have made less significant inroads into the position of Media Buyer and advertising in general. Industry observers estimate the percentage of minorities in advertising at under 5 percent. Opportunities for advancement should increase for members of minority groups.

Unions/Associations

There are no unions that represent or serve as bargaining agents for Account Executives. There are, however, many groups that give support to, and provide a professional forum for, advertising agencies and executives. Most prominent are the American Association of Advertising Agencies (4As) and the American Advertising Federation (AAF).

MARKET RESEARCHER

CAREER PROFILE

Duties: Obtaining and analyzing information essential to marketing and advertising decisions

Alternate Title(s):   Researcher/Planner; Research Analyst; Research Specialist

Salary Range: $21,000 to $36,000

Employment Prospects: Good

Advancement Prospects: Fair

Prerequisites:

Education—Undergraduate degree in business administration; market research; advertising, or mass communication

Experience—Some experience in a research firm or research department outside the advertising industry

Special Skills—Analytical aptitude; statistical skill; orientation to detail; ability to communicate; computer literacy

CAREER LADDER

```
┌─────────────────────────────────────┐
│    Senior Analyst; Project Director  │
└─────────────────────────────────────┘

┌─────────────────────────────────────┐
│         Market Researcher            │
└─────────────────────────────────────┘

┌─────────────────────────────────────┐
│         Junior Researcher            │
└─────────────────────────────────────┘
```

Position Description

A Market Researcher in an advertising agency acquires and analyzes the information on which profitable marketing and advertising decisions are made. Many of the ads seen on TV are purchased for the advertiser by an agency only after a considerable amount of research has been done.

Research data may come from interviews, questionnaires, library study, government agencies, or trade magazines and associations. The goal of advertising research is to determine who will buy a product and why. Research also explores the potential market and helps to determine how a new product can best be presented or how an existing product can be presented more attractively.

Research at a large advertising agency may be conducted by a research department, with a director supervising several project directors and Market Researchers. At a small agency, such responsibility may be handled by one person. Research duties at very small agencies may be added to those of another staff member, but more often all research is subcontracted by the agency to an outside independent research organization.

There are usually three areas of advertising research, and a Market Researcher may work in all of them or, in a larger agency, specialize in a single area. One area centers on the advertising markets. Research must uncover who the poten-

tial consumers are, how they think, how they are most likely to respond to a televised commercial message, and what advertising techniques will appeal to them most strongly.

Another area concentrates on the product to be advertised. It is the responsibility of the Market Researcher to determine what the product does, how it is used, the impact of packaging and pricing on consumers, how to attract buyers, why consumers will (or will not) buy it, and how the competition treats these questions.

A third area of research analyzes the effectiveness of the advertising. This follow-up work, done after television commercials have appeared, evaluates the specific ad campaign and provides guidelines for future advertising of the client's products. This aspect of research examines the viewers' degree of product awareness before and after advertising, their buying motivations, and the direct results, in sales, of the advertising.

The good Market Researcher must be able to think and write clearly, to take a creative, intellectual approach to projects, to design a research methodology, to interpret data from all areas of study, to analyze and verbalize results, and to present data in clear, concise, sound conclusions that address specific marketing problems of the client and the product. Equally important is an understanding of human behavior, particularly consumer motivations, and the ability to interpret that behavior.

Additionally, the Market Researcher

- determines the most efficient manner of obtaining the necessary research;
- analyzes already-published research and statistical data relating to products, markets, consumer preferences, and buying trends;
- designs and prepares questionnaires and supervises field or telephone research; and
- makes recommendations that are utilized by the media and creative departments.

Salaries

Salaries for Market Researchers at advertising agencies range from a beginning level of $21,000 per year to a high of $36,000 for personnel with about five years experience, according to informal industry surveys.

Employment Prospects

There is a reasonable amount of mobility among advertising research people, which creates some openings. While some smaller agencies contract for all research services with outside independent research firms, most agencies employ Market Researchers on staff. In addition, many major market stations employ Market Researchers to assist their advertising sales staff.

In the past, agencies have considered this position as an entry-level job; and the position is now often filled by young college graduates.

Advancement Prospects

Opportunities for promotion are only fair because of heavy competition and this circumstance is not likely to improve. The bright and dedicated Market Researcher, however, can sometimes move up to the position of research director at a larger advertising agency. At smaller companies, promotion to more responsible positions in other areas of the agency is possible.

Some Market Researchers join, or return to, independent research organizations at higher salaries to advance their careers. Still others utilize their skills and experience to obtain similar positions in the sales departments of major market television stations or in the cable industry.

Education

An undergraduate degree from an accredited college or university is mandatory for individuals seeking the position of Market Researcher at an advertising agency. A degree in business administration or marketing research with a solid liberal arts background, or a degree in advertising or mass communications with some marketing and statistical analysis coursework is desirable. An MBA is even more valuable. Courses in psychology and sociology are helpful.

Experience/Skills

Some analytical experience in research methodology and design is helpful. Computer literacy is assumed. Most useful is some actual experience, either with an independent research firm or in the research department of a company in a nonrelated field. Several industry sources have noted that they want to hire marketing or advertising people who have experience in research, not researchers who happen to work in advertising. Because the position may be an entry-level job, part-time work in college, at an agency, or at a research organization can provide valuable experience in advertising, marketing, and research techniques. A Market Researcher should be skilled at statistical interpretation and have the patience to carry out detailed projects. The ability to write clearly and logically is essential in this job.

Minority/Women's Opportunities

Opportunities in market research are predicated more on ability, talent, and performance than on sex or race. Women and minority group members, therefore, should find ample opportunity in advertising (including research). The majority of Market Researchers are female.

Unions/Associations

No union serves as a representative or bargaining agent for Market Researchers, but membership groups such as the Advertising Research Foundation provide professional guidance and support.

ADVERTISING COPYWRITER

CAREER PROFILE

Duties: Writing copy for television commercials

Alternate Title(s): None

Salary Range: $22,000 to $75,000

Employment Prospects: Fair

Advancement Prospects: Good

Prerequisites:

  Education—Undergraduate degree in journalism, advertising, English, or mass communications

  Experience—Amateur or professional advertising or writing background helpful

  Special Skills—Exceptional writing ability; originality; understanding of human motivation

CAREER LADDER

```
┌─────────────────────────────┐
│     Senior Copywriter;       │
│     Creative Director        │
└─────────────────────────────┘

┌─────────────────────────────┐
│    Advertising Copywriter    │
└─────────────────────────────┘

┌─────────────────────────────┐
│     Junior Copywriter;       │
│        Secretary;            │
│     Traffic Coordinator      │
└─────────────────────────────┘
```

Position Description

An Advertising Copywriter works in the creative department of an advertising agency and conceives and writes the announcements, voice-overs, dialogue, special effects, and expository material heard on a television commercial. This work requires more than a mastery of the language. It demands an understanding of the total advertising campaign, a clear perception of the potential audience, and a knowledge of the client's marketing philosophy about the product being advertised.

The Copywriter does not become involved with an ad plan or campaign until after the analysis of the product or service and the market, when the market research has been completed and the media and market approach has been determined. The Copywriter does become directly involved at this point, drawing on all this information in the creation of the advertising copy.

The Copywriter confers with the Account Executive to determine the overall thrust of the commercial message and to become knowledgeable about the product, the competition, and the intended audience. Working with the Art Director, this creative team develops the advertising concept that ensures an imaginative, integrated, informative commercial that attracts the attention of the potential consumers and motivates them to respond.

In addition to preparing a final copy, the Copywriter also writes the material for the storyboard (a preliminary treatment that is a rough representation of the frame-by-frame action of a television commercial).

Good Copywriters use the English language to meet the needs of clients, and to stimulate buying impulses and product acceptance by the consumer. In addition to being writers, they are part salespeople, part word inventors, and part artists.

Additionally, the Advertising Copywriter

- creates slogans and catchy phrases for products to ensure viewer recognition and acceptance; and
- writes copy for brochures and promotional pieces used in advertising campaigns.

Salaries

Salaries for Advertising Copywriters vary considerably, depending on the geographical location and the local competition and the experience of the writer. Industry salary surveys indicate various salary levels, but in general college-trained beginners can expect to start at about $22,000 per year. A survey by *Advertising Age* in 1997 indicated a range of $42,000 to $60,000 for Copywriters and revealed a large disparity in compensation for men and women. The average salary for men Copywriters at agencies with annual revenues of $15 million or more was $70,700 in 1997 versus $50,900 for women. The more gifted and experienced Copywriter working in a major market may command as much as $75,000 per year. Some advertising firms have introductory training programs that provide valuable basic education and give the trainee a head start on the salary scale.

Employment Prospects

With 13,000 advertising agencies in the United States, many with multiple offices, and in larger agencies, with several Copywriters have on staff, there are many employment possibilities. However, while there are many aspiring writers in the world, few have the necessary training and understanding of television production, the talent to create concise copy, and the marketing insights needed. A good writer who has training or experience in these areas and a knack for writing advertising copy will have an advantage in the job market.

Copywriting is often considered an entry-level position, but many Copywriters have found their niches and stay in the position for years. Those who show a particular flair for the creative side of advertising are often promoted to more responsible agency positions in the creative department, and still others move to larger agencies or markets, at higher salaries, thus creating openings for beginners.

Secretarial or clerical work or any entry-level position in an agency can be a springboard to a copywriting position for a talented, ambitious individual.

Advancement Prospects

The inspired, creative Copywriter with an instinct for advertising and who has grasped the broader concepts of creating a commercial, a plan, or a campaign should have no trouble advancing within the industry.

Advertising professionals generally pursue highly mobile careers, sometimes by moving upward within the same company but more often by joining another agency at a higher salary or in a more prestigious position. At larger agencies, a Copywriter may be promoted to creative director, a position that is responsible for the entire creative output.

Higher-level positions are also becoming more available in the fast-growing communications area outside the advertising agency field. Although most ad copy is written by agency writers, some television stations and cable TV systems employ Copywriters within the sales department.

Education

Today, a bachelor's degree is virtually a requirement for obtaining a job as a Copywriter at an advertising agency. In 1998, 190 colleges and universities offered a degree in advertising. English and journalism studies are important to aspiring Copywriters, but a broad liberal arts education is equally valuable. Some coursework that includes mass communications, television writing or production, marketing, and psychology is also desirable. In addition, art courses in design and color are helpful in developing effective, coordinated advertising.

Experience/Skills

Extracurricular activities and part-time jobs while in college can be helpful. Campus radio and television stations, school newspapers, yearbooks, and literary magazines often provide practical experience. Any project involving selling, persuasion, marketing, or distribution gives insights into advertising skills. Any writing experience, but particularly short, concise pieces, is extremely valuable. The ability to use language well and to communicate ideas in an original, convincing way are essential. Word processing is a required technical skill. Copywriters must also be able to work well under pressure.

Minority/Women's Opportunities

Industry sources maintain that advancement opportunities within the advertising industry are as available to women and minority-group members as they are to white males.

Unions/Associations

There is no union that specifically represents or negotiates labor contracts on behalf of Advertising Copywriters. Some people maintain membership in the Writers Guild of America (WGA) as a way to improve their skills or gain representation in negotiations in other areas of writing.

PERFORMER

CAREER PROFILE

Duties: Acting, singing, dancing, or otherwise performing in a television production

Alternate Title(s): Talent

Salary Range: Under $10,000 to $100,000+

Employment Prospects: Poor

Advancement Prospects: Poor

Prerequisites:

Education—Post–high school training in performing arts; undergraduate theater arts degree helpful

Experience—Extensive amateur or professional work

Special Skills—Talent; commitment; perseverance; showmanship; poise; imagination; aggressiveness; versatility

CAREER LADDER

```
┌─────────────────────────────────┐
│   Featured Performer; Star      │
└─────────────────────────────────┘

┌─────────────────────────────────┐
│         Performer               │
└─────────────────────────────────┘

┌─────────────────────────────────┐
│   Performer (Other Media);      │
│   College/Professional School   │
└─────────────────────────────────┘
```

Position Description

A television Performer appears on camera to entertain or inform the viewer and can be an actor, singer, dancer, comedian, emcee, magician, talk or game show host, pantomimist, juggler, ventriloquist, and more. Performers are most often actors who play supporting or featured roles in dramatic series, miniseries, or situation comedies, or who are singers or dancers in entertainment specials. Many obtain work as extras or walk-ons in dramatic productions or comedy sketches. Other work in variety shows, made-for-TV movies, dramas, and soap operas.

There are a number of television environments in which Performers work. They can appear in programs for commercial and public TV stations and networks, independent production companies, cable TV systems that do original programming, advertising agencies, and, on occasion, corporate, government, health, and educational TV operations. Performers work in rehearsal halls, studios, and, occasionally, on location. Although they are usually cast and employed by a Producer, they report to the Director of a TV program for rehearsals and for the performance.

When appearing on a TV show, a Performer uses the skills and techniques of the theater but plays to a camera rather than to a live audience. Action, reaction, and movement must conform to the camera's mobility and the type of shots used by the Director. Although movies make similar demands of Performers, television shows are made in such a tight time frame that Performers must learn their roles, lines, and movements much more quickly to accommodate the fast pace and shorter production schedule under which TV operates.

Many Performers work in television commercials, which can be an important source of income and exposure. Most Performers do not limit themselves to TV, however, but perform at every opportunity, in the theater, movies, industrial shows, or nightclubs.

Additionally, the Performer

- attends scheduled readings, camera run-throughs, blocking (position placement) sessions, and rehearsals;
- rehearses independently for his or her specific role or appearance; and
- continues to attend performing arts classes.

Salaries

Most Performers work on a project-by-project, and often a day-to-day, basis. Union pay scales for Performers are extremely complicated and are related to the type and length of a program and to the importance of the part. Performers are most often members of the American Federation of Television and Radio Actors (AFTRA) or the Screen Actors Guild (SAG). A union "day" Performer in a prime-time dramatic program earned $559 per day in 1998, while a Singer (as a soloist or in a duet) earned $505.50 per day in the same year. Payment for low-budget, industrial, and educational programs paid less. Recognized Performers, however, often command fees considerably higher than the minimum, and residual payments are common.

Payment for work in TV commercials is even more complicated. A base session fee is paid whether or not a commercial is aired, and a complex formula defines additional payments once it is broadcast.

A few individuals get work on continuing series, where a featured Performer or star can sometimes earn millions of dollars annually from TV work. Most Performers, however, are fortunate to work even a few weeks each year, and their annual income from television is usually under $15,000. SAG reported in 1997 that Performers earned a minimum daily rate of $559. Most actors earn less than $5,000 a year from acting.

Employment Prospects

In 1996 actors, directors, and producers held approximately 105,000 jobs in the United States, according to the Bureau of Labor Statistics (BLS).

Opportunities are poor. It is difficult to become a Performer of any kind. Full-time, year-long employment is extremely rare. Except for roles in long-running shows, nearly all commercial TV opportunities are limited to one or two performances.

Performers occasionally find work in nonbroadcast areas, including government, health, corporate, and educational media operations. Cable TV networks also use Performers, and opportunities will grow as production increases.

Employment is usually obtained through contacts and by personal recommendations. Acclaimed professional or amateur performances in other media can occasionally lead to a role of some kind in a television production.

Advancement Prospects

In most professions, a good worker is usually rewarded with a promotion, increased responsibility, and a higher salary. This is not generally true of the performing arts, where Performers themselves must get the next job. Although agents are helpful, the Performer must be successful at tryouts, auditions, and callbacks. Talent, exposure, and impressive credits all contribute to the continuing success of a Performer, but, in general, opportunities for advancement are poor.

Very few Performers achieve feature or star status. A few experienced individuals with particular talents become well known and are cast in supporting roles, but even those with TV, movie, and stage credits find it necessary to supplement their incomes with jobs unrelated to performing.

Education

Post–high school training in the performing arts is becoming increasingly necessary and is available from private teachers, schools, workshops, studios, and colleges. Courses in television production techniques are useful. A broad liberal arts education is helpful, and many Performers obtain an undergraduate degree in theater arts. Some actors study at one of the more than 36 conservatory-style acting schools.

Experience/Skills

Experience is more important than education, and an aspiring Performer should work at every opportunity in school and college plays and in variety shows, benefits, local productions, community theater, and workshops.

Talent, of course, is the preeminent essential skill, but a Performer must also be extremely committed, aggressive, poised, and imaginative. A person who expects to work in TV must develop a knowledge of, and an appreciation for, television production techniques. Most Performers are versatile and adapt well to a variety of casting needs. Above all, they are persistent in seeking employment.

Minority/Women's Opportunities

Men and women are in equal demand as Performers in most TV productions. Members of minority groups have found increasing opportunities in television performance during the past 10 years, but the majority of Performers on TV are not minority group members.

Unions/Associations

Joining an appropriate union is often difficult. Individuals sometimes cannot obtain a union card without work but cannot obtain work without a union card.

AFTRA is an open union and can be joined by paying an initiation fee. Membership, however, does not guarantee work, and many people wait until they land their first job to join. Actors must join SAG after their first film job in a principal role.

Four other guilds represent television Performers: Actors Equity Association (Equity), the American Guild of Musical Artists (AGMA), the American Guild of Variety Artists (AGVA), and the Screen Extras Guild (SEG).

WRITER

CAREER PROFILE

Duties: Writing of scripts for television programs and productions

Alternate Title(s):   Scriptwriter

Salary Range: $20,000 to $100,000

Employment Prospects: Poor

Advancement Prospects: Poor

Prerequisites:

Education—Undergraduate degree in English, theater, or
radio-TV

Experience—Writing for any medium; some television or
film production helpful

Special Skills—Writing talent; creativity; television production knowledge

CAREER LADDER

```
┌─────────────────────────────────┐
│      Producer; Director          │
└─────────────────────────────────┘

┌─────────────────────────────────┐
│           Writer                 │
└─────────────────────────────────┘

┌─────────────────────────────────┐
│    Writer (Other Media);         │
│    TV Production Position         │
└─────────────────────────────────┘
```

Position Description

A TV Writer creates a visually oriented script for a commercial or public television drama, documentary, variety, talk
show, situation comedy, or other production. The Writer may
also develop and write scripts for programs produced by health,
education, government, and corporate TV or home video companies. A Writer is either on staff or hired for a particular
program or series, usually by a Producer or Director.

It is essential that Writers understand the television medium. They must think visually and sense the way the camera
will "see" each element.

The television script is a blueprint for production. The
complete script is typed in two columns, "audio" on the right
and "video" on the left. The audio column, or content portion,
contains dialogue or narration, as well as instructions for
music and sound effects. The video side contains major visual
instructions such as camera shots and key production notes
such as timing, set descriptions, and directions to Performers.
The specific details are filled in by the Director. Most good
TV scripts make little sense when only the audio column is
read. Writing for television is demanding. The structure is
tight and the style must be more concentrated, imaginative
and powerful than that of ordinary speech.

When developing scripts, Writers first determine the subject matter, the purpose, and the intended audience of the
program. They then research the subject, organize the material, and develop it in a format that the audience will understand and enjoy. Nonfiction television programs, however,
are often shot before they are written. The Writer is called
upon to match the visual images with prose, using spit-second
timing. Sometimes each word must be written to "hit" a
specific part of the video image.

Writing television scripts for government, private industry, health care, and educational organizations is particularly
demanding. It requires creating the appeal of an entertainment
script while presenting information that trains, educates, or
informs. Considerable research and particular attention to
accuracy and detail are often needed. Often the script must be
reviewed by content experts, and considerable editing is
required.

A general TV Writer usually does not write for news
programs. This activity demands a particular combination of
skills and background and is performed by a News Writer
assigned to the news department.

Additionally, the television Writer

- develops a sequence-by-sequence narrative describing
  events in their proper continuity (called a treatment);
- attends story conferences and planning sessions to change,
  delete, or add to the treatment; and
- attends production meetings and rehearsals and follows up
  with script rewrites, additions, and deletions.

Salaries

In the entertainment field, the Writers Guild of America (WGA) minimum scale for a 30-minute commercial network story and teleplay in 1998 was $16,579. By negotiating rates above union scale, a recognized Writer can earn $100,000 a year or more. The median income for the working half of WGA-West members in 1996 was $84,608, up 12.1 percent from 1995. The beginning freelance Writer in commercial TV, however, makes very little money, and most work at other jobs for a source of regular income.

The salary for a script Writer at nonprofit production centers in hospitals, agencies, and universities was about $26,000, in 1996, according to industry observers.

Employment Prospects

The chances of obtaining a regular full-time position as a Writer are poor. Staff Writers or script supervisors are employed at a few middle and large market commercial and public stations, but there is little turnover in these positions.

A TV Writer can get a start in many ways. Those who write creative scripts may come from a related medium such as movies or theater. Some production workers are asked to fulfill a writing assignment in the course of their regular duties. In business, government, or education, some people become Writers because they have already shown such talent (as copywriters, publicists, or journalists) or because, as subject specialists, they are best able to write the appropriate scripts to educate, train, and inform.

A very few Writers are steadily employed by personalities (Dennis Miller), on network shows (*60 Minutes*), or on shows created by independent production firms (*Dharma & Greg*). Most Writers, however, freelance while pursuing a full-time career in another field, possibly unrelated to television.

Advancement Prospects

Good credits, a reputation for reliability and solid scripts, and personal connections are the ways to ensure continuing assignments. A few established individuals become head writers for commercial TV series. Some Writers become Producers or Directors, but most dedicated individuals continue to do some writing for their own or for other shows. In the noncommercial areas, some Writers become Producers or Directors of informational and instructional programs. Overall, advancement opportunities are poor, unless a Writer wants to assume broader creative or managerial responsibility.

Education

An undergraduate degree, usually in English, is virtually essential, even though it is not always required for employment. Many individuals have an undergraduate or graduate degree in theater or radio-TV. Courses in writing, play writing, and composition, in addition to film and television production, are helpful. Most writers have a broad liberal arts education.

Experience/Skills

Many Writers begin writing at an early age and continue to do so all of their lives. Part- or full-time experience at a TV station is helpful to master the special techniques, opportunities, and limitations inherent in writing for TV.

Creativity and imagination are important, as are a mastery of the language and knowledge of basic construction. A good television Writer is well organized and disciplined, has a perpetual curiosity, and is usually in love with the English language.

Minority/Women's Opportunities

The majority of Writers in the entertainment field are white males, according to industry observers, but women and minorities have increased their representation in this area in the past five years.

The WGA's Employment Access department works with producers, studio and network heads, and writers to increase employment opportunities and the availability of writing assignments for writers who are underrepresented; in addition, CBS has instituted an Employment Diversity Program that encourages such writers to submit scripts. The newer networks—Fox, WB, and UPN—have successfully developed programming created by and for urban audiences, particularly African Americans; meanwhile, other underrepresented groups have yet to make similar progress.

Unions/Associations

Writers in educational or training environments are seldom represented by a union for bargaining purposes. Professional freelance Writers in the entertainment field may be members of WGA, which had nearly 8,000 members in 1998. Union membership is required of Writers who submit a script for network television production. The Screenwriters Guild and the Authors Guild also represent Writers. They may also hold membership in the National Writers Club, as well as in specific content-area professional associations, for purposes of professional growth and support.

MUSIC DIRECTOR

CAREER PROFILE

Duties: Evaluating, selecting, and supervising music for a television production

Alternate Title(s):   Music Supervisor

Salary Range: $50,000 to $100,000

Employment Prospects: Poor

Advancement Prospects: Poor

Prerequisites:

Education—Extensive training in music; undergraduate degree preferable

Experience—Minimum of five years in television or film music

Special Skills—Musical talent; creativity; taste; synthesizer literacy

CAREER LADDER

```
┌──────────────────────────────────────────┐
│  Music Director (Major Film Production     │
│                or                          │
│  Independent Production Company)           │
└──────────────────────────────────────────┘

┌──────────────────────────────────────────┐
│              Music Director                │
└──────────────────────────────────────────┘

┌──────────────────────────────────────────┐
│                Musician                    │
└──────────────────────────────────────────┘
```

Position Description

A Music Director is responsible for evaluating, selecting, and supervising all music for a television program. Music Directors are most often employed in major television film productions or on situation comedy, variety, or dramatic series. They also work on documentary programs and, occasionally, on large-budget education, government, or corporate television productions. Sometimes the title Music Director is used to describe the individual who is in charge of all music during an entertainment or variety special and who conducts the orchestra.

Various types and styles of music are used in television productions to enhance and underscore the visual images. Music Directors determine when and if music should be used for specific scenes to create a mood, capture the attention of the audience, or complement the action. They analyze the needs of each segment or scene and audition, preview, and select musical bridges and segments that appropriately accompany the video portion of the production. After the show has been recorded, they add music to the visual, voice, and nonmusical sound effects material on the existing tape or film, choosing from a variety of music styles and sources.

On major television film programs, the Music Director might commission original compositions from composers who usually work specifically in the film and television industries. In such cases, the Music Director supervises the arrangement of the music, chooses the orchestra size, and oversees the recording, often conducting the orchestra during the recording session and sometimes composing, arranging, and orchestrating the music as well.

As a composer, the Music Director is often called upon to complete a score for a TV movie or miniseries. Some 20 or 30 percent of a typical TV movie may contain background music. Some Music Directors specialize in creating and supervising music for commercials.

Sometimes a Music Director uses existing musical bridges, cues, themes, and other short sections supplied by established music production companies and selects specific portions from the tapes and records maintained by such music libraries, supervising their insertion into the sound track of the television program.

A Music Director may work in recording studios but is most often found in the control room and in videotape and film editing rooms of major production firms or television studios. The Music Director supervises sound editors, audio engineers, and recording engineers. The position reports to the Producer or Director of a television production.

Additionally, the Music Director

- oversees the audio editing of the music sound track for a television production;
- maintains a file of existing music and music sources for possible future use; and

- establishes contacts with musicians, composers, music researchers, and other potential resources.

Salaries

Music Directors are usually employed on a project-by-project basis. Their salaries vary considerably and depend on the scope and extent of music used in a production and on the size of the enterprise. Some top Music Directors with impressive credentials command more than $90,000 for the complete scoring of a major two-hour television drama. More often, however, a Music Director works on simple productions, using prerecorded library music, and will be paid from $8,000 to $20,000. He or she may work on three or four such projects each year. Those who compose music for commercials charge between $10,000 and $25,000 for each job.

Most industry observers indicate that the total yearly income for a Music Director generally ranges from $50,000 for individuals with a modest reputation to well over $100,000 for the established professional with impressive credits.

Employment Prospects

Opportunities for employment in broadcast or cable television are poor. Most talk shows, newscasts, and other formats make little use of music. Although many television programs do include music, the duties of a Music Director in lower-budget productions are often performed by the Producer, the Director, or the sound or music editor. Major market commercial and public television stations use Music Directors only occasionally. The majority of the positions are in Hollywood or New York City, usually on a program-by-program or series-by-series basis. Employment often depends on contacts within the industry. With the proper education, training, and experience, some Musicians may become Music Directors.

Advancement Prospects

Chances for advancement depend on the talent and continuing reputation of the individual. With peer recognition, critical acclaim, and film or theatrical credits come new opportunities for more projects at larger fees.

Some Music Directors increase their earnings by working on major motion pictures. A few in Hollywood are employed on long-lasting television series or become staff Music Directors for independent production companies. A very few Mu-

sic Directors become Producers of television films or musical theater productions after gaining the necessary experience in TV, film, and theatrical production.

In general, opportunities for advancement are poor and the competition is heavy.

Education

Almost all Music Directors are highly trained, extremely talented musicians. They have studied music intensely from childhood and have an educational background that includes music theory, harmony, arranging, and music history. Many have an undergraduate degree in music and a considerable number have graduate degrees.

Experience/Skills

At least five years of experience in the use of music in television or film is frequently required. A knowledge of general production techniques is also a necessity. A Music Director should be familiar with audio recording and have extensive experience in working with short, precisely timed music segments. Music Directors are talented, creative individuals who have a broad knowledge of music styles and a finely honed musical taste. They are adept at manipulating timbres and changing rhythms and developing small motifs and musical "hooks" to create musical imagery. Today, most have had experience with synthesizers and other computer-generated electronic music gear.

Minority/Women's Opportunities

Although some female and minority group employment opportunities have occurred during the past 10 years in smaller-budget productions, more than 90 percent of the Music Directors in television were white males in 1997, according to industry observers.

Unions/Associations

While there are no specific unions that represent or bargain for Music Directors, most belong to the American Federation of Musicians (AFM), including those who occasionally serve as arrangers or orchestrators. Music Directors who are composers and lyricists are often members of the Dramatists Guild; the American Society of Composers, Authors, and Publishers (ASCAP); or to Broadcast Music, Inc. (BMI).

MUSICIAN

CAREER PROFILE

Duties: Playing of an instrument as part of an ensemble for a television production

Alternate Title(s):   None

Salary Range: $20,000 to $50,000+

Employment Prospects: Poor

Advancement Prospects: Poor

Prerequisites:

Education—Extensive private music instruction; undergraduate degree in music preferable

Experience—Minimum of five years of recording studio, nightclub, theater, or radio-TV work

Special Skills—Musical talent; sight-reading abilities; transposition and improvisation skills

CAREER LADDER

```
┌─────────────────────────────────┐
│         Music Director          │
└─────────────────────────────────┘

┌─────────────────────────────────┐
│           Musician              │
└─────────────────────────────────┘

┌─────────────────────────────────┐
│           Musician              │
│    (Other Entertainment Field)  │
└─────────────────────────────────┘
```

Position Description

A television Musician works as part of a music ensemble that provides backup accompaniment for Performers in musical variety or entertainment productions, or music for background use in television films and dramatic or comedy programs. Musicians work in rehearsal halls and in television or recording studios. For many live or taped musical entertainment programs, the Musicians are in one studio and the Performers in another, and the music is brought electronically to the Performers' studio.

Musicians usually specialize in popular music for television production and accompany vocal or instrumental Performers as part of an ensemble. They are sometimes members of jazz combos, rock groups, dance bands, or classical orchestras that appear on television as featured acts or in full-scale concerts.

A television Musician usually freelances on a project-by-project basis and may be part of a rhythm section consisting of as few as three players (piano/guitar, bass, drums) or as many as eight players (drums, bass, three guitars, two keyboards, percussion). A Musician may temporarily become part of a band of 17 to 23 members or a full orchestra of more than 50 Musicians. A few individuals work under contract and play for a regularly scheduled program such as *The Tonight Show*. On occasion, a Musician performs as a soloist during a musical number or as a featured Performer.

This is not a supervisory job, although most large bands or orchestras distinguish between a first chair (lead Musician in a section) and second or third chairs. A Musician reports to the conductor or Music Director during the production of a television program or in a recording session.

Some Musicians act as contractors, bringing together many others in a temporary group, and others serve as musical consultants, copyists, and arrangers.

Additionally, the Musician

- rehearses for recording sessions, run-throughs, and performances;
- keeps abreast of musical trends, new songs, and techniques; and
- performs on more than one type of instrument during a session, when necessary.

Salaries

Minimum union scale for nonsolo (sideman) work on a three-hour TV recording session was $226 in 1993, according to union sources. Rehearsals and run-throughs often add to the minimum scale, depending on the extent of the production. Pay is usually based on specific time segments (double sessions of another three hours).

Salaries above the scale are negotiable and many experienced Musicians can obtain higher rates. In general, however, the pay for Musicians is lower than for most other positions in television, ranging between $20,000 and $50,000 a year for those who work fairly regularly. Because most television work is on a project-by-project basis, most Musicians perform in theaters and nightclubs and teach in order to earn a reasonable yearly salary. Others work at jobs unrelated to music.

Employment Prospects

The possibility for employment is poor. As in most cases in show business, professional contacts are very important in obtaining a position.

According to government and union estimates, there were about 300,000 professional Musicians in the United States in 1996. Most were located in the major urban centers. Jobs, however, are sporadic. An average of 274,000 Musicians held jobs that year; 3 out of 5 musicians worked part-time. Few public or commercial stations or cable systems have a need or budget for Musicians, and the majority of those working in television are in Hollywood and New York City. Of the thousands of Musicians in those cities, less than 10 percent earn any appreciable income from television work. Moreover, computerized instruments are replacing individual Musicians playing conventional instruments in recording and television/film studios. Modern machines can effectively duplicate horn and string sections and drummers, eliminating many jobs. Nevertheless, overall employment of musicians is expected to grow from 21 to 35 percent by 2006, according to the Bureau of Labor Statistics.

Advancement Prospects

There is limited potential for advancement. Very few Musicians obtain star or featured Performer status. Advancement is based on great talent, peer recognition, and superior musicianship on a particular instrument. The skill and talents necessary are seldom transferable to other television positions. A very few Musicians who are qualified obtain full-time employment at major motion picture or television studios. Some become Music Directors. Others with well-developed interpersonal and management skills become contractors who put together ensembles and groups for particular television productions.

Education

While a degree is not a prerequisite to obtaining employment, such disciplined training is helpful in acquiring the necessary skills. Courses in theory, harmony, composition, performance, notation, and music history are useful.

The key to success as a Musician, however, is practice, and lots of it. Most professional Musicians begin studying an instrument at a very early age and continue for the rest of their lives. To acquire great technical skill, musical knowledge, and interpretative ability, intensive and continuous training is required. As a rule, such expertise is developed through years of study with an accomplished teacher, usually in a combination of private classes and academic study at any of the 500 colleges and conservatories of music that offer degrees in performance, theory, and harmony.

Experience/Skills

A minimum of five years of previous experience in recording studios, nightclubs, theater, or radio-TV work is usually required of a Musician.

Most television Musicians are professionals who "know their horns"—a description that implies complete technical mastery of an instrument. Musicians must be able to sight-read and transpose from one key to another with ease. An ability to improvise is required, as well as a knowledge of instrumental literature. A Musician in television must possess skill in ensemble playing and be alert and dependable. The Musician must be able to work from a "lead sheet" (containing only lyrics and chords) and to work out "head" arrangements, which are created verbally between the Musician and the Music Director.

Minority/Women's Opportunities

The majority of Musicians employed in television production and programming in 1998 were white males, according to industry observers, although white female representation in the string and woodwind sections of small orchestras was significant. Employment of minority group Musicians in small bands on television was approximately 50 percent, according to industry sources.

Unions/Associations

Many professional Musicians are members of the American Federation of Musicians (AFM), which represents them in bargaining and salary negotiations. Union membership, however, has declined in the past few years, and many of today's Musicians are only nominal members of AFM or do not belong to any union. Some Musicians who perform as soloists belong to the American Guild of Musical Artists (AGMA).

Musicians who are also composers and lyricists are often members of one or more of the organizations listed in the profile of Music Director.

COSTUME DESIGNER

CAREER PROFILE

Duties: Designing of costumes for major television productions

Alternate Title(s):   Costume Director

Salary Range: $35,000 to $200,000+

Employment Prospects: Fair

Advancement Prospects: Poor

Prerequisites:

Education—Undergraduate degree in fashion or costume design helpful

Experience—Several years of costuming for theater or television productions

Special Skills—Design talent; sewing ability; creative flair, TV production knowledge

CAREER LADDER

```
┌─────────────────────────────────────────┐
│         Costume Designer                 │
│  (Major Theater or Film Production)      │
└─────────────────────────────────────────┘

┌─────────────────────────────────────────┐
│         Costume Designer                 │
└─────────────────────────────────────────┘

┌─────────────────────────────────────────┐
│    Costuming Apprentice (Theater);       │
│      Costume Sketch Artist               │
└─────────────────────────────────────────┘
```

Position Description

The Costume Designer is responsible for creating the designs for all costumes worn in a television production. Since many TV productions call for Performers to wear their own street clothes, the Costume Designer is sometimes called on to approve their on-camera wardrobes. Costume Designers often work at drawing boards in their own studios, but they also spend a considerable amount of time in dressing or fitting rooms and in costume and tailor shops. During television productions they are usually on hand in the studio and control room.

In most instances, a Costume Designer does not actually sew and construct costumes, but these activities are always under his or her supervision. Depending on the size of the project, a Costume Designer may supervise from three to eight workers, including costumers, tailors, and fitters; often they are employees of a costume company owned by the Costume Designer. The position usually reports to the Director of the production.

Costume Designers must be adept at drawing and painting, composition and perspective, and light and shadow renderings. They make sketches, models, silhouettes, choose fabrics, and match clothing swatches so that the costumes will help provide the visual effect necessary for the television drama or entertainment special. The Costume Designer considers lighting, makeup, hair styles, and set design in determining the colors and styles of costumes and must solve many problems, ranging from too much or too little set light to widely differing body shapes.

Costume Designers must be capable of designing costumes for a variety of assignments. For dramatic programs, they may design costumes that are appropriate for a primitive caveman, a 20th-century career woman, or a futuristic alien. For variety programs or entertainment specials, they must be capable of creating exciting costumes for the chorus, supporting players, and featured Performers that complement and add to the overall production. They solve the problems of dancers' costumes (which require movement) and singers' costumes (which require throat and diaphragm freedom). When the performance calls for constant movement of a large cast, the Costume Designer adjusts costumes so that the visual effect remains pleasing and clashes are avoided.

Additionally, the Costume Designer

- studies the script to gain an understanding of the costume requirements of a particular program or series;
- researches the styles of a specific geographic area or historical period, when necessary;
- locates costumes from stock, redesigns existing costumes, or rents appropriate costumes from a theatrical costume supply house; and
- works within an allocated budget when determining the creation or acquisition of costumes.

Salaries

When they are working, top Costume Designers are relatively highly paid, as befits the talent, ability, and training essential for the position. The union minimum for film costume designing was $1,631.04 per week in 1998. A costume design job with a network television series pays a daily minimum of $391.45. Most Costume Designers, however, do not work steadily, and their yearly income is derived from nine months of work, on average. As an individual's reputation or style becomes established, higher rates can be negotiated. Most Costume Designers also work for theatrical productions, films, industrial shows, or nightclub acts, where the pay is usually the minimum union scale but is always negotiable.

Employment Prospects

Opportunities for employment in film are good and in television are fair. Costume Designers freelance on a project-by-project basis. They often own their own companies and in turn employ freelance employees when they get an assignment. In 1998, Disney was the only organization employing in-house costume designers. Major market stations and cable systems do not have the budget or the need for a full-time staff position in this area.

In most cases, only one person is hired for a program or series of programs. When costuming demands are extensive and complicated, the production or costume company may employ one or more costumers who function as assistants to the Costume Designer. Most Costume Designers have been costumers or sketch artists in the early stages of their careers.

Opportunities often become available through connections with other theatrical and television workers. Nearly all of the available positions are in Hollywood or New York City; of the 460 members of the International Alliance of Theatrical and Stage Employees (IATSE) in 1998, 400 were located in Los Angeles.

Advancement Prospects

A successful television Costume Designer who has worked for relatively small productions on meager budgets may move into costume design for motion pictures in Hollywood or make a transition to the Broadway stage. Many Costume Designers work on both coasts and in a variety of settings to advance their careers. Peer recognition and reputation and a distinctive style lead to more important assignments and higher salaries. Opportunities are so limited, however, that prospects for advancing to more prestigious positions are very poor.

Education

Style and design abilities are more important than a formal education in obtaining a position as a Costume Designer. An undergraduate degree in fashion or costume design from an art, design, or fashion institute can, however, be useful. Instruction in life drawing, color theory, and composition are necessary, as well as studies in costume history, television production, and theater arts. Coursework in staging and lighting techniques for television and theater are extremely helpful.

Experience/Skills

Most Costume Designers have spent a considerable amount of time in an informal apprenticeship in the theater as costumers, dressers, wardrobe assistants, tailors, and a wide variety of other backstage jobs. They have sometimes served as Craftpersons and occasionally performed in school or college in plays and summer stock.

A candidate for the job should have a balanced portfolio that includes design sketches for musicals, operas, Shakespearean dramas, and entertainment or nightclub shows. The individual must be expert at sewing and possess excellent drawing, painting, and graphic art skills. An understanding of the techniques, limitations, and capabilities of television production is required. The applicant must also have a creative flair and sense of style and be excellent at interpersonal relationships, inasmuch as costume design is a collaborative effort.

Minority/Women's Opportunities

The percentage of women and men in costuming and design in 1998 was about even, according to industry observers. Minority group members have been less well represented, but opportunities are increasing, according to industry sources.

Unions/Associations

For bargaining purposes, Costume Designers on the East Coast are represented by United Scenic Artists and, on the West Coast, by the Costume Designers Guild. Some belong to the IATSE.

MAKEUP ARTIST

CAREER PROFILE

Duties: Designing and applying makeup needed by Performers in a television production

Alternate Title(s): None

Salary Range: $35,000 to $50,000+

Employment Prospects: Fair

Advancement Prospects: Poor

Prerequisites:

Education—Post–high school TV and theater arts courses in makeup required; undergraduate degree preferable

Experience—College or amateur theater; apprenticeship in legitimate theater

Special Skills—Creativity; visual imagination; familiarity with television techniques

CAREER LADDER

```
┌─────────────────────────────┐
│      Makeup Director         │
│   (Major TV, Theater, or     │
│      Film Productions)       │
└─────────────────────────────┘

┌─────────────────────────────┐
│       Makeup Artist          │
└─────────────────────────────┘

┌─────────────────────────────┐
│    Theatrical Apprentice     │
└─────────────────────────────┘
```

Position Description

A Makeup Artist is responsible for ensuring that the physical appearance of on-camera talent is in keeping with the style and needs of a television program. The person holding this position consults with the Director to determine the proper effects that makeup should achieve for a particular production.

The application of makeup to Performers in a television production usually serves one of two purposes. The first is to enhance the natural features of the Performer, compensate for the washed-out effects that lighting can produce, and generally improve the Performer's appearance in much the same way as street makeup is intended to do. The TV camera can exaggerate blemishes and skin tones, and most Makeup Artists working in TV devote the greater portion of their time to applying straight (non-character) makeup that will minimize flaws and make the Performer appear natural to the viewer. Makeup Artists work on entertainment programs, network newscasts, series, and soap operas, and television films, putting makeup on supporting players, stars, dancers, singers, and other on-camera talent. The element of time is important to a Makeup Artist. In television production, time is money, and one hour to prepare a Performer for a regular appearance is standard in the industry.

The second function of TV makeup is to distinctly alter a Performer's appearance so that it conforms to the character being portrayed. Applying character or corrective makeup is a more ambitious and challenging undertaking than is straight makeup work, sometimes requiring the Makeup Artist to devise and apply artificial features. Such challenges, however, are only required for the most complex dramatic or entertainment productions on television. Individuals may be made to look older or younger. They may be changed to assume particular racial characteristics, or their appearances may be altered to resemble historical figures. Through the skillful use of makeup and props, a Makeup Artist can create an illusion of swollen limbs, hunchbacks, added weight, or other body and facial changes appropriate to the character being portrayed.

Occasionally, Makeup Artists must create the special effects that simulate the results of excessive violence, such as blood, broken noses, or knife wounds. Less frequently, they are called upon to transform Performers into characters appropriate to science fiction or horror productions. Many of these specialized makeup effects have been accomplished only after elaborate testing and experimentation. The skillful use of makeup gives a TV Performer an additional advantage in portraying a character.

When no Hair Stylist has been employed for a TV production, the Makeup Artist may also assume those responsibilities. The job is not normally a supervisory one, and the Makeup Artist usually reports to the Director of a TV production.

Additionally, the Makeup Artist

* maintains a file of facial pictures of all historical periods and nationalities and of unusual and interesting characters; and
* develops and maintains a collection of cosmetic supplies, application devices, and other equipment.

Salaries

Most Makeup Artists are nonsalaried and work on a freelance basis. Union scales are complex. For studio work, the daily pay averaged $250 in 1998. Makeup Artists at television stations earn less. A select few in Hollywood earn upward of $120,000 per year. It is not unusual for Makeup Artists to work a total of about 8 to 10 months in any 1 year. This generally produces a minimum annual income of approximately $35,000. People who work more steadily usually earn in excess of $60,000.

As the Makeup Artist acquires experience and a reputation and his or her skills become more highly developed, salaries considerably higher than scale can be negotiated with an employer. Those who specialize in special effects makeup command significantly high minimum rates and can go on to earn well in excess of $100,000 per year.

Employment Prospects

Opportunities are generally considered to be fair, and the competition is heavy. Most Makeup Artists are freelance, and the completion of one job is the beginning of a search for another.

Very few TV stations employ Makeup Artists. The networks do hire them, but employment is irregular and sporadic. Independent television production companies employ them, too, usually in Hollywood or New York City. Most Makeup Artists also work for stage, theatrical plays, films, and industrial shows on a project basis.

Advancement Prospects

Advancement and continued employment are dependent on building a good reputation, making and developing con-

tacts, and luck. Some Makeup Artists do advance to the position of makeup director in major television dramas or theatrical or motion picture productions. Competition, however, is heavy, and advancement prospects are poor.

Education

Courses in television and stage makeup are vital and can be acquired at a college or university with a strong TV or theater arts curriculum or at a specialized institute, studio, or workshop. Courses in staging and lighting, television production, and costume design are helpful. While a degree is not necessary, studies leading to an undergraduate or graduate degree can provide good basic training.

Experience/Skills

Some experience with television and theatrical makeup is mandatory and may be acquired in college or any of the many community, regional, summer stock, or dinner theaters. An apprenticeship in the theater is the best way to gain the broad makeup experience necessary.

Minority/Women's Opportunities

Women comprise about one half of the union membership for Makeup Artists and are well represented in television, according to industry observers. Industry sources report a substantial degree of minority group representation among Makeup Artists.

Unions/Associations

For bargaining purposes, Makeup Artists are represented by a local unit of the International Alliance of Theatrical Stage Employees (IATSE) in New York City and in Hollywood. At some major market stations, they are represented by the National Association of Broadcast Employees and Technicians AFL-CIO (NABET). They may also belong to the National Hairdressers and Cosmetologists Association in order to meet their peers and share mutual professional concerns.

HAIR STYLIST

CAREER PROFILE

Duties: Responsibility for styling and dressing the hair of Performers in a television production or series

Alternate Title(s): Hairdresser

Salary Range: $35,000 to $50,000

Employment Prospects: Fair

Advancement Prospects: Poor

Prerequisites:

Education—Minimum of high school diploma and special training; certificate from beauty school preferable

Experience—Minimum of two or three years of hair styling for men and women, commercially or in the performing arts, preferably television

Special Skills—Creativity; manual dexterity; familiarity with TV lighting and camera techniques

CAREER LADDER

```
┌─────────────────────────────────────┐
│         Hair Stylist                 │
│ (Major Theater or Film Productions)  │
└─────────────────────────────────────┘

┌─────────────────────────────────────┐
│         Hair Stylist                 │
└─────────────────────────────────────┘

┌─────────────────────────────────────┐
│      Commercial Hairdresser          │
└─────────────────────────────────────┘
```

Position Description

A Hair Stylist is responsible for creating and maintaining the hair styles of Performers in a television production. The job is not a supervisory one, and a Hair Stylist usually reports to the Director of the production.

While certain dramatic productions and musical-variety programs may require styles that are elaborate and extreme, most Hair Stylists mainly work with those that are considered natural, fashionable, and attractive by today's standards.

Hair styling for a television production differs from theatrical hair styling because the television camera reveals more detail than is visible to the naked eye in a theater. As with makeup, hair styles for television are usually subtle and natural. A Hair Stylist must also solve problems caused by television lighting, which generates a considerable amount of heat, often making it difficult to maintain hairdos throughout the course of a production.

Hair Stylists are employed by large independent production companies and networks for a particular television show or series. In small and middle-size production organizations, hair styling is often done by the individual who serves as the Makeup Artist.

Lavish, large-scale TV productions that involve a great many feature and supporting Performers may require more than one Hair Stylist. Many superstars negotiate a contractual arrangement that provides them with a personal Hair Stylist.

Other stars employ their own person who travels with them on a regular basis. In most instances, and for relatively simple productions, a Hair Stylist works alone on a project-by-project basis.

A Hair Stylist works in the dressing room before a television show and is available in the studio for touch-ups and adjustments during the actual production.

Additionally, the Hair Stylist

- shampoos, cuts, shapes, and trims hair, when necessary, in the course of styling;
- works with the Costume Designer and Makeup Artist when designing particular hair styles;
- designs hair styles to complement and enhance Performers' specific facial shapes;
- creates hair styles that suggest personality traits of specific characters; and
- uses hair coloring agents, accepted styling techniques, standard and specialized equipment, wigs, hairpieces, falls, and other accessories to achieve desired effects.

Salaries

Hair Stylists usually freelance on specific projects, although a few are steadily employed as part of the production team for a network series or soap opera.

Minimum union scale averaged $250 per day in 1998. The union usually requires a weekly minimum. Most Hair Stylists work in television irregularly during the year, and they generally earn a minimum of about $35,000 annually. People who work steadily may have an income of more than $50,000 per year. After Hair Stylists become established in the industry, fees may be negotiated that are higher than union scale. If they work regularly, they may earn more than $75,000 a year.

Employment Prospects

The prospects for employment at the network level or at an independent production firm are generally fair. Relatively few positions exist in the television industry, turnover is extremely low, and employment is traditionally periodic and often seasonal. Industry observers are generally not optimistic about increased opportunities in the near future, although there will always be a need for some Hair Stylists in major television production operations.

Personal contacts and connections account for much of the employment of successful Hair Stylists. These contacts are usually acquired as a result of previous assignments in television or through the recommendation of an influential friend or relative. Most Hair Stylists have additional opportunities for employment by working in other show business environments, including theaters and nightclubs. Some are occasionally employed at production/facilities companies.

Advancement Prospects

Advancement is achieved by developing a reputation, thus ensuring continued employment and higher pay. Television Hair Stylists occasionally move to major motion picture or Broadway theater productions. A very few individuals become personal Hair Stylists for stars.

It is generally recognized that getting started in the profession is the most difficult step and that, as one's credits and reputation grow, additional and more important assignments follow more easily. Overall, however, advancement prospects are poor.

Education

A high school diploma with some additional specialized training in hair styling is usually the minimum educational requirement. A certificate or diploma from an accredited beauty culture school that specializes in hair styling is also a common prerequisite. Most vocational schools offer courses leading to a hair styling specialty.

Experience/Skills

Virtually all Hair Stylists begin their careers by working on a daily basis in a commercial beauty salon. The opportunities for employment in television production increase in proportion to the experience an individual acquires. A minimum of two or three years of previous professional work in the theater or in television production is usually necessary, and experience in hair styling for commercial photography studios or in modeling is also useful. Because of the particular technical requirements of television, some experience in staging, lighting, and production is helpful. Participation in school or community theater productions can also serve as good training.

A television Hair Stylist needs all of the skills of a creative commercial hair stylist, including style, artistic flair, and manual dexterity. Good interpersonal skills are also necessary. In some instances, graphic arts skills and the ability to research and copy period hair styles are helpful.

Minority/Women's Opportunities

Industry sources indicate that hair styling today is a field that is equally accessible to men and women, whether members of minority groups or not. About an equal number of men and women held the position in 1998, according to industry observers.

Unions/Associations

For bargaining purposes, Hair Stylists are represented by a local unit of the International Alliance of Theatrical Stage Employees (IATSE) in New York City and Hollywood. Membership in the union, however, is not required for employment in the television industry. Some Hair Stylists working for TV stations belong to the National Association of Broadcast Employees and Technicians AFL-CIO (NABET).

A few Hair Stylists belong to the National Hairdressers and Cosmetologists Association for purposes of professional growth and support.

SCENIC DESIGNER

CAREER PROFILE

Duties: Designing of the scenery and sets for a television production

Alternate Title(s):   Scenic Director; Set Designer; Art Director

Salary Range: $50,000 to $75,000+

Employment Prospects: Poor

Advancement Prospects: Poor

Prerequisites:

Education—Undergraduate degree; master's degree in theater helpful

Experience—Minimum of five years in theatrical and television set design

Special Skills—Creativity; graphic arts talent; artistic flair; knowledge of TV production; interpersonal abilities

CAREER LADDER

```
┌─────────────────────────────────────┐
│         Scenic Designer              │
│ (Major Theater or Film Productions)  │
└─────────────────────────────────────┘

┌─────────────────────────────────────┐
│         Scenic Designer              │
└─────────────────────────────────────┘

┌─────────────────────────────────────┐
│     Assistant Scenic Designer        │
└─────────────────────────────────────┘
```

Position Description

A Scenic Designer for a TV production designs the sets and scenery, oversees their construction, and determines how they will be dressed (the addition of finishing touches). Responsibilities include conceiving, designing, and supervising the creation or acquisition of backdrops, exteriors, interiors, furniture, and the decorative and functional details of all sets and scenery. The Scenic Designer decides the background color and brightness as well as the material to be used, such as paint or wallpaper.

After reading the script and working closely with the Producer and Director, the Scenic Designer ascertains the purpose of the production as well as the place, time, and mood of the action and translates their concepts into physical settings. This is accomplished by making preliminary sketches, illustrations, and perspectives and drafting all set plans and elevations. In the case of major productions, three-dimensional models of sets are occasionally constructed in the design process.

The Scenic Designer must visualize the set as it will appear in various camera shots, including closeups and long shots from specific angles. Building on the Director's concept, the Designer takes into account the activity and physical movement that the sets and scenery will have to accommodate. During preproduction stages, a floor plan is created which indicates where each set will be situated, where major equipment (such as cameras) are positioned, where permanent lighting fixtures and outlets are located, and where scenery and furniture will be placed.

Scenic Designers are usually employed only by networks and independent production companies for entertainment or dramatic programs, such as musicals, specials, game shows, commercials, ongoing situation comedies, dramatic series, or soap operas.

A Scenic Designer works at a drafting board and at the computer in an art studio during the design period, in carpentry and scene shops while overseeing construction, and in a television studio during setup and production. The person in this position occasionally supervises an assistant, a "chargeman," a journeyman scenic artist, set dressers, a Property Master, and others on a project-by-project basis. A Scenic Designer usually reports to the Director or Producer of the TV program.

Additionally, the Scenic Designer

- works closely with the Costume Designer and Lighting Director;
- researches particular historical periods and geographic locations to ensure accuracy of set detail;
- maintains inventory of sets, scenery, backdrops, and furniture; and
- supervises the dismantling of sets.

Salaries

Scenic Designers are usually paid on a project-by-project basis. Minimum union scale for the related title of Set Decorator was $1,706.13 per week in 1998. Recognized professionals with a reputation for skill and talent command considerably higher fees. While employment is seasonal and irregular, an experienced Scenic Designer often earns between $50,000 and $75,000 or more a year.

Employment Prospects

Most employment is for one-time-only jobs, but a Scenic Designer may occasionally get continuing employment on a weekly series or a daily soap opera, which often use several different sets in each show.

Even after being an assistant scenic designer for years, it is very hard to land that critical first job as a full Scenic Designer, whether on a specific project or as a staff member. With good personal contacts and a high degree of talent, however, it becomes somewhat easier to get work.

Opportunities are no longer confined to Hollywood and New York. The omnipresence of sophisticated technology coupled with financial incentives and advantageous currency exchange rates offered by various municipalities and countries competing to host film and television productions have created new industry hot spots, which in the late 1990s included Florida, the Carolinas, and Canada.

Advancement Prospects

This is a highly competitive field and advancement opportunities are poor. A few individuals move into more responsible, higher-paying scenic design jobs on a regular staff basis. Others try to advance by contracting for larger and more frequent projects. The very best Scenic Designers advance their careers by broadening their base to include work for major theatrical and motion picture productions along with television programs.

Education

Style and design capabilities are more important in getting a job than a formal education. An undergraduate degree in art and design, radio-TV production, theater arts, or architectural design is usually necessary, however, and a master's degree in theater arts can be of additional help. Courses in stagecraft, TV production, drafting, architecture, and the principles of color and composition are essential as well as study in drawing, painting, sculpture, and graphic arts.

Experience/Skills

A minimum of five years in television and theatrical scene design on a professional level is usually required for the job. A number of people work as "chargeman" or journeyman scenic artists before they move to the top position. Most have spent a considerable amount of time as apprentices in the theater, working in a variety of backstage roles such as scene painters and carpenters, or in other Craftperson roles.

A Scenic Designer must have creativity, fine graphic arts skills, an artistic flair and style and, since the work is a collaborative effort, excellent interpersonal abilities. A feel for color and texture is necessary, as well as a strong sense of shadow and light. A Scenic Designer must be dextrous. A knowledge of television production techniques is also required. Most important, perhaps, is possessing the talent to understand the relationship among time, space, and movement.

Minority/Women's Opportunities

The number of women working as Scenic Designers is quite high and increasing each year, according to industry sources. Minority group members are less well represented, but the number has increased within the profession in recent years and observers believe this trend will continue.

Unions/Associations

For bargaining purposes Scenic Designers are often represented by United Scenic Artists. Many also join graphic and visual arts associations in order to share ideas and advance their careers. Others are members of the International Alliance of Theatrical Stage Employees (IATSE) in New York and Hollywood.

PROPERTY MASTER

CAREER PROFILE

Duties: Providing, maintaining, and positioning all props used in a major television production

Alternate Title(s): None

Salary Range: $50,000 to $70,000+

Employment Prospects: Poor

Advancement Prospects: Poor

Prerequisites:

　Education—College or other training in TV or theater production

　Experience—Minimum of one year as a set dresser or Stagehand/Grip

　Special Skills—Artistic flair; knowledge of TV/theater carpentry and production; detail orientation; precision; "scavenging" ability

CAREER LADDER

```
┌─────────────────────────────────┐
│      Property Master            │
│  (Theater or Film Production)   │
└─────────────────────────────────┘

┌─────────────────────────────────┐
│      Property Master            │
└─────────────────────────────────┘

┌─────────────────────────────────┐
│   Set Dresser; Stagehand/Grip   │
└─────────────────────────────────┘
```

Position Description

A Property Master is in charge of the acquisition, maintenance, use, storage, and disposition of properties (props) used in a major TV production, series, or television film. This individual arranges to get the small items that add to and visually enhance a set, such as lamps, ash trays, pictures, and other decorative or functional pieces. The Property Master also supplies hand articles essential to Performers, hosts, guests, or the plot of a drama, such as magazines, canes, guns, drinks, and other paraphernalia.

Props are an integral part of any performance, and the TV camera reveals, with closeup clarity, any flaw or error in any part of the set or its props. The Property Master determines exactly what props are required by studying the script and consulting with the Scenic Designer, the Director, the Performers, and, occasionally, the Producer. Responsibilities include purchasing or renting properties or obtaining them from storage, along with maintaining a list of props and seeing that they are in place, in good condition, and available for each scene. When props cannot otherwise be obtained because of special requirements or budgetary restrictions, it sometimes becomes necessary to supervise their construction.

When selecting props for a period or historical program, the Property Master first researches the era or geographic location to ensure authenticity. For contemporary entertainment programs or dramas, the finishing touches to a set or scene are added by providing props that complement the presentation and stylistic setting.

The title Property Master, a term borrowed from the legitimate theater, is normally used only in major dramatic TV programs. Property Masters are employed at network television studios, independent production companies, or film sound stages in New York or Hollywood, and occasionally they work on location. At most TV stations, the Property Master's duties are handled by the Floor Manager and a Production Assistant.

Property Masters sometimes supervise assistants, called set dressers or set decorators, who physically place and arrange props in the appropriate locations on a set. For some major TV productions, a Property Master may supervise a property buyer, who purchases necessary items, or a property maker, who works with the scenic design crew, and Craftpersons in constructing special items. Property Masters usually report to a Scenic Designer or the Director.

Additionally, the Property Master

- maintains and cleans props that are scheduled for repeated use;
- monitors expenditures and stays within budget;

- packs and unpacks props when accompanying a show on location;
- arranges for the shipping and transportation of props; and
- strikes (removes) props from the set after production, returns rented or borrowed items, and arranges for storage or appropriate disposition of others.

Salaries

Union scale was $27.79 per hour for Property Masters who were employed on a pilot or first- or second-season television program in 1998. The minimum guarantee was for eight hours of work per day. The minimum was $1,672 a week for studio productions, a rate that is often negotiated upward by an experienced Property Master with a solid reputation for efficiency and capability. On location the pay is greater. Opportunities are not common, and long periods between jobs are normal. Annual incomes usually range from a low of $50,000 to a high of $70,000 or more.

Employment Prospects

Opportunities for employment are poor and depend heavily on contacts and relationships in the entertainment field. Most Property Masters freelance on a project-by-project basis.

Set dressers, who function as assistants to the Property Master in major television productions, and Stagehand/Grips are the most likely candidates for promotion to the job of Property Master.

The seasonal nature of television production results in lengthy periods of unemployment. Most individuals work in theatrical and other entertainment fields to augment their income from television.

Advancement Prospects

Property Master is usually the top rung of a career ladder that may have begun at one of the entry-level jobs in television, film, or theatrical production. Because many individuals consider working in the Broadway theater or motion pictures to be prestigious, they often seek to become the staff Property Master with a theater or film studio to advance their careers. Prospects for getting one of these jobs, however, are poor, since they usually go to people with years of experience and many contacts.

Education

Some post–high school training in television or theatrical production at a college, university, or special theatrical workshop is strongly recommended. Studies in art, theater history, scenic design, and construction are useful. An undergraduate degree in theater arts is also helpful. Apprenticeships of two to three years are sometimes available through one of the appropriate local branches of the International Alliance of Theatrical Stage Employees (IATSE).

Experience/Skills

At least one year of experience as a set dresser or Stagehand/Grip is usually necessary before an individual can assume the position of Property Master.

Artistic flair is a must, as are a basic knowledge of theatrical and television carpentry and construction and TV production techniques. Successful Property Masters are also detail oriented and precise.

A Property Master is a master "scavenger." He or she has the contacts, abilities, and skills to find and obtain the perfect items from stores, theatrical supply houses, thrift shops, museums, art galleries, and the homes of friends and relatives.

Minority/Women's Opportunities

Both women and members of minority groups are well represented in the field. Industry sources indicate that women occupied about half of the positions in 1998.

Unions/Associations

Property Masters are represented by local units of IATSE in New York City and Los Angeles for negotiating and bargaining purposes. Those working at television stations are sometimes represented by the National Association of Broadcast Employees and Technicians AFL-CIO (NABET).

STAGEHAND/GRIP

Duties: Setting up, moving, and dismantling sets for a major television production.

Alternate Title(s): Staging/Lighting Assistant

Salary Range: $20,000 to $60,000

Employment Prospects: Fair

Advancement Prospects: Fair

Prerequisites:

Education—High school diploma; undergraduate degree in radio-TV or theater preferable

Experience—College/amateur scenic work in TV or theater helpful

Special Skills—Knowledge of TV or film production techniques; physical strength; esthetic sense

```
┌────────────────────────────────────────┐
│  Assistant Scenic Designer; Property    │
│              Master;                     │
│    Floor Manager; Unit Manager           │
└────────────────────────────────────────┘

┌────────────────────────────────────────┐
│           Stagehand/Grip                 │
└────────────────────────────────────────┘

┌────────────────────────────────────────┐
│         High School/College              │
└────────────────────────────────────────┘
```

Position Description

After sets have been constructed or requisitioned and delivered to a television studio, the Stagehand/Grip assembles them according to the designated plan created by the Scenic Designer. The person holding this position puts together and sets up backdrops, scenery, and set pieces for rehearsals and production. Other duties are positioning furniture and placing props and technical equipment in their proper studio locations. The Stagehand/Grip also sees that the furniture and sets are moved or changed as required by the script. As necessary, this individual assists in maintenance, adjustment, and alteration of scenery and set pieces. When a production is completed, the Stagehand/Grip strikes (dismantles) and stores them in the scene shop or prepares them for transport to outside storage.

The terms *stagehand* and *grip* are borrowed from the theatrical and film worlds, respectively, and the responsibilities of the job in TV are similar to those in the theater or motion pictures. There are differences, however, that are directly related to television production techniques. Unlike the theater, complete removal of one set and setup of another during production is rarely required in TV.

A Stagehand/Grip performs strenuous physical tasks, such as moving heavy furniture, as well as less arduous chores, such as rearranging small props. In some major market TV stations, the Stagehand/Grip may also hold time or cue cards, place microphones, or handle camera cables during production.

As a rule, a Stagehand/Grip works at independent television and film production companies. Work is often confined to Hollywood or New York City, but some major market stations also employ people in this position. Occasionally, a Stagehand/Grip will work on location. The individual in the position usually reports to a Unit Manager prior to production, or to a Floor Manager during production. In large productions, the Stagehand/Grip may be assigned to a Property Master. Some major film and TV programs designate a senior individual as a key or chief grip, with some supervisory duties over other staging employees.

Additionally, the Stagehand/Grip

- helps the Lighting Director in preparing or positioning lighting equipment;
- assists in moving camera cranes, booms, and dollies during production; and
- keeps the studio, staging, and storage areas neat and orderly.

Salaries

Salaries for the union position of Stagehand/Grip are relatively good. In 1998, freelance people working on a per diem basis were paid a minimum of $24.72 per hour when covered by an International Alliance of Theatrical Stage Employees (IATSE) contract. Overtime work paid more. Rates for working on commercials were slightly higher. Per diem work, however, is not regular or continuous, but most grips work an average of 10 months per year, according to union sources. Nonunion positions are paid less, ranging from $20,000 to $28,000 at most stations or production/facilities companies.

Employment Prospects

Opportunities for this entry-level job are fair. Employment is normally confined to major productions in New York City or Hollywood or at one of the top 20 major market commercial or public TV stations, but television and film productions occur in virtually every state. Work in the late 1990s was steady. As a lower-paid entry-level job at some major market stations, however, the turnover is relatively high and openings do occur from time to time as those in the position are promoted or leave for other jobs.

Advancement Prospects

Opportunities for bright, ambitious individuals are fair and depend largely upon personal initiative and talents. The job can sometimes serve as an informal apprenticeship for scenic designing, and with the proper education, experience, talent, and aggressiveness a bright Stagehand/Grip can advance to the position of assistant scenic designer. Some Stagehand/Grips become Property Masters for major film and television productions. A Stagehand/Grip who becomes extremely proficient at the job might move to a larger production company at a high salary, where there is involvement with more ambitious and complex programs. In nonunion shops and at some major market TV stations, the Stagehand/Grip may have the opportunity to move to the position of Floor Manager or Unit Manager.

Education

Education credentials beyond high school are not required, but an ambitious candidate who views the job as an entry into television production should have a college degree in radio-TV or theater. Courses in theatrical staging, lighting, and television and film production are extremely helpful.

Experience/Skills

Professional experience in television production is not required. Any experience in set construction or related scenic responsibilities in college television or theater or in any amateur or community theater production is a decided advantage.

A Stagehand/Grip should have some knowledge of television or film production techniques, physical strength, and a sense of esthetics.

Minority/Women's Opportunities

Industry sources indicate that both women and members of minorities are well represented in this position. Women comprised approximately 40 percent of union membership in 1998, while employment of minority group members was somewhat higher, according to a spokesperson for IATSE.

Unions/Associations

Stagehand/Grips are sometimes represented by a New York or Hollywood unit of IATSE. Some individuals at major market television stations belong to the National Association of Broadcast Employees and Technicians AFL-CIO (NABET) for representation in labor negotiations.

CRAFTPERSON

CAREER PROFILE

Duties: Construction and painting of sets, backdrops, props, and other scenic pieces for use in a television production

Alternate Title(s): Shop Craftsman; Shopman; Painter; Prop Maker; Chargeman; Scenic Artist

Salary Range: $25,000 to $60,000+

Employment Prospects: Fair

Advancement Prospects: Poor

Prerequisites:

Education—Trade or vocational school

Experience—Apprenticeship in carpentry and painting; some background in TV or theatrical production or construction

Special Skills—Good carpentry and painting skills; manual dexterity; logical mind; ability to work rapidly and under pressure

CAREER LADDER

```
┌─────────────────────────────────┐
│         Shop Foreman            │
└─────────────────────────────────┘

┌─────────────────────────────────┐
│         Craftperson             │
└─────────────────────────────────┘

┌─────────────────────────────────┐
│   Vocational/Trade School;      │
│   Carpenter/Painter's Helper    │
└─────────────────────────────────┘
```

Position Description

A Craftperson is responsible for painting and constructing the sets used in television programs. This person is normally employed in the scene shop of a television network or independent production company or in a commercial scenery studio that specializes in building sets for television, theatrical, and motion picture production. Although most such studios are located in Hollywood and New York City, they are increasingly found in other major urban centers that have significant theatrical, film, and television activities. Craftpersons usually specialize in carpentry or painting but also work on set decoration, props, special effects, etc.

Carpenters called "Prop Makers" work from blueprints, sketches, floor plans, and instructions from the Scenic Designer and a foreman. A Prop Maker works with painters, assistant scenic designers, and other carpenters and skilled workers in constructing sets. A Prop Maker uses a variety of hand and power tools and works with different materials, such as wood, plastic, fiberglass, and muslin. In the construction industry, carpentry is commonly divided into two categories—rough and finish. Prop Makers who build television and theatrical scenery deal only with finish carpentry.

Painters work with various materials to achieve the effects called for in the scenic design. They use brushes, air guns, cloths, rollers, and other tools to cover and finish set construction. Painters mix and match colors, using a knowledge of paint composition and color harmony. They use varnishes and lacquers, plaster appliqué, and various types of paints to supply texture to surface covering. Painters are also responsible for wood graining, marbleizing, and spattering.

Craftpersons work on various types of sets, including three-sided rooms of all kinds, backdrops, panels, furnishings for game shows and news broadcasts, and outdoor set (exterior) pieces, as well as special furniture and props. Most television scenery is realistic, but on occasion it may be fanciful or abstract. Sets are not usually constructed for permanence or structural integrity. They are often built in units or sections to facilitate storage and reassembly.

Building and painting television scenery is somewhat different from theatrical set construction. Because TV frequently uses closeup shots, the scenery usually has a finished and natural appearance, and the set generally seems to be realistic and detailed. Since in a theater the audience is further removed from the scenery, specific detail may be omitted while certain significant features may be exaggerated.

Carpentry and painting work in television is generally completed on a tight deadline. When working on scenery for a TV production, a Craftperson usually has little time to spare. For *Saturday Night Live,* for example, preliminary sketches are ready on Tuesday, final instructions on Wednesday, and six or eight sets are completed by early Saturday.

Additionally, the Craftperson

- checks the accuracy of construction with levels, rulers, and framing squares;
- paints colors and designs on backdrops and panels; and
- devises ways to solve special construction problems in consultation with the Scenic Designer and foreman.

Salaries

Craftpersons are usually members of a union. Union scales and regulations are extremely complex. The payment depends on a number of factors. Television shop craftsmen are reasonably well paid. A coordinator earned a weekly minimum of $1,660.19 per week on a pilot or first- or second-season television program, while a set decorator earned $1,706.13 in 1998. The minimum "call" was for eight hours per day, and rates are based on straight time—although most jobs include overtime.

Employment Prospects

The opportunities for employment are fair. The demand for Craftpersons in Hollywood is low because of an overabundance of job candidates; however, film and television production is greatly increasing in other areas of the country, and work is far more plentiful. Such areas included Florida, the Carolinas, and Canada in 1998, according to industry sources. Most scenery shops employ some Craftpersons on a full-time basis and augment the crew with temporary help to accommodate a heavy schedule. Because there are often slack periods for television Craftpersons, they usually supplement their television income with general carpentry, construction work and painting. Most Craftpersons work six to nine months of the year.

Advancement Prospects

The opportunities for promotion are poor. Some union Craftpersons advance their careers through promotion to shop foreman. This position is scarce, however, and there is very little turnover. The freelance (temporary) Craftperson generally considers frequent or continuous employment to be the equivalent of advancement.

Education

Basic carpentry and painting skills may be learned at a vocational or trade school or through apprenticeship. The latter is usually a three-year program of on-the-job training accompanied by classroom instruction. Industry sources, however, recommend that an individual obtain special training in motion picture or television production to be adequately prepared for the special requirements of TV scenery construction.

Experience/Skills

Competence in basic carpentry and painting techniques, which may be acquired as an apprentice or carpenter's or painter's helper, is required. Additional experience in television or theatrical production construction and painting is generally considered a prerequisite. An apprenticeship, which is sometimes available through a local union branch, is excellent training.

Craftpersons must have good basic carpentry and painting skills, a considerable degree of manual dexterity, and a logical approach to problems. They should be able to work rapidly and under some pressure.

Minority/Women's Opportunities

Industry sources report that many women and members of minority groups are becoming active as Craftpersons. Women reportedly comprised approximately 20 to 30 percent of union membership in 1998. Estimates regarding minority involvement vary, but industry sources indicate that opportunities for members of minorities have more than doubled over the past 10 years.

Unions/Associations

Craftpersons employed on a freelance basis in television are represented by a local New York or Hollywood unit of the International Alliance of Theatrical Stage Employees (IATSE) for negotiating and bargaining purposes. Some belong to the United Scenic Artists (USA) for the same purpose. Some individuals are also members of the United Brotherhood of Carpenters and Joiners of America, which is a bargaining agent for carpenters in all areas of construction.

PART II
CABLE, VIDEO, AND MULTIMEDIA

INDUSTRY OUTLOOK

A remarkable change is occurring in communications. Rapid technological advances are transforming a television industry based on the physics of scarcity* into one of electronic diversity. New ways of transmitting and receiving messages abound, mostly based on nonbroadcast technology. Some observers believe that we are undergoing a communications revolution. To others, it's an evolution in which newer technologies have developed from the older forms to create unprecedented new possibilities in the ways we transmit and receive information.

The number of technological systems, devices, and methods of reception that can be—and are—used with a modern television set is staggering: broadcast TV; basic cable television; pay cable; home computers; video games; videodiscs; videocassettes; low-power television (LPTV); multichannel multipoint distribution services (MMDS); "wireless cable"; direct broadcast satellite (DBS); satellite master antenna systems (SMATV); Web TV, high-definition television (HDTV), and digital television (DTV); digital versatile or videodisc (DVD); and teletext and videotext. Only broadcast television and basic cable TV were in existence 25 years ago (see Table II-1)!

The television set is beginning to play a dramatically different role in our lives. From a limited number of programs broadcast to a mass audience, we are now in an era of "narrowcasting." Specific messages or programs that reach small targeted audiences with specialized interests are now available to an increasing number of professionals, students, and consumers. We can play back instructional programs on videodiscs or cassettes, watch first-run movies transmitted by MMDS or pay cable TV operations, listen to a special music-only cable channel, play a video game alone or with others, receive important information in written form (teletext), shop on the Internet, and receive entertainment or information programs via DBS and SMATV to our homes. We can now use the TV screen with computers and can receive programs from LPTV stations that offer specialized programs to viewers in small geographic areas.

The standard 21-inch television is being replaced by large screen television. Stereo TV is commonplace, and HDTV, which produces exceptionally clear pictures with more electronic line formations, is now a reality.

These new devices and technologies are not limited to home viewers. Schools, colleges, private industry, government, and health agencies are using them with increasing frequency. This astonishing proliferation has created new businesses along with a need for people to develop, manage, market, service, and operate their systems and products. While employment statistics for most of these newer industries are not available, all observers predict a generally increasing number of career opportunities for many types of workers.

DEFINITIONS

The oldest form of the alternative transmission services is cable TV, which began as a means of providing better reception of regular broadcast television channels. The technology was used in the mountains of Pennsylvania in 1948, when a master antenna was raised on a mountain peak and the houses in the valleys were linked to it by coaxial cable, enabling home viewers to receive a clear picture. The system was called Community Antenna Television (CATV), but the acronym now generally stands for "cable TV." In education, private industry, health, or government, a cable system that operates within or between buildings in a "closed loop" fashion is called a closed circuit TV (CCTV) system.

The word *video* is often used to describe the use of television production in nonbroadcast settings. When used in the context of the home video industry, it includes the manufacture and distribution of consumer electronics products and programs such as videocassette recorders (VCRs), videodisc machines, and prerecorded programs on cassettes and discs.

Video is also used to describe independent companies that produce video programs or offer postproduction services, editing, and studio and remote facilities to other producers. In many instances, such firms are called "video/film production houses."

The use of communications equipment and programming in business and industry is often called "corporate TV," "organizational TV," or "private TV."

The use of satellite-delivered programming to and from many locations is termed *teleconferencing,* but often the term *videoconferencing* is used to distinguish the transmission from strictly audio transmissions.

Many in the field of education use the term *instructional technology* or *educational technology* to describe their use of media.

Some observers commonly combine *all* uses of television other than traditional broadcasting under the general term *nonbroadcast TV* to distinguish the newer uses from the older technology.

More accurately, many experts use the general term *telecommunications* to describe all means of audio and visual transmission of signals from one point to another. Broadcast television, radio, telephone, and telegraph are part of the

---

*This phenomenon effectively limits the number of over-the-air transmissions that can be made without mutual interference.

Table 11-1—Services to the TV Set, United States, 1998

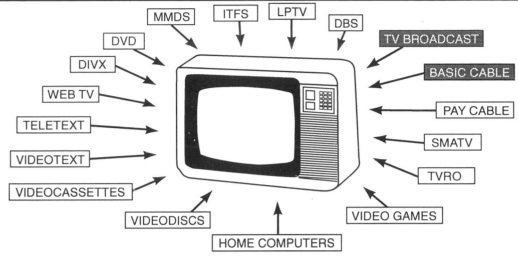

Only these services were available in 1975

telecommunications industries. The term has commonly been used to describe an interconnection method linking two or more electronic points in which an exchange of information takes place. Partly to distinguish their use of technology from the show-business image of broadcast television, some educators and other nonbroadcast specialists use the term to imply a more serious (often interactive) use of the electronic media for information and instruction. Increasingly, however, the term *telecommunications* is used more specifically to describe teleconferencing, electronic mail, data transmission, and the use of telephone networks in communications.

Today, many analysts simply use the term *media* to encompass all nonbroadcast technology, including print and nonprint materials. The term is used in many departments in health, education, private industry, and government organizations to describe their functions. Some professionals use the term *electronic media* to distinguish it from the print media. The term *multimedia* denotes a combination of media such as text, video, audio, and photography accessed through a common interface, usually via computer. In the interest of simplification, the generic term *media* is used throughout Part II.

Following is a discussion of the seven major areas of cable, video, and multimedia, highlighting the present state, the future growth, and employment opportunities of each area. The major positions in these sections are profiled in the 38 descriptions that follow this Industry Outlook.

SECTION 1: CABLE TV AND MMDS

Several types of alternative television transmission and reception systems have been introduced in the past 35 years. Many offer increased opportunities for employment, while others are temporary systems that may be overshadowed in the competitive marketplace.

All of the services were originally designed to reach specific targeted audiences. Unlike broadcast television, these systems charge the viewer a fee to receive the programs.

Cable TV

Cable Systems   Cable TV in all its forms has come a long way in the past 10 years. The growth has been the result of the advances in satellite technology, more diverse programming, and the deregulation of the industry at the federal level.

There were more than 11,000 individual cable systems in the fall of 1998, according to the National Cable Television Association. They served more than 63 million people, or 66 percent of the nation's TV homes.

Some systems are small, serving fewer than 1,000 subscribers, while many have 250,000 or more customers. A number of systems, however, merged in the mid-1990s or were purchased by a large firm and are now owned by a single company, known as a multiple system operator (MSO). Nearly 14 million cable subscribers were served in 1998 by the largest MSO, TCI, at that time.

Cable revenues from subscribers and advertisers in 1998 reached over $30 billion, more than double the amount in 1988.

The technical emphasis in cable TV is on the electronic and physical connection of a subscriber's TV set to the "head end" (control center) by fiber optics and coaxial cable. The system transmits signals received in any of four ways: from satellites, from off-air signals of TV stations, via microwave, and from local origination (whether live, videotaped, or computer generated). The signals are sent from processing equipment and amplifiers at the head end to a series of major trunk cable lines, then to feeder trunk lines that run to clusters of homes, and finally to drop lines that connect the individual home by coaxial cable directly to the system.

Most cable systems offer 30 channels to subscribers, but any system constructed after 1972 must have at least a 20-channel capacity, according to Federal Communications Commission (FCC) regulations. Nearly 46 percent of the systems in 1998 offered 54 or more channels. Systems under construction today (and those being rebuilt) offer 36, 54, or more channels in various program or channel groupings called "tiers," and the subscriber can select from among a number of packaging arrangements called "availabilities."

All subscribers pay a fee to receive basic cable service that covers the reception of local stations, two or three stations from outside their geographic area, and special religious, arts, or music channels. These channels are supported by advertising revenues. Most subscribers pay additional fees to receive pay cable service, which usually includes first-run Hollywood movies and other special entertainment programs.

Cable Program Services   Broadcast television reaches a large mass audience and is the most powerful "electronic newspaper" of all time. Cable TV is perhaps the most powerful "electronic magazine." Its appeal is directed toward a smaller targeted audience that, in its aggregate, constitutes a sizable number of viewers. While hundreds of cable systems had significant amounts of locally originated production in 1998, the majority of programming is supplied by national cable satellite program services. Theatrical films and original programs are supplied by HBO, Showtime, and the Disney Channel. Other networks, such as Lifetime and ESPN, offer special women's lifestyle shows and sports programs. Still others, including the Science Fiction Channel and Telicare, serve particular audience preferences.

The programming must become more general to attract advertisers (for the basic channels that are supported largely by advertising) and to retain subscribers (for the pay channels). Faced with the competition from videocassette machines and a high disconnect (churn) rate by subscribers, many cable systems are offering pay-per-view (PPV) programming.

With PPV, the viewer orders and is charged for a specific program (usually a top sporting event or a newly released film), rather than for a channel of programs. PPV programs are normally offered in a home through addressable converters that can be controlled by a computer at the cable head end. The pay-per-program rather than the pay-per-channel offers increased revenue for cable systems as well as for program suppliers.

The national program services scramble their satellite signals (to curb piracy) and embrace more sophisticated marketing techniques. As cable TV reaches maturity, it has moved out of its engineering/construction stage into a programming and marketing/promotion era. Cable must, however, deal with a vital home video industry and other competing technologies. Nevertheless, the future for cable TV is bright.

Cable Employment   In 1996, 120,530 people were employed at cable television systems in the United States, according to the FCC. This total falls short of the 146,616 people employed at commercial and public television stations in that year.

At the local cable systems, 14 percent of the people were employed as officials/manager, 4 percent as professionals, and 14.5 percent as technicians in 1996. Some 9 percent were employed in sales, 33.5 percent in office/clerical work, and 13.7 percent as operatives in that year.

Women held 41.7 percent of all of the jobs at local cable systems in 1996. This was an increase from 39.8 percent in 1988. Minorities held 28.1 percent of the jobs in 1996, an increase of 6.5 percent from 1988, according to the FCC.

The number of jobs in cable will continue to increase gradually through 2006 as more communities award franchises and as subscribers increase. Opportunities will be generally good in engineering, sales, marketing, and customer relations. As cable systems increase their local programming efforts opportunities should increase in production jobs (see Table II-2). While cable TV faces stiff competition, excellent jobs will be available to dedicated people through 2006.

MMDS

Multichannel Multipoint Distribution Service   Cable TV operations are referred to as systems or plants. MMDS operations are often referred to as stations because they are licensed to broadcast through the air. The video signal either arrives at the station from a satellite or originates locally at the station. It is then broadcast in a modified form on a specially assigned frequency to subscribers' homes, where a special antenna relays the signal to a device (box) at the TV set. The signal is down-converted to a lower frequency by the box and is sent to the subscriber's TV set for normal viewing. Because these stations broadcast over the airwaves, they are licensed by the FCC as common carriers but are commonly known as over-the-air pay-TV services.

This technique of transmission broadcasts a signal by microwave over a 20- to 30-mile radius to private homes, multifamily dwellings, and office buildings.

Originally a business communications service offering one channel (MDS), the operations have been authorized to increase their channel capabilities. Regulatory changes by the FCC in 1983 offered the MMDS industry the opportunity to expand to multichannel transmission through the licensing of additional spectrum space and the leasing of instructional television fixed service (ITFS) channels (see Part II: Education). MMDS can now theoretically become a "cable of the air" system offering 20, 30, or more channels in each location. The viewer pays to receive the MMDS signal and for the converter to unscramble the signal.

The industry is small but growing. Systems now serve 5 million customers in 90 nations, with more than 1 million customers in 250 systems in the United States. In 1989, some 39 systems had only 350,000 subscribers, according to the Wireless Cable Association International.

Because of its potential in currently noncabled areas and in rural areas where cable television may never be constructed, the 1983 FCC ruling drew more than 16,000 applications for licenses. As a "wireless cable system" offering many channels of programming, some observers believe that MMDS will emerge as a cable competitor in some markets in the future. It may also serve many of the 22 million homes (largely rural) that will never receive cable television. Some job opportunities will occur in MMDS in the engineering, sales, and customer service areas, but program, production, and advertising sales opportunities will be slim.

Direct Broadcast Satellite, Satellite Master Antenna Systems, Television Receive-Only Dishes   Since the launch of the Early Bird satellite in 1965, engineers, broadcasters, venture capitalists, and futurists have predicted the imminent international use of satellite transmissions direct to any home. For 35 years, high-powered satellites capable of sending many television signals to a small receiving dish on a rooftop have been just around the corner.

By 1997, DBS had captured 14 percent of the multichannel video market.

American TV set owners have purchased television receive-only 6- to 8-foot (diameter) satellite dishes for installation in their back yards, as well as much smaller dishes. An estimated 2 million TVROs capable of receiving signals from C-Band and domestic satellites were installed by 1989. During the following decade, American TV set owners purchased millions more TVROs, also called DTH (direct-to-home).

Many of the TVROs are being purchased and installed to serve apartment houses, other multiple dwelling units, and hotels. These satellite master antenna systems receive the satellite signals at one location and redistribute them to subscribers in the individual housing units.

As the national cable program services began to scramble their signals, however, a synergy between cable operations and TVROs developed. By scrambling, the current low-power C-Band domestic satellite program services have become a de facto DBS system. Descramblers are sold by cable companies, and the local cable systems may increase their efforts to wire multidwelling housing.

Digital satellite TV service was launched in 1996, with 646,000 units shipped, compounding several million analog systems already in use.

There will be some job opportunities in the DBS, TVRO, and SMATV systems in the near future. The majority of positions available will be in engineering and sales.

SECTION 2: CONSUMER ELECTRONICS AND HOME VIDEO

Consumer Electronics

The consumer electronics industry has created a host of entertainment and educational products that have had an incredible impact on our society. The items for sale include radios, television sets, video games, videocassette recorders/players, videodisc machines, programs on video-cassettes and discs, personal computers, stereo systems, large-screen TV projectors, and many other electronic marvels.

Home Video Machines

Although videotape recording has been used to record and play back TV programs for broadcast since the late 1950s, it was not generally available for home or school use until the 1970s. Small format videocassette machines became available in 1975 and have now settled into the basic system known as VHS. It uses half-inch videotape on cassettes inserted into the machine, which is attached to a TV set. VHS can record programs on blank cassettes from a television set, record sound and pictures from a home video camera and microphone, and play back prerecorded programs on the television set. A new, smaller unit, the 8mm videocassette machine, was introduced in 1985. Designed for and marketed to the home movie maker to be used as a "camcorder," the machine can also be used to record from and play back through the television set, and in the late 1990s, digital camcorders made their appearance. Camcorder sales in all formats have increased dramatically in recent years.

Unlike VCRs, which can record, the newer videodisc machine, first introduced in 1978, can only play back prerecorded programs on a TV screen. The Laservision optical videodisc uses a laser to "read" encoded electronic impulses on a 12-inch disc, similar to an audio record. When the machine is connected to a TV set, the images appear in clear, full color, often accompanied by stereo sound. The optical disc became the de facto standard in 1984, when RCA discontinued the manufacture of its stylus CED disc machine, which failed to win mass market success.

The videodisc was eclipsed by the CD-ROM, which became a standard platform by the mid-1990s and Digital Video Discs, which could store up to 17 gigabytes—a great deal of video, audio, and texture information.

The future of the videodisc may lie in the business, health, and education fields in the United States. An optical disc has the capacity to store 108,000 individual still frames, enabling the disc to act as a video encyclopedia. When used with a small computer, the interactive capabilities can be utilized for individual training and instructional purposes (see Part II: Education; Health).

Home Video Programming

The astonishing growth of home video in the past few years has seen a corresponding growth in the number of prerecorded programs that can be rented or purchased for playback with a VCR or videodisc machine. Some are designed strictly for use in educational settings, but others were available for home use, according to *Bowker's Complete Video Directory*. The same feature films available on cable and MMDS systems constitute many of the titles.

Employment Opportunities

The boom in home video and consumer electronics has created a need for counter sales and rental clerks in retail stores. And the American public's love affair with electronic devices has also created a need for people to service and repair the machines. Video on demand may change all that in another 10 years.

Still, the Bureau of Labor Statistics (BLS) of the federal government expects retail clerk jobs to grow faster than the average of all occupations through the year 2006.

There was a consolidation of many smaller video program regional distributors into larger national concerns in the latter part of the 1980s, and the middle-man role in the two-step video distribution process may be diminished somewhat by the wholesale manufacturers selling directly to retail accounts. Good jobs, however, will be available in marketing and sales at these distribution companies.

In addition, the number of independent production companies developing programs for the home video market is expected to increase.

Many of these companies specialize in programs for education, training, and health, while the home video industry is dominated by the Hollywood studios and a few large independent production companies. As VCR penetration has grown, however, many new firms have been formed to develop, produce, and distribute programs specifically designed for home video. Sports titles, music videos, how-to and instructional programs, and children's shows have become an increasing part of the home video industry. Book publishers are also becoming more involved in home video by adapting books to video formats for this ancillary program market.

Production positions (see Table II-2) will become more available in such companies by 2006. More jobs should also be available at the facilities companies that provide services for home video producers. In addition, more positions should be open in the Performance/Arts/Crafts areas (described in Part I) at those companies producing original programming for home video. Job opportunities will increase in all areas of home video.

SECTION 3: EDUCATION

Simple audiovisual (AV) devices have been used in the United States for more than a century in formal and informal educational settings by teachers who have sought new ways to enrich and supplement traditional classroom and individual learning. Since 1900 the phonograph, radio, magnetic wire and tape recording, stereo, sound, programmed learning machines, and, more recently, television, video, and computers have been used for educational purposes. The use of media in schools and colleges grew quite slowly until the end of World War II, when a veritable explosion occurred. Sparked by the threat of Russian dominance in space, the U.S. Congress passed legislation in 1958 that made the use of educational media to improve instruction a national policy.

Since that time, many traditional AV centers have expanded their functions to embrace all media, including the newer electronic forms, and act as service units for their parent institutions by providing equipment, assisting in curriculum development, producing or acquiring appropriate materials, and maintaining media libraries. Although the growth has slowed in the past 10 years, every school system, college, and university in the United States makes some use of audiovisual technology. Television, video, and computers, as well as traditional AV tools, serve the needs of teachers and students at every level of education.

Instructional Television

In 1998, public television delivered instructional materials to 30 million students and 2 million teachers in over 63,000 K–12 schools nationwide, according to the CPB.

The CPB's 1997 Station Activities Survey reports that a total of 144, or 81 percent of all public television stations in the United States, provided programming to elementary schools, and nearly as many provided programming to secondary schools (141, or 79 percent of all stations). The National Instructional Satellite Service feeds nearly 1,000 hours of instructional programs per year to K–12 students. Moreover, through the Satellite Educational Resources Consortium, spearheaded by CPB, students in 28 states study advanced science, math, and language courses in high schools without teachers for these subjects.

The most popular means of delivery was the full-power broadcast channel, which was used by approximately three out of four stations that provided instructional programming.

The production and use of instructional television (ITV) programs in the classroom may increase in the next five years, due to the inauguration of programs provided by private cable organizations and other commercial providers of educational services via KU-Band satellites.

Closed Circuit Television

Some schools and colleges transmit and receive their ITV programming through closed circuit television (CCTV) systems linking buildings and classrooms by a closed-loop coaxial cable. CCTV systems are largely in operation at colleges and universities, where they transmit ITV programming during the day to classrooms on campus. Some programs are produced in campus television studios and recorded for later transmission or use on campus. Nearly all of the 3,706 institutions of higher education used television for some instructional purposes in 1997, according to the U.S. Department of Education. Nearly one-half made some use of a CCTV system. Some large secondary schools also operate CCTV systems.

Instructional Television Fixed Service

A few schools and colleges transmit and receive their ITV programming via ITFS operations. This transmission system is technically identical to MMDS, although the channels are reserved for educational purposes. Both use low-power, over-the-air microwave signals to transmit to receiving locations within a 24-mile area.

While separately programmed cable channels were used by 17 percent of public television stations, ITFS services were less popular, used by only 10 percent of stations to deliver elementary school programming and by 11 percent to deliver secondary school programming.

There are two predominant audiences served by ITFS systems, according to a CPB study: kindergarten through grade 12 and the adult learner in industry. The numbers of individual learners reached range from less than 100 to more than 400,000. ITFS systems transmit live courses for adults, often in the evening hours, and prerecorded ITV programs for schools.

Telecourses

The arena of distance learning, including telecourses, has expanded to include digital technologies such as the PBS teleWEBcourses[sm]. In fact, the field now commonly called "instructional technology" refers to education of individuals in various locations that is facilitated by personal computers, CD-ROMs, multimedia, hand-held devices, and software, as well as distance modalities such as the Internet, videos, television, satellite, radio, cable, fiber optics short wave, and microwave technologies.

Telecourses, however they are delivered, enable students to study independently from work or home. Most telecourses are a cooperative venture between a college and a public television station. Where broadcast by a local station isn't feasible, other means of delivery can be arranged, such as cablecasts on a college cable channel, delivery through ITFS, the Internet, or videocassette loan. According to PBS, each year more than 400,000 students at nearly 2,000 institutions nationwide enroll in its Adult Learning Service distributed telecourses.

Teleconferencing

Many colleges, universities, and school districts are involved in teleconferencing. This "distant learning" technique uses existing unused time on domestic satellites to transmit live seminars, college courses, or workshops to adult learners or students at predetermined sites. Often the teleconferences (or videoconferences) use ITFS systems for local redistribution of the programs, which sometimes offer lectures and discussions along with correspondence work and computer-assisted instruction (CAI). The videoconferences can be interactive, with both students and instructors capable of seeing and hearing one another, or they can consist of a one-way video lecture from the instructor or presenter and two-way audio. Occasionally, audio-only teleconferences are used as a cost-effective way to link teacher and students together over long distances.

Uplink satellite and teleconferencing services are offered by a number of commercial firms, including IBM, Holiday Inn, and World Communications. Downlinks (reception satellite dishes) are permanently installed at all PBS stations and portable ones are offered for rent by commercial firms. These TVRO dishes are used to receive the signal for retransmission to classrooms or meeting places at local sites.

According to the National Center for Education Statistics, in 1997 22.9 percent of all public schools, K–12, were equipped to receive satellite-delivered programming, whereas 8.7 percent of private schools had a satellite dish. Many schools opted to work in conjunction with local PBS stations for such program delivery.

Two organizations that provide satellite-related programming and services to primary and secondary schools, as well as to universities, are the Satellite Education Resources Consortium (www.serc.org), which is a consortium formed by the partnership of public television and state departments of education, and the National Educational Telecommunications Association (NETA, at www.netaonline.org).

Video

The growth of home video has fostered a growth in the use of video in schools and colleges. Although slow to initially accept the new devices, there has been an explosion in the use of videocassette machines in the schools.

There has been a corresponding growth in the number of prerecorded video programs available for use in schools. Many national producers specifically develop and market programs for use in instructional settings. Increasingly, "crossover" programming, originally distributed for home viewing, is being adapted for or used in a school setting as the VCR replaces the 16mm motion picture projector in education. Videocassette machines are also becoming common in higher education. Most university departments now have a machine or access to one.

School/College Media Centers

The increase in VCRs and use of computers in education have created an expansion in the scope of the activities of university and school media centers. Many colleges and large school districts now operate circulating libraries of videocassettes in addition to 16mm film, film-strips, audio tapes, and the other traditional AV materials.

Public Libraries

Corresponding to the growth of home video (see Part II: Consumer Electronics and Home Video), public libraries have increased their circulation of half-inch videocassettes. Libraries are adding videocassettes to their 16mm and 8mm film collections, and they often share videocassettes with other libraries. Libraries often carry nonentertainment (or auxiliary) videocassettes, including how-to programs, self-improvement lessons, language courses, and performing arts programs, in addition to the usual theatrical films. The circulation of video by libraries will continue to grow in the next few years.

Instruction

Not surprisingly, Communications and Media Instructors use television and video in their classroom teaching. Communications Instructors teach television production, introduction to broadcasting, mass communication courses, and other courses related to broadcasting. Increasingly, courses in cable TV and industrial or corporate communications are taught by Communications Instructors.

Media Instructors teach media production, instructional technology, instructional television, and related topics. Courses in instructional design and multimedia applications in education are also taught by Media Instructors. (For a list of colleges and universities that offer coursework in these fields, see Appendix I.)

Employment Opportunities

The overall opportunities for employment in educational media have been relatively stagnant for the past 10 years. Federal, state, and local educational budgets have not grown in proportion to the U.S. economy.

There is every indication, however, that a new emphasis on education is being embraced by all sections of society. And the impetus given the educational world by private industry will continue.

There will, therefore, be an increase in jobs available in the next five years in the general area of educational media, as administrators and the private sector look for innovations and new accomplishments. Additional job openings will be made available in private, commercial companies that seek to provide programs to the educational market.

In addition to those specific jobs listed in the Education section in Part II, other production jobs are sometimes available in education. For a listing, see Table II-2—Crossover Jobs.

SECTION 4: PRIVATE INDUSTRY

Industrial and corporate managers have used traditional audiovisual tools since the early part of this century as aids for employee training, for improving interoffice communications, and for public relations purposes. Corporate use of new technologies grew rapidly, however, during the mid-1970s. Many companies in virtually all industries established media or audiovisual centers to house, purchase, and produce media programs, usually with a modest staff.

The use of television in business is alternately called "private television," "corporate TV," "professional video," "organizational TV," or "industrial TV." Under whatever label, the use of media and technology in the corporate world has grown consistently in the past few years. The use of television and video has been widely supplemented by multimedia presentations, often incorporating video and audio prepared in such software programs as Macromedia Director for access via the World Wide Web or CD-ROM, according to Fitch, Inc., a strategic business consultancy and design firm.

The largest corporate use of TV and video (as well as multimedia) is usually for training purposes. National companies use videocassettes to transmit product information, new sales techniques, and motivational lectures to employees in various locations. Many companies use video to train production-line workers in new methods or to instruct middle managers in supervisory skills. Still others use media for such internal corporate communications as periodic company video newsletters, a "video memo" from the boss, on-the-job safety programs, or new employee orientations. Many large companies use television and video for annual stockholders' reports or for public and community relations.

Corporations are increasingly using teleconferencing and videoconferencing to conduct companywide meetings or to introduce new products to sales personnel. Some companies are beginning to use video and multimedia for point-of-purchase (POP) displays of products at the retail level. Additionally, organizations have taken to promoting their products and services on CD-ROM as well as via the Internet. With sophisticated production tools including Macromedia Director and Cyberstudio, these interactive media provide retailers and consumers with fast access to detailed information, which can contribute to a company's productivity as well as enrich the end-user's experience.

Training or human resource development (HRD), however, continues to be a major purpose for the use of media in business and industry. Almost all of the training programs involve technology or media in some way. While the one-half-inch and three-quarter-inch videocassette machine is the predominant device used, CD-ROMs are also used extensively.

Many of the programs used on the videocassette and videodisc machines are purchased from outside production/distribution firms. The prerecorded programs are rented or purchased by the video center at the corporation and redistributed through a network of video stations. In the past 10 years, a number of firms have been started to provide "off-shelf" or outside training materials, hardware, and services to organizations.

Many major corporations today, however, produce their programs in-house but they also use outside production facilities.

Outside facilities, equipment, and services are often used to further develop original material produced at the corporate video center. Most corporate facilities are relatively small but have state-of-the-art equipment.

The use of video, however, does not fit neatly into most corporate structures. Video centers within corporations report to a variety of departments within a given corporation. Many report to training departments, but others report to corporate services or administration, public relations, marketing, or the photographic or film department. The full-time video staff ranges from one to three people in small companies, to 21 or more in larger video centers. The full-time staff is often augmented by part-time freelance personnel on a project-by-project basis. While the number of videos and multimedia productions has increased dramatically in recent years, so has the number of producers and facilities, and industry sources estimate that the typical video center produces 10 to 60 programs each year, usually of 10 to 20 minutes in length.

Some video centers are fully funded by the corporation, which pays for all equipment, services, production, and salaries as a part of the corporate overhead. Others are financed through a system of chargebacks whereby the using department in the corporation pays for all services and the video center is viewed as a self-sufficient center. In this manner, the true cost effectiveness of the use of video can be more accurately measured. Partial chargeback systems, however, are most common in private television, where all costs except salaries and office overhead are charged to the using department. Some AV centers rent their facilities to users outside of the corporation to help defray operating costs and minimize downtime in their studios.

The use of media in the corporate world is not limited to video. Corporations are increasingly turning to teleconferencing (or videoconferencing) as a cost-effective way of reaching employees in scattered locations. Information can be disseminated more quickly, and consistent information is transmitted on a company-wide basis. Marketing training and product introduction are the two main purposes for videoconferencing. Corporations such as the Ford Motor Company, Merrill Lynch, and J.C. Penney use one-way satellite-beamed programs.

Teleconferencing is expected to grow. Although most corporations now use ad hoc networks, the establishment of permanent networks is expected to increase.

Employment Opportunities

With growth predicted in the corporate use of telecommunications and video, there are opportunities for employment in production, and engineering. Positions other than Manager of Audiovisual Services and Supervisor of Media Services, fully profiled in this book, are also available in private television. For a list of those jobs, see Table II-2—Crossover Jobs. In addition, many freelance positions are available in private television. Opportunities for positions for those people who are employed at outside production facilities, which serve corporate television departments, are particularly good. Corporate video departments are decreasing the number of people on staff and doing less in-house production. They are increasing their use of facilities companies, opening up opportunities for many production and engineering jobs.

SECTION 5: GOVERNMENT

Almost every government agency of any size at the local, state, or federal level operates and maintains audiovisual equipment. Sometimes the equipment consists of only an overhead or 16mm film projector used for internal training purposes or public information activities. Many establish a media center with a small staff to acquire, store, circulate, and occasionally produce media programs. Some government agencies maintain extensive television and video operations.

The federal government is the largest user of video programs. Expenditures in audiovisual activities include production, duplicating, library operations, and off-the-shelf purchases. The vast majority of production is done on videotape. And most of the production is done by outside commercial production freelance companies or by a combination of in-house agencies and outside firms. This continues a trend toward using commercial companies to produce federal video programs. Still, many of the products are produced at government-owned and -operated facilities.

Government agencies use TV and video for internal training and public information. Training programs are also developed or purchased by many state and local government agencies. Training in the public sector includes programs in management skills and development, clerical/secretarial skills, communication skills, new methods and procedures, technical and supervisory skills, and retraining.

Government agencies at all levels do as much in-house design of training programs as does private industry, and a considerable number of such programs involve media. Videocassettes, videodiscs, computers, and multimedia combinations provide support for most training programs, and many specific programs are designed around audiovisual devices.

At the state governmental level, public health, agriculture, youth services, law enforcement, and transportation agencies use TV and video to reach and instruct employees throughout the state, as well as for internal training purposes. Many of these agencies use the media to retrain their employees or to introduce new techniques and information. In addition, fire fighters, postal employees, and clerks and typists in local or state agencies receive an increasing amount of their training and retraining with media support materials.

Many of the television programs developed at local and state governmental agencies are one-camera, on-location shows with a minimum of production and editing. Still others utilize the techniques of broadcasting and the facilities of production and postproduction houses to produce more sophisticated programs.

In addition to video and television, some federal and state agencies utilize ITFS systems for training programs. Federal agencies are also utilizing teleconferences to communicate with their counterparts at the local and state levels.

Local and state agencies (as well as those at the federal level) continue to use television and video as public information tools. A number of agencies develop and produce their own videocassettes to reach their publics and to inform them of their specific missions.

The use of television and video in government agencies, however, has not grown as fast as it has in business and industry or in other nonprofit sectors, such as education. Most observers predict small growth in the next five years.

Employment Opportunities

Some state agencies employ as few as three people in all areas of media, with perhaps only one individual serving as the local Audiovisual Program Officer. Employment in media (including television and video) is more prevalent at the federal level. Some observers have estimated that there are more than 20,000 individuals directly involved in audiovisual activities at federal agencies around the country, but this does not include private consultants and agencies hired as a result of recent government downsizing, so the actual number could be much higher. Many of the larger federal agencies in Washington operate their own television production units and employ production, engineering, and other employees in jobs similar to those in broadcast TV. For a chart listing such crossover jobs, see Table II-2. Part-time positions on a project-by-project basis are also occasionally available. Generally, however, employment opportunities in video, television, and media at the local, state and federal levels have not greatly increased in the past five years. Most observers do not see any significant growth in the future.

SECTION 6: HEALTH

Health care specialists have been using traditional audiovisual materials for a number of years and in a variety of ways. Today, medical schools make use of videocassettes to demonstrate surgical and medical procedures and to present patient case histories. Hospitals use video along with

other media for patient education, for training, and for public and community relations. Physicians subscribe to teleconference networks for continuing education, conferences, demonstrations, and seminar programs that help them to complete state, medical association, or board requirements for Continuing Medical Education (CME) credits.

The health care services industry and the use of media within it can be divided into eight major types of organizations/institutions: (1) Teaching centers associated with university hospitals and (2) Veterans Administration hospitals reportedly make the most use of media. (3) Private independent, state, and local hospitals also make some use of media. (4) School health centers make occasional use of media, but budget constraints inhibit the use of video or media in this area, as well as in (5) nonprofit public health organizations. (6) Clinics and special health care facilities (drug and alcohol rehabilitation or health care facilities for the elderly), and (7) private physicians' offices reportedly make slight use of video and other media. (8) Veterinary medicine makes some use of media to support teaching programs.

In the academically related media facilities, media are used for instruction and to support professional personnel with exhibits and displays. Media are also used to support in-service training, but only incidentally for patient or public education.

In private, state, local, or VA hospitals, media are most often used for in-service training for professional personnel, including physicians and nurses. Patient education and public information programs in these settings do not utilize media to support their activities to a major extent. Not surprisingly, those public health organizations using media concentrate on patient education.

Overall, the major use of media in all health-related facilities is to support in-service training and instruction. Training in health facilities is used to enhance management skills and development and to improve clerical and supervisory skills. Media are used to help instruct personnel in new methods and procedures and in technical skills and knowledge updating. The use of media to support training and teaching programs is greatest at the nation's medical schools.

Most university-affiliated teaching hospitals operate media centers, which serve as the central acquisition, storage, and distribution centers for media support materials. The medical school media centers also produce materials.

The most sophisticated and large centers are located at the institutions that are members of the Association of Biomedical Communications Directors (ABCD). The Universities of Michigan, Nebraska, and Florida and Indiana University operate large medical media centers. In the private school environment, Georgetown, Boston University, and Baylor maintain and operate large medical school media facilities.

Biomedical communications centers provide a number of services to their parent institutions. They provide medical illustration and photography services and supply television production and traditional AV services. The biomedical communications centers also supply graphic design and print shop services.

Some of the centers' budgets are received from a charge-back system similar to that used in private industry media centers and, to a lesser extent, similar operations in education. Under this system, departments within the parent institution using the services and facilities are charged for the services and an interdepartmental transfer of funds is made. The other major use of media in health care facilities is in the Veterans Administration hospitals.

Most of the use of media in the health care field, however, is not as organized or centralized as in the medical schools or at the VA hospitals. Personnel who are involved with video and other media are often scattered throughout various departments in health care facilities. Some may be found in the public information department, in the research, personnel, and training departments, or in nursing or library services.

Each of these hospitals has some traditional audiovisual equipment, such as slide and filmstrip machines and 16mm film and overhead projectors. Nearly every one has acquired one-half-inch or three-quarter-inch videocassette equipment, or has access to such equipment. The VCR machines are largely used as playback devices for training and patient education. One staff member is usually responsible for the use of media in such settings. Many obtain prerecorded videocassettes from a circulating audiovisual library at the National Library of Medicine (NLM).

Many hospitals, however, also use the VCR equipment to produce and record short programs on videocassette for patient education, in-service training, and to document patient illness. These projects often involve a staff of two but are essentially one-camera productions.

An estimated 1,500 hospitals maintain a significant media and video operation that employs from three to four people, according to observers. The programs often support the educational services and nursing departments in training and patient education.

In such circumstances, the use of multimedia is seldom under the organizational control of the librarian at the hospital. Although to be accredited by the Joint Commission on Accreditation for Hospitals (JCAH) a hospital must maintain or have access to a library, the majority of medical library holdings are printed materials.

Because of budgetary constraints, the American Hospital Association (AHA) no longer produces or sponsors satellite teleconferences; independent vendors are hired as needed by health care facilities for such delivery of medical forums, training, and business communications, according to the public affairs office of the AHA.

Like virtually every other industry, however, hospitals and related health care operations have a strong presence on the World Wide Web. Web sites proliferated during the 1990s and are expected to remain a mainstay that requires regular management, according to industry observers.

Employment Opportunities

The opportunities for employment in media in the health care field during the next five years are fair.

The cost of health care in the United States, which reached new heights during the 1990s, created demands for cost cutting and made most medical care facilities' budgets come under closer scrutiny. Some hospitals and health care facilities closed in the 1990s. Media budgets stabilized, however, according to most observers, but little growth is seen in the future.

Opportunities for positions as librarians specializing in media will remain only fair, as in the other educational areas, in the next five years. Photographer and graphic artist positions should remain stable because of turnover and retirement. Opportunities for employment in specific television production jobs will not grow appreciably by 2006 in the health care field, but some positions in engineering should remain in demand.

As more health care facilities slowly expand their use of video, however, there will be some opportunities for the media generalist who can serve as a Producer, Director, Camera Operator, Writer, Lighting Director, and Videotape Operator/Editor of one-camera ENG productions in smaller health care institutions. While there is a general lack of financial support for video in the health care field and the policy of sharing prerecorded video programs would seem logical, there is, paradoxically, a large number of small local productions. These unique and specialized programs, which are not distributed to other health care facilities, are a part of the "not invented here" (NIH) syndrome in the health care field, according to observers. As a result of this emphasis on local production, some crossover production positions (see Table II-2) should be available in the future at the larger medical care facilities on a part-time basis.

In general, however, the opportunities for employment in video and media positions at health care facilities are poor. The media field has yet to become a cohesive force in or a vital part of the health care profession.

SECTION 7: MULTIMEDIA DEVELOPMENT

Multimedia as it is known today was barely emerging in the early 1990s, but during that decade, this burgeoning force, which employs a computer interface to combine text, video, audio, photos, and animation, came into its own and showed signs of becoming a dominant player in the global economy. Many have dubbed the new millennium the multimedia age, and its proponents point to its role in the broader category of information technology (IT), whose share of total nominal gross domestic product growth was running almost double its

Table II-2—Crossover Communications Jobs in Cable, Video, and Multimedia

The following jobs are profiled in Part I and Part II	Cable/MMDS Large systems involved in original production and local origination	Consumer Electronics/Video Independent companies involved in original production	Independent Production Companies Companies involved in original production	Education Larger organizations involved in original production	Private Industry Larger companies involved in original production	Government Larger organizations involved in original production	Health Larger organizations involved in original production	Multimedia Larger organizations involved in original production
Business Manager		•	•					•
Accountant		•		•			•	
Receptionist/Office Clerk	•	•	•	•	•	•	•	•
Film/Tape Librarian	•		•		•	•		
Director of Publicity/Promotion	•	•						
Publicity/Promotion Assistant	•	•	•					
Production Manager	•			•				•
Executive Producer		•	•					•
Producer	•	•	•	•	•	•	•	•
Associate Producer		•	•					
Director	•	•	•	•	•	•	•	
Assistant Director	•	•	•					
Floor Manager	•		•	•	•		•	
Production Assistant	•	•	•	•	•	•	•	
Production Secretary	•	•	•	•	•	•		
Lighting Director		•	•					
Art Director		•	•					
Graphic Artist	•		•	•	•	•	•	•
Cinematographer/Videographer	•	•	•	•	•	•	•	
Film/Tape Editor	•		•	•	•	•	•	
Engineering Supervisor	•	•	•	•	•	•	•	•
Audio/Video Engineer	•	•	•	•	•	•	•	
Videotape Engineer/Editor	•	•	•	•	•	•		
Engineering Technician	•		•	•	•	•	•	
Camera Operator	•	•	•	•	•	•	•	
Account Executive/Sales	•							
Site Flow Architect								•
Programmer								•
Multimedia Writer	•	•	•	•	•	•	•	•

Jobs unique to Cable/MMDS, Video, Education, Private Industry, Government, Health, and Multimedia are profiled in Part II share of the economy, at close to 15 percent in 1998, according to the U.S. Department of Commerce.

Multimedia is developed for use on the Internet, more specifically the World Wide Web, and stand-alone products that include CD-ROMs, CD-Is, and proprietary games produced by companies such as Nintendo. As information transmission and storage capacity increase and computer processing speeds and data compression technology improve, the presence of multimedia on the World Wide Web is expected to escalate dramatically. Its role will encompass communication, education, entertainment, and electronic commerce—meaning that organizations in the public and private sectors will find having an Internet presence essential. That in turn translates into plentiful work for individuals involved in multimedia development. Projections made by the Bureau of Labor Statistics (BLS) in 1998 estimated that through 2006, an additional 2 million workers will be needed to fill jobs in the IT field, including multimedia.

The potential impact of multimedia on the global economy and the culture at large is staggering. In 1993 only 5 million people around the world were using the Internet. By 1997 the number had risen to 100 million, and during that year traffic was doubling every 100 days. Some experts project that by 2005, 1 billion people will be connected, according to the U.S. Department of Commerce. Businesses in virtually every sector of the economy have begun to use the Internet as a tool in research, development, sales, and marketing, leading to the conclusion that information technology and electronic commerce may well drive economic growth for years to come.

At its best, multimedia is an interactive forum that enables the consumer to make choices concerning how the product is to be used, or navigated. In addition to exploring the product or World Wide Web site via various paths, eliciting information, or being passively entertained, multimedia allows the consumer to enter information—often in real-time exchanges—and influence the results, arriving at different destinations based on the multitude of nonlinear paths available.

The buzz word of the day is *convergence*. Among the provisions of the Telecommunications Act of 1996 was the repeal of cable-telephone cross-ownership restriction. This in effect allowed cable operators to offer telephone services and vice versa, opening the floodgates to investment in and competition for meeting a spectrum of business and consumer telecommunications needs: television, telephone, and Internet services. In response, the cable industry invested $11 billion in 1998 alone in new technology and programming, according to the National Cable Television Association, as it banked on the transmission superiority of broadband technology over telephone lines and tried to stave off the threat of

direct broadcast satellite (DBS) services, which in 1998 already held 14 percent of the multichannel distribution television market.

Employment Opportunities

Regardless of how content is ultimately transmitted and received, the fact remains that much of that content will be multimedia, which will have to be conceived of and produced. The eight multimedia job descriptions in this section represent the areas of management, programming, and content development or production. Individuals who would like to pursue a career in writing, designing, programming or managing multimedia development would do well to review these job descriptions; they offer guidance on desired skills and aptitude, educational requirements, and career paths. Most experts agree that as the multimedia industry was in its infancy, most people who entered the field were self-taught, motivated professionals who had media and management skills that transferred well to the creative, logistical demands. As the discipline grows and stabilizes, however, conventional wisdom indicates that more job candidates will earn degrees in multimedia and its related fields and build a body of experience to launch their careers. Those with higher levels of education and training as well as a variety of specialized skills will advance most quickly.

Crossover Positions/Job Descriptions

Part II contains 38 descriptions of jobs in the area of Cable, Video, and Multimedia. The positions are divided among seven sections: Cable Television; Consumer Electronics; Education; Private Industry; Government; Health; and Multimedia Development.

In addition to the jobs specifically profiled in Part II, there are often other job possibilities.

Table II-2 lists those jobs fully profiled in Part I (Television) and in the multimedia section that are also often available in cable video, private industry, government, education, and health agencies involved in original productions or local originations. The jobs listed in Table II-2 are *full-time* positions, usually available only in the larger organizations or firms in those nonbroadcast fields. The reader interested in obtaining specific production and engineering positions in cable, video, and other nonbroadcast areas should check the specific jobs listed in the crossover positions in Table II-2. Full descriptions of each of the jobs are given in Part I. Other *part-time* jobs profiled in the Performance/Arts/Crafts section of Part I are also often available at those companies and organizations described in Part II that are involved in original production.

SYSTEM MANAGER

CAREER PROFILE

Duties: Managing the operation of a cable TV system or an MMDS station

Alternate Title(s):   Station Manager; General Manager

Salary Range: $40,000 to $95,000+

Employment Prospects: Fair

Advancement Prospects: Fair

Prerequisites:

Education—Undergraduate degree; graduate degree in communications or business preferable

Experience—Minimum of three years in business management, preferably in telecommunications

Special Skills—Organizational skills; leadership qualities; good judgment; technical knowledge; sense of responsibility

CAREER LADDER

```
┌─────────────────────────────────────────┐
│  System Manager (Large System or         │
│  Station);                               │
│  District or Regional Manager            │
└─────────────────────────────────────────┘

┌─────────────────────────────────────────┐
│           System Manager                  │
└─────────────────────────────────────────┘

┌─────────────────────────────────────────┐
│      Marketing Director;                  │
│  Chief Technician; Chief Engineer         │
└─────────────────────────────────────────┘
```

Position Description

A System Manager of a cable television system or a multichannel multipoint distribution service (MMDS) station is in charge of the overall management of the operation, including income and expenses, programming, sales, and engineering. Responsibilities include maintaining good relationships with local governmental agencies, the community, and all outside contacts, and directly supervising all departments of the organization. As the chief operating officer of a small telecommunications firm, a System Manager is responsible for managing a program service that may reach from 2,500 to more than 200,000 subscribers. In cable TV, the person in this position is referred to as the System Manager and in MMDS operations as the Station Manager, but the functions are similar. The responsibilities parallel those of a General Manager at a commercial or public full-power television station.

The System Manager determines the types of basic program and pay TV services to be offered to customers, the number of channels to be used, and the charges for services. Another important function is the planning for new facilities such as satellite receiving stations, increased channel capacity, and production equipment. The System Manager must plan and budget so that the operation can keep up with technology, increase its subscriber base, and earn a healthy profit.

If a cable system sells advertising time, a System Manager also establishes rates and supervises Salespersons in selling commercials. In small systems, the System Manager may also be the chief Advertising Salesperson.

A System Manager oversees the operation of a cable system or an MMDS broadcast station in accordance with all Federal Communications Commission (FCC) regulations and with all other federal, state, and local laws. The individual in this position keeps informed about construction laws, tariffs, and access charges, and works closely with local utility companies and governmental agencies to provide a profitable public service to the community. A System Manager serves as the company's most visible representative within the community and is ultimately responsible for all customer relations.

A System Manager is sometimes an owner or part-owner of the company. In other cases, the individual is a salaried employee who reports to a board of directors. In many organizations the System Manager is part of a management team that represents a group owner. A System Manager may also serve as the local manager for one or two of a company's systems in a particular geographic area.

Additionally, the System Manager

- forecasts monthly and annual income and expenses;
- evaluates and approves all marketing and sales efforts;

- hires all employees and monitors their performance; and
- handles customer complaints and billing and payment disagreements.

Salaries

Salaries for System Managers depend on the size of the operation, the number of subscribers, and the geographic location. Salaries in cable TV systems ranged from $40,000 in the smaller systems to $95,000 in major markets in 1997, according to the Women in Cable and Telecommunications Foundation survey. Station Managers at MMDS companies were paid somewhat less in 1997, according to industry observers. Many companies offer excellent benefit plans, including a company car, health and pension plans, and profit sharing. Most offer bonus plans and reasonable expense accounts.

Employment Prospects

Opportunities for bright, diligent individuals are fair. MMDS operations (largely in rural areas) will grow by 2006. The position is not an entry-level job, however, and while many operations are opening, it is usually only the person with some experience who is selected as System Manager.

A talented Marketing Director, Chief Technician, or (from broadcasting) Chief Engineer can often become a System Manager.

Advancement Prospects

The opportunities for advancement are fair, and the competition is heavy. Many System Managers move to larger, competing systems or stations in other markets with more responsibilities and at higher salaries. Some successful Managers are transferred within their own organizations to larger existing systems or to other communities to establish new franchises or licenses. Other people are promoted to district or regional manager positions within a Multiple System Operator (MSO). Still others move to middle management positions at their parent companies' headquarters.

Education

As in most management positions in telecommunications, an undergraduate degree is expected, and an advanced degree is desirable. Most System Managers for national MSOs have undergraduate degrees in business administration or marketing. A few have graduate degrees in communications, computer science, or electrical engineering.

Experience/Skills

A minimum of three years in general business management, but preferably in telecommunications, is required. Some System Managers have been Chief Technicians in cable or MMDS, or Chief Engineers at broadcast stations where they gained considerable experience in engineering practice. Individuals with marketing backgrounds are being sought as System Managers as cable has matured.

A candidate should be a self-starter with initiative and leadership qualities. Sound business judgment, acceptance of responsibility, a respect for profits, and organizational skills are required, as are poise and social skills for dealing with a variety of community leaders and agencies.

Minority/Women's Opportunities

According to FCC statistics, 35.9 percent of all officials and managers in cable television were females in 1996, and 15.5 percent were minority group members. The percentage of women in management positions is much higher in cable television than in other segments of the media industry. Because cable has been largely a rural operation, however, there is a relatively low percentage of minority employment.

Unions/Associations

There are no unions that serve as bargaining agents for System Managers. Most cable companies belong to the National Cable Television Association (NCTA), and many System Managers represent their companies in that association. Many cable System Managers also belong to a state or regional cable association to share mutual concerns and advance their careers.

Managers of MMDS companies often belong to the Wireless Cable Association to share common industry concerns.

OFFICE MANAGER

CAREER PROFILE

Duties: Managing the office and business functions at a cable TV system or MMDS station

Alternate Title(s):   Accounts Receivable Clerk

Salary Range: $24,000 to $45,000

Employment Prospects: Good

Advancement Prospects: Good

Prerequisites:

  Education—High school diploma; college degree preferable

  Experience—Minimum of one year in office management and bookkeeping

  Special Skills—Accuracy; reliability; organizational ability; good interpersonal skills

CAREER LADDER

```
┌─────────────────────────────────┐
│      Business Manager;           │
│    Accountant/Bookkeeper         │
└─────────────────────────────────┘

┌─────────────────────────────────┐
│        Office Manager            │
└─────────────────────────────────┘

┌─────────────────────────────────┐
│   Customer Service Representative │
└─────────────────────────────────┘
```

Position Description

The Office Manager of a cable TV system or multichannel multipoint distribution service (MMDS) company is responsible for the smooth operation of daily business activity. The major function of the position is to relieve the System Manager from as many routine day-to-day office obligations as possible and to coordinate all financial and office functions so that they support the marketing and engineering staffs. The Office Manager also works as a troubleshooter in solving specific office problems.

The Office Manager is often second in command of the business aspects of the operation and is in charge of many of the financial transactions of the company. One of the primary responsibilities of the position is to monitor the accounts receivable status to ensure that money that is owed to the company is paid as promptly as possible. The Office Manager prepares regular accounts receivable reports in association with the marketing and sales department. Another of the duties of the position is to supervise the monthly billing of subscribers and to authorize service disconnections for non-payment. The Office Manager often has the responsibility for directly dealing with the delinquent account customer. The accurate maintenance of all of the company's financial records and journals is an additional function of this position.

In most circumstances, the Office Manager reports directly to the System Manager. In some larger organizations,

the person in this position reports to a business manager or to the senior accountant/bookkeeper.

The Office Manager usually directly supervises from 1 to more than 20 people, depending on the size of the operation. The majority of local cable systems and MMDS organizations, however, are small business enterprises, employing as few as 5 full-time workers. At such companies, the Office Manager, along with a Customer Service Representative, often performs the duties of an accounts receivable clerk, a service dispatcher, a billing clerk, and an accountant/bookkeeper. In larger operations or station organizations, as many as six individuals may perform these functions, with each individual responsible for a particular area. Today, the majority of cable and MMDS operations rely on computer systems to handle office records, billings, accounts receivable and payable, budgeting, and office record keeping.

In whatever situation, the Office Manager is vital to the day-to-day operation of the organization and is the principal middle management coordinator, ensuring that the company's overall business activities mesh smoothly with the efforts of the Marketing Director and sales staff.

Additionally, the Office Manager

- supervises the activities of the customer service department, assuring prompt handling of all accounts and complaints;

- selects, hires, trains, and supervises office staff;
- maintains all employee payroll records; and
- schedules the work of Installers and Technicians, in association with the Chief Technician.

Salaries

Despite the responsibility of the position, salaries for this job in cable TV are relatively low, ranging from $24,000 to $45,000 in 1997, with an average annual salary of $32,688, according to the Women in Cable and Telecommunications Foundation survey. Salaries at MMDS companies in 1997 were comparable, according to industry sources.

Employment Prospects

While this is not an entry-level job, there are openings for capable individuals. Positions open up frequently as Office Managers are promoted or move to more responsible jobs in broadcast, media-related or nonmedia-related companies. Some experienced, talented Customer Service Representatives are promoted to this position. The opportunities in general for aggressive, bright individuals are good, and the skills required are readily transferable to other businesses.

Advancement Prospects

The possibilities for advancement for bright individuals are good. Some Office Managers at large firms are promoted to the position of business manager or accountant/bookkeeper at their own companies or at other stations or systems owned by the parent organization. Some take more responsible financial or office supervisory jobs at new systems or MMDS stations. Still others use their office management skills to obtain better-paying positions in nonmedia-related industries.

Education

A high school diploma and a year or two of training at a business or vocational school are required, and a college degree in business administration is preferable. Courses in bookkeeping and accounting are essential. Some training with spreadsheet software or management information systems is helpful, inasmuch as the sales, billing, and accounting records in virtually every company are computerized.

Experience/Skills

One or two years of actual office management and bookkeeping is required. Experience in television, cable, or the newer media industries is desirable, but background in a responsible position in a nonvideo-related industry is useful.

Office Managers are usually bright, young, well-organized, and aggressive individuals who can handle complicated tasks easily and accurately. The ability to balance conflicting demands and requests routinely is a must, as is reliability. The Office Manager must also have good interpersonal skills and be capable of supervising office workers. A familiarity with office calculating machines is mandatory. Experience with computers or word processing machines is also necessary.

Minority/Women's Opportunities

Opportunities for women are good. According to the Federal Communications Commission (FCC), 47.8 percent of the professional employees (including Office Managers) in cable TV in 1996 were females. The percentage of minorities in these positions was 52.2 percent in 1996, according to the FCC.

Unions/Associations

There are no unions or professional organizations that represent Office Managers in cable television or MMDS operations.

CUSTOMER SERVICE REPRESENTATIVE

CAREER PROFILE

Duties: Coordinating installation and service requests and complaints at a cable TV system or MMDS company; converting inquiries into orders

Alternate Title(s):   None

Salary Range: $22,000 to $36,000

Employment Prospects: Good

Advancement Prospects: Good

Prerequisites:

Education—Minimum of high school diploma; some college preferable

Experience—Minimum of one year of office work

Special Skills—Detail ability; numerical aptitude; organizational capability; service orientation; sales talent; computer literacy

CAREER LADDER

```
┌─────────────────────────────────────┐
│           Office Manager             │
└─────────────────────────────────────┘

┌─────────────────────────────────────┐
│   Customer Service Representative    │
└─────────────────────────────────────┘

┌─────────────────────────────────────┐
│      High School/Business School;    │
│         Clerk; Secretary             │
└─────────────────────────────────────┘
```

Position Description

A Customer Service Representative coordinates all customer requests for service with the sales, marketing, and engineering staffs of a cable television system or a multichannel multipoint distribution service (MMDS) station. The Representative is essential in helping to maintain successful and profitable rapport with potential and current subscribers. The person in this position usually reports directly to the Office Manager in small organizations and, increasingly, to the Marketing Director in larger ones. In either case, this is usually not a supervisory position. The Customer Service Representative's job is to serve, sell, and satisfy subscribers.

Representatives receive all requests and complaints concerning information, prices, and services from subscribers and make certain they are dealt with promptly. They must also be able to convert a casual inquiry into a firm sale and to upgrade an installation request into a higher-priced service. Some industry statistics indicate that more than 20 percent of all initial customer contacts are made from incoming telephone calls to the main office. It is the Customer Service Representative's job to explain the benefits and costs of the various program services to the caller. Representatives also discourage disconnect requests through the application and reinforcement of sales strategies. At some systems or stations, Customer Service Representatives take a more active involvement in telemarketing (telephone) sales by initiating such calls.

At a small system or station, a Customer Service Representative may deal with as many as 2,500 subscriber orders during a year. In many small firms, this person also performs the duties of a billing clerk (invoicing subscribers), a work order control clerk (expediting installations and service calls), or service dispatcher (scheduling Installers and Technicians). In most systems and stations today, such logistics and record keeping are tracked with computerized equipment. In larger companies, the Representative concentrates on providing over-the-counter and telephone responses to potential customers or current subscribers. Larger companies often have more than one Customer Service Representative. Some larger firms employ six or more Customer Service Representatives full-time.

In small systems with few or no sales personnel, Customer Service Representatives are crucial to subscriber growth. In addition to performing public relations, sales, and service roles, they ensure the timely coordination between subscribers' orders and requests and the company's proper fulfillment and response. Customer Service Representatives are also important in reducing the disconnect (churn) rate of an operation. A friendly and persuasive telephone manner can often dissuade discontented customers from canceling the service.

Additionally, the Customer Service Representative

- maintains accurate records of all calls and of dispatcher and work orders;
- processes all phone-in or over-the-counter orders from new customers and assigns them to appropriate Salespersons; and
- prepares preliminary invoices for monthly billings to subscribers and calls delinquent accounts for payment.

Salaries

Compensation for Customer Service Representatives in cable TV is relatively high. Some cable systems offer commissions on sales, bonus plans, or incentive sales plans during the year, which add to the basic salary. Customer Service Representatives are often paid by the hour. Experienced individuals earned from $22,000 to $36,000 in 1997, according to authoritative sources within the cable TV industry. Salaries in MMDS stations were comparable, according to industry sources.

Employment Prospects

The position is often an entry-level job. Many diligent clerks and secretaries are promoted to Customer Service Representative. Because of the growing number of telecommunications companies and the relatively high turnover rate in this job, there are many opportunities for employment. The recent high school or business school graduate should also find it relatively easy to become a Customer Service Representative. Part-time positions are often available at MMDS and cable operations.

Advancement Prospects

The opportunities for advancement are reasonably good for those with some initiative and experience. A person can learn many of the fundamental aspects of customer service, telecommunications operations, and general office functions. As the company grows, many Customer Service Representatives are eventually promoted to more responsible jobs in various intermediate supervisory roles. After some years of experience, an individual may move into the position of Office Manager within the company or at a competing firm. Still others obtain more responsible jobs at higher salaries in nonmedia service-related industries.

Education

A high school diploma is a minimum requirement for the job. Individuals with some business or vocational school training are preferred. Courses in computer operations and training in management information systems can be extremely helpful.

Experience/Skills

Although the position is often considered an entry-level job, candidates are usually expected to have had at least one year of office experience. A working knowledge of standard office equipment is required and experience with computers or word processors is essential. Experience in "one-on-one" telephone relations gained by working with telephone or credit card companies or airlines is very useful.

Most Customer Service Representatives are bright young people who have a penchant for detail and an ability to work with numbers. They are organized and capable of dealing with a variety of tasks and people on a day-to-day basis. Some are homemakers who have reentered the job market.

Interpersonal skills in managing and coordinating internal logistics between departments are necessary and a service-oriented and pleasing personality is helpful. A Customer Service Representative should possess good telephone manners, tact, and courtesy in dealing with subscribers and potential customers. A Customer Service Representative also must be able to reinforce sales strategies during over-the-counter or telephone contacts. An ability to sell or resell a service is mandatory in obtaining the position.

Minority/Women's Opportunities

In the majority of cable TV systems or MMDS firms, the position of Customer Service Representative is held by women. Of all workers in the office clerical category (which includes Customer Service Representatives) in cable TV in 1996, 84.2 percent were females, according to the Federal Communications Commission (FCC). Minorities held 36.5 percent of such positions in 1996.

Unions/Associations

There are no unions or professional organizations that represent Customer Service Representatives at cable TV systems or at MMDS companies.

MARKETING DIRECTOR

CAREER PROFILE

Duties: Developing and coordinating all marketing activities for a cable TV system or an MMDS station

Alternate Title(s): Marketing Manager

Salary Range: $35,000 to $75,000+

Employment Prospects: Good

Advancement Prospects: Good

Prerequisites:

Education—Undergraduate degree in marketing, advertising, or communications; graduate degree preferable

Experience—Minimum of three years of experience in telecommunications sales or marketing

Special Skills—Aggressiveness; leadership qualities; organizational skills; outgoing personality; promotional talent

CAREER LADDER

```
┌─────────────────────────────┐
│      System Manager         │
└─────────────────────────────┘

┌─────────────────────────────┐
│     Marketing Director      │
└─────────────────────────────┘

┌─────────────────────────────┐
│      Sales Manager          │
└─────────────────────────────┘
```

Position Description

A Marketing Director of a cable TV system or a multichannel multipoint distribution service (MMDS) operation is responsible for providing the income that allows the company to operate profitably. This individual is responsible for all marketing, promotion, publicity, and advertising activities and for all direct sales to subscribers.

The major objective of a Marketing Director is to obtain—and retain—as many customers as possible for the organization. Responsibilities include the development of sales campaigns that will reach a reasonable percentage of the potential subscribers in the system's or station's area. The byword of these consumer-oriented organizations is customer satisfaction. The viewer "votes" every month by payment of the bill or by a request for a disconnect. It is an ongoing and complicated marketing challenge to attract, connect, satisfy, and retain subscribers, and thus to maximize the volume of sales without increasing the costs to the company.

One of the most important duties of a Marketing Director is to select, train, and supervise the sales staff, which may have from 2 to more than 20 Salespersons, and to coordinate and monitor all sales activities. The Marketing Director also conceives and develops sales tools, including print brochures and advertising displays, to assist all sales efforts.

The Marketing Director often performs important programming duties. In cooperation with the System Manager, the person in this position researches and selects the types of basic and premium pay television services the company will offer subscribers. The Marketing Director may also pick programs from existing national satellite services, negotiate with pay-TV program companies, or deal directly with suppliers to obtain particular programs.

Marketing Directors report directly to System Managers. Not all companies, however, employ Marketing Directors. They are usually found only at systems that have 10,000 or more subscribers. At smaller operations, the duties are either performed by the System Manager alone or are divided between the System Manager and the Sales Manager.

Additionally, the Marketing Director

- establishes rates, discounts, and special offers for program services, in consultation with the System Manager;
- recommends and researches new subscriber services, such as pay-per-view programming, home security, and interactive customer response systems;
- designs and monitors research to determine subscriber satisfaction; and
- creates incentive sales plans for Sales Managers and Salespersons.

Salaries

Salaries for Marketing Directors in 1997 ranged from $35,000 at medium-size cable TV operations to more than $75,000 for experienced individuals with seniority at systems with a large number of subscribers, according to the Women in Cable and Telecommunications Foundation survey. A company car, a bonus or profit-sharing plan, a reasonable expense account, and a health and pension plan are usually provided. In some instances, the Marketing Director is also paid a commission on overall yearly sales above quotas. Salaries at MMDS operations were somewhat lower during 1997, according to industry observers.

Employment Prospects

Opportunities at a cable TV system or MMDS station are good. While the position is not an entry-level job and requires some experience in telecommunications marketing, there is considerable turnover. In addition, the growth of these industries creates opportunities at new systems and stations for alert and qualified individuals. Some talented, experienced Sales Managers become Marketing Directors. Cable TV has moved out of the engineering/construction stage into a marketing and service era. More emphasis is being placed on attracting and retaining subscribers and more sophisticated marketing techniques are being employed. There is a need for qualified personnel to lead such efforts.

Advancement Prospects

Opportunities are good, but the competition is strong. Most Marketing Directors are ambitious and seek new challenges and opportunities in the telecommunications arena. After achieving a successful sales record and high profits for one company, some move to a similar but higher-paid job at a new operation. Still others become System Managers in similar or smaller markets. Successful Marketing Directors also take more responsible marketing or programming positions at the headquarters of cable TV multiple system operators (MSOs) or join pay television service companies such as Home Box Office and the Discovery Channel.

Education

An undergraduate degree in marketing, advertising, or communications is essential at all companies. A master of business administration (MBA) in marketing is virtually a requirement at large urban organizations. Courses in sales management can be useful. In addition, training in computer science is necessary, inasmuch as the customer service and billing operations make extensive use of computers, management information systems, or word processing systems to track and service subscribers.

Experience/Skills

A minimum of three years of previous experience in telecommunications sales or marketing is usually required. This can often be gained in the Sales Manager position.

A Marketing Director should be aggressive and capable of providing motivation and leadership to a diverse group of Salespersons. The candidate should be well organized and have some background in actual sales work. An outgoing and positive personality, a good feel for logistics, statistics, and research, and a flair for promotion and publicity are required.

Minority/Women's Opportunities

The number of women and minority group members occupying the position has been increasing during the past 10 years, according to industry observers. Many are joining the marketing and program staffs of the national pay-cable program suppliers. Those that offer special opportunities for members of minorities include the Black Entertainment Network (BET). Minority males serve as Marketing Managers at many of the local cable or MMDS systems that are located in urban centers or in rural areas with large minority populations. The majority of the Marketing Director positions, however, were held by white males in 1997, according to industry sources.

Unions/Associations

There are no unions that represent Marketing Directors. Many individuals belong to the organizations listed in the System Manager profile, particularly Cable and Telecommunications: A Marketing Society (CTAMS).

Some female Marketing Directors (and women in other positions) belong to Women in Cable and Telecommunications (WICT).

SALES MANAGER

Duties: Direct responsibility for all sales at a cable TV system or MMDS company

Alternate Title(s): Director of Sales

Salary Range: $35,000 to $50,000+

Employment Prospects: Good

Advancement Prospects: Good

Prerequisites:

Education—High school diploma; college degree preferable

Experience—Minimum of two years in sales

Special Skills—Aggressiveness; leadership qualities; persistence; organizational skills; dependability; sales ability

```
┌─────────────────────────────┐
│    Marketing Director        │
└─────────────────────────────┘

┌─────────────────────────────┐
│    Sales Manager             │
└─────────────────────────────┘

┌─────────────────────────────┐
│    Salesperson               │
└─────────────────────────────┘
```

Position Description

A Sales Manager is in charge of all of the sales activities of a cable television system or a multichannel multipoint distribution service (MMDS) operation. The main responsibility of the position is to direct a sales operation that tries to convince 2,500 to 200,000 potential individual customers to purchase the company's program services.

The Sales Manager usually reports directly to the Marketing Director and recruits and trains all Salespersons employed by the company. Depending on the size of the operation, a Sales Manager may have a staff of 3 to more than 20 Salespersons who sell by telephone or in the field. Part of the responsibility of the job is to assign these individuals to particular areas or accounts and directly supervise their activities on a daily basis.

A successful sales force is essential for a profitable cable or MMDS operation. The Sales Manager's role in training Salespersons is, therefore, a vital one, working with new individuals to make sure they clearly understand the company's services and how to sell them effectively to potential subscribers. The Sales Manager usually works with each Salesperson to develop a selling technique appropriate for that individual. The Sales Manager's success is directly tied to that of the sales staff. It is in the best interest of all, therefore, to train a highly motivated and successful selling team.

The job is more than simply a supervisory one. A Sales Manager is often involved in consumer sales on an individual,

even door-to-door, basis. This individual actively sells to and services current customers as well as new subscribers and initiates bulk sales to apartment houses or other multi-unit buildings. A Sales Manager is expected to spend at least three-quarters of the time aggressively selling program services to potential subscribers, setting the performance standards for all Salespersons. A Sales Manager must successfully meet individual goals as well as other established quotas for contacts and actual sales.

In conjunction with the Marketing Director, the Sales Manager maps out sales campaigns and establishes overall goals and quotas for specific geographic areas and time periods and devises strategies for reaching potential customers and convincing them to subscribe. The Sales Manager also develops ways to persuade current customers to purchase added program services. Through constant contact with the public, the Sales Manager can judge the effectiveness of the company's sales pieces and displays and then make recommendations to the Marketing Director as to what kinds of promotional materials and sales messages are likely to be successful.

Additionally, the Sales Manager

- keeps all Salespersons informed of changes in service prices, discounts, special offers, and organizational policies;
- maintains records of Salespersons' progress and activities;

- recommends price adjustments and new program services to the Marketing Director; and
- implements and monitors incentive sales plans for Salespersons.

Salaries

Sales Managers at MMDS and cable TV companies are usually paid in any or all of three major ways: with a relatively small salary, a commission on each sale, and an "override" payment for each commissionable sale made by all Salespersons. The compensation for Sales Managers in cable TV ranged from $35,000 to $50,000 in 1997, according to authoritative sources within the cable TV industry. Male managers, in general, reported an average salary of $53,502, and women managers earned $44,607, according to the Women in Cable and Telecommunications (WICT) Foundation survey. Salaries at MMDS companies were comparable, according to industry observers. Sales Managers often receive health, vacation, and insurance benefits and a company car or automobile allowance.

Employment Prospects

Opportunities for employment are good at MMDS and cable systems. As the cable industry has moved from the construction stage to sales and service the importance of increasing the subscriber base has commanded increased attention by system and station owners. Although the position is not an entry-level job, there is a constant need for qualified Sales Managers with good leadership abilities in cable TV and MMDS companies. In addition to the number of new media operations opening each year, there is a considerable turnover in existing sales positions. Many experienced and talented Salespersons are promoted to this more responsible position. Aggressive individuals with some "outside" (door-to-door) sales experience should be able to find jobs if they have management, organizational, and leadership skills.

Advancement Prospects

There is a relatively high turnover rate in the new media industry (particularly in sales), and some Sales Managers obtain more responsible sales or marketing positions within the industry. The competition is severe, however, and advancement is achieved only by those with initiative and strong managerial skills who obtain further education and training.

Sales Managers are usually ambitious and upwardly mobile. They often seek higher-paid jobs at larger market cable or telecommunications organizations. Some are promoted to the position of Marketing Director within their parent organizations and are assigned to new systems or stations. Still others may apply their sales experience to companies in nonmedia fields. Overall, opportunities for advancement are good.

Education

A high school diploma and some college education are required. Courses in business, marketing, interpersonal relations, and psychology are helpful. A college degree is sometimes required at large multiple system operator (MSO) companies. A formal education is less important, however, than the ability to motivate, train, and lead a sales staff. Leadership and management abilities are musts.

Experience/Skills

The position is not an entry-level job. A minimum of two years of sales experience with a consistent and reliable performance record is required. An additional year of sales management experience or a thorough knowledge of cable or MMDS services and sales operations is also a common requirement.

A candidate should be capable of being an aggressive supervisor who leads by example. A Sales Manager must be persuasive, persistent, enthusiastic, and dependable. The individual must also be well organized and consistent and have a genuine love of, and talent for, sales work.

Minority/Women's Opportunities

According to statistics compiled by the Federal Communications Commission (FCC), 44.2 percent of the sales workers (including Sales Managers) in cable television in 1996 were females, and 28.4 percent were minority group members. Minority females held 14.9 percent of the sales positions in that year, according to the FCC. The employment level of white women is much less than in comparable positions in commercial television, but the percentage of minority group members is much higher.

Unions/Associations

There are no unions or professional organizations that represent Sales Managers in cable TV or MMDS operations. Some belong to regional associations or societies to share industry concerns and advance their careers.

SALESPERSON

CAREER PROFILE

Duties: Selling cable television and MMDS program services directly to homes

Alternate Title(s):   Sales Representative

Salary Range: $25,000 to $50,000

Employment Prospects: Excellent

Advancement Prospects: Excellent

Prerequisites:

  Education—Minimum of high school diploma; college degree preferable

  Experience—Some retail or phone sales

  Special Skills—Sales ability; persistence; dependability; persuasiveness; initiative; competitive drive

CAREER LADDER

```
┌─────────────────────────────┐
│      Sales Manager          │
└─────────────────────────────┘

┌─────────────────────────────┐
│      Salesperson            │
└─────────────────────────────┘

┌─────────────────────────────┐
│   High School/College;      │
│   Door-to-Door Sales        │
└─────────────────────────────┘
```

Position Description

A Salesperson for a cable TV system or a multichannel multipoint distribution service (MMDS) station is responsible for selling the company's program service to individuals in homes within the franchise or coverage area. Sales are made in person or on the telephone.

A Salesperson is the backbone of the cable TV and MMDS industries and is immediately responsible for the financial success or failure of a company. This person must be able to describe the various program services offered in order to help the customers understand what they are purchasing. A good Salesperson represents the company in day-to-day contacts with potential subscribers in an accurate, honest, and personable manner. Sales calls are made during the daytime hours as well as during the evening. Sales are directed toward signing new customers for the system or service as it becomes available in a geopolitical area (new builds) or in selling new customers in territories already serviced (remarketing).

Most operations employ between 2 and 10 Salespersons, depending on the time of year, workload, and market situation. At some organizations, Salespersons work part-time, or a small full-time sales staff is augmented by additional help during a particular sales drive. At other organizations, the majority of the sales work is contracted to an outside firm that specializes in door-to-door selling of telecommunications services.

Sales quotas and goals are set for each Salesperson by the Sales Manager and Marketing Director. The Salesperson is expected to achieve specific levels of performance, such as contacting 90 percent of the individuals in the assigned territory. Some industry professionals feel that at least 30 percent of the potential customers contacted will purchase the basic program service and another 20 percent will purchase 5 premium services. The Salesperson's job is to reach and sell to those customers, thus increasing the company's subscriber base and income.

Although most sales efforts are directed toward individual homeowners, some Salespersons are assigned to multiple unit dwellings (apartment houses, hotels, and condominiums) and make sales calls on the managers of those buildings, who arrange for cable TV or MMDS program services for all tenants either with cable or with a satellite master antenna (SMATV) system. While the majority of a Salesperson's efforts are person-to-person, some sales are made by telephone and from the local office, either by answering inquiries or through "cold" calls to prospective subscribers. Other sales are made through follow-up calls designed to interest current customers in subscribing to additional program services.

In most instances, a direct sales effort follows an advertising campaign that is launched on radio or television, by direct mail or outdoor billboards, or by doorknob or mailbox drops. Salespersons are then provided with brochures, program guides, pamphlets, teaser material, and other sales tools to use in their pitch.

Additionally, the Salesperson

- attends daily sales meetings to receive assignments, new policies, procedures, goals, quotas, and sales literature; and
- maintains accurate sales logs, field sales order forms, and other records.

Salaries

Salespersons are usually paid in either, or both, of two ways: a small base monthly salary, and a graduated retroactive commission structure based on the sales made each week. Some work strictly on a commission basis as independent contractors with the cable system or MMDS station. Commissions are often paid at the close of the sale, although some companies pay after the actual installation or hookup of equipment at the subscriber's home. Most companies offer incentive bonus plans in addition to commissions and salaries. Incentive plans usually run for a short period of time and on occasion are offered by a national satellite cable network in conjunction with the local cable system. They often take the form of contests for cash, merchandise, or vacations. Other bonus plans reward Salespersons for the retention of subscribers after the initial sales order.

In 1997, total compensation—including salary, bonus, and commissions—for associate level professional/technical employees, including salespersons, averaged $29,902 for men and $31,133 for women, according to the Women in Cable and Telecommunications (WICT) Foundation survey. The salary range at MMDS companies was $25,000 to $50,000, according to industry observers. Most Salespersons who work on a contract basis, however, do not receive health, insurance, or pension benefits.

Employment Prospects

The position is usually considered an entry-level job and overall opportunities for employment are excellent. Qualified Salespersons are in demand at all MMDS, and cable TV companies. With the emphasis on sales in these industries through 2006, and with the relatively high turnover of sales employees, the prospects for Salespersons remain bright.

Advancement Prospects

Opportunities are excellent for successful Salespersons to move up. There is a constant need for qualified sales manage-ment personnel in all areas of the new media industries. Many Sales Managers leave companies for opportunities elsewhere, creating vacancies that must be filled. Some aggressive and successful Salespersons move to higher sales positions at competitive companies in larger markets. Others find sales jobs in fields unrelated to telecommunications.

Education

A high school diploma is a minimum requirement for employment. Some college training with courses in business is often preferable. A candidate's aptitude for and ability at selling, however, are more important than a formal education.

Experience/Skills

Although Salesperson is often an entry-level job, most employers prefer to hire people with some sales background. Experience in retail store or telephone sales is useful.

A gregarious nature, competitive drive, and evidence of initiative and perseverance are important qualities. An ability to relate to others, to listen, and to be quietly persuasive are very important. A neat appearance is essential, as are the ability to express ideas well and the possession of imagination. Above all, the candidate must be dependable, must like to sell, and must be interested in making money.

Minority/Women's Opportunities

Employment of women and minority group members in cable TV sales jobs is relatively high. According to the Federal Communications Commission (FCC), 44.2 percent of the people designated as sales workers (which includes Salespersons) were women and 28.4 percent were minorities in 1994. Female minorities held 14.9 percent of the positions in that year, according to the FCC. The employment of white women is the same as in comparable positions in commercial television, but the percentage of minority group members is higher. Minority opportunities in cable companies will increase, according to industry observers.

Unions/Associations

There are no unions or professional organizations that represent Salespersons in cable TV or MMDS companies.

DIRECTOR OF LOCAL ORIGINATION

CAREER PROFILE

Duties: Producing programming at a cable TV system

Alternate Title(s):   Manager of Local Origination; Production Director; Director of Public Access

Salary Range: $24,000 to $30,000

Employment Prospects: Fair

Advancement Prospects: Poor

Prerequisites:

  Education—Undergraduate degree in radio-TV or communications

  Experience—Minimum of three years in television production

  Special Skills—Creativity; organizational abilities; leadership qualities

CAREER LADDER

```
┌─────────────────────────────┐
│     Production Manager       │
└─────────────────────────────┘

┌─────────────────────────────┐
│         Director of          │
│      Local Origination       │
└─────────────────────────────┘

┌─────────────────────────────┐
│      Producer; Director      │
└─────────────────────────────┘
```

Position Description

A Director of Local Origination is in charge of local production originated by a cable TV system. As the manager of a cable system's production schedule, a Director of Local Origination occupies a position parallel to that of a Production Manager at a full-power commercial or public television station. The scope of the responsibility, however, is usually narrower at a cable TV system. The position is also similar to a Supervisor of Media Services at a corporate television center.

The responsibilities of the position include developing and monitoring budgets for all local productions, including costs for materials, capital equipment, supplies, and expenses. The Director of Local Origination determines the needs of the community through studies conducted by the marketing staff or by personal surveys and develops local programs to meet those needs. The major responsibility of the position is to supervise all phases of the creation of programs, from inception of the idea and the writing of the script through the technical production of the show. The resulting programs include local newscasts, talk shows, public affairs programs, entertainment or talent shows, sports events, and remote coverage of community events. For those programs that are sponsored, the Director of Local Origination is responsible for supervising the production of commercials that will accompany the program.

In some of the larger cable TV systems, two individuals oversee locally produced programs. The Director of Public Access is responsible for the operation of channels that are allocated for use by the public and must train, supervise, and assist volunteers in the production of programs for those channels. In those circumstances, the Director of Local Origination concentrates on productions that are conceived, developed, and produced by the full-time staff of the cable system. In most midsize and small cable TV operations, the two positions are combined, and the Director of Local Origination also oversees the production of community-developed programs.

The Director of Local Origination supervises the design of simple sets, art, and graphics for remote and in-studio productions. The responsibilities of the position also involve scheduling rehearsals, production dates, and personnel for all locally produced programs.

The number of staff members supervised ranges from three to eight, depending on the size of the system and its emphasis on local origination. The staff includes Camera Operators, Directors, Production Assistants, Graphic Artists, and other production support personnel. During productions, some engineering personnel and Technicians are often under the temporary supervision of the person occupying the position. The Director of Local Origination usually reports directly to the Systems Manager.

Additionally, the Director of Local Origination

- monitors standards of quality in all local productions;
- schedules equipment and facilities for local productions; and
- implements research and feedback mechanisms to evaluate the effectiveness of local productions.

Salaries

Salaries for Directors of Local Origination are relatively low, ranging in 1997 from $24,000 to $30,000, according to authoritative sources within the cable TV industry. Salaries are higher at the larger cable TV systems in urban areas.

Employment Prospects

The opportunities for this position are only fair. Most cable franchises granted by communities require that the system provide for local, governmental, educational, or access programming, with the signal originating at the local system's headend (electronic control center). In practice, however, many originations are simple, character-generated community bulletin boards, slide or one-camera shows, or videotape playbacks of programs produced by outside agencies and transmitted over access, educational, or government channels. There were more than 11,600 cable systems in the United States in 1997, with more than 60 percent of households subscribing to cable, according to the National Cable Television Association. Through the Telecommunications Act of 1996, the cable industry has gained entry into telephone and Internet services, which are expected to expand its reach.

The job market for this position is limited to the systems that have local origination or nonautomatic origination capabilities, and to the usually nonprofit or public organizations (schools, agencies, groups) that produce programs for transmission over the access channels of the local cable system.

Local origination and access programming has had an underground reputation for uneven production values, and System Managers and owners often believe that it is more expensive than it is worth in subscriber interest and loyalty. As cable TV reaches its maturity in the 1990s, however, more emphasis may be placed on its unique capabilities. Local origination brings visibility, community goodwill, and occasional income to a cable system, and jobs in production and as Director of Local Origination should increase in the future.

Advancement Prospects

Most people employed as Directors of Local Origination believe that their chances of advancement are poor. The opportunities for promotion within the local cable system are extremely limited, inasmuch as most systems are distributors rather than creators of programming. The skills and talents of production personnel are seldom transferable to sales, engineering, or management positions. Some Directors of Local Origination advance their careers by moving to larger cable TV systems at higher salaries. Others joins corporate television centers or education, government, or health TV operations in similar supervisory positions but at higher salaries. A few with the requisite experience and skills find advancement opportunities in production supervisory jobs at public TV or commercial stations.

Education

While it is not essential for the job, most Directors of Local Origination have an undergraduate degree in radio-TV or communications. Some have graduate degrees. Courses in television production, particularly with smaller video equipment, are necessary.

Experience/Skills

Most Directors of Local Origination are between the ages of 25 and 35. All have had some prior experience in television production. Most have had experience as Camera Operators, Directors, and Producers. In most instances, Directors of Local Origination have had at least three years of experience in television production.

Organizational ability and leadership qualities are important talents in a Director of Local Origination. Some creativity and an ability to work with and supervise people in complex tasks is a necessity. The Director of Local Origination must be able to supervise the transformation of elusive ideas and concepts into visually exciting cable programs.

Minority/Women's Opportunities

The opportunities for employment as a Director of Local Origination for women and minorities are limited. While 47.8 percent of all professional employees (including Directors of Local Origination) were women in 1996, according to the Federal Communications Commission (FCC), the statistics are deceiving. The vast majority holding the specific position of Director of Local Origination were white males, according to industry observers. The percentage of minority males and females in the position was less than 15 percent in 1996, according to industry sources.

Unions/Associations

There are no unions representing Directors of Local Origination.

CHIEF TECHNICIAN

Duties: Overseeing all on-site technical installation, transmission, and operation at a cable TV system or MMDS company

Alternate Title(s): Chief Engineer; Technical Operating Manager

Salary Range: $25,000 to $50,000+

Employment Prospects: Good

Advancement Prospects: Good

Prerequisites:

Education—High school diploma and some technical training required; college degree in electrical engineering, physics, or a related field preferable; certification

Experience—Five years in broadcast or cable TV engineering

Special Skills—Technical aptitude; administrative ability; leadership qualities; design skills

```
┌─────────────────────────────────────┐
│  Chief Technician or Chief Engineer  │
│      (Large System or Station);      │
│        Director of Engineering       │
└─────────────────────────────────────┘

┌─────────────────────────────────────┐
│           Chief Technician           │
└─────────────────────────────────────┘

┌─────────────────────────────────────┐
│              Technician              │
└─────────────────────────────────────┘
```

Position Description

A Chief Technician is responsible for the day-to-day leadership and supervision of the technical staff of a cable TV system or a multichannel multipoint distribution service (MMDS). The foundation of any such company rests on that technical staff. A Chief Technician may supervise from 3 to more than 30 employees.

In MMDS companies, a Chief Technician is sometimes called a Chief Engineer. In cable television, however, the title of Chief Engineer usually implies broader responsibilities, including more administrative duties and planning and developing new services. Many small cable systems and MMDS companies contract with outside professional engineering firms to provide the services of a Chief Engineer.

In the absence of an on-site Chief Engineer, the Chief Technician is the senior and most highly skilled member of the engineering staff and is responsible for all engineering aspects of the operation, including the construction and installation of antenna towers, satellite receiving stations (dishes), amplifiers, signal processing equipment, and the head end (electronic control center).

If the system originates local programming, the Chief Technician is responsible for the selection and purchase of television production equipment and supervises its installation and operation. The Chief Technician also aligns the various electronic elements of incoming satellite or microwave signals and processes them for retransmission to subscribers' homes. At a cable TV system, the Chief Technician is also responsible for obtaining the necessary permits from local electrical and telephone utility companies for the use of their poles or underground facilities. The Chief Technician determines the number of connections for each pole, diagrams the layout of the cable system, and supervises the connection, installation, and servicing of the system's equipment in subscribers' homes.

In addition to the engineering duties, a Chief Technician sometimes serves as the system or station manager of a small facility, and may be an owner or part owner of the operation or may be assigned to a particular locality by the parent company or multiple system operator (MSO).

Additionally, the Chief Technician

- evaluates and purchases all technical and transmission equipment;
- ensures the system's compliance with all federal, state, and local utility and safety regulations;

- designs and installs systems to deliver new program services, including interactive (two-way) communications, teletext, and data transmissions;
- prepares all necessary technical applications, including construction permits, proof of performance tests, and license renewals and modifications for the Federal Communications Commission (FCC); and
- supervises the preventive maintenance program for all technical and electronic equipment.

Salaries

While the salaries for Chief Technicians in cable TV or MMDS operations are somewhat less than for their peers in the broadcast industry, they are still relatively high. Chief Technicians' salaries at cable systems ranged from $25,000 to $50,000 or more, according to authoritative sources within the cable TV industry, and it's the one category in which women have achieved pay parity with men—although only 7.1 percent of technicians were women in 1997, according to the Women in Cable and Telecommunications (WICT) Foundation survey.

Employment Prospects

The chances of obtaining this position are good. In 1997, there were often more Chief Technician positions available than there were qualified candidates to fill them. The rapid growth of the new telecommunications industries during the past five years has created a general shortage of engineering and technical personnel. Experienced and capable engineers should have little difficulty in obtaining positions, particularly if they have some background in managing a small business. Some Technicians who have pursued further study and training and who possess the requisite leadership qualities are promoted to the position.

Advancement Prospects

The lack of qualified engineering personnel in cable TV systems and MMDS stations has created good opportunities for advancement, even though there is heavy competition for top jobs. Some Chief Technicians in cable television are promoted to new and larger systems, or to positions as Chief Engineers of regional or system-wide operations within their own MSO companies. In MMDS operations, some obtain director of engineering positions in the parent company, in charge of the planning and construction of other stations. Others advance their careers by joining competitive operations at higher salaries. Still others join manufacturing companies as design engineers, field service managers, or construction/engineering managers.

Education

A high school diploma and one or two years of training in electronics are minimum requirements for the position. Most large systems or stations prefer that candidates have some college education or an undergraduate degree in electrical engineering, physics, or a related science. A Restricted Radio Telephone Operator permit from the FCC is required for Chief Engineers in MMDS station operations. Many employers require certification from a study program from one of the industry groups such as the Society of Broadcast Engineers (SBE).

Experience/Skills

A minimum of five years of experience in broadcast electronics or a related field involving highly complex transmission equipment is a prerequisite for the position. Solid experience with all types and models of technical gear, a good understanding of the principles of electronics, and experience with FCC rules and regulations are also required.

A Chief Technician must be able to combine good technical design skills with hands-on experience and must exhibit leadership qualities, be budget conscious, and be a capable administrator.

Minority/Women's Opportunities

The number of female Chief Technicians or Chief Engineers at any MMDS station is small. Less than 10 percent of such positions in cable television were held by minority males in 1997, according to industry estimates. However, organizations such as the Society for Hispanic Professional Engineers and the American Indian Council of Architects and Engineers are seeking to cultivate minorities in the technical and engineering professions.

Unions/Associations

There are no unions that serve as bargaining agents for Chief Technicians or Chief Engineers in cable systems or MMDS stations. Some Chief Technicians belong to the Society of Cable Telecommunications Engineers (SCTE) to share common concerns and advance their careers. Some Chief Engineers belong to the Society for Motion Picture and Television Engineers (SMPTE) or the SBE for the same purposes.

TECHNICIAN

Duties: Maintaining and servicing technical equipment at a cable TV system or an MMDS station

Alternate Title(s): Plant Technician; Bench Technician; Maintenance Technician; Service Technician; Trunk Technician

Salary Range: $20,000 to $38,000

Employment Prospects: Excellent

Advancement Prospects: Excellent

Prerequisites:

Education—High school diploma and technical school training; college degree preferable

Experience—Minimum of six months on-the-job training

Special Skills—Technical aptitude; reliability; conscientiousness; curiosity; analytical ability

```
┌─────────────────────────────┐
│      Chief Technician        │
└─────────────────────────────┘

┌─────────────────────────────┐
│        Technician            │
└─────────────────────────────┘

┌─────────────────────────────┐
│         Installer            │
└─────────────────────────────┘
```

Position Description

Technician (or Plant Technician in cable television) is the general title for the person who maintains, repairs, and installs equipment at a cable system or a multichannel multipoint distribution service (MMDS) station. This position reports to a Chief Technician or Chief Engineer. In smaller operations, the Technician may perform a variety of technical duties. In large settings, a Technician may concentrate in one of several areas.

In cable TV, the technical emphasis is on the electronic and physical connection of subscribers' homes to the head end (the central originating point of the system) by coaxial cable. Technicians are responsible for maintaining equipment at both ends as well as the cable itself and all support gear along its route. Since MMDS stations transmit their signals over the air, their operations are somewhat less complicated than cable systems. Technicians in MMDS are responsible for the transmission equipment as well as the receiving devices in subscribers' homes. A Technician must have an understanding of the television spectrum and a knowledge of amplifiers and be capable of conducting electronic calculations utilizing sophisticated equipment.

The specialized Technician positions include

Bench Technician—(in cable) diagnoses and repairs broken or malfunctioning subscriber converter boxes, prepares equipment for installation in homes, and repairs testing devices.

Maintenance Technician—(in cable) repairs damaged cable between telephone poles and fixes equipment damages caused by adverse weather conditions; (in MMDS) repairs testing equipment, amplifiers, transmitting antennas, and pay-TV signal scrambling units.

Service Technician—(in cable) repairs malfunctions in subscribers' equipment, fixes signal amplifiers, and electronically scans the system to spot problems before breakdowns occur; (in MMDS) repairs faulty receiving antennas and subscriber descrambling units.

Trunk Technician—(in cable) corrects problems in the main cable lines that transmit the signal and in amplifiers that enhance it and wires and maintains electronic components in the field.

Additionally, the Technician

- services television production equipment (cameras, program switchers, audio consoles, etc.); and
- maintains videotape and satellite equipment used to send programs to subscribers.

Salaries

Salaries in 1997 for Technicians in the cable TV industry ranged from $20,000 for beginners to $38,000 for experienced individuals, with the average salary for men in the professional/technical category being $29,902, and for women, $31,133, according to the Women in Cable and Telecommunication (WICT) Foundation survey. In general, Bench, Trunk, and Service Technicians are paid at a slightly higher rate than are Maintenance Technicians. The salary levels for Technicians at MMDS stations are comparable, according to industry sources.

Salaries at cable TV systems and MMDS companies have risen in the past few years because of the supply-demand factor and are now only slightly lower than those for similar positions in the broadcast field. As an additional incentive to prospective employees, many multiple system operators (MSOs) offer company stock purchase plans, life insurance, and medical and dental plans.

Employment Prospects

The opportunities for employment for Technicians are excellent. The demand is expected to continue through 2006 at MMDS stations and cable systems. Many small and medium-size cable systems and MMDS stations employ three to five Technicians. Larger operations may have more than 30 on staff. In addition to the new systems and stations being constructed, there is generally high turnover, and qualified Technicians are constantly in demand. Many Installers complete additional study and training courses and are promoted to Technician positions.

Advancement Prospects

Chances for advancement for diligent individuals with some initiative are excellent. A major problem in the industry is the raiding of trained and qualified Technicians by competing companies. Most operations promote from within the organization to fill the vacancies that result. At some major MSO cable systems, bright, reliable Technicians are paid to attend classes that will qualify them for better-paying positions. The experienced and highly capable Technician with a background in all technical areas can be promoted to Chief Technician.

Some Technicians advance their careers by moving into slightly higher-paying jobs in broadcasting or to computer or electronics engineering positions in nontelecommunications industries.

Education

A high school diploma and some technical or electronics trade school training are minimum requirements. Given increasingly sophisticated technologies, a college degree is often preferable. Some new employees qualify because of experience they have received in the armed forces. Some larger MSOs operate their own training facilities for Technicians.

Candidates for jobs at MMDS operations should have a Restricted Radio Telephone Operator permit from the Federal Communications Commission (FCC).

Experience/Skills

Candidates should have at least six months of actual on-the-job experience in the Technical position being sought.

A Technician must be a reliable and conscientious individual who has an inquisitive mind, mechanical and technical aptitude, and a basic understanding of electronics and physics. The ability to read and interpret schematic diagrams is also necessary. Most good Technicians are excellent problem solvers and troubleshooters. Technicians must also be able to overcome any fear of heights, since roof climbing, pole climbing, and bucket truck aerial work are routine aspects of many Technician positions. An analytical mind is mandatory.

Minority/Women's Opportunities

Females occupied 7.1 percent of the Technician positions in cable TV in 1997, according to the WICT Foundation survey. Minority women held 1.7 percent of the Technician positions in 1996. Minority males held 21.5 percent of all Technician jobs in cable TV in that year, according to the FCC.

Unions/Associations

There are no national trade unions that act as bargaining agents for Technicians at cable TV systems or MMDS operations. Some local and state utility and technical organizations represent Technicians in particular geographic areas.

Technicians often belong to the associations detailed in the Chief Technician profile. In addition, the Society of Cable Telecommunications Engineers (SCTE) has a program leading to certification as a Professional Cable Television Engineer, and many Technicians participate in the program in order to advance their careers.

INSTALLER

Duties: Installing receiving equipment for a cable or MMDS operation or DBS service

Alternate Title(s): None

Salary Range: $20,000 to $40,000

Employment Prospects: Excellent

Advancement Prospects: Good

Prerequisites:

Education—High school diploma and technical school training

Experience—School training in electronic equipment

Special Skills—Mechanical aptitude; technical ability; courtesy; physical strength

```
┌─────────────────────────────┐
│         Technician          │
└─────────────────────────────┘

┌─────────────────────────────┐
│          Installer          │
└─────────────────────────────┘

┌─────────────────────────────┐
│      Technical School       │
└─────────────────────────────┘
```

Position Description

An Installer ensures that the signal and programming of a telecommunications operation are received in the homes of its subscribers. It is the usual entry-level technical position at a multichannel multipoint distribution service (MMDS) station, a cable TV system, or a direct broadcast satellite (DBS) operation.

Many small companies contract with special firms that provide installation services. At some large operations, Installers are full-time employees of the cable franchise, the MMDS license holder, or DBS service. Virtually all systems, however, use contract Installers at some time.

Although Installers usually work in private homes, they can also connect their companies' equipment in apartment houses, hotels, or office buildings.

The duties of an Installer vary, depending on the type of operation. In cable, an Installer prepares the customer's home for the reception of the television signal by running wire from a telephone pole or underground terminal and attaching it to the connector box(es) and television set(s) within the home. An Installer working for an independent contractor often performs the initial construction work for a cable system, which includes digging trenches, relocating telephone poles, and stringing cable between poles. Often three-quarters of such work is contracted to outside companies, according to industry sources. After construction is completed, an Installer

works closely with, and sometimes performs some of the duties of, a Technician.

An Installer working for MMDS operations attaches a special antenna to the roof of the subscriber's house, tests and adjusts it to receive the station's signal, and connects it to a descrambling device and to the television set(s) in the customer's home. DBS Installers work in a similar manner.

Installers who are employed full-time by media companies receive their assignments from the Customer Service Representative or the dispatcher in the main office of the company. They report, however, to the Chief Technician, Chief Engineer, or other technical supervisor. Installers who work for independent companies receive their assignments from a supervisor who works closely with the Chief Technician of the media company or directly with the DBS retail management.

Additionally, the Installer

- explains and demonstrates the operation of the system to subscribers and describes available channels and programs;
- performs minor repairs and adjustments in subscribers' homes;
- (in cable TV) adds or deletes program services by adjusting customers' cable connections and disconnecting their equipment when requested; and
- collects payments for installation or service calls, when employed by small systems.

Salaries

Installers working directly for cable systems, DBS, or MMDS operations are usually paid on an hourly basis. In 1997, rates in cable TV ranged from $12.00 an hour for beginners to $22.00 an hour for experienced individuals with some seniority, according to authoritative sources within the cable TV industry. This amounted to an annual salary of $20,000 to $40,000 in 1997 for a 40-hour, 50-week work cycle. Most Installers work overtime hours, which are usually paid at a time-and-a-half rate.

Employment Prospects

Opportunities are excellent. The construction of new cable TV systems has slowed, but there will be some growth in urban centers and throughout the country through 2006. In addition, the disconnect rate (churn) in many established cable systems can be as high as 33 percent annually. New customers to replace those who move or disconnect for whatever reason require new installations and the services of an Installer. MMDS operations and DBS retail companies also offer many prospects for employment. In most of the nation, there are more positions open than there are candidates.

Small companies or systems employ 3 to 5 Installers, and at large cable systems, an installation staff of 20 individuals is not uncommon. The greatest number of opportunities, however, is with independent contracting firms.

Advancement Prospects

Opportunities are good for diligent individuals who apply themselves to daily tasks in a responsible manner. Many Installers seek additional electronics training and technical improvement and become Technicians in cable TV operations. Others move to supervisory construction positions at new systems owned by the parent multiple system operator (MSO). Still others advance their careers by joining competing companies or other independent contractors at higher wages. Installers who work for independent contracting firms are exposed to many potential employers, which creates increased advancement possibilities for them.

Education

A high school diploma and some post–high school education at a technical school is usually required. Training can also be obtained in the military service. Many major MSOs and cable TV trade associations offer training sessions and seminars. At MMDS operations, a Restricted Radio Telephone permit from the Federal Communications Commission (FCC) is usually necessary.

Experience/Skills

Little previous professional experience is required. Interest and schooling in electronics and in the repair, maintenance, and operation of electronic equipment are, however, essential. MMDS operations often require more technical education in broadcast engineering than is necessary for an Installer in a cable system.

Installers need mechanical aptitude and some technical ability with electronic equipment. Candidates should also possess physical strength and good health and have no fear of heights. Since there is close contact with subscribers, an Installer should be courteous and generally enjoy working with the public. Installers working for independent contractors must be willing to travel and live away from home for long periods of time because such companies move from city to city.

Minority/Women's Opportunities

The majority of Installers for MMDS companies, DBS retail outlets, and cable TV systems are white males, according to industry sources. Females were employed in 12.1 percent of the laborer positions (including Installers) in cable TV in 1996, according to the FCC. Male minorities, however, occupied 29 percent of the positions in that year.

Unions/Associations

There are no national unions or professional organizations that represent Installers in cable TV, DBS, or MMDS operations at the present time. Some local and state utility and construction unions, however, do represent them in specific locations.

VIDEO MARKETING MANAGER

Duties: Supervising all national marketing and distribution for a consumer electronics product or program company

Alternate Title(s): VP, Marketing; National Sales Manager; Director of Marketing

Salary Range: $50,000 to $150,000+

Employment Prospects: Poor

Advancement Prospects: Poor

Prerequisites:

Education—Undergraduate degree in business administration or marketing

Experience—Minimum of five years in consumer electronics marketing

Special Skills—Leadership qualities; organizational ability; good judgment; persuasiveness; business acumen

```
┌──────────────────────────────────────────┐
│  President or Chief Executive Officer      │
│  (Consumer Electronics Company)            │
└──────────────────────────────────────────┘

┌──────────────────────────────────────────┐
│  Video Marketing Manager                   │
└──────────────────────────────────────────┘

┌──────────────────────────────────────────┐
│  Video Distribution Manager                │
└──────────────────────────────────────────┘
```

Position Description

A Video Marketing Manager is the top sales executive for a large video-related company. As such, the person in this position is in charge of all national and, sometimes, international marketing, sales, advertising, and promotion activities associated with the company's consumer electronics products. It is the responsibility of this individual to aggressively and successfully market the product line(s) or video program label(s) to the home consumer.

There are more than 500 consumer electronics companies in the United States selling videocassette and videodisc machines, audio/stereo outfits, video games, electronic accessories, traditional audiovisual equipment, blank videotapes, and satellite earth station receivers (television receive-only dishes, or TVROs). ITA, International Recording Media Association reported a 10 percent increase in global replication of all optical media formats between 1996 and 1997 with an unit increase to 6.42 billion from 5.84 billion. Projections called for an additional 8 percent increase in 1998. Despite this, many experts agree that the superior image and sound quality of the digital media will make the VHS cassette obsolete before long. Additionally, with 1997's introduction of DIVX—a rental-only system allowing the user to download an encoded movie by modem to a disposable disc—and

the emergence of e-commerce as a viable direct sales channel, traditional retail outlets face a serious challenge, as renting or buying video products online becomes a widespread form of distribution.

The success or failure of the company's total sales efforts depends on the abilities of the Video Marketing Manager in strengthening marketing strategies, improving the visibility and consumer awareness of the equipment, tape, or video programs, and maximizing the volume of sales while maintaining costs. The Video Marketing Manager provides marketing research to assist in product development, creates the marketing strategies to introduce products and support sales, and establishes company-wide policies on pricing, discounts, special sales, rentals, returns and exchanges, and other terms of sale.

The Video Marketing Manager usually reports directly to the company's president or chief executive officer and is normally located at its national headquarters. The Video Marketing Manager supervises a staff that may have as few as 5 or more than 200 people.

Additionally, the Video Marketing Manager

- supervises retail sales and distribution channels through company branch offices, independent firms, and authorized dealers;

- oversees all print, radio-TV, and Internet advertising, promotional literature, billboards, and point-of-purchase displays and other in-store merchandising; and
- manages all marketing and sales employees and, often, the advertising and promotion staffs as well.

Salaries

The financial rewards for Video Marketing Managers are usually considerable, although they vary with the size of the company, its sales volume, and the type of products or programs manufactured or distributed. Salaries range from $50,000 at relatively small companies with limited product lines to well over $150,000 for senior and experienced individuals at major national and international firms. The total yearly earnings usually include a base salary, bonus arrangement, liberal expense account, stock options, profit sharing, and extensive life insurance, health, and retirement plans. Some also receive a small commission on overall yearly sales. Membership in social or country clubs, a company car, and other prerequisites are often offered as part of a compensation package for a Video Marketing Manager.

Compensation for Video Marketing Managers at companies selling prerecorded video programs to the health, education, and business markets are considerably lower. Many of the companies are nonprofit, and compensation ranged from $30,000 to $60,000 in 1997, according to industry estimates.

Employment Prospects

The opportunities are poor and limited to the 500 or so consumer electronics companies that employ Video Marketing Managers. Although the majority sold specialized programming to the school, health, or business markets, many concentrated on the home video market. There are many Video Marketing Manager positions, but competition for the job is severe. Only the most able and successful marketing professionals reach the position, and then only after many years of demonstrated ability. Most have had extensive experience as Video Distribution Managers within the company, in a related consumer electronics firm, or in the packaged product field.

Advancement Prospects

The opportunities for advancement are poor. For many, the assumption of a Video Marketing Manager position at a major company is the peak of a successful marketing career. Some may move upward to assume overall control of a company as its president or chief executive officer. The majority of such positions in the United States in 1997 were held by individuals with strong marketing backgrounds. Some Video Marketing Managers advance their careers by forming their own consumer electronics firms or by joining larger companies.

Education

Many Video Marketing Managers have undergraduate degrees in business administration or marketing and many have a master's degree. A few do not have a degree but do have considerable experience in the field.

Experience/Skills

Most Video Marketing Managers at major companies have obtained the job after 5 to 10 years of product, program, or packaged goods marketing experience. In some smaller companies, less experience is required, but an extensive background in advertising and promotion is still necessary.

Video Marketing Managers are poised, confident business leaders with good organizational skills. Many have a flair for promotion and public speaking, are good conceptualizers, and are extremely persuasive. The successful individual must be capable of making sound business judgments and possess leadership skills.

Minority/Women's Opportunities

The percentage of women holding top marketing management positions in consumer electronics has increased during the past 10 years. Minority employment has also risen somewhat in smaller companies, according to industry sources. The position, however, is usually occupied by a white male.

Unions/Associations

There are no unions that represent Video Marketing Managers. Many companies belong to and participate in industry trade associations, including the ITA, International Recording Media Association; the Electronic Industry Alliance (EIA); the International Communications Industries Association (ICIA); and the Motion Picture Association of America (MPAA). Video Marketing Managers often represent their companies at trade meetings of these groups. In addition, some belong to the American Management Association (AMA) and similar associations to share mutual concerns and develop policies and procedures.

VIDEO DISTRIBUTION MANAGER

CAREER PROFILE

Duties: Managing an office or firm that distributes video software, hardware, and accessories to retail stores

Alternate Title(s):   Branch Office Manager; Independent Representative

Salary Range: $45,000 to $70,000+

Employment Prospects: Fair

Advancement Prospects: Poor

Prerequisites:

　　Education—Minimum of high school diploma; undergraduate degree in marketing, advertising, or business administration preferable

　　Experience—Minimum of five years in product or program sales or marketing

　　Special Skills—Business acumen; leadership ability; organizational aptitude; aggressiveness; persuasiveness; persistence

CAREER LADDER

```
┌─────────────────────────────────┐
│    Video Marketing Manager      │
└─────────────────────────────────┘

┌─────────────────────────────────┐
│   Video Distribution Manager    │
└─────────────────────────────────┘

┌─────────────────────────────────┐
│      Video Salesperson;         │
│     Video Store Manager         │
└─────────────────────────────────┘
```

Position Description

The title Video Distribution Manager is a general term used to describe a sales executive in the middle of the chain of distribution in the consumer electronics industry. A Video Distribution Manager acquires products from manufacturers or wholesalers and sells or rents them to retail stores. The position is that of an executive in charge of a sales organization that serves as an intermediary between either a national original equipment manufacturer (OEM) or a national video program or blank tape wholesaler and a retail outlet. The main responsibility of the job is to establish and meet the sales goals in the territory covered and supervise the activities of Video Salespersons.

The majority of national manufacturers and wholesalers distribute their equipment, programs, or blank tapes to retail stores in one of two ways: through company-owned district branches or through nonaffiliated, regional, independent distribution companies of various types. The stores then sell or rent the products to consumers.

A Video Distribution Manager who is employed full-time and exclusively by the national wholesaler or manufacturer (but is stationed away from the home office) is usually called a Branch Office Manager. This person supervises a staff that takes orders, makes sales calls, provides promotional materials, and sometimes stocks the products in retail stores; a Video Distribution Manager in this situation usually reports to the Video Marketing Manager of the parent company.

Independent companies often act as distribution firms and are under contract by one or more national wholesalers or manufacturers to represent them and to distribute their products or labels. Independent reps are the middlemen between suppliers and retailers. These independent companies may or may not stock any or all of the lines they represent. The Video Distribution Manager in charge of such a company is known as an independent representative (rep), and the company usually has exclusive distribution in a given territory or region. He or she supervises a staff that sells and distributes to the retail store.

Many OEMs and national video program or tape wholesalers employ 8 to 10 district branch office managers. These executives supervise sales to retail stores in a specific geographic territory (Southwest, Tristate area, etc.). Independent distribution companies also usually operate in a prescribed area.

Additionally, the Video Distribution Manager

- provides overnight or special catalog order fulfillment to retailers in the assigned territory;
- maintains and balances inventory in warehouses or distribution points for redistribution to retail stores;

- supervises the servicing of all retail accounts and actively seeks and acquires new ones;
- recommends stocking of products, accessories, hardware, and programs to Video Store Managers; and
- suggests new products, product lines, or product improvements to a manufacturer or wholesaler.

Salaries

The salary for a Video Distribution Manager who serves as a branch office manager varies according to the extent of the territory, the size of the company, its policies, and the individual's experience. Earnings range from $45,000 to $70,000, according to industry sources. Many branch office managers are paid a base salary and a relatively small commission for sales within their territories. Some work on a sales quota and receive a bonus for exceeding it. Others work largely on a commission basis. Programming (software) positions sometimes pay more than equipment (hardware) positions. Fringe benefits are quite liberal and usually include a reasonable expense account, a company car, and the retirement and health benefits of the parent company.

Most independent reps own all or a portion of their distribution company and receive all or a portion of the profits. They earn considerably more than Branch Office Managers, but their income is based solely on the amount of their sales.

Employment Prospects

This is not an entry-level position. Most job openings for branch office managers occur when people move to another industry job. While there is considerable turnover in these sales management positions, the competition is severe, and the prospects for employment are only fair. National manufacturers or wholesalers often select bright and aggressive Video Salespersons for the position.

The industry has been consolidated. The entry of mass merchants into the field during the last 20 years has led to the large-scale acquisition or elimination of smaller companies, streamlining the distribution channel nationwide. Industry observers note that there are still jobs to be had, but much overlap between former competitors has been done away with: for example, previously, where two smaller companies competing within a region would each have video distribution managers, now one larger organization assigns one person to direct operations within that region.

Some successful Video Store Managers establish their own distribution operations to serve their own and other stores and, in effect, become independent rep companies. The vast majority handled consumer electronics equipment. There were fewer than 80 independent video program distribution companies in the United States in 1997, and most of the sales were handled by 20 large firms, according to the National Association of Video Distributors. The growth of consumer electronics and home video, however, through the 1990s should open up some new job opportunities at new companies as well as at expanding consumer electronics firms.

Advancement Prospects

The opportunities for moving up are generally poor. Some Branch Managers are promoted to a more responsible marketing or sales position, such as Video Marketing Manager, in their companies' national headquarters. Others may take similar sales jobs at increased salaries at other industry-related firms. Some start their own consumer electronics operations. Independent reps usually advance their career by expanding the territories they cover and the product lines they represent.

Education

All national companies that employ branch office managers require a minimum of a high school diploma. Most prefer additional training in sales, sales management, or marketing and sales distribution. Most large national employers require an undergraduate or graduate degree in marketing, advertising, or business administration. The ability to motivate and lead a sales staff, however, is usually more important than a formal education for both branch office managers and independent reps.

Experience/Skills

Employers at national companies usually require a minimum of five years of sales or marketing experience in appointing branch office managers. Middle management experience in sales is preferred.

Branch office managers and independent reps must be good businesspeople with sales and marketing backgrounds. They must display leadership qualities and be aggressive, competitive, and persistent. Most are persuasive and well organized and have respect for profits.

Minority/Women's Opportunities

The percentage of women and minority Video Distribution Managers employed as branch office managers has increased in the past 10 years, according to industry sources. Most branch office managers and independent reps in 1997, however, were white males.

Unions/Associations

There are no unions that serve as bargaining agents for Video Distribution Managers. Some independent reps belong to the Electronic Representatives Association (ERA) to share trade concerns and advance their careers.

VIDEO SALESPERSON

Duties: Selling video programs, consumer electronics equipment, and accessories to retail stores

Alternate Title(s): Sales Representative; Sales Agent; Marketing Representative

Salary Range: $30,000 to $50,000+

Employment Prospects: Good

Advancement Prospects: Fair

Prerequisites:

Education—High school diploma; some college or vocational school courses in sales or marketing preferable

Experience—Minimum of two years in consumer electronics or other sales

Special Skills—Dependability; persistence; persuasiveness; aggressiveness; initiative

```
┌─────────────────────────────────┐
│   Video Distribution Manager    │
└─────────────────────────────────┘

┌─────────────────────────────────┐
│       Video Salesperson         │
└─────────────────────────────────┘

┌─────────────────────────────────┐
│     Video Store Manager;        │
│     Video Sales Clerk           │
└─────────────────────────────────┘
```

Position Description

A Video Salesperson sells and services video programming, video equipment, and consumer electronics accessories to retail outlets for resale to consumers. Most Salespersons are employed at independent video distribution companies or at branch offices of national video- related wholesalers or manufacturers. Video Salespersons sell direct broadcast satellite (DBS) and television receive-only satellite dishes (TVROs), blank tapes, prerecorded videocassettes, videocassette or videodisc machines, video cameras, projection television units, cables, connectors, and traditional audiovisual equipment, including film cameras, projectors, and photographic supplies.

At a branch office, the Video Salesperson concentrates on selling the products of an individual national original equipment manufacturer (OEM) or of a video program wholesaler. A Salesperson for a hardware (equipment) company may handle cameras or videocassette machines and their accessories for a particular equipment company (such as Sony or RCA), whereas a Salesperson for a video program wholesaler sells the videocassette or videodisc releases of a particular label or line (such as Paramount or Disney).

A Video Salesperson working for an independent distribution company usually sells programs or equipment for a variety of national manufacturers or program wholesalers. Many such firms handle products from more than 15 national companies.

A Video Salesperson usually reports to a Video Distribution Manager (either a branch office manager or an independent rep) and either works in a prescribed geographic territory or is assigned specific retail accounts. In some cases, Video Salespersons report directly to the home office of the national wholesaler or manufacturer.

Most Video Salespersons travel quite a bit, visiting and servicing from 30 to more than 50 retail accounts in a given territory. Many are assigned to phone sales duty (telemarketing) at the branch office or headquarters of the Video Distribution Manager. A Video Salesperson visits or calls retail stores once a week or once a month depending on the volume of purchases made by the store.

Additionally, the Video Salesperson

- acquires new accounts in the assigned territory;
- delivers merchandise to and collects payment from some stores;
- trains retail Video Sales Clerks in the operation of new equipment and accessories;
- distributes sales literature, point-of-purchase displays, brochures, posters, and other merchandising materials to stores;
- keeps track of the competition and their products; and
- coordinates sales incentive programs, contests, and catalog (noncurrent) sales of video programs.

Salaries

Video Salespersons are paid either a straight salary, a small salary plus a commission, or a draw against commission. There is no industry-wide pattern, but less than 15 percent of sales employees work on a straight salary basis, according to industry estimates. Some companies offer commissions on gross sales, others on gross profits from an individual's sales, and still others on a sliding scale tied to the gross profit received by the company for a particular item.

Compensation ranges from less than $30,000 for personnel with a small company or distribution firm to $50,000 and more for experienced individuals who deal in expensive products. Since payment is usually tied to sales results in one way or another, yearly earnings are a direct result of the sales success of the individual. For hardware sales, the commissions are slightly less than 10 percent of the gross income received by the company for the sale of the product. When commissions are calculated on the gross profit to the company, the return to the Salesperson ranges from 20 to 40 percent of that profit on an item.

Most companies provide sales samples, a small entertainment account, and telephone and auto expenses. Some provide a company car and hospitalization and pension plans. A few offer the individual an opportunity to participate in a company profit-sharing plan.

Employment Prospects

Many branch offices of the larger national manufacturers employ seven or more Video Salespersons. Independent distribution companies within a region usually employ three to five. According to the National Association of Video Distributors, the 20 large distributors have sales staffs of from 50 to 100 people. There is considerable turnover of sales employees in consumer electronics. As a result, the job opportunities for the bright, capable, sales-oriented individual are good.

Advancement Prospects

Despite the relatively high turnover rate of sales employees in the consumer electronics industry, the opportunities for advancement are only fair. The competition for more responsible positions is heavy. Many Video Salespersons use their skills and experience in one product line or label to obtain a better-paying sales job at a competitive company. Some advance within their own company and become Video Distribution Managers (at branch offices) or move to middle management marketing positions at the home office. Others seek sales positions in other industries.

Education

A high school education and some evidence of coursework in sales or marketing at a community college or vocational school is usually required. A few employers prefer to hire individuals with undergraduate degrees. While a major in marketing is desirable, an undergraduate degree in any field is helpful. Some training in motivation, sales techniques, and marketing is also valuable. The ability to sell, however, is more important than a formal education.

Experience/Skills

Although the position of Video Salesperson is occasionally an entry-level job, individuals who have at least two years of direct sales experience are usually preferred. Some Video Salespersons gain this experience in fields other than consumer electronics, while others have worked as Video Store Managers or Video Sales Clerks.

A Video Salesperson must be dependable and display a considerable amount of initiative. Persistence and persuasiveness in sales efforts, an outgoing, gregarious personality, and a service orientation are required. A good Video Salesperson has excellent face-to-face verbal skills and responds intuitively to customer cues. The candidate must be adept at identifying customers' characteristics and understanding their behavior patterns and product needs. His record of success is often based on the success of the Video Store Manager. Above all, a Video Salesperson must like to sell and to make money.

Minority/Women's Opportunities

The percentage of women occupying video sales positions has increased dramatically in the past few years, according to industry observers. While the number has increased more in the programming (or software) areas, a number of women are now Video Salespersons for equipment manufacturers. The percentage of minority employees has also increased, according to industry observers.

Unions/Associations

There are no unions that serve as bargaining agents for Video Salespersons. Many individuals attend company-sponsored sales training sessions or those sponsored by the Consumer Electronics Group (CEG) of the Electronic Industries Alliance (EIA) and the International Communications Industries Association (ICIA) to learn new sales techniques and methods.

VIDEO STORE MANAGER

CAREER PROFILE

Duties: Managing and operating a video or consumer electronics retail store

Alternate Title(s):   Video Retailer; Video Dealer

Salary Range: $18,000 to $40,000+

Employment Prospects: Good

Advancement Prospects: Fair

Prerequisites:

　Education—Minimum of high school diploma

　Experience—Minimum of two years of experience in retail sales

　Special Skills—Video product knowledge; sales talent; business acumen; merchandising instinct

CAREER LADDER

```
┌─────────────────────────────────┐
│   Video Distribution Manager;    │
│      Video Salesperson           │
└─────────────────────────────────┘

┌─────────────────────────────────┐
│                                  │
│      Video Store Manager         │
│                                  │
└─────────────────────────────────┘

┌─────────────────────────────────┐
│                                  │
│       Video Sales Clerk          │
│                                  │
└─────────────────────────────────┘
```

Position Description

A Video Store Manager is responsible for the day-to-day operation and management of a retail store that deals in consumer electronics and related accessories and supplies. This person is in charge of all income and expenses, all short- and long-range planning, and the general profitability of the store. A Video Store Manager may be the owner or part-owner of an independent store, manager of the daily operations of an outlet that is part of a chain, or head a video-TV-CD department within a department store.

Many video retailers belong to the Video Software Dealers Association, whose membership in 1999 numbered more than 3,500 companies ranging from smaller, independently owned retail video outlets to large, multi-store video chains. The VSDA membership also includes the home video divisions of all major and independent motion picture studios, major distributors and a host of other businesses connected to the home video industry.

In any situation, however, a Video Store Manager directs the operation and supervises all Video Sales Clerks and occasionally, Video Service Technicians. In some stores, the Manager acts as the video buyer, selecting what products are carried. The individual is ultimately responsible for the success or failure of the enterprise.

Additionally, the Video Store Manager

- develops advertising and promotional campaigns and in-store displays;

- establishes special sales and discount policies;
- determines the level of investment in inventory of hardware, accessories, and prerecorded and blank videocassettes and maintains inventory controls;
- stays informed of industry trends, new products, and new rental, sales, and returns policies; and
- develops and supervises training and retraining programs for employees.

Salaries

Earnings for Video Store Managers vary considerably according to the geographical location, size, and profitability of the store. Compensation ranged from $18,000 to more than $40,000 in 1997. The Manager who is also the owner usually collects a weekly salary and shares in or retains any profits the store returns during the year. Such individuals earn $40,000 or more annually, depending on the store's success in a given year. Those who do not own a share of the store are usually compensated by a combination of salary and commission or yearly bonus.

Employment Prospects

The opportunities for employment as a Video Store Manager are good for ambitious, aggressive people. It is not an entry-level position, however, and many Managers are owners or co-owners of stores and have financial and sales experience in the retail trade. Although some young entrepreneurs have operated video stores successfully, many such outlets have folded because of undercapitalization, competition, or their owners' lack of experience. Many successful owners of consumer electronics stores, however, expand by opening other stores and promoting capable Video Sales Clerks to managerial positions. Department stores sometimes promote bright and successful Video Sales Clerks with leadership qualities to handle the video, audiovisual, or CD departments.

Overall employment in the retail trade is expected to increase dramatically by 2006. The national demand for managerial people, however, will grow more slowly than most occupations, according to the Bureau of Labor Statistics (BLS).

Advancement Prospects

The prospects for advancement from the position are generally fair. There is considerable competition. For many Video Store Managers, the position is the successful realization of a desire to be one's own boss by owning and operating a store; many have fled the corporate world. They may seek advancement and additional success by owning and operating more stores. Some salaried managers use the contacts they have acquired to advance their careers by becoming Video Salespersons for particular consumer electronics products or labels. A few become Video Distribution Managers for national wholesalers and manufacturers. Managers who work for large department stores sometimes move to more responsible middle management positions in their stores or elsewhere in the chain.

Some owner/managers in the audiovisual equipment field participate in the certification program of the International Communications Industries Association (ICIA). Becoming an ICIA-certified media specialist can help in career advancement.

Education

Employers require a minimum of a high school diploma in assigning or promoting people to this position. In many department store chains, an undergraduate degree in management or retailing is required.

Experience/Skills

The video program retailing business is a unique blend of the entertainment and package goods industries. The majority of Video Store Managers in the consumer electronics industry have had at least two years of experience in retail sales prior to assuming the position. Some day-to-day experience as a Video Sales Clerk is a prerequisite for the job.

Video Store Managers must be well organized and display leadership qualities. In addition, initiative and sound business judgment are required. Video Store Managers should have a thorough knowledge of the products they sell and they should have some knowledge of and experience with business computers. They are experts in media and video equipment and programming, understand local tastes and desires, and are good merchandisers. Above all, Video Store Managers are excellent salespeople who enjoy selling to and serving retail customers.

Minority/Women's Opportunities

Women have become increasingly involved in video retail management in the past five years, particularly as co-owners. The percentage of minority group owners or owners/managers, however, remains rather low, except in urban centers or certain geographic locations.

Unions/Associations

There are no unions that represent Video Store Managers. Many, however, belong to such associations as ICIA, the National Association of Recording Merchandisers (NARM), or the North American Retail Dealers Association (NARDA) to keep abreast of the industry and share common concerns. Many Managers and store owners attend the annual trade exhibitions and seminars of the Consumer Electronics Group (CEG) of the Electronic Industries Alliance (EIA). The semiannual Consumer Electronic Shows (CES) sponsored by the EIA offer the largest display of new electronics products available for resale.

Many Video Store Managers dealing with motion pictures belong to the Video Software Dealers Association (VSDA).

VIDEO SALES CLERK

CAREER PROFILE

Duties: Selling video hardware and software at the retail level

Alternate Title(s):   None

Salary Range: $12,000 to $25,000

Employment Prospects: Excellent

Advancement Prospects: Good

Prerequisites:
  Education—High school diploma
  Experience—Some retail sales background preferable
  Special Skills—Good interpersonal skills; sales aptitude; initiative; dependability

CAREER LADDER

```
┌─────────────────────────────────┐
│   Video Store Manager;           │
│   Video Salesperson              │
└─────────────────────────────────┘

┌─────────────────────────────────┐
│   Video Sales Clerk              │
└─────────────────────────────────┘

┌─────────────────────────────────┐
│   High School/College;           │
│   Retail Salesperson             │
└─────────────────────────────────┘
```

Position Description

A Video Sales Clerk is responsible for selling video hardware (equipment) and software (programming) to customers at a retail store. In many instances, the Sales Clerk also sells video and audiovisual accessories, including connecting boxes, cables, blank videocassettes, bulbs, reels, and other supplies. In stores that specialize in video programming, the Sales Clerk is involved in the rental of videocassettes and videodiscs for customer use.

Video Sales Clerks usually report directly to the Video Store Manager or owner. In small stores, Clerks are responsible for selling or renting all displayed merchandise. In larger operations, they may specialize in either software or hardware or in a particular line of equipment.

It is the responsibility of Video Sales Clerks to service customer requests and to inform the customer about the merchandise offered by the store. They outline the various options available, demonstrate equipment and programs, and persuade the customer to rent or buy.

Video Sales Clerks operate in a dynamic environment that can be challenging and rewarding. New products, new equipment, and new label lines and programs are constantly being introduced, as are new merchandising techniques, discounts, and special sales. In addition, different people move through the store daily. It is the Video Sales Clerk's responsibility to balance all of these factors and devise new sales methods that meet customers' needs and that increase sales for the store.

Video stores are located in "stripcenters," suburban shopping malls in small towns, and in major urban centers. Video Sales Clerks usually work in one location, but in multiple-store companies they may be transferred periodically to other branches.

Additionally, the Video Sales Clerk

• studies the operation or user characteristics of each new product offered for sale or rental by the store;
• assists in setting up in-store and window merchandising displays; and
• maintains inventory records and sales files.

Salaries

Compensation for Video Sales Clerks is relatively low. The majority of video retailers pay a straight salary, a salary and commission, or a salary and a bonus. Most employers start beginners with a small salary and a relatively large commission on each sale. As the individual progresses, the salary is raised and commissions are lowered. Some stores have other incentive sales plans and rewards in order to motivate employees. Most Video Sales Clerks are paid on an hourly basis.

In 1997, the yearly compensation for Video Sales Clerks ranged from $12,000 for inexperienced full-time individuals to $25,000 for experienced employees with good track records, according to the Bureau of Labor Statistics (BLS).

Benefits are usually minimal, with only the larger stores and chains offering medical and retirement plans.

Employment Prospects

The Video Sales Clerk's position is an entry-level job at most retail stores. The majority of video stores employ two to six workers in sales for various shifts and assignments. The average store also employed nine part-time employees in that year.

According to the BLS national demand for retail clerks will increase 21 to 35 percent by 2006. There will be increased opportunities in book, music, and drug stores, along with other mass merchandising outlets, for Video Sales Clerks. There is a large turnover among Video Sales Clerks, and as a result employment opportunities are excellent. Many large department stores provide in-service training in sales merchandising for apprentices. Others seek bright, aggressive high school or college students to work part-time or on weekends. After graduation, they are often employed full-time.

Advancement Prospects

Most Video Sales Clerks seek advancement in video or audiovisual retail sales or in other consumer electronics fields. The opportunities for advancement are good. Some diligent individuals are appointed video or appliance department managers at larger chain operations, and others move into branch management for a video store chain. Some aggressive Video Sales Clerks use their retail sales experience to move to more responsible positions as sales managers at stores that sell products unrelated to video or audiovisual equipment. A few advance their careers by becoming Video Salespersons for particular consumer electronics products or manufacturers' lines. Some sales personnel in the audiovisual equipment field participate in the Certified Media Specialist Program of the International Communications Industries Association (ICIA). Such certification is valuable in obtaining more responsible positions within the industry.

Education

A high school diploma is usually required. Some junior college or college coursework is preferred by a few larger department store chains and an undergraduate degree is sometimes required. Some experience in business computers or training in computers is preferred, since virtually all of the stores have computer systems. The ability to sell, however, is more important than a formal education or training.

Experience/Skills

Some previous experience in retail sales in any field is often required. Experience with computers is highly desirable. Most Video Sales Clerks have an outgoing personality, an ability to relate to others, initiative, and an aptitude for selling. A neat appearance and a gregarious manner are most important. The most successful individuals are friendly, service-oriented, and somewhat competitive and aggressive. Above all, a good Video Sales Clerk must like to sell and be interested in making money.

Minority/Women's Opportunities

The opportunities for women and minority group members as Video Sales Clerks are good. There has been a marked increase in employment opportunities for both in the past 10 years, according to industry observers.

Unions/Associations

There are no unions that represent Video Sales Clerks. Some individuals, however, belong to ICIA to advance their careers. In addition to the certification program, ICIA holds training seminars in sales and new products. Other Video Sales Clerks attend periodic sales conferences and seminars held by the North American Retail Dealers Association (NARDA) or the Electronic Representatives Association (ERA) to improve their skills.

VIDEO SERVICE TECHNICIAN

CAREER PROFILE

Duties: Repairing and servicing equipment at a consumer electronics retail store

Alternate Title(s): Maintenance Technician; Bench Technician; Service Technician

Salary Range: $17,000 to $50,000+

Employment Prospects: Fair

Advancement Prospects: Good

Prerequisites:

　Education—High school diploma; some vocational or technical school training

　Experience—Minimum of six months of maintenance experience preferable

　Special Skills—Mechanical ability; electronic aptitude; manual dexterity; inquisitiveness

CAREER LADDER

```
┌─────────────────────────────────────┐
│  Maintenance Engineer; Technician;   │
│         Media Technician             │
└─────────────────────────────────────┘

┌─────────────────────────────────────┐
│      Video Service Technician        │
└─────────────────────────────────────┘

┌─────────────────────────────────────┐
│      Vocational/Technical School     │
└─────────────────────────────────────┘
```

Position Description

A Video Service Technician is responsible for the maintenance and repair of electronic equipment. This individual works in a consumer electronics store or in a repair center and usually reports to the manager of the facility. A Video Service Technician works on customers' videocassette recorders and videodisc machines as well as on other audiovisual equipment, such as film cameras, slide projectors, and stereo systems. This individual also maintains the technical equipment owned by stores. Today's Video Service Technician must be familiar with the digital electronics, microprocessors, and integrated circuitry used in highly complex electronics gear.

At a retail store, this person is also responsible for setting up and maintaining a comprehensive repair service that can become a profit center for the store. The presence of a good repair department can bring customers back for new purchases and help to build the store's reputation. Usually, only one Video Service Technician is employed in an average retail outlet. In many instances, a central group of Video Service Technicians operates out of one main store and repairs equipment sent to them from branch locations. From 4 to 10 Video Service Technicians may be employed at a repair center that operates as a separate business and provides electronic repair work for many stores, regardless of their ownership.

Additionally, the Video Service Technician

- interprets diagrams and schematic charts of video equipment;
- attends training programs to keep abreast of new equipment and service techniques;
- works with manufacturers' field service representatives or design engineers to isolate equipment problems; and
- maintains an inventory of supplies, accessories, and test gear used in servicing equipment.

Salaries

In 1996, median weekly earnings for full-time electronic equipment repairers were $619, with the middle 50 percent earning from $444 to $802, according to the Bureau of Labor Statistics (BLS).

Salaries often depend on the geographical location of the store and the competition from other outlets in the area. Video Service Technicians are also usually financially rewarded for completing factory repair certification training or other in-service training programs. A few large chains offer excellent benefit programs. There are often many opportunities for overtime work.

Employment Prospects

The opportunities for employment are fair. By 2006, jobs in the field are expected to grow more slowly than the average for all occupations. According to the BLS, 396,000 people were employed as electrical/electronic technicians in 1996, 93,000 of whom were repairers of home, commercial and industrial electronic equipment.

Many Video Service Technicians move to other firms at higher salaries, leaving positions open for promising newcomers. With more than 100,000 retail stores, chains, department stores, and other outlets selling video, audiovisual, stereo, and photographic equipment, the opportunities for employment do exist.

Advancement Prospects

Many Video Service Technicians improve their skills and, with further training, advance their careers by moving into broadcast-related electronics as Maintenance Engineers or become Technicians at cable TV systems or multichannel multipoint distribution service (MMDS) stations. A few seek advancement and security as Media Technicians in educational institutions. Some advance their careers by finding employment at a manufacturers' facility. An increasingly promising route will be the transition to computer and office machine repair, and job openings will be plentiful while electronic home entertainment equipment repair jobs will decline, according to the BLS.

Education

A high school diploma and some evidence of vocational or technical school training is usually required. Coursework in the basic sciences, algebra, and physics is helpful. Drafting courses that help an individual understand spatial relationships and physical characteristics are also useful. Specialized training is available at technical schools, community colleges, extension divisions of colleges/universities, and public or private vocational/technical schools. Some training may be taken by correspondence study. Many new employees qualify because of experience they receive in the armed forces. Some manufacturers operate their own training centers.

Experience/Skills

Although six months to a year in electronics or audiovisual repair work is preferred, lengthy experience is not necessary in obtaining an entry-level position. Many employers hire recent vocational or technical school graduates and train them on the job.

Most Video Service Technicians serve an apprenticeship. After four years of work experience, an individual can qualify for a voluntary examination leading to certification as a Journeyman Certified Electronic Technician (CET) under the auspices of the International Society of Certified Electronic Technicians (ISCET). Some students and beginning employees who do not have the experience for a Journeyman certificate pass the Associate Level test and are so certified by the ISCET. Still others pass the certification requirements of the Association of Communications Technicians (AACT). Some states require Video Service Technicians to pass a proficiency test.

Some experience in the operation of video, photographic, audio, and audiovisual equipment is necessary. Video Service Technicians need inquisitive minds and should enjoy solving technical problems. They should also have good manual dexterity and an aptitude for electronics. An ability to do detailed work with a high degree of accuracy is needed, as is the ability to work independently.

Minority/Women's Opportunities

Although historically the job has been filled by white males, the percentage of minority group members holding the position has increased in the past few years, according to industry observers. The opportunities for women are excellent, but relatively few train or apply for positions as Video Service Technicians.

Unions/Associations

There are no unions that serve as bargaining agents for Video Service Technicians. Some belong to the Institute of Electrical and Electronics Engineers (IEEE) or the National Electronic Service Dealers Association (NESDA). Some also belong to ISCET or AACT to share concerns and advance their careers.

DIRECTOR OF MEDIA SERVICES

CAREER PROFILE

Duties: Administering media services, including television video, and multimedia/Internet support, in a school district, college, or university

Alternate Title(s): Director, Instructional Technology; Director, Learning Resources; Director, Educational Media

Salary Range: $25,000 to $60,000+

Employment Prospects: Fair

Advancement Prospects: Poor

Prerequisites:

Education—Master's or doctorate degree in education

Experience—Minimum of two to three years of educational media experience; classroom teaching

Special Skills—Verbal and writing talent; persuasiveness; leadership qualities; supervisory ability; good interpersonal skills; inquisitiveness

CAREER LADDER

```
┌─────────────────────────────────────────┐
│  Director of Media Services (Larger      │
│  Institution);                            │
│  Dean; Assistant Superintendent (School  │
│  System)                                  │
└─────────────────────────────────────────┘

┌─────────────────────────────────────────┐
│  Director of Media Services              │
└─────────────────────────────────────────┘

┌─────────────────────────────────────────┐
│  Media Librarian; Instructional Designer;│
│  Director of ITV                          │
└─────────────────────────────────────────┘
```

Position Description

A Director of Media Services is the senior administrative official in charge of providing instructional support materials to schools and colleges that use media as part of their curricula and training. The person holding this position ensures that well-selected materials and equipment are easily accessible to teachers and students for classroom use. Directors of Media Services work in elementary and secondary schools, community and four-year colleges, and universities.

In addition to the traditional audiovisual equipment and materials such as 16mm films, slides, charts, filmstrips, overhead transparencies, and audio tapes and records, there is a vast new array of technological devices. These new media include computers and videotape, videocassette, videodisc equipment and programs, and the Internet and World Wide Web. It is the responsibility of the Director of Media Services to coordinate the use of this new technology within the instructional process.

The Director of Media Services is an educational and technological generalist who views television/video programming as one component of a multimedia service. As part of the overall responsibility of the job, the Director of Media Services evaluates and purchases media equipment and programs to supplement and enrich classroom instruction and often supervises their use.

Directors of Media Services operate in a variety of administrative situations. In some cases, they have overall responsibility for an instructional television (ITV) operation, including the production of programs that are shown through a school-owned TV system. Sometimes the Director of Media Services oversees all print (library) and nonprint (media) services for a school or college and is in charge of the day-to-day distribution of video and other equipment and instructional programs.

In higher education, media services departments are complex and often employ more than 30 individuals who handle a variety of tasks. A Director of Media Services manages various units such as film production, audio production, graphic arts, technical and maintenance, and video/film booking. In smaller school systems, these functions may be handled by as few as five people.

A Director of Media Services in a school system usually reports to an assistant superintendent or, at a college or university, to a vice president of academic affairs.

Additionally, the Director of Media Services

- provides equipment and operators for classroom use;
- supervises the maintenance of equipment; and
- develops budgets, reports, research, and other data relevant to program circulation.

Salaries

Salaries for experienced personnel ranged from $25,000 to $60,000 with the most common range between $30,000 and $50,500 in 1998. Fifty percent of those surveyed earned $37,717 in that year, according to the International Television Association (ITVA). The average salary for a Director of Educational Media Services was $40,000, according to industry observers, and the median salary for a Director of Learning Resources at a university was $36,434 in that school year, according to that association.

Employment Prospects

With the general decline of support for education and media in recent years, the opportunities for employment are only fair. The majority of placements for media graduates has been in elementary/secondary schools.

This is not usually an entry-level job. Although some small school systems employ individuals who have just received their college degrees, most seek more experienced people. A significant number of graduate students return to their former positions.

Most states have a unit concerned with statewide media coordination, and many circulate classroom and in-service materials to schools. In addition, most school districts, community and four-year colleges, and universities have media centers. There is relatively little turnover, however, and openings are often filled from within.

In some organizations, the Media Librarian or an Instructional Designer is promoted to the position. In other cases, the Director of Instructional Television moves up to the Director of Media Services slot.

Advancement Prospects

Opportunities are poor compared to other video and telecommunications areas. For many senior-level Directors of Media Services at large school systems or at higher education institutions, the position is the climax of a successful career in educational communications and media. A few take administrative posts at larger universities as deans of instructional resources or at larger school systems as assistant superintendents.

Most advance their careers by moving to larger school systems, colleges, or universities that offer higher salaries and more prestige. Some obtain higher-paying positions in government, health, or business media centers, but such a move often requires a willingness to specialize in a particular field of interest.

Education

A bachelor's degree in education is a minimum requirement, and all but the very small school systems require a master's degree. A master's is a minimum requirement at colleges and universities, but most higher education institutions prefer a doctorate.

A candidate should have earned a degree in education with the major field of study in educational media, instructional technology, or learning resources. Courses in curriculum design, educational administration, educational psychology, and computer operations are necessary.

Experience/Skills

While some small schools or colleges employ recent graduates, the majority require a minimum of two to three years of educational experience. A broad knowledge of all technology, including the traditional audiovisual equipment, is necessary. Equally important is classroom teaching experience that provides insight into the day-to-day instructional process and environment.

Most good Directors of Media Services are expert practitioners of various teaching and learning techniques and are eager to discover new methods that work. They possess strong verbal and writing talents, are articulate and persuasive, and have excellent interpersonal skills. They have good leadership qualities and are able to supervise a number of individuals in various tasks.

Minority/Women's Opportunities

The opportunities for women and members of minorities are excellent. More women are seeking graduate degrees in educational media, and constitute more than 50 percent of recent graduates in the field. Many institutions and schools report that they have a difficult time finding minority applicants, however, and most positions are held by white males, according to professional sources.

Unions/Associations

There are no unions that specifically represent Directors of Media Services. Some individuals belong to the National Education Association (NEA) or American Association of University Professors (AAUP), which may represent them as faculty members.

Most Directors of Media Services belong to the Association for Educational Communications and Technology (AECT) or the American Library Association (ALA) in order to share mutual concerns and advance their careers.

INSTRUCTIONAL DESIGNER

CAREER PROFILE

Duties: Assisting teachers in the design of new instructional techniques using video, media, and computers

Alternate Title(s):   Curriculum Specialist; Curriculum Writer

Salary Range: $26,000 to $50,000

Employment Prospects: Good

Advancement Prospects: Good

Prerequisites:

Education—Undergraduate degree in education; master's degree preferable

Experience—Minimum of one to two years in media, training, and instruction

Special Skills—Interpersonal skills; logic; organizational ability; knowledge of media equipment; statistical aptitude

CAREER LADDER

```
┌─────────────────────────────────┐
│    Director of Media Services    │
└─────────────────────────────────┘

┌─────────────────────────────────┐
│      Instructional Designer      │
└─────────────────────────────────┘

┌─────────────────────────────────┐
│    Graduate Assistant; Teacher   │
└─────────────────────────────────┘
```

Position Description

An Instructional Designer is a learning facilitator who assists faculty members (in college), teachers (in schools), and trainers (in business, health, or government) to improve instruction and learning. This person takes advantage of the instructional capabilities of media to help design effective means of teaching. An Instructional Designer is alert to new instructional methods and technologies and is familiar with the uses of television, non-broadcast video, computers, and telecommunications systems in education.

The position of Instructional Designer is a relatively new one, incorporating the traditional functions of a curriculum specialist and a curriculum writer. Instructional Designers are usually employed by large school systems, colleges, or universities. Increasingly, they work in private industry, health, and, on occasion, government training projects and programs.

In whatever setting, Instructional Designers are responsible for assisting subject experts to design or redesign entire courses, specific lessons, individual lectures, or professional training sessions. They help to develop the content and to design the most effective method for teaching it, making use of media technology. Instructional Designers develop units, modules, and courses of instruction. In addition, they recommend and update instructional materials, including video programs. When appropriate, they organize and plan new

media programs and often write, edit, and rewrite scripts for instructional video use.

An Instructional Designer sometimes works independently but more often is a member of a team, which may include a content or subject specialist (faculty member in a specific discipline), Media Technician, Media Librarian, Graphic Artist, and, often, a Producer or Director. Today they often work with computer Software Engineers, Programmers, and Multimedia Writers.

This is not generally a supervisory position and the Instructional Designer usually reports to a Director of Media Services or Director of Instructional Television.

Additionally, the Instructional Designer

- consults with faculty and supervisors regarding instructional needs and designs:
- develops cost-benefit and accountability studies for media use; and
- evaluates the effectiveness of new instructional techniques, equipment, and video programs.

Salaries

Salaries in 1997 ranged from $26,000 for beginners to more than $50,000 for experienced individuals, according to industry sources. Salaries for Instructional Designers in a college or university were higher than those employed in school systems. Salaries for persons employed in business and industry were higher than school or university personnel. Almost all employers offer excellent fringe benefits, including health and pension plans. In most instances, salaries are a reflection of the individual's level of education and of his or her particular skills and achievements.

Employment Prospects

In spite of a general decline in educational media opportunities, Instructional Designers are in some demand, and employment prospects for this specialty are good. Increasing costs have caused administrators to examine all possible ways to improve teaching and training and to manage it more efficiently. The sound application of new technology is one of the more viable approaches.

Positions in education are usually available at the larger school districts and universities, which are involved with extensive media programs, telecommunications, and video. Some elementary and secondary school teachers who have worked in curriculum development get further training in this new discipline and find jobs as Instructional Designers.

In addition to the opportunities in education, there are an increasing number of positions available in private business and industry and in health areas. Most observers predict that this trend will continue and that such organizations will provide the major marketplace for graduates of instructional development programs in the future.

Advancement Prospects

Some Instructional Designers serve in joint academic appointments and teach instructional development, educational psychology, or other courses in colleges or universities. As such, their career advancement is often tied to their academic achievements—papers, research, teaching competence, etc. Some Instructional Designers advance their careers by moving to more responsible positions as Directors of Media Services at smaller colleges or school systems. Still others join private industry for better-paid positions. The opportunities for advancement are good.

Education

An undergraduate degree in education is a minimum requirement, and a master's degree is usually required. Individuals who seek employment at a major university must have a doctorate.

Coursework in educational psychology, curriculum design, sociology, and computers is required. Courses in educational media, including television, video, cable, and other nonbroadcast technology, are mandatory.

Experience/Skills

One to two years of experience, either as a graduate assistant or as an elementary or secondary school or college teacher is usually required.

Knowledge of and experience with the various theories of learning and of the use of a wide range of media resources and technology is essential. Skill in the operation and use of video equipment and in writing and editing video and television programs is required. Computer skills are a must.

Instructional Designers must possess interpersonal skills, inasmuch as there is constant contact with faculty and staff members of an organization. An inquisitive mind, a penchant for creative and logical thought, and statistical aptitude are necessary. Most Instructional Designers have had some teaching experience and are excellent motivators and cooperative leaders.

Minority/Women's Opportunities

Opportunities for women are excellent. In 1997, one half of all Instructional Designers were females, according to industry observers. The opportunities for members of minorities are plentiful.

Unions/Associations

There are no unions that serve as bargaining agents for Instructional Designers. Some individuals who also serve as faculty members at schools and colleges belong to the American Association of University Professors (AAUP) or the National Education Association (NEA).

Many Instructional Designers belong to the Association for Educational Communication and Technology (AECT) and to its Division of Instructional Development to exchange ideas and advance their careers. Others belong to the American Society for Training and Development (ASTD) and its Media Design and Production Division or to the National Society for Performance and Instruction (NSPI).

MEDIA LIBRARIAN

CAREER PROFILE

Duties: Acquiring, scheduling, and circulating nonprint materials

Alternate Title(s): Learning Information Specialist; Learning Resource Specialist; Media Scheduler; Media Specialist; Audiovisual Librarian

Salary Range: $22,000 to $40,000

Employment Prospects: Excellent

Advancement Prospects: Poor

Prerequisites:

Education—Undergraduate degree; master's degree in education or library science preferable

Experience—Minimum of one year of cataloging, classifying, and circulating media

Special Skills—Organizational ability; detail orientation; responsible nature; interpersonal skills

CAREER LADDER

```
+-------------------------------------+
|  Media or Library Administrator;    |
|          ITV Coordinator            |
+-------------------------------------+

+-------------------------------------+
|          Media Librarian            |
+-------------------------------------+

+-------------------------------------+
|        Librarian; Secretary         |
+-------------------------------------+
```

Position Description

A Media Librarian is responsible for acquiring, previewing, scheduling, and circulating films, videocassettes, videotapes, videodiscs, and other nonprint materials for educational, public, or training use. Duties also include processing customer orders and maintaining records detailing the location and disposition of all such material.

In the past, Media Librarians dealt predominantly with slides, 8mm and 16mm films, audio tapes, and records. Today, they are increasingly becoming responsible for assisting in the selection of videocassettes, videodiscs, and CD-ROMs that a library or media center makes available to its clients or patrons.

In some small media centers, Media Librarians are responsible for checking out and scheduling nonprint instructional support materials. They serve as "bookers" or "schedulers" and perform mainly clerical support functions. Most often, Media Librarians are professional librarians or media specialists, charged with acquiring, evaluating, categorizing, and cataloging film and video materials and are considered members of the professional media support staff. They select video and film titles from a variety of sources, including reviews in professional literature, producer or distributor sales or promotional literature, and exhibits.

Media Librarians are employed by schools and colleges, private industry, government, and health media centers and, increasingly, are important staff members at public libraries. They serve as collectors and distributors of nonprint materials to instructors, trainers, students, and the public. Many librarians at small schools are in charge of both print and media/audiovisual collections. With audiovisual collections, they are responsible for the circulation of video and film materials for on-campus or in-company use. In some large media centers that have extensive collections of film and video materials, or in public libraries, Media Librarians are also responsible for off-campus or public circulation.

Media Librarians often supervise many part-time student workers and, in large media centers, are often responsible for the supervision of one or two full-time employees. Media Librarians employed by schools and colleges usually report to a Director of Media Services. Those employed by a government media operation report to the Chief, Audiovisual Services. A Media Librarian working at a public library reports to the head librarian.

Additionally, the Media Librarian

- monitors the frequency of circulation of videotapes and films as well as the use of the media center;

- supervises the preparation and publication of the media center's film and video rental/sale catalogs;
- responds to inquiries and requests for video and film programs, processes complaints, and resolves circulation and user problems; and
- keeps up-to-date on copyright regulations and licensing agreements.

Salaries

The 1998–99 *Occupational Outlook Handbook* reports that according to the Special Libraries Association, salaries for special librarians (which includes media librarians) with two years or less of library experience averaged $33,100 a year in 1996, while those with three to five years of experience averaged $37,400 a year. Salaries for special librarians with primarily administrative responsibilities averaged $58,400 a year.

In a public library setting, the average starting salary for a Librarian was $28,000 in 1998, according to industry observers.

Salaries are a reflection of a combination of seniority and education. Individuals with professional training in library science or media earn higher beginning salaries and advance more rapidly.

Employment Prospects

Opportunities in education or public library work are excellent due to a shortage of trained librarians in the United States. The number of Master of Library Science (MLS) graduates of schools accredited by the American Library Association (ALA) in the 1990s was about half the level of the mid-1970s.

While some administrators of small media collections choose a secretary experienced in media to fill the job of a "booker," all prefer a trained professional as a Librarian. Positions as Media Librarians in private industry and at health media centers are also increasingly available.

Advancement Prospects

Possibilities for advancement are poor. The competition for better jobs in the library and educational media worlds is great.

Media Librarians can sometimes advance their careers by obtaining positions at larger media centers or public libraries in other geographic areas. Some move within their own organizations into more responsible positions as administra-

tors of media programs in education. In the library field, some move into better-paid positions with the responsibility for acquisition of print as well as nonprint materials.

Education

A master of education or master of library science degree is almost always required, and at libraries a master of library science degree is mandatory. The degree should be from one of the 56 library schools accredited by the ALA.

In smaller media operations where the position has less responsibility for the selection and acquisition of video and film programs, an undergraduate degree is necessary. Courses in media, cataloging, and classification of materials are required, and a broad liberal arts background is helpful.

Experience/Skills

A minimum of one year spent cataloging and classifying media and handling circulation procedures is usually mandatory. In addition, some part-time or full-time experience in the distribution of nonprint materials is often necessary. Since most media centers use computers in their circulation operations, familiarity with word processing equipment and computers is required.

A Media Librarian must be extremely well organized, detail oriented, responsible, inquisitive, and able to relate to users in a friendly and helpful manner.

Minority/Women's Opportunities

More than 60 percent of all librarians in the early 1990s were white females, according to industry observers. More than 7 percent were black. While employment opportunities for members of minority groups have increased in recent years, the number of individuals in the position has not risen proportionately, except in urban settings.

Unions/Associations

There are no national unions that represent and bargain for Media Librarians. Many individuals belong to the ALA and one or more of its divisions, notably the Library and Information Technology Association (LITA). Others hold membership in the Special Libraries Association (SLA). Some Media Librarians also belong to the Association for Educational Communications and Technology (AECT), the Association of Visual Communicators (AVC), and the American Film and Video Association (AFVA) to share common concerns and advance their careers.

MEDIA TECHNICIAN

Duties: Repairing and maintaining media, television, and video equipment at a school or university

Alternate Title(s): Maintenance Technician; AV Technician

Salary Range: $20,000 to $32,000

Employment Prospects: Excellent

Advancement Prospects: Good

Prerequisites:

Education—High school diploma; some vocational or technical school training

Experience—Minimum of six months of audiovisual equipment repair preferable

Special Skills—Mechanical aptitude; electronics skills; inquiring mind; good problem-solving ability; accuracy

Technician; Video Service Technician

Media Technician

Audiovisual Equipment Repair; Technical School

Position Description

A Media Technician maintains, repairs, and services the technical equipment at a school or college media center. This individual repairs traditional audiovisual equipment, including 16mm projectors and cameras, slide and film-strip machines, opaque and overhead projectors, television sets, and videocassette and videodisc machines. In media centers that have television studio equipment, the responsibilities center on repairing cameras, switchers, and associated equipment. A Media Technician must be familiar with a wide variety of audiovisual equipment. Many problems that arise are mechanical, but others require a knowledge of digital electronics, integrated circuit boards, and computerized equipment.

It is the Media Technician's responsibility to develop and maintain an orderly system of preventive maintenance to ensure that the video and other media equipment is in good operating order at all times. This involves developing daily and weekly worksheets and adhering to maintenance schedules.

Small media operations at schools usually employ only one full-time Media Technician while at larger university media centers two to three are required full-time to keep the equipment in good operating condition. In some cases, high school or college students are employed part-time to augment the services of the Media Technician, who supervises and trains them.

A Media Technician usually operates out of a maintenance equipment room at the central headquarters of a media center. In some large media operations with more than one location, Technicians may be assigned to a specific branch or office. On occasion, they are required to do on-location repair work in classrooms or other buildings where equipment is located.

A Media Technician usually reports directly to a Director of Media Services in small operations and to that person's assistant in large organizations.

Additionally, the Media Technician

- maintains an inventory of parts, accessories, and supplies;
- interprets schematic charts and diagrams detailing television, video, and media electronic components and systems;
- works with manufacturers' field service representatives and attends periodic seminars and training sessions to keep abreast of new equipment and techniques; and recommends the replacement of outdated or irreparable equipment.

Salaries

Salaries in 1997 ranged from $20,000 to $32,000, according to industry observers. While such salaries are generally lower than those for similar maintenance positions in multichannel multipoint distribution (MMDS) companies or in the home video field, the fringe benefits and security offered are often considerably better. All school and university health centers offer good employee health, life insurance, and pension plans. An employee credit union is often available, and good vacation schedules are normal.

Employment Prospects

Opportunities are excellent. There is a lack of qualified people in established media centers, and the position does not usually require as much electronics knowledge and training as do the somewhat similar positions of Video Service Technician (in home video) or Technician (in Cable, or MMDS operations), although the basic skills are similar.

There is some turnover in the position as individuals leave for better-paid jobs in private industry. In addition, most government, health, and corporate media centers require Media Technicians. The number of media centers in education, health, and government, however, is not likely to grow. Nevertheless, as in most technical positions in television, video, and media, there are usually more openings than there are qualified candidates.

Advancement Prospects

Opportunities for advancement are good. As in most technical positions in electronics, there is some turnover in the field. Alert and diligent individuals who combine their mechanical and electronic experience with further study can move to better-paid positions as Technicians in MMDS or cable TV operations. Some get jobs in the consumer electronics field as Video Service Technicians with higher pay but fewer benefits. A few move to larger markets to advance their careers.

Education

A high school diploma and some evidence of post–high school training in a trade, technical, or vocational school are usually required. Classes in the basic sciences, as well as in math and algebra, are useful. Drafting, basic electronics, and electrical engineering courses are extremely helpful. A Federal Communications Commission (FCC) license is not required.

Specialized training is available at technical institutes, community colleges, extension divisions of colleges and universities, and public or private vocational/technical schools.

Some training may be taken by correspondence study. Many new employees qualify on the basis of experience they have received in the armed forces. Some Media Technicians study for exams and become certified by the Association of Communications Technicians (AACT) or the International Society of Certified Electronics Technicians (ISCET), whose membership includes more than 25,000 CETs (certified electronic technicians).

Experience/Skills

Most employers prefer to hire those with some experience in the repair of audiovisual equipment. Saturday or evening work at a television repair or consumer electronics store is helpful. Six months to one year of experience is preferred but, because of the scarcity of people for the job, technical school training often serves in lieu of experience for beginners.

A knowledge of the operation of various types of traditional audiovisual equipment and television sets is required, as well as an ability to diagnose mechanical and electronic problems. A Media Technician needs an inquisitive mind, some mechanical dexterity, and an intuitive feel for problem solving. An ability to do detailed work with a high degree of accuracy is necessary, as is the ability to work independently.

Minority/Women's Opportunities

The position of Media Technician was held mostly by white males in 1997, according to industry estimates. Opportunities for women are excellent, but relatively few train or apply for the job. Prospects for minority group members are also excellent, and the number of minority workers in the job has increased, particularly in urban areas, over the past few years. The position, however, remains largely occupied by white males.

Unions/Associations

There are no national unions that serve as bargaining agents for Media Technicians. Most of the jobs in government, school, and college settings and in some health areas are local or federal civil service positions, and employees are represented by the appropriate governmental unions.

Some Media Technicians belong to the International Television Association (ITVA). Others belong to the National Electronic Service Dealers Association (NESDA), the AACT, or the ISCET.

DIRECTOR OF ITV

CAREER PROFILE

Duties: Administering an instructional TV operation at an educational institution

Alternate Title(s): Director of ETV; Assistant Director of Media; Director of Instructional Services; Director of ITV and Telecommunications

Salary Range: $25,000 to $50,000+

Employment Prospects: Fair

Advancement Prospects: Fair

Prerequisites:

Education—Master's degree; doctorate preferable

Experience—Minimum of two years in classroom teaching and instructional TV

Special Skills—Sound educational judgment; good language abilities; interpersonal skills; administrative and leadership qualities

CAREER LADDER

```
┌─────────────────────────────────┐
│    Director of Media Services    │
└─────────────────────────────────┘

┌─────────────────────────────────┐
│         Director of ITV          │
└─────────────────────────────────┘

┌─────────────────────────────────┐
│        ITV Specialist;           │
│      Teacher; Producer           │
└─────────────────────────────────┘
```

Position Description

A Director of ITV (instructional television) is responsible for the operation and administration of an instructional television fixed service (ITFS) station, a closed circuit (CCTV) system, and Internet connectivity at a school, school district, college, or university. The operation provides educational television programs and services to its students in a classroom environment in order to supplement and enrich regular instruction. At most school-owned operations, ITV is also used for in-service teacher training.

Some ITV operations are similar to, although smaller than, public TV broadcast stations and are increasingly becoming involved with telecommunications, including Internet-based instruction. The Director of ITV serves in a capacity that is similar to that of a General Manager of such a station or to the System Manager at a cable TV system. The Director oversees the operation and its schedule in accordance with the regulations of the Federal Communications Commission (FCC) and with the policies of the institution.

A Director of ITV is as much a professional educator as a media or television manager. The person in this position is dedicated to the use of TV to improve classroom instruction and efficiency and helps to identify curriculum areas and courses where ITV may be used beneficially.

Depending on the size and scope of the operation, a Director of ITV may supervise from 4 to 10 people. The small settings usually include only technical and operations employees. At such operations, the Director of ITV is responsible for selecting and renting or otherwise acquiring prerecorded or digital instructional programs for transmission.

At the larger operations at two- and four-year colleges and universities and large school districts, the Director of ITV is sometimes responsible for the production and transmission of original programs. This individual hires and supervises a staff, including production, operations, and engineering people as well as the teachers who will appear on camera.

A Director of ITV sometimes reports to a Director of Media Services. As a rule, however, a Director of ITV heads up a separate department within an educational institution and reports to an assistant superintendent of a school system or a vice president of academic affairs at a college or university.

PTV stations also employ Directors of Instructional Services. In these circumstances, the individual is in charge of all ITV projects for the station and supervises the utilization of the station's ETV schedule. Duties also include coordinating the acquisition of ITV programs with the using schools.

Additionally, the Director of ITV

- develops and manages a budget for operational expenses;
- plans and develops research regarding the effectiveness of instructional television; and
- generates awareness of the ITV operation both within the academic system and among the public.

Salaries

Salaries in 1997 ranged from $25,000 for beginning Directors of ITV at small school operations to more than $50,000, for highly experienced full-time individuals at institutions of higher education, according to professional sources. As is usually the case in education, payment is based on a combination of the individual's academic degree(s), seniority, and experience. In general, Directors of ITV operations at four-year and community colleges earn more than their peers at the school or district level.

At PTV stations, salaries for the position ranged from $20,523 to $86,174 for persons with long-time service, according to the Corporation for Public Broadcasting (CPB). The average salary was $44,211 in that year.

Employment Prospects

The opportunities are fair. The use of ITV programming has declined in the past few years at both the school and college levels; growing commitments toward computer literacy and equal access to Internet resources has led many educational institutions to bolster the use of computers. The emphasis in media has shifted to computer-assisted instruction.

In many school districts, the Director of ITV continues to have other media, teaching, or curriculum duties. Full-time positions are usually available only at colleges, universities, larger school districts and some PTV stations. The number of personnel at PTV stations dedicated to ITV has declined in recent years. Some Producers of ITV are promoted to the position when an opening occurs. More often, a talented ITV Specialist or classroom teacher is promoted to Director of ITV. There is little turnover in the field, and, with little growth in expenditures for education, no new ITV operations are expected in the future.

Advancement Prospects

Opportunities for professional advancement are only fair. There is little turnover and competition is great. Many Directors of ITV see their position as the climax to a successful career. Some, however, become Directors of Media Services for their own school districts, colleges, or universities. Others move to larger systems in other areas, and a few join systems in health or government media operations.

Education

A master's degree is required for the job at the school or community college level or at PTV stations, and a doctorate is usually necessary at four-year colleges or universities. Most Directors of ITV have extensive schooling in educational media development, design, and utilization as well as in television production and communications. Coursework in educational psychology, curriculum design, and instruction is usually mandatory.

Experience/Skills

Some experience in classroom teaching is necessary, particularly in school systems, where actual experience in classroom instruction is usually a prerequisite for the position. Candidates should have at least two to three years of classroom and instructional television experience.

A Director of ITV must be a professional with sound educational judgment. In addition to good speaking and writing abilities, the Director must possess excellent interpersonal skills to deal with colleagues and subordinates and be organized and persuasive. Strong administrative and leadership talents are also important.

Minority/Women's Opportunities

Opportunities for women are excellent. According to professional estimates, more than 50 percent of such positions at the school district level were occupied by white females in 1997. The number of white females employed as Directors of ITV in higher education is lower, and the number of minority group members in the position was even fewer, except in urban settings. At PTV stations, more than 50 percent of those holding comparable positions were women and less than 15 percent were minorities in 1997, according to observers.

Unions/Associations

There are no national unions that represent Directors of ITV for bargaining purposes.

As teachers or faculty members, they are represented by the American Association of University Professors (AAUP), the National Education Association (NEA), or the American Federation of Teachers (AFT). Many belong to the Association for Educational Communications and Technology (AECT) and, in particular, to its Division of Telecommunication (DOT).

ITV SPECIALIST

CAREER PROFILE

Duties: Coordinating the use of instructional television programs at a school, school district, or public broadcasting station

Alternate Title(s): ITV Coordinator; Education/Utilization Specialist; School Services Assistant (public TV)

Salary Range: $18,000 to $35,000

Employment Prospects: Fair

Advancement Prospects: Fair

Prerequisites:

Education—Minimum of an undergraduate degree in education; master's degree in media preferable

Experience—Minimum of one to two years of experience in classroom teaching or as a Media Librarian

Special Skills—Organizational abilities; leadership qualities; interpersonal and language skills

CAREER LADDER

```
+---------------------------------------------+
|              Director of ITV                |
+---------------------------------------------+

+---------------------------------------------+
|               ITV Specialist                |
+---------------------------------------------+

+---------------------------------------------+
|  Elementary/Secondary School Teacher;       |
|            Media Librarian                  |
+---------------------------------------------+
```

Position Description

An ITV (instructional television) Specialist is responsible for facilitating the most effective use of televised programs and telecommunications resources in a school district or regional educational agency. Specialists also serve at individual elementary and secondary schools, where they collaborate with classroom teachers to devise and help implement methods to improve the learning process with the use of instructional television programming.

ITV Specialists are employed directly by a school district or system, where they work mainly with elementary and middle (junior high) school teachers, or, sometimes, are assigned to work with a public TV station. Some are full-time members of that station's staff. Approximately one-third of the public stations employ such people. ITV Specialists are not employed in institutions of higher education.

ITV Specialists often work out of a school district office or administrative headquarters and spend most of their time in schools and classrooms, helping teachers to get full use of television programs in an educational setting. They conduct in-service training programs on the use of instructional television for groups of teachers, either via TV or in person.

An ITV Specialist tries to develop a team-teaching environment in which an instructor appearing in an ITV program supplements the classroom teacher with informative and highly visualized television presentations. The ITV Specialist also prepares and distributes lesson guides, manuals, and ancillary materials for use by the classroom teacher. The teacher then prepares the students for the TV lesson, supervises the actual viewing, answers questions, leads discussions, makes assignments, and gives tests on the material. The ITV Specialist encourages this learning approach and assists the teacher in making maximum use of television instructional materials.

Some large school districts employ two ITV Specialists, each assigned to a particular geographic area or grade level. In small systems, the duties are often combined with those of other ITV or media employees, such as the Media Librarian.

As a rule, an ITV Specialist reports to a Director of Instructional Television or a Director of Media Services. The position is not usually a supervisory job.

Additionally, the ITV Specialist

- helps classroom teachers and curriculum specialists to acquire, preview, and select ITV programs;
- develops ITV transmission schedules with classroom teachers and administrators; and
- conducts research and evaluates the extent and effectiveness of ITV use in classrooms.

Salaries

Earnings in 1997 ranged from $18,000 for relatively inexperienced individuals to more than $35,000 for those with extensive background and seniority, according to professional estimates. As in other educational occupations, salaries are based on the level of academic achievement, teaching status, and seniority. Individuals with graduate degrees and substantial experience in a school system often earn more, particularly in large urban systems.

At public TV stations, ITV Specialists usually earn more than their peers in school systems.

Employment Prospects

Only large school districts employ full-time ITV Specialists. Many smaller districts combine the responsibilities with that of the Audiovisual or Media Librarian. There is little turnover in the field, and the use of ITV in today's educational environment has decreased. Chances of getting a job as a full-time ITV Specialist are fair.

Advancement Prospects

The possibilities for career advancement are fair, according to professional observers. Most ITV Specialists are professional teachers who seek or are assigned to the position, and their career progress often depends upon increasing their subject area competence or administrative abilities in the system.

There is little turnover at the next level, the more responsible position of Director of ITV, and the competition is heavy. Those who wish to advance are usually required to seek other media and Director of ITV positions in larger school systems or at universities or community colleges. A few find opportunities in national educational organizations, which occasionally employ specialists in the use of ITV.

Education

A bachelor's degree in education is required, and a master's degree in media is preferable. Courses in television and media production, curriculum design, and educational psychology are necessary in obtaining the position, as well as some in-service training or seminars in instructional television use. The position usually requires basic teaching credentials.

Experience/Skills

One or two years of classroom teaching and some work in television, video, and other media production or use are preferable. The experience may be gained at an organization producing ITV programs or in a classroom where extensive use is made of instructional television and video. Work as a Media Librarian with ITV responsibilities for at least one or two years is also considered sufficient background for the position.

ITV Specialists must be enthusiastic proponents of televised instruction. They should be well organized and have leadership qualities and excellent interpersonal and language skills.

Minority/Women's Opportunities

The majority of ITV Specialists in 1997 were white females. There were twice as many women as men in the field in 1997, according to observers. Most were in the 30–50 age bracket. Minority group employment is considerably lower and is mainly in urban centers and large school systems and districts.

Unions/Associations

There are no unions that serve as representatives or bargaining agents for ITV Specialists. As teachers, however, some are represented by the National Education Association (NEA) or the American Federation of Teachers (AFT).

Many individuals belong to the Association for Educational Communications and Technology (AECT) and its Division of Telecommunications (DOT) or to the Association of Visual Communicators (AVC) to share mutual concerns and advance their careers.

COMMUNICATIONS INSTRUCTOR

CAREER PROFILE

Duties: Teaching college-level courses in advertising, journalism, film, and television

Alternate Title(s): Assistant Professor; Associate Professor; Professor

Salary Range: $25,000 to $75,000+

Employment Prospects: Fair

Advancement Prospects: Fair

Prerequisites:

Education—Doctorate degree preferable

Experience—Some college-level teaching; professional experience helpful

Special Skills—Teaching aptitude; verbal and writing abilities; leadership qualities; ability to motivate others

CAREER LADDER

```
┌─────────────────────────────────────┐
│    Department Chairperson; Dean      │
└─────────────────────────────────────┘

┌─────────────────────────────────────┐
│      Communications Instructor       │
└─────────────────────────────────────┘

┌─────────────────────────────────────┐
│  Graduate Assistant; Graduate School │
└─────────────────────────────────────┘
```

Position Description

Communications Instructor is a general title for someone who teaches courses in any of the communications disciplines. Only courses that have a relationship to television, however, will be discussed here, including advertising, journalism, film, TV, and multimedia. They may be taught at a community college, four-year college, or university. Such an Instructor can hold any rank in the teaching hierarchy, from lecturer to full professor, and may teach in an undergraduate, graduate, or continuing education program.

No two colleges are alike. Communications courses are taught in various departments and schools at different institutions. Some have full curricula and others offer only a few courses in a particular field. There are universities that have separate schools of communications or journalism. Many smaller colleges teach only a handful of TV-related courses and offer them through the theater, English, speech, or other department. There is no clear-cut pattern in the way college-level communications classes are presented.

Communications Instructors specializing in advertising are frequently members of a business or journalism school or department. In addition to introductory advertising courses, they may teach classes in specific areas such as television and radio commercials, copywriting, or market research.

A journalism Instructor is often a faculty member of a separate school or department of journalism or of a depart-

ment that is part of a communications school. Because of the importance of television news, there are frequently specialized courses offered. An Instructor may teach classes in news writing, news gathering techniques, and news management as related to broadcasting.

Since radio, film, television, and multimedia are so closely connected, many schools teach them in a single department. If there is a large media arts curriculum, it is often taught in a separate communications school. A Communications Instructor can teach in any of a number of areas, including mass communications theory, the history of broadcasting, television production, filmmaking, and broadcast management.

Additionally, the Communications Instructor

- advises students regarding registration, special projects, internships, and graduate theses;
- serves on department and university committees for administrative or curriculum policy making; and
- develops proposals for research grants in his or her specialty and administers grant projects.

Salaries

Salaries for Communications Instructors are generally lower than for their peers in other disciplines. The average salary at public institutions ranged from $25,000 for Instructors to $75,000 for full professors in 1997, according to industry experts. Salaries at private colleges were slightly lower. The average salary for Communications Instructors in 1996–97 was $29,396 at public institutions and $30,373 at private institutions, according to the College and University Personnel Association's survey of four-year colleges.

Employment Prospects

Chances of getting a position as a Communications Instructor are only fair. This appointment requires considerable academic study and apprenticeship. Some professional experience in the field being taught is extremely helpful.

There are an increasing number of part-time or adjunct teaching (lecturer) jobs available. This trend is expected to continue in the future as tenure-track jobs decline.

Advancement Prospects

Faculty at institutions of higher education usually begin as instructors and are promoted through the successive ranks of assistant professor, associate professor, and, finally, to full professor. Occasionally, a Communications Instructor can become chairperson of the department and, in some instances, dean of the school. Although there is relatively little turnover, some Communications Instructors get more rewarding positions and career advancement at more prestigious or larger institutions.

Promotion is usually based on publishing in professional journals and a good teaching record. Most colleges and universities emphasize research and writing. Sometimes recognition is given for professional activity in the field, such as producing a documentary. Overall advancement opportunities are fair.

Education

A beginning Communications Instructor should have a doctorate from a recognized and accredited university, although some departments or schools will employ an experienced individual with particular expertise in a discipline and a master's degree. Community colleges prefer to employ Ph.D.s but will accept master's degree holders. A few accept individuals with bachelor's degrees, but extensive coursework and, perhaps, a growing reputation in a specific field are required. Most Communications Instructors have their graduate degrees in communications with an emphasis on a particular discipline.

Experience/Skills

Most colleges and universities expect beginning instructors to have had some experience as graduate teaching assistants. It is extremely helpful if the candidate has also had some professional experience in his or her field.

For assistant, associate, and full professors, successful teaching background is usually a requirement, but the emphasis is on the individual's record of research, published works, projects in the field, and standing in the professional world. Community colleges usually place more emphasis on teaching experience and less on research and writing.

Communications Instructors must have good verbal and writing skills, good leadership qualities, the ability to motivate, and excellent interpersonal skills. Good Instructors are creative, imaginative, and often innovative. Above all, they like to teach.

Minority/Women's Opportunities

Only 29 percent of college and university faculty members were white women in 1997, according to *Diversity Digest,* while 7.7 percent were minority men and 4.4 percent were minority women. According to most academic observers, about 35 percent of Communications Instructors in 1997 were white females. The percentage of minority group members was considerably lower. Most public institutions of higher education are extremely active in affirmative action and equal employment opportunity (EEO) programs and aggressively recruit minority and female employees.

Unions/Associations

Some faculty members belong to the American Association of University Professors (AAUP), the American Federation of Teachers (AFT), or the National Education Association (NEA), which bargain for salary increases and benefits on their behalf. Some are members of a state educational association. Many are not represented by any organization.

Many Communications Instructors who teach television studies belong to the Broadcast Education Association (BEA) and the Speech Communications Association (SCA) to share common professional concerns. Journalism Instructors may belong to the Association for Education in Journalism and Mass Communications (AEJMC). Some female Communications Instructors belong to Women in Communications Inc. (WIC).

MEDIA INSTRUCTOR

CAREER PROFILE

Duties: Teaching college-level courses in educational media

Alternate Title(s):   Assistant Professor; Associate Professor; Professor

Salary Range: $30,000 to $55,000+

Employment Prospects: Good

Advancement Prospects: Fair

Prerequisites:

  Education—Minimum of a master's degree in education; doctorate degree preferable

  Experience—Minimum of one to two years in teaching and media laboratory supervision

  Special Skills—Teaching aptitude; knowledge of media; verbal and writing abilities; leadership qualities; ability to motivate others

CAREER LADDER

```
┌─────────────────────────────────────┐
│   Department Chairperson; Dean       │
└─────────────────────────────────────┘

┌─────────────────────────────────────┐
│         Media Instructor            │
└─────────────────────────────────────┘

┌─────────────────────────────────────┐
│  Graduate Assistant; Graduate School │
└─────────────────────────────────────┘
```

Position Description

Media Instructor is a general title for someone who teaches courses that pertain to the educational uses of a wide variety of media, including television, video and multimedia. The courses are offered for undergraduate, graduate, or in-service teacher education credit at a community college, four-year college, or university. The Instructor teaches people who are, or are going to be, teachers as to when, how, and why to use media as part of the classroom instructional process.

Theoretical courses taught by the Media Instructor explain how media work in the learning process to spark interest, enhance classroom instruction, and supplement printed materials. In practical courses and laboratories, the Media Instructor discusses specific media and their advantages, availabilities, limitations, and costs. In addition, the Instructor explains what kinds are appropriate for various learning situations, how to operate equipment, what programs can be used, and how to create media projects inexpensively.

In the past, Media Instructors dealt with the traditional supplementary materials, such as filmstrips, slides, and 16mm films. While they continue to use these formats, most are also teaching about new resources, including computer-assisted instruction, which includes the Internet and CD-ROMs, television, and video. It is the Media Instructor's responsibility to educate and train students in the theory, use, and techniques of all such learning aids.

A Media Instructor not only teaches classes but also may be involved with his or her institution's media center, which is where media are produced or obtained for other faculty members teaching any subject. The Media Instructor also conducts individual laboratory sessions detailing how to run and operate specific equipment, holds seminars on new techniques, and lectures in other education classes to highlight media use. The Instructor advises other educators about media applications in their subjects. As a result, Media Instructors are not only members of the faculty but also serve as administrative and support employees. They sometimes teach only one or two classes each semester.

As a rule, a Media Instructor is a member of the faculty of a school or department of education and can hold any rank from lecturer to full professor.

Additionally, the Media Instructor

- evaluates and selects instructional materials and equipment for classroom use and lab training;
- supervises student workers at media instructional or learning resource centers; and
- prepares grant proposals for additional media support.

Salaries

Salaries for instructors at four-year colleges and universities averaged $30,800, according to the 1995–96 survey by the American Association of University Professors (AAUP).

Salaries for humanities faculty tended to be lower. The average of all ranks was $51,000 in that school year. Salaries are dependent on faculty rank, geographic location, and research and publishing reputation. Media Instructors in community colleges make lower salaries for both part- and full-time work. Media Instructors enjoy the standard institutional fringe benefits, including group health and life insurance and retirement plans if they are full-time employees, and salaries are usually based on nine-month work schedules.

Employment Prospects

In the past, Media Instructors were in great demand. The federal, state, and local emphasis on education, and particularly on new techniques of instruction, created a demand for qualified teachers in the new media. This is less true today, but employment prospects remain good, especially with the advent of the Internet and the World Wide Web. Many of the available jobs are in the teaching of media production.

Those who are willing to relocate geographically stand a better chance of obtaining positions. There are also a considerable number of adjunct or part-time teaching positions at both four-year and community colleges. This trend is expected to continue in the future. Individuals entering the profession may expect to be awarded only three-year contracts.

Candidates are usually screened by a search committee. Selection is made on the basis of academic credentials, references, professional writing, research reputation, and on whether the particular academic strengths meet an instructional need at the institution. Many Media Instructors are chosen from the ranks of graduate school students or graduate assistants.

Advancement Prospects

Opportunities for advancement are fair. Teachers usually move up from assistant professor to associate professor and finally to full professor. Promotion is competitive and is based largely on an individual's research, publication of papers, and teaching abilities. A Media Instructor may become chairperson of the media or education department or may, in some cases, become dean. Some leave the educational profession for higher-paying positions in private industry. Others use their video, media, and training skills to obtain more financially rewarding jobs in business or health media operations.

Education

A Media Instructor should have at least a master's degree in education, although a doctorate is preferred. Courses and training in educational psychology, communications, learning theory, and curriculum design are also required.

Experience/Skills

Media Instructors must have experience operating all media equipment, including television cameras, audio gear, and videotape and videodisc players and accessories. At least one or two years of experience in teaching and media laboratory supervision is generally required. Media Instructors are usually excellent teachers with knowledge of the traditional instructional support equipment and of the new media, their operation, and their use in education.

Good verbal and writing skills are essential, as are creativity, an innovative approach to problem solving, and leadership qualities. Individuals should enjoy teaching and be able to motivate students.

Minority/Women's Opportunities

Only 29 percent of college and university faculty members were white women in 1997, according to *Diversity Digest;* more than 12 percent were minorities. Prior to 1975, most Media Instructor positions were held by white males. In 1997, more than 35 percent of Media Instructors were white females, according to academic observers. In 1993, minorities represented only 12.2 percent of all full-time faculty and 9.2 percent of full professors; minority representation in the general population was 25 percent that year. All public institutions are actively involved in affirmative action and equal employment opportunity programs and actively seek women and minority employees.

Unions/Associations

Some Media Instructors belong to the American Federation of Teachers (AFT), the AAUP, or the National Education Association (NEA), which act as bargaining agents for salary increases and benefits. In addition, most are active in the Association for Educational Communications Technology (AECT) and in their own state associations of that organization to share mutual concerns and advance their careers. Some belong to the University Film and Video Association (UFVA).

MANAGER OF MEDIA SERVICES

CAREER PROFILE

Duties: Responsibility for the development and use of audiovisual media in private industry

Alternate Title(s): Manager of AV Services and Telecommunications

Salary Range: $30,000 to $75,000

Employment Prospects: Fair

Advancement Prospects: Poor

Prerequisites:

Education—Undergraduate degree in communications, educational media, or radio-TV; master's degree preferable

Experience—Minimum of three to four years in broadcast TV or educational media

Special Skills—Organizational ability; knowledge of media; administrative talent; computer literacy

CAREER LADDER

```
┌─────────────────────────────────────┐
│        Training Director;            │
│  Director of Corporate Communications│
└─────────────────────────────────────┘

┌─────────────────────────────────────┐
│     Manager of Media Services        │
└─────────────────────────────────────┘

┌─────────────────────────────────────┐
│    Supervisor of Media Services      │
└─────────────────────────────────────┘
```

Position Description

A Manager of Media Services is in charge of a corporate media center within an industry and is responsible for the planning, development, and use of audiovisual and media services to satisfy the company's training and communication needs. The Manager develops ideas for media projects that use traditional audiovisual materials as well as film, television, multimedia, and video to support corporate policies and objectives for employee training, public relations, marketing, sales, and internal communications.

To meet the requirements of corporate communications, a Manager of Media Services supervises the selection and use of a wide range of media formats. This may include creating videocassettes or overseeing production of a CD-ROM for training or to introduce manufacturing procedures or new company policies. Projects may also include the production of periodic company video newsletters or video memos, video product displays, slide, film, or video presentations, annual video stockholder reports, and public and community relations videotapes.

For a large company with many employees, the Manager of Media Services establishes video playback stations in a number of geographic locations and distributes TV training and employee communications videocassettes to them. In smaller firms, this individual is responsible for contracting with outside TV or media production companies to produce videocassettes, films, slides, or multimedia shows for internal company use.

In a major company, the Manager of Media Services may supervise from 1 to 20 or more people and oversees the Supervisor of Media Services, who produces the projects. In a small firm, the Manager of Media Services may be the only media person in the company. The position usually reports to the training director of the company or to the director of corporate communications.

Additionally, the Manager of Media Services

- determines overall policies and budgets for audiovisual and media use in the corporation;
- establishes specific budgets and schedules for in-house or outside production services; and
- develops research and evaluation systems to measure the effectiveness of audiovisual use.

Salaries

Managers of Media Services earned from $30,000 to $75,000, according to industry observers. Most salaries for persons with seniority and experience fell between $40,000 at small companies and $60,000 at larger firms. In general, the larger the staff and responsibilities, the higher the salary. Salaries were higher for Managers of Media Services at financial firms and at insurance and manufacturing companies than at retail firms. Most companies provide liberal fringe benefits, including health and life insurance and retirement plans. Some individuals participate in stock option programs, and a few receive annual bonuses based on performance goals.

Employment Prospects

Although this is not usually an entry-level job, except in small companies, the opportunities for employment are fair because of some growth in the field. In larger companies, the Supervisor of Media Services is frequently promoted to the position when openings occur.

Most industry observers expect that the use of media in corporate training and communications will increase at the rate of 20 percent annually in the next few years. But much of the growth will be provided by projects produced by outside production facilities and producers. Some corporate media staffs have been reduced in the past few years, but the top job of Manager is usually maintained. He or she contracts for many production services with outside facilities companies.

Advancement Prospects

To some, the job is a climax to a successful career. Opportunities for advancement are poor because of the heavy competition and the fact that many corporate officers believe that the individual is limited to his expertise in media. To advance, the Manager of Media Services must usually broaden and increase his knowledge in other areas of the corporate world. Some Managers of Media Services become training directors within their own companies on the strength of new knowledge and of their experience and media background. At larger organizations where external communication is emphasized, an individual may be promoted to director of corporate communications. Some Managers of Media Services move to the same position in larger companies to advance their careers, and others take positions as training directors or directors of corporate communications in smaller companies in other industries. Some begin their own production firms.

Education

An undergraduate degree in communications, educational media, or radio-TV is the minimum requirement, and a master's degree is usually required.

Courses in media, education, educational technology, and instructional development are important. Studies in mass communications or radio-TV and coursework in television production, videotape editing, and multimedia production, along with some training in traditional audiovisual materials, are also helpful.

Experience/Skills

Three to four years of experience in broadcast television or educational media is necessary. Experience in a training environment is vital, as is familiarity with the use of a wide variety of media and equipment in support of instructional or communications objectives. Experience with computer-generated graphics is necessary.

A Manager of Media Services must be a highly organized media generalist with substantial administrative skills. The candidate must be capable of analyzing the economic results of media use in various applications and of designing and implementing instructional programs. Most are bright, creative, and aggressive individuals with excellent interpersonal skills necessary to "sell" their department to other divisions of the company.

Minority/Women's Opportunities

Opportunities for women are good. In 1997, about 50 percent of the Managers of Media Services were white females, according to industry observers. The opportunities for minority group members are good.

Unions/Associations

There are no unions that serve as bargaining agents for Managers of Media Services. Individuals often belong to a number of professional organizations, however, to share mutual concerns and advance their careers. Among them are the International Television Association (ITVA), the International Association of Business Communicators (IABC), the American Society for Training and Development (ASTD), and the Association for Educational Communications and Technology (AECT).

SUPERVISOR OF MEDIA SERVICES

CAREER PROFILE

Duties: Producing audiovisual projects and managing a media center in business or industry

Alternate Title(s): Media Center Manager

Salary Range: $27,000 to $50,000

Employment Prospects: Fair

Advancement Prospects: Good

Prerequisites:

Education—Undergraduate degree in mass communications, educational media, or radio-TV; graduate degree preferable

Experience—Minimum of two to three years in media production

Special Skills—Technical aptitude; creativity; organizational ability, computer literacy

CAREER LADDER

```
┌─────────────────────────────────┐
│    Manager of Media Services     │
└─────────────────────────────────┘

┌─────────────────────────────────┐
│   Supervisor of Media Services   │
└─────────────────────────────────┘

┌─────────────────────────────────┐
│            Producer              │
└─────────────────────────────────┘
```

Position Description

A Supervisor of Media Services is usually the second in command at a corporate media center, reporting directly to a Manager of Media Services. In the absence of the Manager, this person acts as the top administrator of the center. The main responsibility of the Supervisor of Media Services is to oversee the production of media projects and manage the day-to-day operation of the center. This is accomplished by creating films, slides, audio, and television and videocassette programs for the center and for other units within the company.

Often a Supervisor of Media Services coordinates a number of simultaneous media projects, oversees all preproduction stages, ensures timely and efficient completion, and supervises postproduction editing, either in-house or at a postproduction facilities company. Working relationships exist with Instructional Designers, heads of manufacturing departments, public relations directors, marketing personnel, and training directors to produce multimedia slide presentations, instructional television training programs, corporate image films, other media materials, and desktop videos.

At most media centers in business and industry, the production staff is quite small, with a few individuals who double in many capacities for routine in-house productions.

At smaller audiovisual operations, the Supervisor of Media Services often writes and produces videotape training programs and other media projects. The person in this position often hires and oversees independent commercial production firms or freelancers for writing and actual production. At larger companies, this person acts as Production Manager and supervises the full-time in-house staff, which may include Directors, Instructional Designers, and a number of production and engineering people.

Additionally, the Supervisor of Media Services

- assists in developing overall operating and capital budgets for the department;
- administers budgets for specific media productions; and
- implements research and feedback mechanisms to evaluate the effectiveness of media projects.

Salaries

Salaries in 1997 ranged from $27,000 for people at smaller companies to more than $50,000 for individuals with a good deal of supervisory responsibility, according to industry observers. Salaries are higher at large companies, particularly utility and financial companies. The majority of Supervisors participate in company health, life insurance, and pension plans. Some individuals at major corporations participate in stock option plans.

Employment Prospects

Opportunities in private industry are only fair. The use of corporate television, video, and media has increased and projections indicate continued growth. The use of audiovisual and media techniques for increased productivity and intra-company communications, as well as for teleconferencing, offer fair opportunities for alert and diligent individuals.

A number of corporations, however, have decreased their in-house productions and staffs. Many of the opportunities for similar work will come in creative and production jobs at private production facilities companies that are hired by corporations to produce programs for them. In-house jobs are more available at smaller corporations in smaller markets, where the lack of production facilities companies forces the corporation to do more in-house work.

Advancement Prospects

A well-trained, ambitious communications specialist should find that the opportunities for advancement are good.

With the increasing need for bottom-line efficiency and productivity, newer technologies, such as computers, interactive videodiscs, and teleconferencing networks, are being harnessed by business to improve communications and training. A bright individual with some experience in media who can adapt to other methods of originating, processing, and transmitting information should find opportunities for career growth.

Some Supervisors of Media Services assume broader responsibilities as Managers of Media Services within their own companies, but there is relatively little turnover in that position. Some move to smaller firms in other industries or to government, health, or education operations to assume more general media responsibility, often in a public relations capacity. A few retrain to become information processors, working with and for data processing and telemetrics companies to develop new techniques of transmitting and sharing information.

Education

A bachelor's degree in mass communications, educational media, or radio-TV is usually the minimum requirement, and a graduate degree in one of these fields is often preferable. Undergraduate or graduate-level courses in instructional design, television and film production, scriptwriting, photography, and industrial psychology are also helpful. Many colleges and universities now offer full course sequences in corporate or organizational television, and the number is expected to increase in the future. Some schools emphasize programs in the field.

Experience/Skills

Two to three years as a Producer or Director of media projects and programs is usually necessary for the job, as is experience in all media production techniques, including audio, video, television, slides, film, and still photography. Some instructional design experience is often mandatory. Familiarity with computer-generated graphics is required.

A candidate should have initiative, enthusiasm, and good technical skills and be a creative self-starter. A Supervisor of Media Services must be organized and have excellent verbal and script writing abilities as well as strong interpersonal skills.

Minority/Women's Opportunities

The employment of women in this position has increased rapidly in the past five years, according to industry observers. The opportunities for members of minorities are very good.

Unions/Associations

There are no unions that serve as bargaining agents for Supervisors of Media Services. Some individuals, however, belong to the organizations cited in the profile of the Manager of Audiovisual Services. In addition, some are members of the Association for Multi-Media International (AMI); Association of Visual Communicators (AVC) and the Division of Educational Media Management (DEMM); the Division of Telecommunications (DOT); and the Media Design and Production Division (MDPD) of the Association for Educational Communications and Technology (AECT).

CHIEF, MEDIA SERVICES

CAREER PROFILE

Duties: Administering media services for a government agency

Alternate Title(s):   Director of Audiovisual Services; Media Resources Director; Director, Visual Information

Salary Range: Under $39,000 to $66,000

Employment Prospects: Poor

Advancement Prospects: Poor

Prerequisites:

Education—Minimum of an undergraduate degree in radio-TV, communications, or educational media; graduate degree preferable

Experience—Three to five years in educational media or communications and media administration

Special Skills—Organizational abilities; leadership qualities; administrative and interpersonal skills

CAREER LADDER

```
┌─────────────────────────────────┐
│      Director of Public Affairs;    │
│    Director of Communications;      │
│         Training Director            │
└─────────────────────────────────┘

┌─────────────────────────────────┐
│      Chief, Media Services          │
└─────────────────────────────────┘

┌─────────────────────────────────┐
│      Media Program Officer          │
└─────────────────────────────────┘
```

Position Description

A Chief, Media Services is responsible for the administration of media services at a local, county, state, or federal government agency for training, internal communications, and public information purposes. It is the responsibility of the person in this position to help identify the agency's training and information needs that can best be satisfied with media support. Government agencies use media primarily for specialized and distinct internal staff training needs, particularly to inform and instruct employees who are geographically separated from the organization's headquarters, and to promote and explain the department's service to the general public.

After consulting with administrators, agency heads, and public information officers, the Chief, Media Services plans media support materials. This person supervises the production of original charts, graphs, slides, film, video, and other media programs or obtains them from outside sources and notifies agency heads and administrators about the availability of video and other formats for agency use.

The federal government is the largest employer of audiovisual specialists. About 61 executive departments and agencies are actively involved in the production or acquisition of slides, video programming, and other media. The largest is the Department of Defense, but agencies ranging from the Department of Agriculture to the Veterans Administration use and produce audiovisual materials. Some state government executive and legislative branches also operate media departments. At the county and city level, police, fire, or safety departments occasionally maintain media centers.

A Chief, Media Services may supervise from 2 to more than 20 workers, depending on the size of the agency and the extent to which it uses video and other media. In small operations, these workers may be Media Specialists, Media Librarians, and, occasionally, Media Technicians. In larger centers that produce video programs, the person in this position may supervise Media Program Officers and their small staffs. At most levels of government, the Chief, Media Services reports to a director of public affairs or information or to a director of training, communications, or personnel.

Additionally, the Chief, Media Services

- evaluates, previews, rents, or purchases video programs and films for internal training use;
- supervises the operation of audiovisual and video equipment; and
- develops and administers capital and operating budgets for the media center.

Salaries

Salaries for government employees are determined by the grade of the position within a local, state, or federal civil service classification system. The federal government classifies its employees according to a GS (government service) rating that assigns a salary range for specific job occupations, from GS-1 to GS-18. Most local, county, and state governments operate under a similar system.

Most Chiefs, Media Services in the federal civil service system are ranked at GS-13 or GS-14 (or higher levels); starting salaries in 1998 were $56,951 and $93,431, respectively. Most have worked for some time in the position and earn up to $83,000, depending on their length of service and on their automatic annual increases. Those in similar positions at nonfederal government agencies, however, usually receive lower salaries, starting at under $25,000 depending on the size of the agency and the classification of the position. All government employees have health insurance and pension plans available.

Employment Prospects

Almost every government agency maintains some audiovisual equipment and materials, and most have access to a videocassette machine. The general tightening of budgets in local, county, and state agencies, however, has created cutbacks in audiovisual production. Nevertheless, Media Program Officers with management skills and seniority are occasionally promoted. Overall opportunities for the position of Chief, Media Services at this time, however, are poor.

Advancement Prospects

The general lack of growth in audiovisual and other media expenditures at all levels of government has made opportunities extremely limited. A move to a larger agency in a similar position within the same governmental structure often means only a lateral transfer of responsibility, with little or no increase in grade or salary.

The position is viewed by many as the climax to a successful career, but some take similar positions in business for advancement. A few further their education and obtain higher GS ratings as directors of public affairs, directors of communications, or training directors within other governmental systems.

Education

A preclassification evaluation is usually necessary for civil service positions, and the candidate must meet at least the minimum established requirements for the job. Most requirements are extremely broad in nature, but this job usually requires a minimum of a bachelor's degree in radio-TV, communications, or educational media. In a few cases, a master's degree in one of the fields is required. At some agencies that use media primarily for external public information, degrees and coursework in communications and radio-TV production are helpful. At agencies where the emphasis is on media production for internal training, coursework in educational media and instructional design is useful.

Experience/Skills

Federal civil service usually requires three to five years of experience in some area of educational media or communications and a background in media administration.

Candidates must be well organized and capable of leadership and administration. They should possess excellent interpersonal skills to work with a diversity of people and be enthusiastic promoters of governmental use of video and other audiovisual techniques.

Minority/Women's Opportunities

Despite strong affirmative action programs in recent years and the requirements of the Equal Employment Opportunities Act, the majority of Chiefs, Media Services in 1997 were white males. Female and minority employment has increased greatly in the job, however, particularly in the federal service in Washington, D.C.

Unions/Associations

There are no unions that specifically represent Chiefs, Media Services as bargaining agents. Some government employees are represented by the American Federation of State, County, and Municipal Employees (AFSCME). Some belong to the Association for Educational Communications and Technology (AECT) and to the International Television Association (ITVA).

MEDIA PROGRAM OFFICER

CAREER PROFILE

Duties: Operating a specific media section in a government agency

Alternate Title(s):   Audiovisual Branch Head; Media Specialist; Training Aids Officer; Education Specialist

Salary Range; $57,000 to $93,000

Employment Prospects: Poor

Advancement Prospects: Poor

Prerequisites:

Education—Undergraduate degree in radio- TV, communications, or educational media

Experience—One to two years of college production courses or professional media work in education and training

Special Skills—Creativity; writing ability; interpersonal skills; supervisory talent

CAREER LADDER

> **Chief, Media Services**

> **Media Program Officer**

> **Media Specialist; College**

Position Description

A Media Program Officer is in charge of the daily operation of a department within a larger media center in a federal, state, city, or local government agency. The specific department may concentrate on exhibits, photography, graphics, motion pictures, radio-TV, or video. It is the responsibility of the officer to develop and produce training and public service programs and media support materials in response to requests from various divisions or departments within the agency.

At the federal level, such individuals are sometimes referred to as Audiovisual Branch Heads. At smaller media centers of the federal government and at state agencies, the person may be classified as a Media Specialist, working in (and occasionally supervising employees who are assigned to) specific media areas, including radio-TV and video. At the very small media centers of local and county governments, Media Specialists often perform general, more diverse audiovisual duties.

In most settings, however, a Media Program Officer specializes in a particular media area and provides operational and support activities in that area as part of the overall service of the media center to the entire agency. The Program Officer usually works on assignment and conceives and develops productions and supporting materials to meet defined agency

goals and objectives. This individual consults regularly with department heads and administrators to identify media projects and to report on progress.

When video production is undertaken within the government facility, the Media Program Officer serves in a capacity similar to that of a broadcast Production Manager and may supervise a Director, Floor Manager, Camera Operator, and, on occasion, Technicians. Often, the Program Officer writes and coordinates a particular project, contracting the actual production to a commercial production firm.

A Media Program Officer usually supervises a team of one to four employees who develop and produce programs and video materials for specific projects. The position usually reports to the Chief, Media Services.

Additionally, the Media Program Officer

- develops the cost analysis and budgeting for particular programs or services;
- prepares the capital and operating budget for his or her unit;
- assists in the development of research and utilization studies that evaluate the effectiveness of specific training programs; and
- supervises outside production services on specific projects.

Salaries

Most governmental salaries are determined by the grade level assigned to a particular position. The federal government grades most Media Program Officers at GS-11 or GS-12, with a beginning salary range in 1998 of $39,960 to $66,485. Most earn more, however, since many agencies rank the job at a higher grade and since salaries are affected by seniority. A Media Program Officer with several years of experience could earn $45,000 or more.

At the state, county, or local governmental level, salaries are generally lower and depend on the size of the agency, its media involvement, the grade level of the job, and seniority. Earnings at a smaller agency range from $18,000 for a beginning employee to more than $30,000 for an experienced person with seniority. In all government situations, salaries ranged from $27,000 to $36,000 or more in 1997, according to industry observers. All government employees have insurance and pension plans available.

Employment Prospects

The general tightening of funds at all levels of government has meant fewer opportunities for employment in media in general and for Media Program Officers specifically. Fewer new audiovisual services are expected to be developed. Many existing media center budgets have been lowered, and a few centers may be eliminated. Opportunities for employment at this time are poor.

The best source for obtaining a federal position is the newspaper *Federal Career Opportunities* or the web site www.opm.gov, maintained by the U.S. Office of Personnel Management. Both list job openings worldwide. Applicants are given numeric ratings (based on experience and education) and placed on a register for a particular job. The applicant then must be "in reach" of the agency seeking to fill a position for a job interview.

Advancement Prospects

Opportunities for advancement are also poor at all levels of government at present. Some individuals with management skills and seniority, however, are promoted to the position of Chief, Media Services when openings occur. Others

seek similar positions in the private sector in health, business or industry to advance their careers.

Education

For most government positions at any level, a preclassification is required and the results must be compared with the minimum requirements for the job. When hiring a Media Program Officer, most state and federal agencies require a bachelor's degree or equivalent experience in radio-TV, communications, or educational media. Specific coursework in television and video production is necessary. At agencies that emphasize the development of training programs, coursework in instructional design is helpful.

Experience/Skills

One to two years of college coursework in production techniques or professional experience as a Media Specialist in the health care field or in a similar position in another education and training setting is usually required. Military training and experience is helpful.

Minority/Women's Opportunities

Many women and minority group members hold the job, particularly at the federal level, but the majority of Media Program Officers in 1998 were white males, according to government sources.

There are more opportunities for women and members of minorities in government than in similar positions in nongovernmental organizations. Affirmative action programs and the Equal Employment Opportunity Act have opened up more opportunities for minorities and women in the past 10 years.

Unions/Associations

There are no specific unions that act as bargaining agents for Media Program Officers, although some are represented by local or state government employees unions. Others belong to the Division of Telecommunications (DOT) or other sections of the Association for Educational Communications and Technology (AECT) to share mutual concerns and advance their careers. Many belong to the International Television Association (ITVA).

MEDIA RESOURCE MANAGER

CAREER PROFILE

Duties: Administration of media services in a health care facility

Alternate Title(s):   Director of Media Services; Director of Audiovisual Services; Director of Biomedical Communications

Salary Range: $32,000 to $50,000+

Employment Prospects: Poor

Advancement Prospects: Poor

Prerequisites:

Education—Minimum of an undergraduate degree in radio-TV, communications, or educational media; graduate degree preferable

Experience—Minimum of three to four years of multimedia production for a health care or teaching facility

Special Skills—Organizational ability; knowledge of media technology; leadership qualities; administrative capability; interpersonal skills

CAREER LADDER

```
┌─────────────────────────────────┐
│   Director of Health Education;  │
│   Director of Health Training    │
└─────────────────────────────────┘

┌─────────────────────────────────┐
│     Media Resource Manager       │
└─────────────────────────────────┘

┌─────────────────────────────────┐
│        Media Specialist          │
└─────────────────────────────────┘
```

Position Description

A Media Resource Manager is the chief administrator of the audiovisual center serving a hospital or health care facility. The person in this position is an expert in the cost-efficient development and application of a variety of media to health care education and training. The Media Resource Manager works at hospitals and at nursing, veterinary, dental, allied health care, and other health-related schools. The individual is often in charge of the media support activities for a medical school.

In whatever facility, a Media Resource Manager develops programs for human resource development, training, continuing and patient education, internal communications, and public relations that meet the specific objectives of professional departments of the institution. The Manager consults regularly with training directors, physicians, nurses, and faculty regarding their use of media support programs. It is the responsibility of the Manager to identify the training and communications needs to be satisfied and to determine the best media approach. The Media Resource Manager supervises the production of health-oriented multi-image slide presentations, instructional films and video programs, and other audio or visual projects, including multimedia presentations and the use of computers. The person holding this position informs the health administrative staff of available media programs and equipment.

A Media Resource Manager may supervise one to four employees, including a Media Specialist, Media Technician, Instructional Designer, Media Librarian, and Cinematographer. When TV and video training is an integral part of the media services, duties may also include overseeing a unit of up to seven employees, including production and engineering professionals. A staff of this size, however, is employed only in the larger hospitals and video facilities.

In the medical media facilities at colleges of medicine, an individual with the related title of director of biomedical communications fills the role of the Media Resource Manager but has a more extensive educational background and greater responsibilities. At those schools, a director of biomedical communications supervises audiovisual services, medical television, biomedical photography, medical illustration, educational development, printing services, and other units.

At most hospitals, the Media Resource Manager reports to a director of health education, but in some small institutions the Manager reports directly to the hospital administrator. At medical schools/hospitals, the director of biomedical communications reports to the dean or vice president.

Additionally, the Media Resource Manager

- selects, evaluates, and purchases media equipment and programs;
- provides for the operation of media equipment for health care workers or patients; and
- develops and administers capital, operating, and staffing budgets for the media center.

Salaries

In 1997, salaries for Media Resource Managers ranged from $32,000 for people with degrees and some background in small hospitals to more than $50,000 for experienced individuals with seniority at major hospitals, according to industry observers.

Salaries for directors of biomedical communications were higher.

Salaries for individuals in hospitals and health care teaching centers vary according to the size of the operation and its geographic location.

Employment Prospects

Opportunities are poor, with the best chances for employment in large medical schools and hospitals. The extensive experience and education required for the position and the need to persuade hospital administrators that qualified media experts are necessary have tended to limit employment opportunities. In general, the use of video and other media at health education facilities has grown very little in the past five years.

Advancement Prospects

There is little turnover in the field, promotion opportunities are generally poor, and competition is strong. Advancement is generally limited to the extent of the individual's academic study and experience. Candidates should also be willing to move to a new location to get a better position.

To many individuals, becoming a Media Resource Manager is the climax of a successful career in communications and media in the health field. Others get further training in patient education, management, and instructional and organizational development in order to become directors of health education at smaller health facilities. Still others move to similar but better-paid positions in media and audiovisual services at larger organizations. Many use the position as background for moving into health care administration.

Education

A bachelor's degree in radio-TV, communications, or, preferably, educational media is usually required for a Media Resource Manager's job, and a master's degree is preferred. Courses in instructional development, manpower training, and medical education are helpful. To become a Director of Biomedical Communications, a master's degree is virtually mandatory, and a doctorate is preferable.

Experience/Skills

A minimum of three to four years of experience in multimedia production at a health care or teaching facility is usually required. Most Media Resource Managers have been Media Specialists and have had experience in producing media training programs. Directors of Biomedical Communications have usually had at least 10 years in educational and instructional development and training.

A Media Resource Manager, or Biomedical Communications Director, must be well organized and knowledgeable about a variety of media and must have excellent interpersonal skills to deal with a diversity of professional colleagues. The candidate must be a good administrator and leader with an enthusiastic desire to improve the use of the media in the health sciences. Because many medical media centers operate with a chargeback financial system, business and accounting skills have become increasingly important.

Minority/Women's Opportunities

In 1997, the majority of Media Resource Managers in hospitals were white males, according to industry observers. A small percentage of white females and members of minorities have held the position in the past 10 years.

Unions/Associations

There are no unions that serve as bargaining agents for Media Resource Managers, or Directors of Biomedical Communications. Some individuals, however, belong to the American Society for Healthcare Human Resources Administration of the American Hospital Association (AHA) to share ideas and concerns in health and training. For the same reasons, others belong to the Association for Educational Communications and Technology (AECT). Nearly all Directors of Biomedical Communications belong to the Health Sciences Communications Association (HeSCA) and to the Association of Biomedical Communication Directors (ABCD).

MEDIA SPECIALIST

CAREER PROFILE

Duties: Responsibility for the production and utilization of media in a hospital or health care facility

Alternate Titles(s): Audiovisual Specialist; Media Resource Specialist; Media Coordinator

Salary Range: $22,000 to $30,000+

Employment Prospects: Poor

Advancement Prospects: Poor

Prerequisites:

Education—Minimum of undergraduate degree in educational media, radio-TV, or communications; master's degree preferable

Experience—One or two years in an education or training media center, or equivalent part-time work in a college

Special Skills—Multimedia production capability; technical aptitude; creativity; writing abilities; interpersonal skills

CAREER LADDER

```
┌─────────────────────────────────────┐
│      Media Resource Manager;         │
│ Director of Biomedical Communications│
└─────────────────────────────────────┘

┌─────────────────────────────────────┐
│         Media Specialist             │
└─────────────────────────────────────┘

┌─────────────────────────────────────┐
│      Media Center Experience         │
└─────────────────────────────────────┘
```

Position Description

A Media Specialist develops and plans for the use of a wide variety of audiovisual support materials to satisfy the instructional, training, continuing education, and community relations needs within a health care or training facility. The person in this position either produces the necessary materials or selects video and other media programs from outside sources that will best assist in meeting defined educational goals and objectives.

Usually, a Media Specialist works on assignment and conceives and develops film and video programs and slide and multimedia presentations. The position may be in a hospital or in a school of medicine, dentistry, nursing, veterinary medicine, allied health care, or other health specialty. The Media Specialist consults with physicians, nurses, and the training staff to determine their media needs and conducts demonstrations and trains staff in the use of equipment.

In the larger media centers at medical schools or hospitals, a Media Specialist may be a Producer or Director of short demonstration or training programs or may serve in another capacity in video production. In medium-size centers, this individual usually serves as an audiovisual generalist, adept at and experienced with a wide range of equipment and media, including video and computers.

In the smaller health care audiovisual centers, Media Specialists are often responsible for producing many of the traditional educational materials used in patient education or staff training. These may include a series of slides, overhead transparencies, or audio tapes. In many facilities, the Media Specialist is the only individual on staff with audiovisual experience.

It is often the responsibility of a Media Specialist to plan and execute simple television instruction and demonstration programs using nonbroadcast video equipment. Frequently, these programs are shot and recorded on location in various parts of the facility and are played back later. For these simple productions, a Media Specialist acts as a one-person production team.

A Media Specialist normally reports to a Media Resource Manager or to the related position of director of biomedical communications. It is not usually a supervisory job.

Additionally, the Media Specialist

- assists in the development of studies on the effectiveness of media instruction;
- schedules the playback of media programs within the health facility; and
- helps to prepare and administer the capital and operating budgets for the media center.

Salaries

Salaries in 1997 ranged from $22,000 at small hospitals to more than $30,000 for experienced individuals with seniority at larger hospitals, according to industry observers. Media Specialists in hospitals and medical schools participate in all staff benefits, including health insurance and pension programs.

Employment Prospects

The opportunities for getting a job as a Media Specialist in the health care industry are poor. The use of media in health has not grown appreciably in the past five years, and observers do not see much growth in the immediate future. The majority of positions available will be in the larger hospitals and health care facilities.

Advancement Prospects

A Media Specialist who has the technical expertise, personal skills, and necessary education may be promoted to Media Resource Manager in a hospital, and, on occasion, to director of biomedical communications in a medical or other school of health care. Competition for these positions is heavy, however, and opportunities for such growth are poor.

Personal interests or talents lead others to seek career opportunities at larger health care facilities by concentrating on video as a Producer or Director, or occasionally, on curriculum or training development as an Instructional Designer. Usually, however, the ultimate goal is still to become a Media Resource Manager or a director of biomedical communications. Some Media Specialists use their skills to obtain more specialized positions in business, education, or government media centers.

Education

A minimum of a bachelor's degree in educational media, radio-TV, or communications is usually required. Many larger health training facilities and hospitals require a master's degree, but fewer than 25 institutions of higher education offered specialized health media training programs in 1998. Courses in the production of all types of audiovisual materials and in television and film production are necessary. Some courses in the health sciences, health science education, and instructional design are useful.

Experience/Skills

One or two years of general audiovisual experience in an education or training media center or part-time employment (while a student) in a college's media or television production unit is usually required.

Media Specialists should have strong backgrounds in audiovisual and video production and know how to operate a variety of technical equipment including computer graphics gear. Most good Media Specialists are creative and have good writing abilities and excellent interpersonal skills.

Minority/Women's Opportunities

Opportunities in the health education field are increasing for both women and minority group members. Nearly 35 percent of the Media Specialists in hospitals were white females, according to industry observers. While the percentage of minority group employment is not as high, opportunities have increased for both males and females during the past five years.

Unions/Associations

There are no unions that specifically represent or bargain for Media Specialists, but some individuals are represented by unions as a part of their staff memberships in hospitals or health care facilities. Many belong to the American Society for Healthcare Education and Training (ASHET) of the American Hospital Association (AHA) to share common concerns and advance their careers. In addition, some Media Specialists belong to the Association for Multi-Media International (AMI), the Association for Educational Communications and Technology (AECT), and the International Television Association (ITVA).

EXECUTIVE PRODUCER/MULTIMEDIA

CAREER PROFILE

Duties: Managing the overall production process of a multimedia project or line of products, from preparing budgets and schedules to hiring and managing project execution by the creative/production teams

Alternative Title: Developer

Salary Range: $50,000 to $90,000+

Employment Prospects: Good

Advancement Prospects: Good

Prerequisites:

Education—Bachelor's degree in design, communications, humanities, or business; advanced degree preferred

Experience—Five to 10 years experience in television production; two to five years' experience in multimedia production

Special Skills—Keen organizational skills; ability to conceive of and manage overall process while paying attention to detail

CAREER LADDER

```
┌─────────────────────────────────┐
│    VP, Multimedia Production     │
└─────────────────────────────────┘

┌─────────────────────────────────┐
│  Executive Producer/Multimedia  │
└─────────────────────────────────┘

┌─────────────────────────────────┐
│    Producer/Project Manager     │
└─────────────────────────────────┘
```

Position Description

The Executive Producer/Multimedia is the top decision-maker in the process of creating a multimedia product, which can be delivered in a number of formats, or "platforms," including a CD-ROM for use with Windows or on a Macintosh; a World Wide Web site, or an interactive game. Typically, a company hires an Executive Producer/Multimedia to be the chief planner for a line of multimedia products, and in that capacity, the Executive Producer writes short- and long-range plans to build the line by identifying appropriate products for development, putting the best-suited production teams into place, and creating time lines and budgets for completion.

In smaller companies and nonprofit organizations, the Executive Producer can also assume more operational responsibilities, including researching funding institutions and writing proposals to secure adequate financing; negotiating rights and contracts with the authors and vendors who provide content including text, video footage, stock photographs, audio clips, and other materials; and cultivating relationships with various constituents, including distributors and cross-marketing partners.

On a day-to-day basis, the Executive Producer is charged with ensuring that the final product is of the best quality possible and is brought in as efficiently as possible—that is, the Executive Producer/Multimedia sees that the job gets done right, is finished on schedule, and stays within budget. To accomplish this, she or he often has to keep a close and careful eye on the details of a project while also keeping in mind the broader goals of line development. Working closely with the producer, the Executive Producer is apprised of the work flow of graphic designers, programmers, animators, writers, sound designers—the entire production team—and applies pressure where needed to execute a seamless process.

Additionally, the Executive Producer/Multimedia

- serves as the key coordinator of communication and project implementation among senior management, engineering, and the creative team;
- acts as product spokesperson when media inquiries are received; and
- assesses how to maximize use of available resources.

Salaries

In the field of multimedia, the average annual salary for an Executive Producer in 1997 was $71,000, according to the "AV Video and Multimedia Producer's Salary Survey," conducted by the Survey Center for *Multimedia Producer* magazine.

Location plays a significant role in the income of multimedia producers, with those working in Los Angeles earning far more, on average, than the next-highest paid group—those working in New York, Boston, and the San Francisco Bay area. The Pacific Northwest and the Midwest trail the field. Another factor affecting income is the number of people reporting to the Executive Producer: the more reports, the higher the income. Somewhat surprisingly, the size of the company, as measured in annual revenue, had little to do with salary levels reported in 1997.

Employment Prospects

Far from being limited to the spheres of games and entertainment, multimedia, much like video and the telephone before it, will touch virtually every industry, finding a purpose through web sites for organizations as diverse as a fleet specializing in whale watch expeditions and vast government agencies such as the Internal Revenue Service. CD-ROMs can be used to train and educate employees or to present the debut of the latest computer-aided design (CAD) capabilities at a trade show. The possibilities are virtually endless, therefore the opportunities will be plentiful during the next 10 years, according to industry observers.

Advancement Prospects

Even though Executive Producer/Multimedia is near the top of the organizational structure, meaning there are few positions to attain once it's achieved, movement to larger production companies or to a top executive post at a smaller organization will be a strong possibility for years to come, industry experts say.

Education

By the late 1990s, those who had assumed the role of Executive Producer came from a wide range of educational backgrounds including bachelor's degrees in the humanities, business, and mass communication. Most had gone on to learn multimedia production as the industry was emerging, and a few were among the first to obtain certificates and advanced degrees in the field, while others had worked for years in television and were ready for the transition. In the coming decade, those who earn an undergraduate degree in media arts or in the humanities and gain as much project experience as possible will have an advantage.

Experience/Skills

The Executive Producer/Multimedia should have worked as a Producer or Production Manager and learned, as a result, the detailed planning involved in getting a project off the ground, the ability to anticipate and overcome typical disruptions to work flow, and a command of project management including reasonable budgeting and realistic scheduling of the various players in the process. Skills required encompass the vision to know how the project should take shape long before it has begun, the ability to work under extreme pressure since deadlines are usually very demanding, and a knack for managing different types of contributors, from illustrators and animators to programmers and navigation experts. In short, the Executive Producer must possess grace under fire.

Minority/Women's Opportunities

Industry experts stated consistently in 1998 that opportunities were plentiful for minorities and women, observing that women constituted about 50 percent of the workforce and the number of minorities was on the increase. Many observed that fewer women were working as engineers, programmers, and coders, and while technically oriented professions are historically male dominated, women can expect to encounter few barriers.

Unions/Associations

Executive Producer/Multimedias are not represented by any unions, but many are members of the Software Publishers Association as well as regional multimedia councils.

PRODUCER/MULTIMEDIA

CAREER PROFILE

Duties: Managing the day-to-day production process, which involves coordination of Engineers and Programmers, the creative team, and the physical implementation and packaging of the product, whether it is on-line or on disk

Alternative Title: Production Manager/Multimedia

Salary Range: $35,000 to $85,000

Employment Prospects: Excellent

Advancement Prospects: Good

Prerequisites:

Education—Bachelor's degree in media arts, mass communications, computer science required; master's degree in new media desirable

Experience—Two to five years of experience in the production of multimedia products

Special Skills—Facility with multimedia authoring software; strong electronic design skills with industry-standard tools; ability to manage the production cycle and to oversee quality assurance

CAREER LADDER

```
┌─────────────────────────────────────────┐
│  Project Manager; Executive Producer      │
└─────────────────────────────────────────┘

┌─────────────────────────────────────────┐
│  Producer/Multimedia                      │
└─────────────────────────────────────────┘

┌─────────────────────────────────────────┐
│  Production Coordinator                    │
└─────────────────────────────────────────┘
```

Position Description

Reporting to the Executive Producer/Multimedia, the Producer/Multimedia is the hands-on manager of the production process from inception to completion. Versatility is the key to this position, as the Producer must be well versed in multimedia development, which encompasses programming, navigation, design, content, and quality management, and must also be a good overall manager. This position holds direct responsibility for the production scheduling and staffing and in smaller organizations, is often accountable for project budgets and overall scheduling. It's also common for the Producer to shape the creative direction of a project, much as a director does on a film. The Producer has to understand the product thoroughly, coordinate logistics with grace, and manage people effectively.

Excellent communications skills are essential for the Producer, who has to nail down the production schedule and then ensure that the various contributors to the process are getting their work done on time and up to standard. Among the participants in the process overseen by the Producer are production coordinators (who, in larger organizations, are often assigned supervision of particular production groups),

animators, sound designers, Computer Graphic Designers, content writers, and technicians, as well as the Software Engineers, navigation experts, and Programmers. Many steps in the process happen simultaneously, while others have to happen sequentially; it's the Producer who sees that the process moves along at the desired pace.

Typically, the Producer/Multimedia is expected to have a working knowledge of industry-standard tools, which in the late 1990s included Macromedia Director, Visual Basic, Adobe Photoshop and Illustrator, and Javascript; however, with the exceedingly rapid rate of change in multimedia, it's difficult to project which programs and tools will be the standard. The environment of constant change, though, means that a Producer has to stay on top of emerging technologies and industry direction; he or she does this by regularly visiting information-rich web sites such as www.zdnet.com and www.outlook.com.

Salaries

In 1997, multimedia Producers averaged $55,000 in annual income, but that figure varied widely for a number of reasons: The platform for which the product was produced, the number of people reporting to the Producer, and the region of the country all were important factors, according to the first "AV Video and Multimedia Producer's Salary Survey" conducted for *Multimedia Producer* magazine.

Those Producers who created for next-generation game machines such as Sega Saturn, Sony PlayStation, and Nintendo Ultra 64 averaged $65,000 to $85,000 annually, benefiting from a dearth of talent and know-how in this arena; interactive/on-line Producers had average annual salaries ranging from $54,000 to $66,000; and Producers for the PC and Macintosh platforms comprised the lowest-paid tier, still earning a respectable $55,000 to $59,000.

Employment Prospects

Employment prospects are excellent. This field is burgeoning and will influence virtually every area of work and play, which translates into an abundance of opportunity for those who are willing to keep up with emerging technologies and take the reins of a multimedia project. Industry observers have dubbed the new millennium the multimedia age and have expressed confidence that work will be there for those who are willing to gain the expertise and make the effort. The Bureau of Labor Statistics cites that computer-related occupations (along with health-related jobs) will dominate the list of the fastest-growing jobs through the year 2006.

Advancement Prospects

Advancement prospects are good. Multimedia production houses are proliferating; meanwhile, many larger companies and governmental agencies are producing their own web sites and taking an active role in producing larger projects in conjunction with freelancers and independent firms. In addition, the World Wide Web is expanding and Internet service providers (ISPs) and content providers are on the increase—all of which means that Producers who want to move into project management or the role of Executive Producer are likely to find work, often as an independent contractor, but also on a permanent basis.

Education

Multimedia Producers often come from the ranks of television production, but increasingly, they have earned certificates, bachelor's, or master's degrees in multimedia/new media, a discipline that brings together the creation and production of video, audio, photography, animation, and text via a computer interface. A Producer can also benefit from a degree in business. Most employers seek these qualifications but will usually accept a solid portfolio as a substitute for an advanced degree.

Experience/Skills

The multimedia Producer is generally expected to have two to five years' experience in the production of multimedia products, usually as a project director, production coordinator, Programmer or Computer Graphics Designer. The Producer should possess a spectrum of skills including the ability to communicate effectively, manage demanding, multifaceted projects, and work well in a fast-paced environment—often with ambitious deadlines. While this position calls for versatility, knowledge of a particular industry will create an advantage when developing products for that industry. In addition, with more and more business being conducted internationally, the ability to speak a second language is often a plus.

Minority/Women's Opportunities

The multimedia industry prides itself on equal opportunity, and the "AV Video and Multimedia Producer's Annual Salary Survey" did find that the gender gap in 1997 was much smaller than in older, more staid professions. Overall, the average annual salary for female Producers was $51,000, and $56,000, for male Producers. Still, 76 percent of survey respondents were male, and there were no women respondents in three job categories: audio, quality assurance, and staff web designer/programmer. Minority representation in the industry is estimated at 10 to 20 percent, but industry professionals insist that opportunities exist.

Unions/Associations

There are no unions that represent Producers/Multimedia for bargaining purposes. Many producers belong to the Software Publishers Association and state and regional multimedia organizations—the Oregon Multimedia Alliance, or the Massachusetts Interactive Media Council, for instance—to network with peers, attend trainings, and be visible participants in the industry.

WEBMASTER

CAREER PROFILE

Duties: Managing the planning, implementation, evaluation, and maintenance of a World Wide Web site; working with management, Computer Graphics Designers, and Programmers to gather and upload content; tracking site usage statistics; responding to or routing user inquiries

Alternative Title: Web Site Manager

Salary Range: $40,000 to $80,000+

Employment Prospects: Excellent

Advancement Prospects: Excellent

Prerequisites:

Education—Bachelor's degree in computer science, new media, electrical engineering

Experience—At least one year of content development, programming, computer graphic design

Special Skills—Programming knowledge; interface design; application implementation; presentation, management, analytical, and communication skills

CAREER LADDER

```
┌─────────────────────────────┐
│   Director, Communications   │
└─────────────────────────────┘

┌─────────────────────────────┐
│         Webmaster           │
└─────────────────────────────┘

┌─────────────────────────────┐
│  HTML Programmer; Designer  │
└─────────────────────────────┘
```

Position Description

In this quickly evolving field, the title Webmaster means different things to different organizations. Broadly speaking, the Webmaster manages the planning, production, and maintenance of a World Wide Web site by coordinating management goals with the efforts of the creative and programming teams, frequently contributing directly both to strategy and operational efforts and to design and coding. Further, the person in this role ensures that the site's content remains current, that site usage is monitored and reported, that public inquiries are routed to the appropriate person or department, and that the site functions and serves as an effective communications tool.

Depending on the organization, the Webmaster may be a member of the management team involved in the preparation of annual plans for the web site in which strategy is defined, goals are identified, operational objectives are outlined, and budget requirements are iterated. Typically, the Webmaster plays a key role in the design, site architecture, and shaping of the content—as well as its flow and accessibility. In addition, the Webmaster often serves as a technician, ready to fix hyperlinks and hot spots that fail, for example.

It is the Webmaster's responsibility on a day-to-day basis to fashion the look, flow, and functionality of a web site, and to accomplish this, the Webmaster establishes the house style by selecting the fonts, icons, page format, and document organization. These elements should be in concert with the organization's overall corporate and brand identity, as the Web is but one facet of the corporate communications program.

Finally, the Webmaster's knowledge of the World Wide Web places him or her in a position to promote the web site via links from relevant sites, search engines, and online promotional vehicles.

Salaries

The salaries for Webmaster vary greatly depending on the complexity of the site to be managed, the region in which one works, and the scope of responsibilities assumed, since in larger organizations, the Webmaster does less hands-on programming and design, serving instead as the coordinator of specialists. A survey conducted for *Computerworld* magazine determined a median annual salary of $42,500 in 1997, with 20 percent of respondents reporting an annual income of

$40,000. Other industry research indicates a wide salary range that reaches upward of $80,000 annually.

Employment Prospects

Industry observers in 1998 anticipated plentiful job opportunities during the coming decade because of the difficulty in finding people who possess such diverse talents as well as the ever-increasing number of web sites that are fast becoming as ubiquitous and vital as the telephone. Opportunities will exist "in house," or within the structure of the organization whose web site it is, as well as with Web hosting companies, firms that contract with a number of companies to keep their web sites up to date.

Advancement Prospects

In the late 1990s, this industry was still new, and people assuming this role were just getting their feet wet in the expanding scope of the World Wide Web and the software that was rapidly evolving to serve it. Early indications are that Webmasters could move on to roles as Producers/Multimedia or, in some cases, Executive Producers/Multimedia with companies creating multimedia products, or move into management roles within their company, which could include senior positions in marketing, operations, or development, depending on the strengths and goals of the individual.

Education

Most hiring authorities by 1998 were looking for individuals with a bachelor's degree, as well as training in and experience with computer graphic design and/or computer programming for the Web. Because the Webmaster must draw on a variety of skills, the undergraduate degree can be in a number of disciplines including media arts, computer science, electronic engineering, marketing, or liberal arts. Completing a certificate program or advanced degree in multimedia will give a candidate an advantage over someone without such training; the software and programming languages being taught will evolve with the changing demands of the industry.

Experience/Skills

Managing a web site is a sprawling and ongoing project. Considering the spectrum of duties performed by the Webmaster, this person must be versatile. Specifically, she or he must possess standard technical skills in the areas of computer programming and design, an ability to determine which tools will best meet the design and site flow tasks, interpersonal skills that foster clear, effective communication among internal and external clients, and sound organizational skills.

Minority/Women's Opportunities

Industry experts stated consistently in 1998 that opportunities are plentiful for minorities and women, observing that women constituted about 50 percent of the workforce and the number of minorities working as Webmasters was on the increase. Many observed that fewer women were working as engineers, programmers, and coders, and while technically oriented professions are historically male dominated, women can expect to encounter few barriers.

Unions/Associations

There are no unions representing the concerns of Webmasters. A number of national and regional associations and other professional connections enable Webmasters to remain informed about the industry and the multimedia development profession. Among these are the Association for Multimedia Communications, state software associations, and World Wide Web sites including www.developer.com and www.webtechniques.com.

COMPUTER GRAPHICS DESIGNER

CAREER PROFILE

Duties: Conceiving of and executing the design of a multimedia product or World Wide Web site; ensuring that its aesthetic appeal and its functionality meet the objectives set by the producer, art director, and/or client

Alternative Title: Web Designer; Interactive Designer

Salary Range: $20,000 to $60,000+

Employment Prospects: Excellent

Advancement Prospects: Excellent

Prerequisites:

Education—Bachelor's degree in graphic design or fine arts; training in industry-standard design applications, which in 1998 included Adobe Photoshop, Adobe Illustrator, and programming languages such as HTML, Java, and CGI

Experience—One to two years' experience in traditional graphic design and one or more years' experience in multimedia design

Special Skills—An ability to take direction from the art director and develop multimedia elements that will appropriately represent the look and feel of the product; an ability to think in a nonlinear fashion that anticipates and facilitates the end-user's experience; excellent communications skills and affability

CAREER LADDER

Art Director

Computer Graphics Designer

Conventional graphic design

Position Description

The Computer Graphics Designer determines the aesthetic appeal of a multimedia product or web site, but just as important is this person's role in ensuring the product's user-friendliness. The Computer Graphics Designer determines how the computer interface should be constructed to simplify navigation, considers the multitude of paths that an end-user could follow, and takes into account issues of data compression and the functionality of various computer systems and applications. Perhaps the greatest challenge is to think in a nonlinear fashion and bear in mind that the end-user may want to move from point A to point B, or C, or Z; therefore, the designer must weigh the disparate visual, audio, and functional components and create continuity, or a smooth site flow.

As an integral part of the creative team, the Computer Graphics Designer possesses the design talent and the technological sophistication to bring a multimedia product to life.

Working with the Software Engineer, the art director, the Producer, and the Programmers, among others, this person has to listen carefully during planning meetings, absorb the key design objectives of the project, and combine such traditional knowledge as color theory and layout with the programming and computer design tools that convert ideas into a concrete, functional product.

In smaller operations, the Computer Graphics Designer may be responsible for developing the navigational routes, typically collaborating with the Software Engineer or senior Programmer to ascertain the feasibility of site flow. Larger creative teams, however, frequently employ a navigation expert to devise the simplest and most effective system.

Salaries

According to the Bureau of Labor Statistics, nearly 60 percent of all designers are self-employed. In multimedia, this statistic holds true, which means that while Computer

Graphic Designers are reasonably well compensated, many work on a project-by-project basis and are responsible for paying their own federal and state taxes as well as benefits such as health insurance. Still, an ambitious junior graphic designer can expect to earn from $25,000 to $40,000 a year; someone with three or more years' experience can boost that figure to $60,000.

Employment Prospects

Employment of Computer Graphics Designers is expected to grow faster than average through 2006. Competition will increase, and individuals who can distinguish themselves in terms of versatility—artistic talent combined with technological savvy—will make the greatest gains, according to industry observers. The U.S. Department of Commerce in 1998 reported that the number of registered Internet domain names rose from 627,000 in December 1996 to 1.5 million in December 1997. During the next decade, virtually every sector of the economy will be using the Internet to advance its goals, and all will require computer graphic representation.

Advancement Prospects

Advancement prospects are likely to be excellent, as millions of businesses and nonprofit organizations take to the World Wide Web. Where Computer Graphics Designers are needed, so are those to supervise them: art directors, creative directors, and Producers.

Education

In 1997, more than 90 percent of graphic artists possessed a college degree, according to the American Institute of Graphic Arts, and most had majored in graphic design. Approximately 20 percent held advanced degrees. In computer graphic design, through the late 1990s, most had earned a bachelor's degree and were self-taught in terms of computer applications. Industry observers anticipate that this trend will likely change as the field matures, academic and specialized training programs proliferate, and ever-more sophisticated demands are made on the artist.

Experience/Skills

Employers typically look for individuals with one to two years of conventional design work and/or at least one year of multimedia design. The Computer Graphic Designer is expected to be skilled in the use of industry-standard software applications, which in 1998 included Adobe Illustrator, Adobe Photoshop, programming languages such as HTML, DHTML, Java, and CGI, and in some cases have the ability to do more challenging programming toward the creation of proprietary functional designs.

Minority/Women's Opportunities

The field of graphic arts has long been fairly well balanced in terms of the representation of men and women. Industry observers state that in 1998, the ratio was about one to one. Minorities have begun to enter the field, although most observers estimate that the percentage of computer graphic design jobs held by minorities doesn't yet approach their representation in the overall workforce, which stood at 26 percent in 1997. Across the board, however, employers stated that opportunities abound.

Unions/Associations

No unions represent Computer Graphics Designers. Among the associations that support their professional development are the American Institute of Graphic Arts (AIGA) and SIGGRAPH, the Association for Computing Machinery's special interest group on computer graphics.

SOFTWARE ENGINEER

CAREER PROFILE

Duties: Designing and developing multimedia products

Alternative Title: Lead Programmer; Software Developer

Salary Range: $40,000 to $85,000+

Employment Prospects: Excellent

Advancement Prospects: Good

Prerequisites:

Education—Bachelor's degree in computer science, electrical engineering, or related field; advanced degree in computer science, multimedia or related field desirable

Experience—Two to five years' experience in software development

Special Skills—Design and programming experience in various development environments such as Windows and UNIX; knowledge of industry-standard programming languages such as C++, Java, HTML; excellent communications skills

CAREER LADDER

```
┌─────────────────────────────┐
│      Junior Programmer       │
└─────────────────────────────┘

┌─────────────────────────────┐
│      Software Engineer       │
└─────────────────────────────┘

┌─────────────────────────────┐
│      Technical Manager       │
└─────────────────────────────┘
```

Position Description

The Software Engineer is responsible for the design and programming of the software architecture that will support a multimedia product's aesthetic and functional design. This technical design is the framework for the project and must be communicated to programmers and modified as the development process evolves. Whereas the functional design describes the user interface and site flow, or "navigation," through a multimedia product or World Wide Web site, the technical design is the nuts and bolts of the project and involves the determination of development environment, the selection of authoring tools, and the use of programming languages that will most effectively build on those authoring tools to achieve the desired product features.

Frequently, the Software Engineer is brought into the early planning and analysis process to advise the management team on the most efficient ways to implement that functional design. More often, though, the technical design process begins after the functional design has been determined and in a true case of form following function, considers these desired ends—how the product should look and feel—and then figures out how to make it happen using the available resources.

Along with design and development of the product itself, the Software Engineer typically develops methods for ensur-

ing the integrity and performance of the product. The functionality and programming demands of World Wide Web browsers in the late 1990s, for example, varied significantly; these distinctions required individualized technical designs, coding, and testing. Also required of Software Engineers is the development of systems support applications, which address the maintenance and reliability of the product or site.

Salaries

Software Engineers are generally paid quite well; annual salaries in 1997 ranged from $50,000 to $85,000, according to industry resources. The Bureau of Labor Statistics (BLS) states that in 1997, starting salaries for engineers with a bachelor's degree were significantly higher than those of bachelor's degree graduates in other fields, and the pattern holds true as education and experience increase, according to industry observers. Starting salaries for computer engineering graduates in 1997 averaged $39,593, according to the National Association of Colleges and Employers.

Employment Prospects

Employment prospects will be excellent for the next 10 years. In 1998, the World Wide Web was burgeoning, as was multimedia in general. A study conducted by the Interactive

Digital Software Association and Coopers & Lybrand revealed that in 1997, the interactive entertainment industry alone generated $16 billion in economic activity in the United States. Software Engineers are among the highly skilled workers who will be in demand, according to the BLS, which reported in 1998 that more than 2 million employees will be needed to fill such jobs during the next decade.

Advancement Prospects

The same escalating multimedia industry that promises an abundance of employment opportunities will offer advancement opportunities, particularly for those Software Engineers who are versatile and who continue to stay informed of emerging technologies and remain skilled at a number of different operating systems, authoring tools, and programming languages. Industry certification such as that offered by Microsoft and advanced degrees may also be an advantage.

Education

A bachelor's degree in computer science, computer engineering, electrical engineering, or a related field is almost always required of Software Engineers. Hiring authorities also look favorably on job candidates with advanced degrees. As the multimedia industry grows, it's possible that industry-recognized training programs, such as those offered by Microsoft, which certify individuals as "Microsoft Certified Systems Engineers" and "Microsoft Certified Solution Developers," will gain authority and therefore may influence hiring decisions.

Experience/Skills

The Software Engineer, or Lead Programmer, on a project is generally expected to have two to five years' experience in software development and to be knowledgeable about industry-standard development environments, operating systems, authoring tools, and programming languages. Engineers typically think logically and must be adept at organization and process design and execution. Employers also look for individuals who can communicate with other technical staff, project management, and customers and clients; they must be capable of articulating ideas and listening to a variety of audiences.

Minority/Women's Opportunities

The number of minorities and women working in multimedia was on the rise in the late 1990s, according to industry observers, but they were still underrepresented, especially in the technical professions. Nevertheless, no formal barriers to entry exist.

Unions/Associations

There are no unions representing Software Engineers. Many join a number of regional and national associations such as the Interactive Digital Software Association, Association of Computing Machinery, the National Society of Professional Engineers, and the Society of Women Engineers.

SITE FLOW ARCHITECT

Duties: Ensuring that the aesthetic and functional design of a multimedia product or World Wide Web site enables the end user to navigate it in a multitude of ways with ease and effectiveness

Alternative Title: Navigation Expert; Information Designer

Salary Range: $55,000 to $85,000+

Employment Prospects: Good

Advancement Prospects: Good

Prerequisites:

Education—Bachelor's degree in industrial design, graphic design, computer engineering; or a related field

Experience—Two to five years in software development, particularly in the areas of functional design

Special Skills—Excellent organizational skills; process orientation; the ability to work as a team member

```
┌─────────────────────────────┐
│     Executive Producer      │
└─────────────────────────────┘

┌─────────────────────────────┐
│     Site Flow Architect     │
└─────────────────────────────┘

┌─────────────────────────────┐
│   User Interface Designer   │
└─────────────────────────────┘
```

Position Description

The Site Flow Architect is responsible for organizing the multimedia product and user's travels from one screen to another in a medium that is nonlinear and has extensive storage capacity. Unlike designing the layout of a book, which a reader knows will follow a logical, ordered path through a limited number of pages, the Site Flow Architect has to plan the various options for exploration available to the end-user and make the information connect in seamless and sensible ways.

During the early years of multimedia development, it was accomplishment enough to simply transfer printed information to a digital platform through basic design and coding. That stage, however, is over, and multimedia developers are now driven to make their products as easy to use and performance oriented as possible. Therefore, throughout the planning and analysis phase of the project, the Site Flow Architect determines who the users will be and what they'll be trying to attain when using the product; he or she works with the Producer, Software Engineer, Programmers, and content developers to identify the chunks of information to be disseminated, the many ways in which they relate to one another, and how the end user can access them via the graphical user interface (GUI).

Through the final testing phase of the product's beta version, the Site Flow Architect's sense of organization will refine the paths, which must anticipate the sometimes unpredictable movements of a consumer through a product. Far from being a two-dimensional matrix containing solutions or "destinations," the possible courses to chart in multimedia are vast, with as many tangents as a creative mind can muster. The Site Flow Architect must be able to devise systems to structure these potential routes, allow the end-user to walk each path (figuratively speaking), and always be able to return to the starting point or move to relevant screens with ease. The Site Flow Architect makes sure the user doesn't get lost or confused in the expansive realm of multimedia.

Salaries

Executive recruiters in the multimedia industry reported that in 1998, Site Flow Architects were earning from $55,000 to $85,000 annually, with those working in the metropolitan areas considered multimedia hotbeds—the San Francisco Bay area, New York City, Los Angeles, and greater Boston—typically landing on the higher end of that scale. The industry is still new, and this position is even newer, since navigation had been the domain of Software Engineers and Computer Graphics Designers until the medium matured in the late 1990s and firms began making solution integration a priority.

Employment Prospects

Employment prospects for Site Flow Architects are good. The multimedia industry is growing almost faster than anyone can quantify. The number of people connected to the Internet increased from 40 million in 1996 to 100 million in 1997. Labor experts project that computer-related careers will be among the fastest growing. Many firms in need of navigation expertise couple that role with programming or design, however, so only the larger or more specialized companies will hire for this position.

Advancement Prospects

Advancement prospects are good. The Site Flow Architect usually brings other skills to bear on a multimedia project and can go on to a management role in which a thorough understanding of the entire multimedia development process is beneficial, according to industry observers.

Education

Employers tend to hire people with a minimum of a bachelor's degree and usually with a major in a process-oriented field such as engineering, graphic design, or industrial design. There are those who consider a fine arts or liberal arts undergraduate degree advantageous based on their strengths in cultivating cognitive abilities as well as their foundation in the natural interrelatedness of form and function.

Experience/Skills

The discipline of site flow architecture is relatively new, and barriers to entry to the field were low in the 1990s, as the individuals who were hired were merely able to demonstrate an ability to structure a project for clear navigation and communication. In the coming decade, it is expected that this position will be sought after by people with experience in graphic design, user interface design, or process engineering who can organize enormous amounts of information into manageable and accessible segments. Systems administration and database management are among the skill set for this position.

Minority/Women's Opportunities

Approximately 25 percent of Site Flow Architects were women in 1998, according to industry observers, while minorities numbered about 10 percent. Although those figures don't approach either group's representation in the overall workforce, opportunities for entry into this field exist.

Unions/Associations

There are no unions representing Site Flow Architects. Many join such professional associations as the Interactive Multimedia Association.

PROGRAMMER

Duties: Implementing, testing, and maintaining the technical and functional design prepared by the Software Engineer/software architect

Alternative Title: None

Salary Range: $40,000 to $75,000

Employment Prospects: Excellent

Advancement Prospects: Excellent

Prerequisites:

Education—Bachelor's degree is required; association or vendor certification is desirable

Experience—One to two years' experience as a programming technician or junior Programmer working with object-oriented programs or World Wide Web development

Special Skills—Experience with such programs and tools as C++, Java, Visual Basic; the ability to think logically and analytically; persistence in seeking programming solutions; a talent for communicating technical information to nontechnical individuals

```
┌─────────────────────────────┐
│      Software Engineer       │
└─────────────────────────────┘

┌─────────────────────────────┐
│         Programmer           │
└─────────────────────────────┘

┌─────────────────────────────┐
│         Technician           │
└─────────────────────────────┘
```

Position Description

The Programmer is responsible for writing and testing the code, a set of detailed instructions put forth in a particular programming language that tells a computer how to execute the desired functions. In some cases, the Programmer is retained to maintain the program or system, modifying it as necessary and addressing problems as they arise. Multimedia Programmers are proficient in object-oriented languages and tools, which in the late 1990s included C++, Java, and Visual Basic; these were among the more sophisticated tools that enabled programmers to meet the technical and functional design challenges of increasingly complex products.

Programmers frequently work on a contract basis, as opposed to being employed full time by a single employer. In 1996, 20,000 of the 568,000 Programmers working full-time were self- employed, and industry observers expect that number to increase.

Advanced computing technologies and programming languages have elevated the role of Programmers from mere technicians who take a set of design specifications from a Software Engineer and translate them into a programming language to more creative and managerial contributors on a development team. A specialist in a particular programming language may be the one most likely to arrive at a coding solution to meet a design or functional goal. Typically, a Software Engineer will divide a job into numerous modules and assign them to a number of Programmers; this kind of delegation keeps a complicated project ordered and ensures that if a serious error occurs, it can be localized and addressed without contaminating the entire project.

Programmers usually know more than one programming language, have a keen sense of the strengths and pitfalls of each, and because so many languages are similar in nature, learn new ones with relative ease. As new technologies emerge, it is incumbent on Programmers to stay informed and skilled, as they are often called upon to update and modify existing programs.

Multimedia Programmers must test their work for integrity in functioning on various platforms (Windows or Macintosh, for example) or with different World Wide Web browsers such as Internet Explorer and Netscape Navigator. As problems are encountered, the program must be "debugged," that is, fixed, and documented for other technical maintenance staff who may encounter similar problems.

Salaries

The salary range for multimedia Programmers is fairly wide, with income depending on years of experience, the number of programming languages mastered, degrees and certifications, and region of the country. In 1996, median earnings of Programmers who worked full time were $40,100 a year, with the highest-paid 10 percent earning more than $65,200, according to the Bureau of Labor Statistics (BLS). Those figures pertain to all application and systems Programmers. Multimedia Programmers are increasingly in demand, and because of the difficult programming involved, salaries are slightly higher than average, according to industry observers.

Employment Prospects

Employment prospects for multimedia Programmers are excellent. The U.S. Department of Labor projects that the computer and data processing services industry, which encompasses multimedia Programmers, will be the fastest-growing industry through the year 2006. Information technology's share of economic growth, measured as gross domestic product (GDP) will have risen from 6.4 percent in 1993 to 8.2 percent in 1998, according to the U.S. Department of Commerce.

These numbers simply mean that actual and projected growth in this area is dependable, and despite increasing numbers of computer Programmers, there will be ample opportunity, particularly for those who are willing to stay on top of emerging technologies, continue to learn the latest industry-standard languages and tools, and work diligently.

Advancement Prospects

The field holds great promise through the year 2006 at least. Advancement prospects are very good, as Programmers can follow a traditional path toward becoming Software Engineers, broaden their scope by pursuing jobs as systems Programmers, or enter the ranks of management by becoming a Site Flow Architect, project manager, or Producer.

Education

Programming tasks are becoming increasingly complex and competition in the field is growing; therefore, the level of education and training required by employers is also on the increase. The majority of computer Programmers—almost 60 percent—had a bachelor's degree or higher in 1996, according to the BLS, and this percentage is expected to increase. Most hold degrees in computer science, information systems, or mathematics, while others have enrolled in computer training programs after earning a degree in an unrelated field.

Experience/Skills

Multimedia Programmers are expected to be proficient in industry-standard, object-oriented, and Internet/World Wide Web programming languages and tools, which in 1998 included C++, Java, Ada, CGI, and Visual Basic, among others. The degree of responsibility held in a particular job is based on years of experience and areas of specialization. In addition to technical knowledge, the Programmer must be able to think logically, solve problems, and communicate well as a team member.

Minority/Women's Opportunities

There's a dearth of women and minorities in this profession, according to industry observers, but the opportunities are plentiful. In a profession dominated by white males, observers estimate that less than 10 percent of Programmers are women or minorities, but the doors are open to any qualified individuals. Organizations such the Ada Project for Women in Computer Science and Quality Education for Minorities in Mathematics, Science, and Engineering Network offer information on education and professional recruitment.

Unions/Associations

No unions represent the interests of Programmers. Many Programmers join professional associations such as the Association of C and C++ Users to stay abreast of industry changes and pursue career development.

MULTIMEDIA WRITER

Duties: Writing and editing textual content for multimedia products and the World Wide Web, bearing in mind the end-user's nonlinear navigation through the product, as well as how the text can interplay with and be enhanced by audio, video, graphics, and animation

Alternative Title: Content Writer

Salary Range: $45,000 to $80,000

Employment Prospects: Excellent

Advancement Prospects: Good

Prerequisites:

Education—Bachelor's degree in English, journalism, or multimedia required; training/certification in multimedia or an advanced degree desirable

Experience—One to three years' experience writing for multimedia projects or for print, radio or television

Special Skills—Knowledge of the product's subject matter; creativity; ability to conceptualize and organize material in a nonlinear fashion; ability to work as part of a team; proficiency with HTML

```
+-------------------------------+
|     Producer/Multimedia       |
+-------------------------------+

+-------------------------------+
|      Multimedia Writer        |
+-------------------------------+

+-------------------------------+
|  Copywriter/Assistant Editor  |
+-------------------------------+
```

Position Description

The Multimedia Writer is responsible for researching, writing, and editing textual content, that is, the written or spoken word segments of a multimedia product. Just as writers whose work had appeared in print learned to adapt their techniques to writing for electronic media—radio and television or video—so must Multimedia Writers adapt their communications to the new media forum, which incorporates audio, video, graphics, and animation to enrich the textual messages.

A World Wide Web site or multimedia product, by its very nature, enables the end-user to navigate it in a number of ways; therefore, the Multimedia Writer, working with the development team, must be able to anticipate the various nonlinear routes and write seamless transitions from one screen to the next, keeping voice and tone consistent and charting logical conceptual connections among the product's core ideas. The choices exercised by end-users represent the product's interactivity and are generally constructed using a technique called "branching." This structure follows a flow from the general to the specific, in which the home or welcome page contains broad categories for further exploration, and each category branches toward more specific,

specialized information. The best designs (which include the text) enable the end user to detect the current location and easily return to the core categories or move to other key screens. The rule of thumb in multimedia writing and design is to prevent the end-user from getting lost.

In order to create this matrix of nonlinear navigation, the Multimedia Writer must be extremely organized and clear-thinking, yet possess a free-roaming imagination. Usually, before any writing begins, the writer drafts a flow chart that depicts the end-user's spectrum of navigation choices. Along with a keen ability to organize information, the Multimedia Writer must be attentive to the constraints of the medium: the computer screen is still relatively small (or crowded with images) and people's attention spans are often short, so information should be presented in digestible chunks written with punch and concision.

Salaries

Salaries for Multimedia Writers vary widely and are largely dependent on the individuals' years of experience, particularly in the multimedia field, the complexity of the project at hand, and the region of the country. Salaries range from $45,000 to $80,000. In Los Angeles, where the multimedia games and entertainment industry is based, salaries tend to be highest, followed by San Francisco, New York, and Boston, according to industry sources.

Employment Prospects

Employment prospects for Multimedia Writers are excellent. The boom in multimedia will continue well into the next decade, and the areas in which writers will be needed will expand from the current segments of games, entertainment, education, training, promotion, and reference to every discipline imaginable. The need for a World Wide Web site will become as critical for business as is the telephone, as corporations, nonprofit organizations, and educational institutions establish their presence and determine ways to pursue their various missions via multimedia.

Advancement Prospects

Advancement prospects for Multimedia Writers are good. Because of the versatility required of this position—the ability to grasp the complex, nonlinear workings of a multimedia product—writers can move into the position of informational designer, navigation expert, project manager, Producer/Multimedia, or, more predictably, simply on to a post as senior writer or on-line editor.

Education

Employers require a bachelor's degree in English, journalism, or multimedia production or in another field, particularly related to the product's subject matter, and a demonstrated ability to write well. For instance, a financial services company might hire someone with experience in that industry to write the content for its corporate web site. As the nature of these products becomes increasingly complex, individuals with advanced degrees will be at an advantage when job seeking, according to the Bureau of Labor Statistics.

Experience/Skills

Those who have experience in writing for multimedia will surely have an advantage over those without it; however, many hiring authorities are willing to consider other professional writing coupled with a desire to enter the field. The Multimedia Writer has to be exceedingly organized and extraordinarily creative, work well as a member of a team, and in many cases, be proficient with HTML (or the emerging industry-standards, text-oriented languages).

Minority/Women's Opportunities

Industry observers estimated that approximately 25 percent of Multimedia Writers working in 1998 were women, but fewer than 15 percent were minorities. The Writers Guild of America and organizations such as CBS have established programs to cultivate the work of aspiring screenwriters who are members of underrepresented groups. The multimedia industry, as of 1998, had not, however, initiated such efforts. Industry experts say that the nonhierarchical, egalitarian nature of the multimedia business indicates its openness to hiring minorities and women who wish to gain entry.

Unions/Associations

The Writers Guild of America represents writers of interactive/multimedia content. Professional associations include the Interactive Multimedia Association.

APPENDIX I
DEGREE AND NONDEGREE PROGRAMS

A. COLLEGES AND UNIVERSITIES

The preferred minimum educational requirement for the majority of positions discussed in this book is a bachelor's degree. Of the nearly 4,000 accredited four-year colleges and universities and community colleges in the United States, 1,000 offer degrees in communications, while 201 two-year colleges also do, according to www.petersons.com.

Television courses are often taught in several academic departments, and some schools offer interdisciplinary or interdepartmental programs leading to a degree. Although it is sometimes possible to major in another field and minor in communications, educational media, film, journalism, advertising, or radio-TV, many institutions offer degree programs in these communications areas.

This section contains the names and mailing and web addresses of more than 270 four-year colleges and universities

that offer programs emphasizing journalism, communications, or education. These institutions offer a major in (or emphasis on) radio-television or media. Space limitations preclude the listing of all such colleges and universities. More than 133 schools offer courses in nonbroadcast television, according to a study by the University of Missouri–Columbia for the International Television Association (ITVA). Many of these are small colleges and universities.

Information about these and the other colleges and universities offering courses in radio-TV and film can be obtained from the Speech Communication Association (SCA) (5105 Backlick Road, Annandale, VA 22033). Additional information about college courses in television is available from the Broadcast Education Association (1771 N Street NW, Washington, DC 20036).

ALABAMA

Auburn University
Department of Communication
Haley Center 4030
Auburn University, AL 36849
www.auburn.edu

University of Alabama
Department of Broadcast and Film
    Communication, Box 87015
College of Communication
Birmingham, AL 35486
www.uab.edu

ARIZONA

Arizona State University
Walter Cronkite School of Journalism
    and Telecommunication
Tempe, AZ 85287-1305

University of Arizona
Department of Media Arts
Modern Language 265
Tucson, AZ 85721
www.arizona.edu

ARKANSAS

Arkansas State University
Department of Radio-Television
State University, AR 72467-2160

University of Arkansas, Fayetteville
Communication Department
417 Kimpel Hall
Fayetteville, AR 72701
www.uark.edu

University of Arkansas, Little Rock
Department of Radio, TV, and Film
2801 South University
Little Rock, AR 72204
www.ualr.edu

CALIFORNIA

California State University, Chico
Information and Communication
    Studies
Chico, CA 95929-0145
www.csuchico.edu

California State University, Fresno
Department of Telecommunications
Cedar and Shaw Avenues
Fresno, CA 93740-0046
www.csufresno.edu

California State University, Fullerton
Communications Department
Fullerton, CA 92634-4080

California State University, Long Beach
Radio Television, and Film
    Department
1250 Bellflower Boulevard
Long Beach, CA 90840-2803

California State University, Los Angeles
Department of Communication
    Studies
5151 State University Drive
Los Angeles, CA 90034

California State University, Northridge
Radio-TV-Film Department
18111 Nordhoff Street
Northridge, CA 91330
www.csun.edu

Pepperdine University
Communication Division
Malibu, CA 90263
www.pepperdine.edu

San Diego State University
Telecommunications and Film
    Department
5300 Campanile Drive
San Diego, CA 92182-0117
www.sdsu.edu

San Francisco State University
Broadcast Communication Arts
    Department
1600 Holloway Avenue
San Francisco, CA 94132
www.sfsu.edu

San Jose State University
Theatre Arts Department
School of Humanities and the Arts
Seventh and San Fernando
San Jose, CA 95192
www.sjsu.edu

Stanford University
Communication Department
McClatchy Hall
Stanford, CA 94305-2050
www.stanford.edu

University of California, Los Angeles
School of Theater and Film/Television
Department of Film/Television
405 Hilgard Avenue
Los Angeles, CA 90024
www.ucla.edu

University of Southern California
Annenberg School of Communications
University Park
Los Angeles, CA 90089-0281
www.usc.edu

COLORADO

Colorado State University
Department of Technical Journalism
Fort Collins, CO 80523
www.colostate.edu

University of Colorado
School of Journalism and Mass Communication
Campus Box 287
Boulder, CO 80309
www.colorado.edu

University of Colorado, Colorado Springs
Communication Department
PO Box 7150
Colorado Springs, CO 80933-7150
www.uccs.edu

University of Denver
Mass Communications Department
2490 South Gaylord
Denver, CO 80210
www.du.edu

Western State College
Radio-TV Department
Gunnison, CO 81230
www.western.edu

CONNECTICUT

University of Bridgeport
Mass Communication Department
170 Lafayette Street
Bridgeport, CT 06602
www.bridgeport.edu

DISTRICT OF COLUMBIA

American University
School of Communication
Washington, DC 20016
www.american.edu

Gallaudet University
Department of TV, Film, and Photography
Washington, DC 20002
www.gallaudet.edu

George Washington University
Communication Department
Washington, DC 20052
www.gwu.edu

Howard University
Department of Radio, Television and Film
School of Communications
525 Bryant Street NW, Room 226
Washington, DC 20059
www.howard.edu

FLORIDA

Florida Atlantic University
Communication Department
Boca Raton, FL 33431
www.fau.edu

Florida International University
School of Journalism and Mass Communication
North Miami, FL 33181
www.fiu.edu

Florida State University
Department of Communication
356 Diffenbaugh Building
Tallahassee, FL 32306
www.fsu.edu

University of Central Florida
Communication Department
PO Box 25000
Orlando, FL 32816
www.ucf.edu

University of Florida
Department of Telecommunication
2090 Weimer Hall
Gainesville, FL 32611
www.ufl.edu

University of Miami
School of Communication
Coral Gables, FL 33124
www.miami.edu

University of South Florida
Mass Communications Department
College of Arts and Letters
Tampa, FL 33620
www.usf.edu

University of West Florida
Department of Communication Arts
Pensacola, FL 32514- 5751
www.uwf.edu

GEORGIA

Georgia Southern University
Department of Communication Arts
Landrum Box 8091
Statesboro, GA 30460-8091
www.gasou.edu

Shorter College
Division of Communication Arts
315 Shorter Avenue
Rome, GA 30161-4298
www.shorter.edu

University of Georgia
Department of Telecommunications
College of Journalism
Athens, GA 30602
www.uga.edu

HAWAII

University of Hawaii, Manoa
Educational Technology Department
1776 University Avenue
Wist Hall 105
Honolulu, HI 96822
www.hawaii.edu

IDAHO

University of Idaho
School of Communication
Moscow, ID 83843
www.uidaho.edu

ILLINOIS

Columbia College
Television Department, Room 1501
600 South Michigan Avenue
Chicago, IL 60605
www.colum.edu

Eastern Illinois University
Speech Communication Department
Charleston, IL 61920
www.eiu.edu

Illinois State University
Department of Communication
Normal, IL 61761
www.ilstu.edu

Loyola University, Chicago
Department of Communication Arts
820 North Michigan Avenue
Chicago, IL 60626
www.luc.edu

Northeastern Illinois University
Speech and Performing Arts
Chicago, IL 60625
www.neiu.edu

Northern Illinois University
Department of Communication
    Studies
Watson Hall
De Kalb, IL 60115
www.niu.edu

Northwestern University
Radio, Television, and Film
    Department
School of Speech
Evanston, IL 60208-2270
www.nwu.edu

**Southern Illinois University at
    Carbondale**
Department of Radio-Television
Communications Building
Carbondale, IL 62901-6609
www.siu.edu

**Southern Illinois University at
    Edwardsville**
Mass Communications Department
Box 1775
Edwardsville, IL 62026
www.siue.edu

**University of Illinois, Urbana-
    Champaign**
College of Communications
119 Gregory Hall
Urbana, IL 61801
www.illinois.edu

Western Illinois University
Communication Arts and Sciences
    Department
Macomb, IL 61455
www.wiu.edu

Wheaton College
Communications Department
Wheaton, IL 60187
www.wheaton.edu

INDIANA

Ball State University
Department of Telecommunications
Muncie, IN 47306
www.bsu.edu

Butler University
Radio-Television Department
46th and Sunset
Indianapolis, IN 46208
www.butler.edu

Indiana State University
Department of Communication
Terre Haute, IN 47809
www.isu.indstate.edu

Indiana University
Telecommunications Department
Radio and Television Center
College of Arts and Sciences
Bloomington, IN 47405
www.indiana.edu

**Indiana University–Purdue
    University, Indianapolis**
Telecommunications Department
525 North Blackford
Indianapolis, IN 46202-3120
www.iupui.edu

Manchester College
Department of Communication
    Studies
College Avenue
North Manchester, IN 46962
www.manchester.edu

Purdue University
Department of Communication
Heavilon Hall
West Lafayette, IN 47907
www.purdue.edu

Purdue University Calumet
Communication and Creative Arts
    Department
Hammond, IN 46323
www.calumet.purdue.edu

University of Evansville
Department of Communications
1800 Lincoln Avenue
Evansville, IN 47714
www.evansville.edu

IOWA

Buena Vista University
Mass Communications Program
Storm Lake, IA 50588
www.bvu.edu

Clarke College
Communication Department
Dubuque, IA 52001-3198
www.clarke.edu

Drake University
Department of Speech
    Communication
Des Moines, IA 50311-4505
www.drake.edu

Iowa State University
Journalism and Mass Communication
21 Exhibit Hall
Ames, IA 50011
www.iastate.edu

University of Iowa
Division of Broadcasting and Film
Department of Communication
    Studies
Iowa City, IA 52242
www.uiowa.edu

University of Northern Iowa
Educational Media Program
Department of Curriculum and
    Instruction
Cedar Falls, IA 50614
www.uni.edu

KANSAS

Fort Hays State University
Radio-Television/Film Department
Hays, KS 67601-4099
www.fhsu.edu

Kansas State University
A.Q. Miller School of Journalism and
    Mass Communications
Kedzie Hall
Manhattan, KS 66506-1501
www.ksu.edu

University of Kansas
Radio-Television Department
217 Flint Hall
Lawrence, KS 66045
www.ukans.edu

Wichita State University
Speech Communication Department
Wichita, KS 67208
www.wichita.edu

KENTUCKY

Eastern Kentucky University
Department of Mass
    Communications
Donovan Annex 102
Richmond, KY 40475-0941

Murray State University
Journalism and Radio-TV Department
Murray, KY 42071
www.murraystate.edu

Northern Kentucky University
Communications Department
Highland Heights, KY 41076
www.nku.edu

University of Kentucky
College of Communications
Lexington, KY 40506-0042
www.uky.edu

Western Kentucky University
Communication and Broadcasting
    Department
Fine Arts Center
Bowling Green, KY 42101
www.wku.edu

LOUISIANA

Grambling State University
Department of Mass Communication
PO Box 45
Grambling, LA 71245

Louisiana State University
Manship School of Journalism
Baton Rouge, LA 70803
www.lsu.edu

Loyola University, New Orleans
Communications Department
New Orleans, LA 70118
www.loyno.edu

University of New Orleans
Drama and Communications
    Department
Lakefront
New Orleans, LA 70148
www.uno.edu

University of Southwestern Louisiana
Department of Communication
Box 43650 USL
Lafayette, LA 70504
www.usl.edu

MAINE

University of Maine
Department of Journalism and Mass
    Communication
107 Lord Hall
Orono, ME 04469
www.ume.maine.edu

MARYLAND

Towson University
Speech and Mass Communication
    Department
Baltimore, MD 21204-7097
www.towson.edu

University of Maryland
Radio-TV-Film Division
Department of Communication Arts
    and Theatre
College Park, MD 20742
www.umcp.umd.edu

MASSACHUSETTS

Boston College
Speech, Communication, and
    Theater Department
Chestnut Hill, MA 02167
www.bc.edu

Boston University
Department of Broadcasting and Film
College of Communication
640 Commonwealth Avenue
Boston, MA 02215
www.bu.edu

Emerson College
Department of Visual and Media Arts
100 Beacon Street
Boston, MA 02116
www.emerson.edu

Stonehill College
Communications and Theatre Arts
Easton, MA 02357
www.stonehill.edu

University of Massachusetts
Department of Communications
Amherst, MA 01003
www.umass.edu

Worcester State College
Department of Media, Arts and
    Philosophy
486 Chandler Street
Worcester, MA 01602
www.worc.edu

MICHIGAN

Central Michigan University
Broadcast and Cinematic Arts
340 Moore Hall
Mount Pleasant, MI 48858
www.cmich.edu

Eastern Michigan University
Department of Communication and
    Theatre Arts
124 Quirk
Ypsilanti, MI 48197
www.emich.edu

Ferris State University
Television Production Department
IRC 108
Big Rapids, MI 49307
www.ferris.edu

Grand Valley State University
Radio-TV Department
Allendale, MI 49401
www.gvsu.edu

Michigan State University
Telecommunication Department
409 Communication Arts and Sciences
East Lansing, MI 48824
www.msu.edu

Northern Michigan University
Speech Department
Marquette, MI 49855
www.nmu.edu

University of Michigan
Department of Communication
2020 Frieze Building
Ann Arbor, MI 48109-1285
www.umich.edu

Wayne State University
Department of Communication
585 Manoogian Hall
Detroit, MI 48202
www.wayne.edu

Western Michigan University
Department of Communication
Kalamazoo, MI 49008
www.wmich.edu

MINNESOTA

Bemidji State University
Mass Communication
Box 59
Bemidji, MN 56601

Hamline University
Theatre and Communications
    Department
St. Paul, MN 55104
www.hamline.edu

Moorhead State University
Speech Communication/Theatre Arts
Moorhead, MN 56560
www.moorhead.edu

St. Cloud State University
Mass Communications Department
St. Cloud, MN 56301
www.stcloud.msus.edu

**University of Minnesota,
    Minneapolis/St. Paul**
Speech-Communications Department
Minneapolis, MN 55455
www1.umn.edu

MISSISSIPPI

Jackson State University
Department of Mass Communications
PO Box 18590
Jackson, MS 39217-0990
www.jsums.edu

Mississippi State University
Communication Department
PO Drawer PF
Mississippi State, MS 39762
www.msstate.edu

University of Mississippi
Radio and Television Program
Department of Theatre Arts
Oxford, MS 38677
www.olemiss.edu

University of Southern Mississippi
Radio, Television, and Film Department
Hardy Street and US 49
Hattiesburg, MS 39406-5141
www.usm.edu

MISSOURI

Avila College
Communication Department
11901 Wornall Road
Kansas City, MO 64145
www.avila.edu

Central Missouri State University
Department of Communication
Warrensburg, MO 64093
www.cmsu.edu

Lindenwood University
Communications Department
St. Charles, MO 63301
www.lindenwood.edu

Saint Louis University
Department of Communication
3733 West Pine
St. Louis, MO 63108
www.slu.edu

Stephens College
Communications Department
Columbia, MO 65215-0001
www.stephens.edu

University of Missouri, Columbia
Department of Communications
Switzler Hall
Columbia, MO 65211
www.missouri.edu

University of Missouri, Kansas City
Department of Communication Studies
College of Arts and Sciences
5100 Rockhill Road
Kansas City, MO 64110-2499
www.umkc.edu

MONTANA

Montana State University
Department of Media and Theatre Arts
Bozeman, MT 59717
www.montana.edu

University of Montana
Radio-Television Department
School of Journalism
Missoula, MT 59812-0001
www.umt.edu

NEBRASKA

Creighton University
Department of Journalism and Mass
   Communication
California at 24th Street
Omaha, NE 68178-0119
www.creighton.edu

Midland Lutheran College
Journalism Department
Fremont, NE 68025
www.mlc.edu

University of Nebraska
Broadcasting Department
203 Avery Hall
Lincoln, NE 68588
www.unl.edu

University of Nebraska at Omaha
Communication Department
Omaha, NE 68182-0112

Wayne State College
Division of Humanities
Wayne, NE 68787
www.wsc.edu

NEVADA

University of Nevada, Las Vegas
Department of Communication Studies
4505 Maryland Parkway
Las Vegas, NV 89154
www.unlv.edu

NEW HAMPSHIRE

Franklin Pierce College
Mass Communications Department
Rindge, NH 03461
www.fpc.edu

University of New Hampshire
Theater and Communication
   Department
Paul Arts Center
Durham, NH 03824
www.unh.edu

NEW JERSEY

**Fairleigh Dickinson University,
   Teaneck**
Department of Communications and
   Speech
College of Liberal Arts
1000 River Road
Teaneck, NJ 07666
www.fdu.edu

Montclair State College
Speech and Theater Department
Valley Road and Normal Avenue
Upper Montclair, NJ 07043
www.saturn.montclair.edu

Seton Hall University
Communications Department
South Orange, NJ 07079
www.shu.edu

**William Paterson University of New
   Jersey**
Communication Department
300 Pompton Road
Wayne, NJ 07470-2156
www.wilpatterson.edu

NEW MEXICO

Eastern New Mexico University
Communicative Arts and Sciences
Portales, NM 88130
www.enmu.edu

New Mexico State University
Journalism and Mass
   Communication Department
Las Cruces, NM 88003
www.nmsu.edu

NEW YORK

Adelphi University
Communications Department
Blodgett U113
Garden City, NY 11530
www.adelphi.edu

**City University of New York,
   Brooklyn College**
Television/Radio Department
Bedford Avenue and Avenue H
Brooklyn, NY 11210
www.ccny.cuny.edu

**City University of New York,
   Lehman College**
Speech and Theatre Department
Mass Communication Division
Bedford Park Boulevard W
Bronx, NY 10468
www.ccny.cuny.edu

**City University of New York, Queens
   College**
Department of Communication Arts
   and Sciences
Flushing, NY 11367
www.ccny.cuny.edu

**C.W. Post Campus of Long Island
   University**
Department of Theatre and Film
Northern Boulevard
Brookville, NY 11548
www.liu.edu

Fordham University
Communications Department
Bronx, NY 10458
www.fordham.edu

Hofstra University
Communication Arts Department
Hempstead Turnpike
Hempstead, NY 11550
www.hofstra.edu

Ithaca College
Department of Television-Radio
Roy H. Park School of
   Communications
Danby Road
Ithaca, NY 14850
www.ithaca.edu

Marist College
Lowell Thomas Communications
   Center
North Road
Poughkeepsie, NY 12601
www.marist.edu

Medaille College
Media Communications Department
18 Agassiz Circle
Buffalo, NY 14214
www.medaille.edu

New York Institute of Technology, Old Westbury
Communication Arts Department
Wheatley Road
Old Westbury, NY 11568
www.nyit.edu

New York University
Tisch School of the Arts
Institute of Film and Television
721 Broadway
New York, NY 10003
www.nyu.edu

St. Bonaventure University
Department of Mass Communication
St. Bonaventure, NY 14778
www.sbu.edu

St. Francis College
Radio-TV Department
Brooklyn Heights, NY 11201
www.stfranciscollege.edu

St. Thomas Aquinas College
Radio-TV Program
Sparkill, NY 10976
www.stac.edu

State University of New York, Buffalo
Department of Communication
1300 Elmwood Avenue
Buffalo, NY 14222-1095
www.buffalostate.edu

State University of New York, College at New Paltz
Communication Department
New Paltz, NY 12561
www.newpaltz.edu

Syracuse University
Television, Radio and Film Department
S.I. Newhouse School of Public
    Communications
215 University Place
Syracuse, NY 13244-2100
www.syr.edu

NORTH CAROLINA

East Carolina University
Department of Communication
Greenville, NC 27834
www.ecu.edu

Fayetteville State University
Communications and Fine Arts
    Department
Fayetteville, NC 28301-4298

North Carolina State University
Office of Admissions
Box 7103
112 Peele Hall
Raleigh, NC 27695
www.ncsu.edu

University of North Carolina, Chapel Hill
Department of Radio, Television,
    and Motion Pictures
Swain Hall 044A
Chapel Hill, NC 27514
www.unc.edu

Wake Forest University
Speech Communication and Theatre
    Arts Department
PO Box 7347
Winston-Salem, NC 27109
www.wfu.edu

Western Carolina University
Speech-Theater Arts Department
Cullowhee, NC 28723

NORTH DAKOTA

University of North Dakota
School of Communication
College of Arts and Sciences
Grand Forks, ND 58202
www.und.nodak.edu

OHIO

Antioch College
Communication-Video Department
Yellow Springs, OH 45387
www.college.antioch.edu

Bowling Green State University
Department of Radio-
    Television-Film
School of Mass Communication
Bowling Green, OH 43403
www.bgsu.edu

Cedarville College
Communication Arts-Broadcasting
Cedarville, OH 45314-0601
www.cedarville.edu

College of Wooster
Department of Speech
    Communication
Wooster, OH 44691
www.wooster.edu

Kent State University
School of Journalism and Mass
    Communication
130-H Taylor Hall
Kent, OH 44242
www.kent.edu

Miami University
Department of Communication
Oxford, OH 45056
www.muohio.edu

Muskingum College
Radio-TV Department
New Concord, OH 43762
www.muskingum.edu

Ohio Northern University
Communication Arts
Ada, OH 45810
www.onu.edu

Ohio State University
Department of Communication
205 Derby Hall
154 North Oval Mall
Columbus, OH 43210
www.ohio-state.edu

Ohio University
School of Telecommunications
College of Communication
Athens, OH 45701-2979
www.ohiou.edu

University of Dayton
Communication Department
Dayton, OH 45409
www.udayton.edu

University of Toledo
Department of Communications
2801 West Bancroft Street
Toledo, OH 43606
www.utoledo.edu

Xavier University
Communication Arts Department
B-11 Alter Hall
Cincinnati, OH 45207
www.xu.edu

Youngstown State University
Speech Communication and Theatre
Youngstown, OH 44555
www.ysu.edu

OKLAHOMA

Cameron University
Communications Department
Lawton, OK 73505

Oklahoma City University
Department of Mass Communications
2501 North Blackwelder
Oklahoma City, OK 73106
www.okcu.edu

Oklahoma State University
School of Journalism and Broadcasting
Stillwater, OK 74078-0195
www.okstate.edu

Oral Roberts University
Communication Arts Department
7777 South Lewis
Tulsa, OK 74171
www.oru.edu

Southern Nazarene University
Mass Communication Program
6729 NW 39 Expressway
Bethany, OK 73008-2694

University of Oklahoma
H.H. Herbert School of Journalism
   and Mass Communication
Norman, OK 73019
www.ou.edu

University of Tulsa
Communication Department
Tulsa, OK 74104
www.utulsa.edu

OREGON

George Fox College
Video Communication Center
Newberg, OR 97132
www.georgefox.edu

Lewis and Clark College
Communications Department
Portland, OR 97219
www.lclark.edu

Oregon State University
Department of Speech Communication
College of Liberal Arts
Corvallis, OR 97331-6199
www.orst.edu

Southern Oregon University
Communication Department
Ashland, OR 97520

University of Oregon
Telecommunications and Film Area
Department of Speech
Villard Hall
Eugene, OR 97403
www.uoregon.cdu

University of Portland
Department of Communication Studies
5000 North Willamette Boulevard
Portland, OR 97203-5798
www.uofport.edu

PENNSYLVANIA

California University of Pennsylvania
Communication Studies Department
California, PA 15419-1394
www.cup.edu

East Stroudsburg State University
Speech Communication Department
East Stroudsburg, PA 18301
www.esu.edu

Edinboro University of Pennsylvania
Speech Communication
   Department/Radio-TV Center
Compton 208
Edinboro, PA 16412
www.edinboro.edu

Indiana University of Pennsylvania
Communications Media Department
121 Stouffer Hall
Indiana, PA 15705
www.iup.edu

Kutztown University of Pennsylvania
Department of Telecommunications
Kutztown, PA 19530
www.kutztown.edu

La Salle University
Communication Department
20th and Olney Avenue
Philadelphia, PA 19141
www.lasalle.edu

Marywood College
Department of Communication Arts
Scranton, PA 18509
www.marywood.edu

**Pennsylvania State University,
University Park**
School of Communications
201 Shields Building
University Park, PA 16802
www.psu.edu

**Shippensburg University of
   Pennsylvania**
Communications and Journalism
   Department
Shippensburg, PA 17257
www.ship.edu

**Slippery Rock University of
   Pennsylvania**
Communication Department
Slippery Rock, PA 16057
www.sru.edu

Susquehanna University
Department of Communications and
   Theatre Arts
Selinsgrove, PA 17870-1001
www.susqu.edu

Temple University
Department of Radio-
   Television-Film
School of Communications and Theater
13th and Diamond Streets
Philadelphia, PA 19122
www.temple.edu

University of Pennsylvania
Annenberg School of Communications
3620 Walnut Street
Philadelphia, PA 19104
www.upenn.edu

University of Scranton
Department of Communication
Scranton, PA 18510-2192
www.uofs.edu

Villanova University
Communications Department
Villanova, PA 19085
www.vill.edu

Wilkes University
Speech Communication Department
Wilkes-Barre, PA 18766
www.wilkes.edu

York College of Pennsylvania
Department of Music, Art, and
   Speech Communication
York, PA 17403
www.ycp.edu

RHODE ISLAND

Rhode Island College
Communications Department
Providence, RI 02908
www.ric.edu

SOUTH CAROLINA

University of South Carolina
Department of Media Arts
Columbia, SC 29208
www.csd.scarolina.edu

SOUTH DAKOTA

South Dakota State University
Speech Department, Box 2201
Brookings, SD 57007-1197
www.sdstate.edu

University of South Dakota
Mass Communication Department
Vermillion, SD 57069

TENNESSEE

David Lipscomb University
Radio-TV, Department of Speech
   Communication
Nashville, TN 37204-3951
www.dlu.edu

Middle Tennessee State University
School of Mass Communications
PO Box 51
Murfreesboro, TN 37132
www.mtsu.edu

University of Tennessee, Knoxville
Department of Broadcasting
College of Communications
295 Communication and University
   Extension Building
Knoxville, TN 37916

University of Tennessee, Martin
Department of Communications
305 Gooch Hall
Martin, TN 38238
www.utk.edu

TEXAS

Abilene Christian University
Journalism and Mass Communications
PO Box 7568
Abilene, TX 79699
www.acu.edu

Baylor University
Communication Studies Department
Telecommunication Division
Waco, TX 76798-7368
www.baylor.edu

Prairie View A&M University
Communications Department
PO Box 0156
Prairie View, TX 77446-0156

Sam Houston State University
Radio-TV-Film
Box 2207-SHSU
Huntsville, TX 77340
www.shsu.edu

Southern Methodist University
Communication Arts
Dallas, TX 75275
www.smu.edu

Texas Christian University
Radio-Television-Film Department
Fort Worth, TX 76129
www.tcu.edu

Texas Southern University
School of Communication
Houston, TX 77004
www.tsu.edu

Texas Tech University
School of Mass Communication
Box 4710
Lubbock, TX 79409
www.ttu.edu

Trinity University
Department of Communication
715 Stadium Drive
San Antonio, TX 78212
www.trinity.edu

University of Houston
School of Communication
Houston, TX 77204-3786
www.uh.edu

University of North Texas
Division of Radio/Television/Film
PO Box 13108
Denton, TX 76203-3108
www.unt.edu

University of Texas, Arlington
Communication Department
UTA Box 19107
Arlington, TX 76019
www.uta.edu

University of Texas, Austin
Department of Radio-Television-Film
College of Communication
Austin, TX 78712
www.utexas.edu

UTAH

Brigham Young University
Communications Department
E-509 HFAC
Provo, UT 84602
www.byu.edu

Southern Utah University
Communication Department
Cedar City, UT 84720
www.suu.edu

University of Utah
Communication Department
Salt Lake City, UT 84112
www.utah.edu

Weber State College
Department of Communication
3750 Harrison Boulevard
Ogden, UT 84408-1903
www.weber.edu

VERMONT

University of Vermont
Theater Department
Burlington, VT 05405
www.uvm.edu

VIRGINIA

James Madison University
Department of Communication
Harrisonburg, VA 22807
www.jmu.edu

Norfolk State College
Mass Communications Department
2400 Corprew Avenue
Norfolk, VA 23504
www.nsu.edu

Virginia Commonwealth University
Mass Communications Department
901 West Main Street
Richmond, VA 23284-2034
www.vcu.edu

**Virginia Polytechnic Institute and
  State University**
Department of Communication Studies
Blacksburg, VA 24061
www.vt.edu

Washington and Lee University
Department of Journalism and
  Communications
Lexington, VA 24450
www.wlu.edu

WASHINGTON

Central Washington University
Department of Communication
Ellensburg, WA 98926

Eastern Washington University
Radio-Television Department
Mail Stop 104
Cheney, WA 99004
www.ewu.edu

Evergreen State College
Radio-TV Department
Olympia, WA 98505-0003
www.evergreen.edu

Pacific Lutheran University
Communication Arts Department
Tacoma, WA 98447
www.plu.edu

Seattle Pacific University
Communication Department
Seattle, WA 98119
www.spu.edu

University of Washington
School of Communications
College of Arts and Sciences
DS-40
Seattle, WA 98195
www.washington.edu

Washington State University
Department of Communication
Pullman, WA 99164-2520
www.wsu.edu

Western Washington University
Department of Communication
Bellingham, WA 98225
www.wwu.edu

WEST VIRGINIA

Marshall University
Speech Department
Huntington, WV 25701
www.marshall.edu

West Virginia State College
Department of Communications
PO Box 28
Institute, WV 25112
www.wvsc.wvnet.edu

West Virginia University
Communication Studies Department
Morgantown, WV 26506
www.wvu.edu

WISCONSIN

Marquette University
Broadcast Communication Department
Milwaukee, WI 53233
www.marquette.edu

University of Wisconsin, Green Bay
Communication Processes
Green Bay, WI 54311-7001
www.uwgb.edu

University of Wisconsin, LaCrosse
Mass Communications Department
LaCrosse, WI 54601
www.uwlax.edu

University of Wisconsin, Madison
Department of Communication Arts
Vilas Communication Hall
821 University Avenue
Madison, WI 53706
www.wisc.edu

University of Wisconsin, Milwaukee
Department of Mass Communication
Milwaukee, WI 53201
www.uwm.edu

University of Wisconsin, Platteville
Department of Communication
Platteville, WI 53818
www.uwplatt.edu

University of Wisconsin, Stevens Point
Communications Department
Stevens Point, WI 54481
www.uwsp.edu

University of Wisconsin, Whitewater
Communication Department
800 West Main Street
Whitewater, WI 53190
www.uww.edu

WYOMING

University of Wyoming
Department of Communication and
    Mass Media
PO Box 3904
University Station
Laramie, WY 82071-3904
www.uwyo.edu

B. WORKSHOPS AND SEMINARS

The following is a list of selected workshops and seminars with their sponsors' names and addresses and the general subjects they cover. Some last for two or three days, and a modest fee is charged for attending; others are one-day or evening sessions; some are free. Many run for a week at higher fees. The reader should check with the particular sponsor for its current schedule.

American Film Institute
PO Box 27999
2021 North Western Avenue
Los Angeles, CA 90027
(323) 856-7600
(323) 467-4578 (fax)
www.afionline.com

workshops, seminars, conferences on film and TV for a fee

Assistant Directors Training Program
15260 Ventura Blvd, Suite 1200-A
Sherman Oaks, CA 91403
(310) 289-2000
(310) 289-2029 (fax)
www.dgptp.org

seminars in administrative and managerial skills for film and TV industries

Avid Education Seminars
Avid Corporate Education Center
Burbank, CA and Tewksbury, MA
800-867-2843
www.avid.com

various locations nationwide. Beginner-intermediate-advanced courses in digital video production and editing. Media Composer and Effect courses training the professional in 2D and 3D effects, horizontal and vertical effects, sophisticated multilayered effects, keys and titles.

Bay Area Video Coalition
2727 Mariposa St.
San Francisco, CA 94110
(415) 558-2100
www.bavc.org

seminars in careers, basic video, engineering, editing, writing, lighting, production for fees

Crystal Information, Inc.,
30240 SW Parkway Avenue
Wilsonville, OR 97070
503-570-9599

broad range of courses, including AfterEffects, Authorware, Director, EditDV, and Premiere

Institute for Professional Development ICIA/IUPUI
11242 Waples Mill Rd
Fairfax, VA 22030
(800) 659-7469
www.icia.org

summer week-long workshops in AV production and equipment, for a fee

International Television Association
6311 North O'Connor, LB-51
Irving, TX 75039
(972) 869-1112

workshops and seminars several times a year within chapters and regions for modest fees

Knowledge Industry Publications, Inc.
701 Westchester Avenue, Suite 101 W
White Plains, NY 10604
914-328-9157
www.kipinet.com

exposition and seminar program in business/audio/video conferencing, media production

Multimedia Studies Program
San Francisco State University
425 Market Street
San Francisco, CA 94105
415-904-7700

certificate programs include Digital Design and Production, Web Design and Production, 3D Arts, Web Technology

National Academy of Television Arts and Sciences
1560 Broadway, 503
New York, NY 10036
(212) 768-7050

industry-related workshops, seminars, panel discussions, job listings/placement by local chapters in major U.S. cities

National Association of Broadcasters
Employment Clearinghouse
1771 N Street NW
Washington, DC 20036

workshops and broadcast employment seminars for women and minorities

New School for Social Research
66 West 12th Street
New York, NY 10011
email: salmonb@newschool.edu

film and video workshops, courses,
annual Festival of Documentary Center

North American Television Institute
Knowledge Industry Publications, Inc.
701 Westchester Avenue
White Plains, NY 10604

basic, intermediate, and advanced
seminars in video management,
training, lighting, sound, editing, script
writing, directing

School of Visual Arts
209 East 23rd Street
New York, NY 10010
(212) 592-2100
www.schoolofvisualarts.com

short courses in advertising, film, and
video production and postproduction,
animation

Sterling Ledet & Associates, Inc.
2176 Heritage Drive
Atlanta, GA 30345
404-325-3338

Adobe Authorized Training Provider
offering training and support services in
Premiere, After Effects, and Photoshop
for Macintosh and Windows systems

United Digital Artists
FDR Station
PO Box 548
New York, NY 10150-0548
212-777-7200

one- and two-day courses, as well as
seven-day certification programs on the
Internet and multimedia. Courses range
from beginning to advanced.

Vancouver Film School
#401, 1168 Hamilton Street
Vancouver, BC V6B 2s2
www.multimedia.edu

seminars in film and multimedia
production

C. INTERNSHIPS, SCHOLARSHIPS, AND FELLOWSHIPS

The companies and organizations listed below offer intern programs in various media-related disciplines. Some pay a modest stipend, and some offer no money but may grant college credit. (Contact the individual sponsor for specific information.)

There are many other programs throughout the country and the interested applicant should check with local stations (especially public TV), advertising agencies, and cable companies in his or her area for further leads.

In addition to the name of the sponsoring group and its address, each listing provides a brief description of the type of program offered.

For a listing of internships in all fields each year, see *Peterson's Internships 1999,* published annually by Peterson's Guides and cited in Appendix III: Bibliography: Careers.

Many students need financial assistance to begin or complete their studies. Some of the organizations given below award fellowships, scholarships, and grants for training in television, cable, video, and media. These are not usually a part of an internship experience, but a grant may sometimes be used for that purpose, or to defray college expenses.

**Academy of Television Arts and
    Sciences**
Internship Program
5220 Lankershim Boulevard
North Hollywood, CA 91601

28 internships (with stipend) in 24
categories for full-time
undergraduates, grad students, or
recent college graduates

Accuracy in Media
11250 Waples Mill Road, Suite 350
Fairfax, VA 22030

internships in public relations

Aigner Associates
556 Trapelo Road
Belmont, MA 02178

internships in public relations

**American Association of Advertising
    Agencies**
405 Lexington Avenue, Eighth Floor
New York, NY 10174

minority student internship program for
summer position in an ad agency

American Electronics Association
Japan Research Fellowship Program
520 Great American Parkway
Santa Clara, CA 95054

fellowships to graduate engineering
students for a nine-month assignment to
a Japanese high-tech research lab

American Film Institute
2021 North Western Avenue
Los Angeles, CA 90027

internships to observe directing or
editing of feature films/telefeatures
and/or TV shows

American Repertory Theatre
64 Brattle Street
Cambridge, MA 02138

internships in acting, crafts

Boston Globe
PO Box 2378
Boston, MA 02107

internships in advertising

Broadcast Education Association
Scholarship Chairman
200 Stauffers Hall
University of Kansas
Lawrence, KS 66045-2353

national scholarships in broadcasting

**Cable News Network/Turner
Broadcasting**
One CNN Center
PO Box 105366
Hanta, GA 30348

internships in television news; no
stipend

CBS News
51 West 52nd Street
New York, NY 10019

intern opportunities in TV news; some
stipends

Georgia Governor's Office
115 State Capital
Atlanta, GA 30334

student internships in office work, fund-raising, production, public information

Greater Media Cable
95 Higgins Street
Worcester, MA 01606

television internships

Hollywood Internship Program
7083 Hollywood Boulevard, Fifth Floor
Hollywood, CA 90028

internships in production

Home Box Office
1100 Avenue of the Americas
New York, NY 10036

internships in pay cable

International Radio and TV, Inc
Education Programs Coordinator
420 Lexington Avenue, Room 531
New York, NY 10017

broadcasting internships; stipends

Iowa Film Office
200 East Grand Avenue
Des Moines, IA 50309

internships in public relations

KAID-TV
1910 University Drive
Boise, ID 83725

internships in production, fund-raising, public information, technical, office; no stipend

KCTS-TV
401 Mercer Street
Seattle, WA 98109

intern opportunities in tour guide, special events, office, fund-raising, public information, news/current affairs, learning services; no stipend

KERA-FM/TV
3000 Harry Hines Boulevard
Dallas, TX 75201

internships in fund-raising, marketing, office, public information; no stipend

King Broadcasting Company
333 Dexter Avenue
North Seattle, WA 98109

broadcasting internships; with stipend

KLVX-TV
4210 Channel Ten Drive
Las Vegas, NV 89119

internships in office, production, public information, writing, research; no stipend

KOOD-TV
Smoky-Hills Public TV Corporation
Sixth and Elm Streets
Hays, KS 67626

internships in office, production, fund-raising, public information, technical, art; some stipends

KOZK-TV
1101 North Summit
MPO Box 21
Springfield, MO 65801

management, production, public information internships; no stipend

KQED-FM/TV
500 Eighth Street
San Francisco, CA 94103

internships in research, public relations, community affairs, marketing, instructional TV; stipends to work-study students

KRWG-TV
New Mexico State University
Box 30001
Las Cruces, NM 88003

internships in office, fund-raising, production, public information, technical; stipends for college students

KTCA-TV
1640 Como Avenue
St. Paul, MN 55108

internships in office, fund-raising, production, public information; no stipends

KUAT-AM/TV
University of Arizona
Tucson, AZ 85721

office work, fund-raising, special events internships; no stipend

KVAL-TV
PO Box 1313
Eugene, OR 97440

internships for enrolled college students in writing and researching news; no stipend

KVCR-TV
701 South Mount Vernon Avenue
San Bernardino, CA 92410

internships in fund-raising, production, public information, engineering/technical, office work; hourly stipend

KWSU-AM/TV
Edward R. Murrow Communications Center
Washington State University
Pullman, WA 99164

internships in fund-raising, production, public information, technical, office; no stipend

Maryland Public Television
117657 Bonita Avenue
Owings Mills, MD 21117

internships in fund-raising, production, public information, technical, office; college credit, no stipend

Mississippi Educational TV & FM Network
WMAA-FM/TV
PO Box 1101
Jackson, MS 39215-1101

production, engineering, some other internships for qualified students; no stipend

NBC
30 Rockefeller Plaza
New York, NY 10020

internships in network broadcasting; no stipend

New Hampshire Public Television
Box 1100
Durham, NH 03824

internships in fund-raising, production, public information, technical, office

New Jersey Network
1573 Parkside Avenue, CN-777
Trenton, NJ 08625

internships in office fund-raising, production, public information, educational and creative services, news

New York State Education Department
Public Broadcasting Program
Room 10A75 -CEC, Empire State Plaza
Albany, NY 12230

instructional and educational programming internships in public TV in state of New York; some stipends

PBS
1320 Braddock Place
Alexandria, VA 22314
current affairs and promotion internships; no stipend

Prairie Public Radio/Television
207 North Fifth Street
Fargo, ND 58102

internships in fund-raising, production, public information, technical, office; minimum wage stipends

Public Interest Radio and Television Educational Society
P.I.R.A.T.E.S.
c/o Ad Company
1717 North Highland Avenue
Los Angeles, CA 90028

internships in public affairs; with stipend

South Dakota Public Broadcasting Telecommunications Center
414 East Clark Street
Vermillion, SD 57069-2390

SDPTV/Radio Internship Program offers training in many areas to upperclass students in South Dakota colleges/universities; stipend available

UNC Center for Public Television
910 Raleigh Road
Chapel Hill, NC 27515-3508

internships in fund-raising, production, technical, graphic arts; stipends available

University Film and Video Association
Scholarship Awards Program
Department of Communications
University of Nevada, Las Vegas
Las Vegas, NV 89154

scholarships for film/video production and research

Vermont Educational Television
88 Ethan Allen Avenue
Winooski, VT 05404-1097

internships in office, fund-raising, production, public information; no stipend

W*USA-TV
4001 Brandywine Street NW
Washington, DC 20016

intern opportunities in broadcasting; no stipend

WAVE-TV
PO Box 32970
Louisville, KY 40232

internships for minorities in television production and news

WBZ-TV
Human Resources Department
1170 Soldier's Field Road
Boston, MA 02134

internships in television; no stipend

WCAU-TV
Community Affairs
City Avenue and Monument Road
Philadelphia, PA 19131

internships in news, programming, editorial, engineering, research, promotion, finance, press relations, community affairs, traffic

WCBB-TV
1450 Lisbon Street
Augusta, ME 04240

internships in office, fund-raising, production, public information, technical; some stipends

WCBS-TV
524 West 57th Street
New York, NY 10019

internships in TV; no stipend

WCET-TV
1223 Central Parkway
Cincinnati, OH 45214

internships; some high school student opportunities; no stipend

WCHS-TV
PO Box 11138
Charleston, WV 25339

internships in television news

WDIV-TV 4
524 West Lafayette Boulevard
Detroit, MI 48231

television internships; no stipend

WETA-FM/TV
PO Box 2626
Washington, DC 20013

internships in public relations, programming, production, public affairs; stipends available

WFIU-FM/WTIU-TV
Indiana University
Bloomington, IN 47405

internships in office work, production, fund-raising, public information, technical programming, traffic, membership; also instructional TV; credit, no stipend

WFYI/TV
1401 North Meridian Street
Indianapolis, IN 46202

fund-raising, production, programming internships; no stipend

WGBH Educational Foundation
WGBH-FM/TV
125 Western Avenue
Boston, MA 02134

fund-raising and auction internships; no stipend

WHA-TV
821 University Avenue
Madison, WI 53706

internships in office, fund-raising, public information, special events; no stipend

WHYY-FM/TV
150 North Sixth Street
Philadelphia, PA 19106

fund-raising, production, public information internships; no stipend

WJLA-TV
3007 Tilden Street NW
Washington, DC 20008

television internships; no stipend

WKNO-FM/TV
900 Getwell Street
Memphis, TN 38111

production, fund-raising, office internships; no stipend

WLTR-FM/WLRK-TV
Drawer L
Columbia, SC 19150

internships for college students in office, fund-raising, production, public information, news; no stipend

WMFE-TV
11510 East Colonial Drive
Orlando, FL 32817

internships in office work, fund-raising, production; no stipend

WMTJ-TV
PO Box 21345
Fajardo, PR 00928

production and technical internships; no stipend

WMVS-WMVT-TV
1015 North Sixth Street
Milwaukee, WI 53203

office, fund-raising, public information internships; no stipend

WNET-TV
356 West 58th Street
New York, NY 10019

general internships in television production, management, and related fields

WNMU-FM/TV
Northern Michigan University
Marquette, MI 49855

intern assignments in fund-raising, production, public information, technical; with stipend

WNVC-WNVT-TV
8101-A Lee Highway
Fairfax, VA

internships in fund-raising, production, public information, technical, office; no stipend

WNYC-AM/FM/TV
One Centre Street, 32nd Floor
New York, NY 10007

internships in office, fund-raising, production; stipends to cover expenses

WPBT-FM/TV
PO Box 2
Miami, FL 33261-0002

internships in fund-raising, production, news, public information; no stipend

WPBY-TV
Third Avenue
Huntington, WV 25701

internships in fund-raising, production, public information, technical, office, marketing; no stipend

WPSX-TV
Pennsylvania State University
202 Wagner
Clearfield, PA 16830

internships in fund-raising, production, public information, technical, office; no stipend

WSBE-TV
24 Mason Street
Providence, RI 01903

internships in office, development, public relations, production; no stipend

WTOV-TV
Box 9999
Steubenville, OH 43952

internships in all departments

WTTW-TV
5400 North St. Louis Avenue
Chicago, IL 60625

two Harris internships in production annually; with stipend

WTVS-TV
7441 Second Boulevard
Detroit, MI 48202

internships in office, fund-raising, production, public information, development, community outreach; no stipends

WUFT-FM/TV
2104 Weimer Hall
University of Florida
Gainesville, FL 32611

internships in office work, fund-raising, production, public information; stipends available

WXXI-AM/FM/WXXA-TV
280 State Street
Rochester, NY 14614

production, public information, educational services internships; minority program offers minimum wage

WYES-TV
PO Box 24026
New Orleans, LA 70184

public information, production, engineering internships; no stipends

---

D. TRAINING PROGRAMS AND SCHOOLS

In this section, some of the special schools or programs that offer courses in television production, broadcasting, engineering, and electronics are listed. Most offer certificate programs. Students seeking training at any school should inquire about the school's accreditation by the Career College Association (CCA) or licensing by a state board of education.

In addition, there are more than a thousand community and junior colleges and technical schools that are accredited by the regional boards and that offer course sequences leading to an Associate of Arts or Associate of Science degree. Many offer programs in radio-TV, cable, and electronics.

The following chart indicates the approximate number of two-year colleges that offer associate degree programs in nine disciplines related to the jobs in this book.

Discipline	*Number of Colleges*
Journalism	210
Theater Arts/Drama	240
Electronics Engineering Technology	320
Photography	157
Broadcasting	111
Radio/Television Studies	112
Advertising	57
Communication Equipment Technology	64
Educational Media	9

For a list of the schools, the prospective student should refer to a copy of the annual guide titled *Peterson's Two-Year Colleges,* or check with the American Association of Community and Junior College.

Many four-year colleges also offer associate degree programs in journalism, theater arts, electronics, and broadcasting.

American Film Institute
Center for Advanced Film and
   Television Studies
Los Angeles, CA 90027
www.afionline.com

full-time two-year program offering advanced training in film directing, producing, cinematography, screenwriting, and production design

**Assistant Directors Training
   Program**
15503 Ventura Boulevard
Encino, CA 91436
www.dgptp.org

on-the-job training and seminars in administrative and managerial skills for film and TV industries

Bailie School of Broadcast
4045 North Seventh Street
Phoenix, AZ 85014

1731 Technology Drive, Suite 340
San Jose, CA 95110

1100 Stout Street, Ninth Floor
Denver, CO 80204

2517 East Lake Avenue, Suite 100
Seattle, WA 98102

training programs for broadcaster, technician

Broadcast Center
7720 Forsyth Boulevard
St. Louis, MO 63105

courses in TV production, journalism, and copywriting

Broadcasting Institute of Maryland
7200 Harford Road
Baltimore, MD 21234

training in broadcasting

Carolina School of Broadcasting
7003 Wallace Road, Suite 100
Charlotte, NC 28204
www.cbs-radio-tv.com

courses in news, production, announcing, sales

Columbia College Hollywood
925 North La Brea Avenue
Hollywood, CA 90038
www.columbiacollege.edu

training for broadcasting technician, TV production

Connecticut School of Broadcasting
9000 Sweet Valley Drive
Cleveland, OH 44125

broadcasting, technical, TV production training

Electronic Industries Alliance
2500 Wilson Boulevard
Alexandria, VA 22201
www.eia.org

training programs in basic video and TV repair and careers in consumer electronics

Elkins Institute
17430 Campbell Road, Suite 230
Dallas, TX 75252
www.elkinstraining.com

training in broadcasting

International College of Broadcasting
6 South Smithville Road
Dayton, OH 45431

broadcasting training

ITT Technical Institute
5100 Mastheud Street NE
Albuquerque, NM 87109

electronics specialist program

Massachusetts Communications College
142 Berkeley Street
Boston, MA 02116

broadcasting and TV production training

May Technical College
1306 Central Avenue
Billings, MT 59102

broadcaster, electronics specialist, TV production training programs

Miami Technical Institute
14701 NW Seventh Avenue
North Miami, FL 33168

programs for broadcasters, electronics specialist

National Education Center
1225 Orlen Avenue
Cuyahoga Falls, OH 44221

training programs for broadcast technician, electronics specialist, illustrator

New England School of Communications
One College Circle
Bangor, ME 04401

broadcaster and recording specialist training

School of Communication Arts
2526 27th Avenue South
Minneapolis, MN 55406

courses in ENG production and video computer graphics

Specs Howard School of Broadcast Arts
19900 West Nine Mile Road
Southfield, MI 48075

broadcasting and technical training

Technical Careers Institutes
320 West 31st Street
New York, NY 10001

courses in consumer electronics and ENG technology

Western Wisconsin Technical College
304 North Sixth Street
LaCrosse, WI 54602-0908

degree in visual communications technician; courses in audio, media equipment maintenance, photography, graphics

APPENDIX II
UNIONS AND ASSOCIATIONS

A. UNIONS

The unions and associations listed here are all closely related to the careers discussed in this book. Those that are mentioned in the job descriptions are included as well as others that are of importance in the television, cable, video, and multimedia fields. The name and acronym (if one is commonly used) of each group is included in addition to its address and telephone number.

Actors Equity Association (Equity)
165 West 46th Street
New York, NY 10036
212-869-8530
Fax: 212-719-9815

American Association of University Professors (AAUP)
1012 14th Street, Suite 500
Washington, DC 20005
202-737-5900

American Federation of Musicians (AFM)
1501 Broadway, Suite 600
New York, NY 10036
212-869-1330
1777 North Vine Street, Suite 410
Hollywood, CA 90028
213-461-3441
800-237-0988
800-322-2007 (California)
Fax: 213-462-8340

American Federation of State, County and Municipal Employees (AFSCME)
1625 L Street NW
Washington, DC 20036
202-452-4800
Fax: 202-659-0446

American Federation of Teachers (AFT)
555 New Jersey Avenue NW
Washington, DC 20001
202-879-4400
800-238-1133, ext. 4458
Fax: 202-879-4556

American Federation of Television and Radio Artists (AFTRA)
260 Madison Avenue
New York, NY 10016
212-532-0800
Fax: 212-545-1238

5757 Wilshire Boulevard, Ninth Floor
Los Angeles, CA 90036
323-634-8100
Fax: 323-634-8194

American Guild of Musical Artists (AGMA)
1727 Broadway
New York, NY 10019-5284
212-265-3687

American Guild of Variety Artists (AGVA)
184 Fifth Avenue, Sixth Floor
New York, NY 10010
212-675-1003

Authors Guild
330 West 42nd Street, 29th Floor
New York, NY 10036
212-563-5904

Communications Workers of America (CWA)
501 Third Street NW
Washington, DC 20001
202-434-1100

Costume Designers Guild
13949 Ventura Boulevard
Studio City, CA 91423
818-905-1557

Directors Guild of America (DGA)
7920 Sunset Boulevard
Hollywood, CA 90046
213-284-2000
800-421-4173
Fax: 213-289-2029

Dramatists Guild
1501 Broadway, Suite 701
New York, NY 10036
212-398-9366

HTML Writers Guild
110 East Wilshire Avenue, Suite G-12
Fullerton, CA 92832
714-526-4963
Fax: 714-526-4972

1225 Tamiami Trail, Suite B18
Port Charlotte, FL 33953
941-627-6848
Fax: 941-627-6909

International Alliance of Theatrical Stage Employees (IATSE)
1515 Broadway
New York, NY 10036
212-730-1770
Fax: 212-921-7699

International Brotherhood of Electrical Workers (IBEW)
1125 15th Street NW
Washington, DC 20005
202-833-7000

Local 790, Illustrators and Matte Artists,
International Alliance of Theatrical Stage Employees
13949 Ventura Boulevard,
Suite 301
Sherman Oaks, CA 91423
818-784-6555

National Association of Broadcast Employees and Technicians AFL-CIO (NABET)
501 Third Street NW, 880
Washington, DC 20001
202-434-1254

National Education Association (NEA)
1201 16th Street NW
Washington, DC 20036
202-833-4000

Producers Guild of America (PGA)
400 South Beverly Drive, No. 211
Beverly Hills, CA 90212
310-557-0807

Screen Actors Guild (SAG)
5757 Wilshire Boulevard
Hollywood, CA 90036
213-954-1600

1515 Broadway
New York, NY 10036
212-944-1030
Fax: 212-944-6744

Screen Extras Guild (SEG)
3253 North Knoll Drive
Los Angeles, CA 90068
213-851-4301

The Songwriter's Guild
1500 Harbor Boulevard
Weehawken, NJ 07087
201-867-7603

**United Brotherhood of Carpenters
and Joiners of America (UBC)**
101 Constitution Avenue
Washington, DC 20001
202-546-6206

United Scenic Artists (USA)
16 West 61st Street, 11th Floor
New York, NY 10023
212-581-0300
Fax: 212-977-2011

**Writers Guild of America East
(WGA)**
555 West 57th Street
New York, NY 10019
212-245-6180

**Writers Guild of America West
(WGA)**
7000 West Third Street
Los Angeles, CA 90048
213-951-4000
Fax: 213-782-4800

B. ASSOCIATIONS

**Academy of Television Arts and
Sciences**
5220 Lankershim Boulevard
North Hollywood, CA 91601
818-754-2800
Fax: 818-761-2827

Advertising Council
261 Madison Avenue, 11th Floor
New York, NY 10016
212-922-1500
Fax: 212-922-1676

Advertising Research Foundation
641 Lexington Avenue
New York, NY 10022
212-751-5656

**Alliance of Motion Picture and
Television Producers (AMPTP)**
15503 Ventura Boulevard
Encino, CA 91436
818-995-3600
Fax: 818-382-1793

**American Advertising Federation
(AAF)**
1101 Vermont Avenue, NW
Washington, DC 20005
202-898-0089
Fax: 202-898-0159

**American Association of Advertising
Agencies (4As)**
405 Lexington Avenue
New York, NY 10174
212-682-2500
Fax: 212-682-8391

**American Association of Community
Colleges**
1740 N Street NW
Washington, DC 20036
202-775-4667
Fax: 202-223-1297

American Dance Guild
33 West 21st Street, Third Floor
New York, NY 10018
212-627-3790

**American Electronics Association
(AEA)**
PO Box 54990
Santa Clara, CA 95056
408-987-4200

American Film Institute (AFI)
John F. Kennedy Center for the
Performing Arts
Washington, DC 20566
202-828-4000

**American Institute of Graphic
Arts (AIGA)**
164 Fifth Avenue
New York, NY 10010
212-807-1990
800-807-1799

**American Library Association
(ALA)**
50 East Huron Street
Chicago, IL 60611
312-944-6780
800-545-2433
Fax: 312-440-9374

**American Marketing Association
(AMA)**
250 South Wacker Drive
Chicago, IL 60606
312-648-0536
Fax: 312-993-7542

**American Medical Association
(AMA)**
Division of Communications
535 North Dearborn Street
Chicago, IL 60610
312-645-4410

**American Meteorological Society
(AMS)**
45 Beacon Street
Boston, MA 02108-3693
617-227-2425
Fax: 617-742-8718

**American Society for Healthcare
Human Resources Administration**
One North Franklin
Chicago, IL 60606
312-422-3720

**American Society for Training and
Development (ASTD)**
1640 King Street
Box 1443
Alexandria, VA 22313
703-683-8100

**American Society of Composers,
Authors, and Publishers
(ASCAP)**
One Lincoln Plaza
New York, NY 10023
212-595-3050

**American Society of TV Cameramen
(ASTVC)**
4314 Hilary Street
Las Vegas, NV 89117
702-228-6704

**American Sportscasters Association
(ASA)**
5 Beekman Street, Suite 814
New York, NY 10038
212-227-8080
Fax: 212-571-0556

**American Women in Radio and
Television (A.W.R.T.)**
1650 Tysons Boulevard, No. 200
McLean, VA 22102
703-506-3290
703-506-3266

**Armed Forces Broadcasters
Association**
Box 447
Sun City, CA 92586
213-256-3482

Associated Press Broadcasters
c/o Jim Williams
1825 K Street NW, Suite 710
Washington, DC 20006-1253
202-736-1100
Fax: 202-736-1107

Association for Communication Administration (ACA)
5105 Backlick Road, Building E
Annandale, VA 22003
703-750-0533

Association for Computing Machinery
One Astor Plaza
1515 Broadway
New York, NY 10036
212-869-7440
Fax: 212-944-1318

Association for Educational Communications and Technology (AECT)
1025 Vermont Avenue NW, Suite 820
Washington, DC 20005
202-347-7834
Fax: 202-347-7839
Divisions (selected):
Division of Educational Media Management (DEMM)
Division of Instructional Development (DID)
Division of School Media and Technology (DSMT)
Division of Telecommunications (DOT)
Industrial Training and Education Division (ITED)
Media Design and Production Division (MDPD)
Affiliates (selected):
Association for Media and Technology in Education in Canada (AMTEC)
Community College Association for Instruction and Technology (CCAIT)
Consortium of College and University Media Centers (CCUMC)
Federal Educational Technology Association (FETA)
Health Science Communications Association (HeSCA)
Minorities in Media (MIM)

Association for Education in Journalism and Mass Communication (AEJMC)
College of Journalism
University of South Carolina
Columbia, SC 29208
803-777-2005
Fax: 803-777-4728

Association for Media-Based Continuing Education for Engineers (AMCEE)
International Department
1495 Powers Ferry Road, Suite 200-B
Marietta, GA 30067
770-612-9060

Association for Mulitmedia Communications
PO Box 10645
Chicago, IL 60610
312-409-1032

Association for Multi-Media International, Inc. (AMI)
PO Box 270298
Tampa, FL 33688

Association for Women in Communications
1244 Ritchie Highway, Suite 6
Arnold, MD 21012-1887
410-544-7442
Fax: 410-544-4640

Association of America's Public Television Stations
1350 Connecticut Avenue NW
Suite 200
Washington, DC 20036
202-887-1700
Fax: 202-293-2422

Association of Biomedical Communications Directors (ABCD)
Indiana University School of Medicine
1226 West Michigan Street
BR156
Indianapolis, IN 46202
317-274-4083

Association of C and C++ Users
1330 Trinity Drive
Menlo Park, CA 94025

Association of Federal Communications Consulting Engineers
Box 19333, 20th Street Station
Washington, DC 20036
703-534-7880

Association of Independent Commercial Producers (AICP)
11 East 22nd Street, Fourth Floor
New York, NY 10010
212-475-2600

Association of Local Television Stations
1320 19th Street NW, Suite 300
Washington, DC 20036
202-887-1970
Fax: 202-887-0950

Association of Independent Video and Filmmakers (AIVF)
304 Hudson Street
New York, NY 10013
212-807-1400

Association of Maximum Service Telecasters Inc. (MST)
1776 Massachusetts Avenue NW,
Suite 310
Washington, DC 20036
202-861-0344
Fax: 202-861-0342

Association of Schools of Journalism and Mass Communication
c/o Jennifer H. McGill
University of South Carolina
Le Conte College, Room 121
Columbia, SC 29208-0251
803-777-2005
Fax: 803-777-4728

Audio Engineering Society
60 East 42nd Street, Room 2520
New York, NY 10165
212-661-8528
Fax: 212-682-0477

Biocommunications Association International
1819 Peachtree Street, Suite 620
Atlanta, GA 30309
404-351-6300

Broadcast Cable Financial Management Association (BCFMA)
701 Lee Street, Suite 640
Des Plaines, IL 60016
847-296-0200
Fax: 847-296-7510

Broadcast Designers Association
145 West 45th Street, Suite 1100
New York, NY 10036
212-376-6222
Fax: 212-376-6202

Broadcast Education Association (BEA)
1771 N Street NW
Washington, DC 20036
202-429-5354
Fax: 202-429-5343

Broadcast Foundation of College/University Students
89 Longview Road
Port Washington, NY 11050
516-883-2897
Fax: 516-883-7460

Broadcast Music, Inc. (BMI)
320 West 57th Street
New York, NY 10019
212-586-2000
Fax: 212-582-5972

Broadcasting Training Program
PO Box 39696
Los Angeles, CA 90039
818-240-3362
www.theBroadcaster.com

**Cable Television Advertising Bureau
(CTAB)**
757 Third Avenue
New York, NY 10017
212-751-7770

**Cable and Telecommunications:
A Marketing Society (CTAMS)**
201 North Union, Suite 440
Alexandria, VA 23314
703-549-4200
Fax: 703-684-1167

**Cable Telecommunications
Association**
PO Box 1005
Fairfax, VA 22030-1005
703-691-8875
Fax: 703-691-8875

Career College Association (CCA)
750 First Street NE, Suite 900
Washington, DC 20002
202-336-6700
Fax: 202-336-6828

Center for Communication
570 Lexington Avenue, 21st Floor
New York, NY 10022
212-836-3050
Fax: 212-836-2773

**Community College Journalism
Association (CCJA)**
3376 Hill Canyon Avenue
Thousand Oaks, CA 91360
805-492-4440

**Consortium of College and
University Media Centers**
121 Pearson Hall-ITC
Iowa State University
Ames, IA 50011
515-294-1811

**Corporation for Public Broadcasting
(CPB)**
910 E Street NW
Washington, DC 20004
202-879-9600
800-582-8220 job information
www.cpb.org

**Electronic Industries Alliance
(EIA)**
2500 Wilson Boulevard
Arlington, VA 22201
703-907-7500
www.eia.org

**Electronics Representatives
Association (ERA)**
444 North Michigan Avenue
Chicago, IL 60611
312-527-3050

**Electronic Technicians' Association
International**
604 North Jackson Street
Greencastle, IN 46135
317-653-8262
800-359-6706

**Federal Communications Bar
Association (FCBA)**
1722 I Street NW, Suite 300
Washington, DC 20006
202-736-8640

**Federal Communications Commission
(FCC)**
1919 M Street NW
Washington, DC 20554
888-225-5322
www.fcc.gov

**Health Sciences Communications
Association (HeSCA)**
One Wedgewood Drive
Jewett City, CT 06351
860-376-5915

**Hollywood Radio and Television
Society (HRTS)**
13701 Riverside Drive, Suite 205
Sherman Oaks, CA 91423-2467
818-789-1182
Fax: 818-789-1210

**Institute of Electrical and
Electronics Engineers, Inc.
(IEEE)**
345 East 47th Street
New York, NY 10017
212-705-7900

**Interactive Digital Software
Association**
1775 I Street NW, Suite 420
Washington, DC 20006
202-833-4372
www.idsa.com

**Intercollegiate Broadcasting System
(IBS)**
367 Windsor Highway
New Windsor, NY 12553
914-565-6710
Fax: 914-565-7446

**International Advertising Association
(IAA)**
521 Fifth Avenue
New York, NY 10175
212-557-1133
Fax: 212-983-0455

**International Association of
Business Communicators (IABC)**
One Hallidie Plaza
San Francisco, CA 94102
415-433-3400

**International Communications
Industries Association (ICIA)**
11242 Waples Mill Road
Fairfax, VA 22030
703-273-7200
Fax: 703-278-8082

**International Federation of
Advertising Agencies Inc. (IFAA)**
1450 East American Lane
Schaumburg, IL 60173
312-330-6344

**International Interactive
Communications Society (ITCS)**
2120 Steiner Street
San Francisco, CA 94115
415-922-0214

**International Radio and Television
Society (IRTS)**
420 Lexington Avenue
New York, NY 10017
212-867-6650
Fax: 212-867-6653

**International Society for Performance
Improvement**
1300 L Street NW, Suite 1250
Washington, DC 20005
202-408-7869
Fax: 202-408-7972

**International Society
for Technology in Education**
University of Oregon
1787 Agate Street
Eugene, OR 97403
800-336-5191
Fax: 503-346-5890

**International Society of Certified
Electronics Technicians (ISCET)**
2708 West Berry Street
Fort Worth, TX 76109
817-921-9101
Fax: 817-921-3741

**International Technology Education
Association**
1914 Association Drive
Reston, VA 22091-1502
703-860-2100
Fax: 703-860-0353

**International Teleconferencing
Association**
100 Four Falls Corporate Drive
West Conshoshocken, PA 19428
610-941-2020

International Teleproduction Society (ITS)
8230 Boone Boulevard
Vienna, VA 22182
703-641-8770

International Television Association (ITVA)
Dallas Communications Complex
6311 North O'Connor Road, LB-51
Irving, TX 75039
972-869-1112

ITA, International Recording Media Association
182 Nassau Street, Suite 204
Princeton, NJ 08542
609-279-1700
Fax: 609-279-1999

League of Advertising Agencies (LAA)
2 South End Avenue
New York, NY 10280
212-945-4990

Motion Picture Association of America (MPAA)
1600 I Street, NW
Washington, DC 20006
202-293-1966

The National Academy of Television Arts and Sciences
National Office
111 West 57th Street, Suite 1020
New York, NY 10019
212-586-8424
Fax: 212-246-8129

National Alliance of Media Arts and Culture
655 13th Street, Suite 201
Oakland, CA 94612
510-451-2717
Fax: 510-451-2715

National Association of Black Owned Broadcasters (NABOB)
1333 New Hampshire Avenue NW, Suite 1000
Washington, DC 20036
202-463-8970
Fax: 202-429-0657

National Association of Broadcasters (NAB)
1771 N Street NW
Washington, DC 20036
202-429-5300
Fax: 202-429-5343

National Association of College Broadcasters
71 George Street, Box 1824
Providence, RI 02912-1824
401-863-2225
Fax: 401-863-2221
email: NACB@aol.com

National Association of Farm Broadcasters (NAFB)
26 East Exchange Street, Suite 307
St. Paul, MN 55101
612-224-0508
Fax: 612-224-1956

National Association of Government Communicators (NAGC)
669 South Washington Street
Alexandria, VA 22314
703-519-3902

National Association of Recording Merchandisers (NARM)
3 Eves Drive
Marlton, NJ 08053
609-596-8500
Fax: 609-596-3268

North American Retail Dealers Association
10 East 22nd Street, Suite 310
Lombard, IL 60148
312-953-8950

National Association of Video Distributors (NAVD)
700 Frederick Street
Owensboro, KY 42301
502-926-6002

National Broadcast Association for Community Affairs (NBACA)
Cocoa Village
270 Brevard Avenue
Cocoa, FL 32923
407-635-8709
Fax: 407-635-1979

National Cable Television Association (NCTA)
1724 Massachusetts Avenue NW
Washington, DC 20036
202-775-3550
Fax: 202-775-3695

National Cable Television Institute (NCTI)
801 West Mineral Avenue
Littleton, CO 80120-4501
303-797-9393
Fax: 303-797-9394

National Career Development Association
4700 Reed Road, Suite M
Columbus, OH 43220
614-326-1750

National Educational Telecommunications Association
PO Box 50008
Columbia, SC 29250
803-799-5517
Fax: 803-771-4831

National Electronic Service Dealers Association (NESDA)
2708 West Berry Street
Fort Worth, TX 76109
817-921-9061
Fax: 817-921-3741

National Federation of Community Broadcasters (NFCB)
Fort Mason Center, Building D
San Francisco, CA 94123
415-771-1160
Fax: 405-771-4343

National Instructional Television Fixed Service
Box 1130
3421 M Street NW
Washington, DC 20007

National Retail Federation
325 Seventh Street NW
Washington, DC 20004
202-783-7971

National Society of Professional Engineers
1420 King Street
Alexandria, VA 22314
703-684-2800
Fax: 703-836-4875
www.nspe.org

National Translator Association (NTA)
Box 628
Riverton, WY 82501
307-856-3322

National Writers Association
1450 South Havana, Suite 620
Aurora, CO 80012
303-751-7844

NATPE International
2425 Olympic Boulevard Suite 550E
Santa Monica, CA 90404
310-453-4440
Fax: 310-453-5258

P.E.N.
American Center
568 Broadway
New York, NY 10012
212-334-1660
Fax: 212-334-1660

Phi Delta Kappa
Eighth Street and Union Avenue
PO Box 789
Bloomington, IN 47402
800-766-1156
Fax: 812-339-1156

ProMax International
2029 Century Park East, Suite 555
Los Angeles, CA 90067-3283
310-788-7600
Fax: 310-788-7616

Public Broadcasting Service (PBS)
1320 Braddock Place
Alexandria, VA 22314
703-739-5000
Jobs: 703-739-5298

**Public Relations Society of America
(PRSA)**
33 Irving Place
New York, NY 10003
212-995-2230
Fax: 212-995-0757

**Public Telecommunications
Financial Management
Association (PTFMA)**
PO Box 50008
Columbia, SC 29250
803-799-5517
Fax: 803-771-4831

**Radio-Television News Directors
Association (RTNDA)**
1000 Connecticut Avenue NW,
Suite 615
Washington, DC 20036
202-659-6510
Fax: 202-223-4007

**Sales and Marketing Executives
International**
5500 Interstate North Parkway,
Suite 545
Atlanta, GA 30328
770-661-8500

**Satellite Broadcasting and
Communications Association**
225 Reinekers Lane, Suite 600
Alexandria, VA 22314
703-549-6990

**Society for Applied Learning
Technology (SALT)**
50 Culpeper Street
Warrenton, VA 22186
703-347-0055
Fax: 703-349-3169

**Society for Technical
Communication (STC)**
901 North Stuart Street, Suite 904
Arlington, VA 22203
703-522-4114

**Society of Broadcast Engineers
(SBE)**
8445 Keystone Crossing, Suite 140
Indianapolis, IN 46220
317-253-1640
Fax: 317-253-0418
www.sbe.org

**Society of Cable Telecommunications
Engineers (SCTE)**
140 Philips Road
Exton, PA 19341
610-363-6888

**Society of Motion Picture and
Television Engineers (SMPTE)**
595 West Hartsdale Avenue
White Plains, NY 10607-1824
914-761-1100
Fax: 914-761-3115

Society of Professional Journalists
16 South Jackson Boulevard
PO Box 77
Greencastle, IN 46135
317-653-3333

Society of Women Engineers
120 Wall Street, 11th Floor
New York, NY 10005
212-509-9577
Fax: 212-509-0224

**Software and Information Industry
Association**
1730 M Street NW, Suite 700
Washington, DC 20036
202-452-1600
Fax: 202-223-8756

**Speech Communication Association
(SCA)**
5105 Backlick Road, Building F
Annandale, VA 22003
703-750-0533

**Television Bureau of Advertising
(TBA)**
850 Third Avenue, 10th Floor
New York, NY 10022
212-486-1111

**University Film and Video
Association (UFVA)**
c/o Donald J. Zirpola
Loyola Marymount University
Communication Arts Department
Loyola Boulevard, West 80th Street
Los Angeles, CA 90045
310-338-3033
Fax: 310-338-3030

**Video Software Dealers Association
(VSDA)**
16530 Ventura Boulevard, Suite 400
Encino, CA 91436
818-385-1500

**Wireless Cable Association
International**
1140 Connecticut Avenue NW,
Suite 810
Washington, DC 20036
202-452-7823
Fax: 202-223-1288

**Women in Cable and
Telecommunications (WICT)**
230 West Monroe Street, Suite 730
Chicago, IL 60606-4702
312-634-2330
Fax: 312-634-2345

Women in Film (WIF)
6464 Sunset Boulevard, Suite 660
Hollywood, CA 90028
213-463-6040

World Communication Association
c/o Sharon A. Ratliffe
Golden West College
Huntington Beach, CA 92647
714-895-8180
Fax: 714-895-8253

Young Black Programmers Coalition
PO Box 1051
Vicksburg, MS 39181
205-456-9125
Fax: 205-457-8012

APPENDIX III
BIBLIOGRAPHY

A. BOOKS

The following books should be useful in providing further information on the areas discussed in this book. The publications are grouped according to the sections in Parts I and II, with an additional listing of general reference books. In addition to the name of the publisher, the year of publication, number of pages, and price are given, when available. Contact a bookseller before ordering any title to make sure that it is still in print and to learn its current price.

The bibliography was selected from hundreds of titles in the fields of television, cable, video, and multimedia and represents those publications that are most likely to be of interest to the serious reader.

TELEVISION BROADCASTING

Management Administration

Broadcasting in America: A Survey of Electronic Media, 6th edition
by Sydney W. Head and Christopher H. Sterling
Houghton Mifflin
222 Berkeley Street
Boston, MA 02116
617-351-5000
1998, 437 pp., $54.95

Electronic Media Management, 3d edition
by William E. McCavin, Peter K. Pringle, and Michael F. Starr
Focal Press
c/o Butterworth-Heinemann
225 Wildwood Avenue
Woburn, MA 01801
800-366-2665
1994, 425 pp., $44.95

Media Law, 3d edition
by Ralph L. Holsinger and Jon Paul Dilts
McGraw-Hill
1221 Avenue of the Americas
New York, NY 10020
212-512-2000
1996, 693 pp., $60.40

Public Interest and the Business of Broadcasting: The Broadcast Industry Looks at Itself
by Jon T. Powell and Wally Gair
Greenwood Publishing Group
88 Post Road
Westport, CT 06881-9990
203-226-2028
1988, 193 pp., $59.95

Telecommunications Management: Broadcast, Cable and the New Technologies
by B. L. Sherman
McGraw-Hill
1221 Avenue of the Americas
New York, NY 10020
212-512-2000
1995, 431 pp., $72.55

Programming

Announcing: Broadcast Communicating Today, 3d edition
by Lewis B. O'Donnell, Carl Hausman and Philip Benoit
Wadsworth Publishing
10 Davis Drive
Belmont, CA 94002
650-595-2350
1995, 500 pp., $72.95

Audience Ratings: Radio, Television and Cable
by Hugh M. Beville, Jr.
Lawrence Erlbaum Associates
10 Industrial Avenue
Mahwah, NJ 07430-2262
201-236-0072
1988, 424 pp., $89.95

Broadcast-Cable Programming Strategies and Practices, 3d edition
by Susan T. Eastman
Wadsworth Publishing
10 Davis Drive
Belmont, CA 94002
650-595-2350
1996, 608 pp., $66.95

Television and Radio Announcing, 8th edition
by Stuart Hyde
Houghton-Mifflin
222 Berkeley Street
Boston, Massachusetts 02116
617-351-5000
1995, 688 pp., $64.95

Production

1998 Blu-Book of Film and TV Production
Hollywood Reporter
BPI Publications
1998, 500 pp., $69.95

Advanced Animation and Rendering Techniques
by Alan H. Watt and Mark Watt
Addison-Wesley-Longman
One Jacob Way
Reading, MA 01867-3999
781-944-3700
1992, 455 pp., $49.95

The Art of Technique: An Aesthetic Approach to Film and Video Production
by John S. Douglass and Glenn P. Harnden
Allyn & Bacon
160 Gould Street
Needham Heights, MA 02195-2310
781-455-1200
1996, $49.95

Audio for Television
by John Watkinson
Focal Press
c/o Butterworth-Heinemann
225 Wildwood Avenue
Woburn, MA 01801
800-366-2665
1987, 256 pp., $49.95

Creating TV Projects: Video Program and Production Guide
by Norman J. Madoff
Knowledge Industry Publications
701 Westchester Avenue, Suite 101W
White Plains, NY 10604
914-328-9157
1994, 232 pp., $29.95

Digital Television Fundamentals
by Michael Robin
McGraw-Hill
1221 Avenue of the Americas
New York, NY 10020
212-512-2000
1998, 571 pp., $60.00

Directing and Producing for Television: A Format Approach
by Ivan Cury
Focal Press
c/o Butterworth-Heinemann
225 Wildwood Avenue
Woburn, MA 01801
800-366-2665
1998, 336 pp., $34.95

Directing Television and Film,
2d edition
by Alan A. Armer
Wadsworth Publishing
10 Davis Drive
Belmont, CA 94002
650-595-2350
1991, 386 pp., $47.95

Essential Television Handbook
by Peter Jarvis
Focal Press
c/o Butterworth-Heinemann
225 Wildwood Avenue
Woburn, MA 01801
800-366-2665
1996, 192 pp., $37.95

Guide to High Definition Video Production
by Clay Gordon/Rebo Studio
Focal Press
c/o Butterworth-Heinemann
225 Wildwood Avenue
Woburn, MA 01801
800-366-2665
1996, 162 pp., $44.95

Guide to Postproduction for TV and Film
by Barbara Clark and Susan Spohr
Focal Press
c/o Butterworth-Heinemann
225 Wildwood Avenue
Woburn, MA 01801
800-366-2665
1998, 240 pp., $29.95

HDTV: A Global Perspective
by Scott Elliott and Michel Dupagne
Iowa State University Press
2121 South State Avenue
Ames, IA 50014
515-292-0140
1998, 344 pp., $49.95

Introduction to Media Production: From Analog to Digital
by Robert Musberger
Focal Press
c/o Butterworth-Heinemann
225 Wildwood Avenue
Woburn, MA 01801
800-366-2665
1997, 480 pp., $44.95

News

Behind the Scenes at the Local News
by Robert S. Goald
Focal Press
c/o Butterworth-Heinemann
225 Wildwood Avenue
Woburn, MA 01801
800-366-2665
1993, 224 pp., $24.95

Broadcast News Process, 5th edition
by Fred Shook and Dan Lattimore
Morton Publishing Company
925 West Kenyon Avenue, Unit 12
Englewood, CO 80110
303-761-4805
1995, 402 pp., $34.95

Broadcast News Writing and Reporting
by Peter Mayeux
National Association of Broadcasters
1771 N Street NW
Washington, DC 20038
202-429-5300
1996, 432 pp., $44.95

Introduction to Electronic News Gathering
by Bernard Hesketh and Ivor Yorke
Butterworth-Heinemann
225 Wildwood Avenue
Woburn, MA 01801
800-366-2665
1993, 188 pp., $42.95

The New News Business: A Guide to Writing and Reporting
by John Chancellor and Walter R. Mears
Harper Perennial Library
10 East 53rd Street
New York, NY 10022
212-207-7000
1995, 208 pp.

News and Newsmaking: Essays
by Stephen Hess
Brookings Institution
1775 Massachusetts Avenue NW
Washington, DC 20036-2188
202-797-6000
1996, 148 pp., $24.95

Perspectives on American Political Media
by Gary L. Woodward
Allyn & Bacon
160 Gould Street
Needham Heights, MA 02195-2310
781-455-1200
1996, 256 pp., $40.50

Waiting for Prime Time: The Women of Television News
by Marlene Sanders and Marcia Rock
University of Illinois Press
1325 South Oak
Champaign, IL 61820
217-244-8082
1994, 226 pp., $13.95

Writing Broadcast News
by Mervin Block
Bonus Books, Inc.
160 East Illinois Street
Chicago, IL 60611
312-467-0580
1997, 310 pp., $29.95

Engineering

Broadcast Technology Update: Production and Transmission
by Peter B. Seel
Focal Press
c/o Butterworth-Heinemann
225 Wildwood Avenue
Woburn, MA 01801
800-366-2665
1997, 240 pp., $24.95

Dictionary of Television and Audiovisual Terminology
by Moshe Moshkovitz
McFarland & Company
Box 611
Jefferson, NC 28640
336-246-4460
1998, 175 pp., $39.95

Electronic Post-Production and Videotape Editing
by Arthur Schneider
Focal Press
c/o Butterworth-Heinemann
225 Wildwood Avenue
Woburn, MA 01801
800-366-2665
1989, 124 pp., $49.95

Troubleshooting and Repairing Audio Equipment
by Homer L. Davidson
McGraw-Hill
1221 Avenue of the Americas
New York, NY 10020
212-512-2000
1996, 528 pp., $24.95

Video Editing and Post Production
by James Caruso
Prentice Hall
One Lake Street
Upper Saddle River, NJ 07458
201-236-7000
1992, 330 pp., $28.95

Video Editing: A Post Production Primer
by Steven E. Browne
Focal Press
c/o Butterworth-Heinemann
225 Wildwood Avenue
Woburn, MA 01801
800-366-2665
1996, 309 pp., $36.95

Advertising

Advertising and Marketing Checklists, 2d edition
by Ronald B. Kaatz, et al.
NTC (National Textbook Company)
4255 West Touhy Avenue
Lincolnwood, IL 60646
847-679-5500
1994, 240 pp., $22.95

Advertising, Policy and Practice
by John C. Driver
St. Martin's Press
175 Fifth Avenue
New York, NY 10010
212-674-5151
1984, 165 pp., $39.95

Copywriting for the Electronic Media: A Practical Guide
by Milan D. Meeske
Wadsworth Publishing
10 Davis Drive
Belmont, CA 94002
650-595-2350
1997, 295 pp., $53.95

Fundamentals of Advertising Research, 3d edition
by Alan D. Fletcher and Thomas A. Bowers
Wadsworth Publishing
10 Davis Drive
Belmont, CA 94002
650-595-2350
1991, 364 pp., $53.95

Global Perspectives on Advertising Self-Regulation
by Jean J. Boddewyn
Greenwood Publishing Group
88 Post Road
Westport, CT 06881-9990
203-226-2028
1992, 272 pp., $59.95

Performance/Arts/Crafts

Acting for the Camera
by Tony Barr, et al.
HarperCollins Publishers
10 East 53rd Street
New York, NY 10022
212-207-7000
1997, 384 pp., $14.95

Acting in Television Commercials for Fun and Profit
by Squire Fridell and Barry Geller
Crown Publishing Group
201 East 50th Street
New York, NY 10022
212-572-6117
1995, 215 pp., $15.00

Acting in the Cinema
by James Naremore
University of California Press
2120 Berkeley Way
Berkeley, CA 94720
510-642-4247
1990, 316 pp., $15.95

Gaffers, Grips and Best Boys
by Eric Taub
St. Martin's Press
175 Fifth Avenue
New York, NY 10010
212-674-5151
1987, 276 pp., $13.95

How to Write a Selling Screenplay
by Christopher Keane
Bantam Doubleday Dell
1540 Broadway
New York, NY 10036
212-354-6500
1997, 320 pp., $14.00

Screenplay: The Foundations of Screenwriting
by Syd Field
Fine Communications
2 Lincoln Square
60 West 66th Street
New York, NY 10023
212-595-3500
1998, 262 pp., $7.98

The Scriptwriter's Handbook
by William Van Nostran
Focal Press
c/o Butterworth-Heinemann
225 Wildwood Avenue
Woburn, MA 01801
800-366-2665
1989, 403 pp., $37.95

Writing for Television and Radio
by Robert L. Hilliard
Wadsworth Publishing
10 Davis Drive
Belmont, CA 94002
650-595-2350
1996, 496 pp., $53.95

Writing for the Media: Film, Television, Video and Radio, 2d edition
by Paul M. Rubenstein and Martin J. Maloney
Prentice Hall
One Lake Street
Upper Saddle River, NJ 07458
201-236-7000
1988, 290 pp., $65.85

CABLE, VIDEO, AND MULTIMEDIA

Cable TV, MMDS, DBS

The Cable and Satellite Television Industries
by Patrick R. Parsons, et al.
Allyn & Bacon
160 Gould Street
Needham Heights, MA 02195-2310
781-455-1200
1998, $29.95

Cable Television: A Reference Guide to Information
by Ronald Garay
Greenwood Publishing Group
88 Post Road
Westport, CT 06881-9990
203-226-2028
1988, 177 pp., $49.95

Cable TV Advertising: In Search of the Right Formula
ed. by Rajeev Batra and Rashi Glazer
Greenwood Publishing Group
88 Post Road
Westport, CT 06881-9990
203-226-2028
1989, 189 pp., $49.95

Digital Satellite Television
by Frank Baylin
Baylin Publications
1905 Mariposa
Boulder, CO 80302
303-449-4551
1997, $50.00

**Regulation of the Electronic Mass
    Media: Law and Policy for Radio,
    Television, Cable, and the New
    Video Technologies**
by Michael Botein
West/Wadsworth Publishing
10 Davis Drive
Belmont, CA 94002
650-595-2350
1998, 605 pp., $55.95

*Consumer Electronics/
Home Video*

The CET Study Guide
by Joseph A. Risse, et al.
International Society of Certified
    Electronics Technicians
2708 West Berry Street
Fort Worth, TX 76109
817-921-9101
1995, 268 pp., $19.95

**Consumer Electronics' Component
    Handbook**
by Homer L. Davidson
McGraw-Hill
1221 Avenue of the Americas
New York, NY 10020
212-512-2000
1998, 550 pp., $65.00

**Digital Consumer Electronics
    Handbook**
by Ronald K. Jurgin
McGraw-Hill
1221 Avenue of the Americas
New York, NY 10020
212-512-2000
1997, 1,000 pp., $99.50

Film and Video Budgets
by Michael Wiese
Michael Wiese Productions
11288 Ventura Boulevard, Suite 821
Studio City, CA 91604
818-379-8799
1995, 463 pp., $26.95

Guide to Home Video Marketing
ed. by Ellen A. Lazer
Knowledge Industry Publications
701 Westchester Avenue, Suite 101W
White Plains, NY 10604
914-328-9157
1988, $195.00

Lenk's Television Handbook
by John D. Lenk
McGraw-Hill
1221 Avenue of the Americas
New York, NY 10020
212-512-2000
1994, 315 pp., $44.95

Maintaining and Repairing VCRs, 4th
    edition
by Robert L. Goodman
Mc-Graw Hill Professional Book Group
PO Box 545
Blacklick, OH 43004
800-338-3987
1995, $24.95

**Troubleshooting and Repairing
    Consumer Electronics**
by Homer L. Davidson
McGraw-Hill
1221 Avenue of the Americas
New York, NY 10020
212-512-2000
1997, 560 pp., $24.95

TV Repair for Beginners
by Homer L. Davidson
McGraw-Hill
1221 Avenue of the Americas
New York, NY 10020
212-512-2000
1997, 360 pp., $44.95

Private Industry

**Bulletproof News Releases: Help at
    Last for the Publicity Deficient**
by Kay Borden
Franklin-Sarrett Publishers
3761 Vinyard Trace
Marietta, GA 30062
770-578-9410
1994, 176 pp., $18.95

Corporate and Organizational Video
by Alan R. Richardson
McGraw-Hill
1221 Avenue of the Americas
New York, NY 10020
212-512-2000
1992, 358 pp., $54.50

**Corporate Television: A Producer's
    Handbook**
by Ray Dizazzo
Focal Press
c/o Butterworth-Heinemann
225 Wildwood Avenue
Woburn, MA 01801
800-366-2665
1990, 201 pp., $36.95

Corporate Television Programming
by Eugene Marlow
Knowledge Industry Publications
701 Westchester Avenue, Suite 101W
White Plains, NY 10604
914-328-9157
1992, 176 pp., $46.95

Corporate Video Directing
by Howard Hall
Focal Press
c/o Butterworth-Heinemann
225 Wildwood Avenue
Woburn, MA 01801
800-366-2665
1993, 106 pp., $39.95

The Grammar of the Edit
by Roy Thompson
Focal Press
c/o Butterworth-Heinemann
225 Wildwood Avenue
Woburn, MA 01801
800-366-2665
1996, 160 pp., $24.95

Managing Corporate Media
by Eugene Marlow
Knowledge Industry Publications
701 Westchester Avenue, Suite 101W
White Plains, NY 10604
914-328-9157
1989, 198 pp., $44.95

Media for Business
by Robert H. Amend and Michael A.
    Schrader
Knowledge Industry Publications
701 Westchester Avenue, Suite 101W
White Plains, NY 10604
914-328-9157
1989, 241 pp., $46.95

Education/Government/Health

**Designing Health Messages:
    Approaches from Communications
    Theory and Public Health Practice**
by Edward Maibach and Roxanne
    Louiselle Parrott
Sage Publications
2455 Teller Road
Newbury Park, CA 91320-2218
805-499-0721
1995, 304 pp., $24.50

Home Video in Libraries
ed. by Martha Dewing
G.K. Hall
PO Box 159
Thorndike, ME 04986
207-948-2962
1989, 209 pp., $40.00

Information Power: Guidelines for
School Library Media Programs
American Library Association
50 East Huron Street
Chicago, IL 60611
312-944-6780
1988, 171 pp., $35.00

Instructional Media and the New
Technologies of Instruction, 5th edition
by Robert Heinich, Michael Molenda,
and James D. Russell
Prentice Hall
One Lake Street
Upper Saddle River, NJ 07458
201-236-7000
1992, 464 pp., $59.00

Instructional Technology for Teaching
and Learning
by Timothy J. Newby, et al.
Prentice Hall
One Lake Street
Upper Saddle River, NJ 07458
201-236-7000
1996, 367 pp., $52.00

Multimedia

Creating Internet Entertainment:
A Complete Guide for Web
Developers and Entertainment
Professionals
by Jeannie Novak and Pete Markiewicz
John Wiley & Sons
605 Third Avenue
New York, NY 10158
212-850-6000
1996, 454 pp., $39.95

Multimedia Tools for Managers
by Bodhan O. Szuprowicz
AMACOM Books
1601 Broadway
New York, NY 10019-7406
212-586-1670
1996, 288 pp., $35.00

Proposal Savvy: Creating Successful
Proposals for Media Projects
by Elise K. Parsigian
Sage Publications
2455 Teller Road
Newbury Park, CA 91320-2218
805-499-0721
1996, 264 pp., $23.95

Writing for Multimedia Entertainment
by Timothy Garrand
Focal Press
c/o Butterworth-Heinemann
225 Wildwood Avenue
Woburn, MA 01801
800-366-2665
1996, 288 pp., $34.95

Reference

Art and Design Scholarships: A
Complete Guide
by Conway Greene
Conway Greene Publishing Company
1414 South Green, Suite 206
South Euclid, OH 44121
216-691-3870
1995, 324 pp., $20.95

AV Marketplace 1999: The Complete
Business Directory of Audio, Audio
Visual, Computer Systems, Film
Video, Programming with Industry
Yellow Pages
R.R. Bowker Company
121 Chanlon Road
New Providence, NJ 07974
908-464-6800
1999, $165

Banned in the Media: A Reference
Guide to Censorship
by Herbert N. Foerstel
Greenwood Publishing Group
88 Post Road
Westport, CT 06881-9990
203-226-2028
1998, 252 pp., $49.95

The Broadcast Century: A Biography
of American Broadcasting
by Robert Hilliard, with Michael C.
Keith
Focal Press
c/o Butterworth-Heinemann
225 Wildwood Avenue
Woburn, MA 01801
800-366-2665
1997, 320 pp., $39.95

Broadcast Communications
Dictionary, 3d edition
by Lincoln Diamant
NTC (National Textbook Company)
4255 West Touhy Avenue
Lincolnwood, IL 60646
847-679-5500
1991, 255 pp., $27.95

Broadcasting and Cable Yearbook, 1998
R.R. Bowker Company
121 Chanlon Road
New Providence, NJ 07974
908-464-6800
1998, 2 vol., $179.95

Dictionary of Multimedia
by Brad Hansen
Independent Publishers Group
814 North Franklin Street
Chicago, IL 60610
312-337-0747
1996, 343 pp., $16.95

Educational Media and Technology
Yearbook, 1999
ed. by Robert M. Branch and Mary A.
Fitzgerald
Libraries Unlimited
Box 6633
Englewood, CO 80155-6633
303-770-1220
1999, 410 pp., $65.00

The Facts On File Dictionary of
Television, Cable, and Video
by Robert M. and Maxine K. Reed
Facts On File, Inc.
11 Penn Plaza
New York, NY 10001
212-967-8800
1994, 240 pp. $27.95

Film Encyclopedia, 3d edition
by Ephraim Katz, et al.
Harper Perennial Library
10 East 53rd Street
New York, NY 10022
212-207-7000
1998, 1,504 pp., $28.00

Gale Directory of Publications and
Broadcast Media
ed. by Carolyn Fischer
Gale Research
835 Penobscot Building
Detroit, MI 48226-4094
313-961-2242
1998, 4,100 pp., $658.00

Hollywood Creative Directory
Hollywood Creative Directory, Inc.
3000 West Olympic Boulevard
Santa Monica, CA 90404
310-315-4815
1998, 260 pp., $49.50

Mass Media, 98–99
by Joan Gorham
McGraw-Hill
1221 Avenue of the Americas
New York, NY 10020
212-512-2000
1998, 240 pp., $12.25

O'Dwyer's Directory of Corporate
Communications, 1998
J.R. O'Dwyer Company
271 Madison Avenue
New York, NY 10016
212-679-2471
1998, $130.00

Standard Directory of Advertising
Agencies, 1999 (The Red Book)
National Register Publishing Company
121 Chanlon Road
New Providence, NJ 07974
908-464-6800
1999, 3 vol., $599.00

Video Register and Teleconferencing Resources Directory, 1991–92, 12th edition
Knowledge Industry Publications
701 Westchester Avenue, Suite 101W
White Plains, NY 10604
914-328-9157

1992, $74.50

Careers

1997 NAB/BCFM Television Employee Compensation and Fringe Benefits Report
National Association of Broadcasters
1771 N Street NW
Washington, DC 20038
202-429-5300

1997, $125.00

Acting Professionally: Raw Facts About Careers in Acting, 5th edition
by Robert Cohen
Mayfield Publishing Company
1280 Villa Street
Mountain View, CA 94041
650-960-3222

1997, 177 pp., $15.95

Adams Electronic Job Search Almanac 1997
ed. by Emily E. Ehrenstein
Adams Media Group
260 Center Street
Holbrook, MA 02343
781-767-8100
1997, 320 pp., $11.95

Careers for Speech Communication Graduates
by Al R. Weitzel
Sheffield Publishing Company
Box 359
Salem, WI 53168
414-843-2281
1987, $10.50

Hard News: Women in Broadcast Journalism
by David H. Hosley and Gayle K. Yamada
Greenwood Publishing Group
88 Post Road
Westport, CT 06881-9990
203-226-2028
1987, 208 pp., $49.95

Harvard Guide to Careers in the Mass Media
by John Noble
Adams Media Group
260 Center Street
Holbrook, MA 02343
781-767-8100
1989, 192 pp., $7.95

How to Sell Yourself as an Actor
by K. Callan
Alan Gordon Enterprises
1430 Cahuenga Boulevard
Hollywood, CA 90028
213-466-3561
1996, 259 pp., $17.95

Internships: Perspectives on Experiential Learning
by Andrew Ciafolo
Krieger Publishing Company
PO Box 9572
Melbourne, FL 32902-9572
407-724-9542
1992, 263 pp., $34.50

Job Bank Guide to Health Care Companies
Adams Media Group
260 Center Street
Holbrook, MA 02343
781-767-8100
1998, 608 pp., $16.95

B. PERIODICALS

The following list of important periodicals includes magazines, newsletters, newspapers, and membership reports of unions and associations. They provide information and trade news about various aspects of television, cable, video, and multimedia. The list conforms to the major occupational sections used in this book but many of the publications cover more than one field.

In most cases, the name, publisher, address, and telephone number of each periodical is included below, as well as the type and frequency of publication, price, and a brief description of its focus. Readers should be aware that many periodicals also have World Wide Web sites with up-to-date information; the address is typically "www.(name of periodical).com."

This list represents a core group of professional periodicals. In addition, a number of consumer-oriented publications can be found on newsstands.

TELEVISION BROADCASTING

Management and Administration

Broadcasting and Cable
Broadcaster Publications, Inc.
1705 DeSales Street NW
Washington, DC 20036
202-659-2340
magazine, weekly, $129/year
news for television, cable and satellite management with extensive job listings for all industry positions

Communications Daily
Warren Publishing, Inc.
2115 Ward Court NW
Washington, DC 20037
202-872-9200
newsletter, daily
covers all aspects of broadcast/non-broadcast events

Electronic Media
740 North Rush Street
Chicago, IL 60611-2590
312-649-5200
magazine, weekly, $109/year
news of broadcast programming, syndication, and media

Journal of Broadcasting and Electronic Media
Broadcast Education Association
1771 N Street NW
Washington, DC 20036
202-429-5355

magazine, quarterly, $40/year
scholarly articles about trends and
research; reviews, criticism

ProMax International
2029 Century Park East
Los Angeles, CA 90067
310-788-7600
magazine, monthly
directed to promotion and marketing
executives in electronic media

Tape Disc Business
Knowledge Industry Publications
701 Westchester Avenue, Suite 101W
White Plains, NY 10604
914-328-9157
magazine, monthly, $74/year
for the international community of
magnetic and optical media
manufacturers, dealers, and duplicators

TV Today
National Association of Broadcasters
1771 N Street NW
Washington, DC 20038
202-429-5300
magazine, biweekly
articles for TV, radio, and cable TV
management

Programming

Film Quarterly
2120 Berkeley Way
Berkeley, CA 94720
510-643-7154
journal, quarterly, $25/year
scholarly articles about film production,
history, and culture

Hollywood Reporter
5055 Wilshire Boulevard, Sixth Floor
Los Angeles, CA 90036
213-525-2000
newspaper, daily, $199/year
trade news of the film and
entertainment industry; includes job
listings

Programmer
NATPE International
2425 Olympic Boulevard, Suite 550
Santa Monica, CA 90404
310-453-4440
magazine, biweekly
TV industry, programming, syndication
news

Public Relations Strategist
Public Relations Society of America
33 Irving Place
New York, NY 10033
212-460-0360

magazine, monthly
articles of interest to the public relations
professional

Television Broadcast
460 Park Avenue South, Ninth Floor
New York, NY 10016
212-378-0400
magazine, monthly, $29.95/year
articles on all facets of television

Production

American Cinematographer
PO Box 2230
Hollywood, CA 90078
323-876-4973
magazine, monthly
news and articles for directors and
cinematographers

Film and Video
Knowledge Industry Publications
701 Westchester Avenue, Suite 101W
White Plains, NY 10604
914-328-9157
articles for professionals in motion
pictures, teleproductions, commercials
and interactive entertainment

News

Quill
Society of Professional Journalists
16 South Jackson Street
Greencastle, IN 46135
765-653-3333
magazine, monthly $29/year
all aspects of journalism

RTNDA Communicator
Radio-Television News Directors
    Association
1000 Connecticut Avenue NW,
    Suite 615
Washington, DC 20036
202-659-6510
magazine, monthly $75/year (free to
members)
news of interest to RTNDA membership

Engineering

Broadcast Engineering
9800 Metcalf Avenue
Overland Park, KS 66212
913-341-1300
magazine, monthly, $150/year
technical articles and news information
about broadcast engineering

Satellite Choice
Cardiff Publishing Company
PO Box 308
Fortuna, CA 95540

magazine, monthly, $52/year
features, news, tips on new and future
technology and equipment

SMPTE Journal
Society of Motion Picture and
    Television Engineers
595 West Hartsdale Avenue
White Plains, NY 10607
914-761-1100
magazine, monthly, $90/year
articles reviewing technology and
developments in broadcast journalism

Videography
460 Park Avenue South, Ninth Floor
New York, NY 10016
212-378-0400
magazine, monthly
trade and consumer news concerning
engineering, production, technology,
management

Advertising

Advertising Age
Crain Communications
740 North Rush Street
Chicago, IL 60611
312-649-5200
magazine, weekly, $99/year
trade news about all types of
advertising; extensive job listings

ADWEEK
1515 Broadway, 39th Floor
New York, NY 10036
212-764-7300
magazine, weekly, $125/year
all aspects of advertising; surveys; job
listings

Journal of Advertising Research
Advertising Research Foundation
641 Lexington Avenue
New York, NY 10022
212-751-5656
magazine, bimonthly, $100/year
research for the advertising community
with insights into new ideas and
developments

Performance/Arts/Crafts

Backstage/SHOOT
Backstage Publications
1515 Broadway, 39th Floor
New York, NY 10036
212-764-7300
newspaper, weekly, $79/year
theater news, casting calls, listings of
specialty schools in performing, crafts,
and commercial and video production

Billboard
Billboard Publications
1515 Broadway, 11th Floor
New York, NY 10036
212-536-5141
newspaper, weekly, $229/year
international news of music and home
entertainment

Daily Variety
249 West 17th Street
New York, NY 10010
212-337-6900
newspaper, daily
news of the entertainment industry;
some job listings

Emmy
Academy of Television Arts and
    Sciences
5220 Lankershim Boulevard
North Hollywood, CA 91601
818-754-2800
magazine, bimonthly, $23/year
news, reviews, and bios of the
television industry

IATSE Official Bulletin
International Alliance of Theatrical
    Stage Employees
1515 Broadway, Suite 601
New York, NY 10036
212-730-1770
magazine, quarterly
union news and reports; production
articles; agent listings

Screen Magazine
16 West Erie Street
Chicago, IL 60610
312-664-5326
magazine, weekly, $75/year
Chicago-oriented news of the motion
picture industry

Variety
5700 Wilshire Boulevard, Suite 120
Los Angeles, CA 90036
213-857-6600
newspaper, weekly, $129/year
news of television, home video, films,
and theater; some job listings

CABLE, VIDEO, AND MULTIMEDIA

Cable TV, MMDS

Broadcasting and Cable
245 West 17th Street
New York, NY 10011
212-645-0067
magazine, weekly
news, technology, programming for the
broadcast and cable industries

Kagan Newsletters:
    Cable Program Investor
    Cable TV Technology
    Internet Advertising
    Pay TV Newsletter

Paul Kagan Associates
126 Clock Tower Place
Carmel, CA 93923
408-624-1536
newsletters, monthly, prices vary
news for various sections of the cable
industry

Multichannel News
245 West 17th Street
New York, NY 10011
212-645-0067
newspaper, weekly
news of cable, STVA, MMDS; job
listings

Consumer Electronics and Home Video

ProService
National Electronic Sales and Service
    Dealers Association
2708 West Berry
Fort Worth, TX 76109
817-921-9062
magazine, bimonthly, $12/year
consumer electronics repair and services

Sales and Marketing Management
355 Park Avenue South
New York, NY 10010
212-463-6999
magazine, monthly, $99.90/year
business articles for sales and
marketing executives in consumer
electronics

**TWICE (This Week in Consumer
    Electronics)**
245 West 17th Street
New York, NY 10010
212-463-6802
magazine, semiweekly, $35/year
news of home video industry; program
charts; classifieds

Private Industry

Videography
460 Park Avenue South, Ninth Floor
New York, NY 10016
magazine, monthly
news, trends, analysis of video industry;
calendar

Education, Government, and Health

AT&T Technical Journal
600 Mountain Avenue, Room 3C443
Box 636
Murray Hill, NJ 07974
201-871-0679
journal, bimonthly, $50/year
articles focused on research and
development in telecommunications

Communication Arts
410 Sherman Avenue
PO Box 10300
Palo Alto, CA 94303
650-326-6040
magazine, eight times/year, $53/year
news, reviews, trends in the field of
design

Current
1612 K Street NW, Suite 704
Washington, DC 20006
202-463-7055
newspaper, 10 times/year, $54/year
news and opinion on public
broadcasting industry; job, seminar,
workshop listings

Educational Technology
700 Palisade Avenue
Englewood Cliffs, NJ 07632
201-871-4007
magazine, bimonthly, $119/year
articles in media, instructional design,
AV methods, video, media for educators

Feedback
Broadcast Education Association
171 N Street NW
Washington, DC 20036-2891
202-429-5355
magazine, quarterly, free/members
articles relating to broadcast education
and news of the association

**Journal of Business and Technical
    Communications**
2455 Teller Road
Thousand Oaks, CA 91320
805-499-0721
journal, quarterly, $44/year
articles on communication applications
and technology

Journal of Health Communications
Emerson College/Tufts University
    Program
c/o Emerson College
100 Beacon Street
Boston, MA 02116
617-824-7831

journal, quarterly
scholarly articles, case studies
concerning and shaped by the health
care industry

Mass Comm Review
Washington State University
School of Communications
Pullman, WA 99164
509-335-5608
journal, quarterly, $45/year
scholarly articles concerning the theory
and practice of mass communications

MediaFile
814 Mission Street, Suite 205
San Francisco, CA 94103
415-546-6334
newspaper, bimonthly, $25/year
news and features covering the mass
media

Tech Trends
Association for Educational
    Communications and Technology
1025 Vermont Avenue NW, Suite 820
Washington, DC 20025
202-347-7834
magazine, bimonthly
news and articles on education and
training

Telemedicine and Telehealth Networks
600 Harrison Street
San Francisco, CA 94107
415-905-2200
magazine, bimonthly
emerging technological trends in
medicine and allied health industries

Training and Development
American Society for Training and
    Development
1640 King Street
Alexandria, VA 22313
703-683-8100
journal, monthly
news and articles on current trends in
industry training practices

Multimedia

3D Artist
PO Box 4787
Santa Fe, NM 87502
505-982-3532
magazine, bimonthly, $20/year
addresses creative and technical
opportunities within computer-based
graphic arts

AV Video and Multimedia Producer
Knowledge Industry Publications Inc.
701 Westchester Avenue
White Plains, NY 10604
914-328-9157
magazine, monthly, $53.00/year
production and presentation technology
for the audio and video industries

Computerworld
500 Old Connecticut Path
Framingham, MA 01701
508-879-0700
newspaper, weekly, $48/year
news, product and book reviews on the
computer industry, including
multimedia/interactive

IEEE Multimedia
445 Hoes Lane
Piscataway, NJ 08855
732-981-0060
journal, quarterly, $295/year
analysis of current developments in the
field of multimedia, published by the
Institute of Electrical and Electronics
Engineers

Mac Week
50 Beale Street, 14th Floor
San Francisco, CA 94105
415-243-3500
magazine, weekly, $125/year
news and analysis concerning the
Macintosh operating system and related
software

Technology and Learning
600 Harrison Street
San Francisco, CA 94107
415-905-2200
magazine, 10 times/year, $24/year
examines the ways in which technology
supports learning, effective
applications, proposes uses

INDEX

269